British Vocational Qualifications

British Vocational Qualifications 2010

12TH EDITION

A directory of vocational qualifications
available in the United Kingdom

KoganPage

LONDON PHILADELPHIA NEW DELHI

331.114

BRI

Publisher's note

Every possible effort has been made to ensure that the information contained in this book is accurate at the time of going to press, and the publishers and authors cannot accept responsibility for any errors or omissions, however caused. No responsibility for loss or damage occasioned to any person acting, or refraining from action, as a result of the material in this publication can be accepted by the editor, the publisher or any of the authors.

Twelfth edition published in Great Britain and the United States in 2010 by Kogan Page Limited

120 Pentonville Road	525 South 4th Street, #241	4737/23 Ansari Road
London N1 9JN	Philadelphia PA 19147	Daryaganj
United Kingdom	USA	New Delhi, 110002
www.koganpage.com		India

© Kogan Page Limited, 2010

The right of Kogan Page Limited to be identified as the author of this work has been asserted by them in accordance with the Copyright, Designs and Patents Act 1988.

ISBN   978 0 7494 5881 2
E-ISBN 978 0 7494 5897 3

British Library Cataloguing-in-Publication Data

A CIP record for this book is available from the British Library.

Typeset by AMA DataSet Limited, Preston
Printed and bound in Great Britain by MPG Books Ltd, Bodmin, Cornwall

CONTENTS

HOW TO USE THIS BOOK

British Vocational Qualifications is divided into five parts:

Part One provides a brief overview of the provision of vocational education for the 19-plus age group within the United Kingdom at the time of publication. It provides current information on regulatory authorities and the main awarding bodies and an overview of the National Qualifications Framework. The main types of vocational qualifications are included within this publication and are described in full.

Part Two is the directory of vocational qualifications. Qualifications are listed under subject headings and sub-categories covering a wide range of professional and careers areas. For each heading the qualifications are set out in alphabetical order by award type. Under each heading qualifications are listed alphabetically by title and then by ascending level. Sections do not contain all types of award, they contain only the qualification types available for that particular professional or career area. Each entry gives details of the type of qualifications, course title, level and awarding body.

Part Three consists of a list of acronyms of the awarding bodies together with their full titles and addresses of awarding bodies and sources of further information. Sources of further information include contact details of industry lead bodies and professional institutions and organisations.

Part Four is a directory of Further Education colleges offering vocational qualifications, listed alphabetically by area.

Part Five is an index of all qualifications listed, together with the number of the page on which the entry appears. Qualification titles (with level) are listed in alphabetical order.

Part 1

Introduction

Vocational education in the UK is continuing the change and reorganization that got underway in recent years. These developments are in response to various Government strategies which have set out to create a new economic mission for further education (FE) with providers of learning and skills supplying a more specialist service. There is also an enhanced role for employers and learners in shaping development and new entitlements to learning and support for those who need it most. Ensuring that vocational training and development remains in line with the rapidly changing needs of the economy requires a highly responsive system which can operate within a framework of quality to keep standards as high as possible.

There are also a number of new bodies that influence qualifications provision at sector and regional level and work together to develop and oversee the education and training provision across the sector/subject classifications set by the regulatory authorities. These bodies include:

- **Learning and Skills Councils (LSCs)**. Responsible for all funding for young people aged 16–19 in colleges, schools and training providers. From April 2010 the LSC will be replaced by two new systems: 16–19 funding will transfer to local authorities with the support of a new Young People's Learning Agency; a new Skills Funding Agency (SFA) will cover adult learning.
- **Alliance of Sector Skills Councils (ASSC)**. Comprising all 25 licensed UK Sector Skills Councils (SSCs).
- **Regional Development Agencies (RDAs)**. Create regional workforce plans through focusing on regional priorities which will drive economic growth.
- **Sector Skills Councils (SSCs)**. Industry-specific bodies that ensure education and training provision respond to employer requirements.

The involvement of these bodies reflects the opening up of a variety of settings in which vocational qualifications can be studied. Further education colleges, distance learning, workplaces and higher education institutions are now able to offer vocational qualifications in a new and dynamic way and the increased involvement by industry through the SSCs will inevitably see a continued growth in workplace and home-based provision of vocational education.

This edition of *British Vocational Qualifications* provides an updated listing of vocational qualifications offered in the United Kingdom for the 19-plus age group. While the national framework starts at introductory level and goes up to level 8, this publication offers a listing of qualifications from levels 1 to 5 in keeping with the qualifications most likely to be offered by further education colleges. However, contact details for awarding bodies are also included to ensure that readers are able to identify providers of qualifications that might be offered outside the traditional further education setting. Vocational courses offered by Higher Education institutions can be found in *British Qualifications* (40th edition), also published by Kogan Page.

REGULATORY AUTHORITIES AND AWARDING BODIES

Central to the organization of vocational education is the relationship between the regulatory authorities and the awarding bodies. The checks and balances built into this relationship ensure quality assurance, standardization of awarding bodies and the qualifications they offer and, with the involvement of the Sector Skills Councils, an adequate response to employer and student requirements for qualifications that respond to market needs.

Regulatory authorities

Responsibility for regulating external qualifications lies with three regulatory authorities in England, Wales and Northern Ireland. The Office of the Qualifications and Examinations Regulator (Ofqual), together with Ofqual Northern Ireland, the Department for Children, Education, Lifelong Learning and Skills (DCELLS), in Wales, Qualifications and Curriculum Group and the Council for the Curriculum, Examinations and Assessment in Northern Ireland (CCEA) are responsible for establishing a coherent and comprehensive national framework for qualifications in England, Wales and Northern Ireland. The Scottish Qualifications Authority (SQA) regulates qualifications in Scotland. A description of qualifications regulated by the SQA is provided further on in this section.

National Vocational Qualifications (NVQs), other vocational qualifications and key skills qualifications are accredited by the regulatory authorities and are components of the framework. Candidates for these are assessed by awarding bodies, which award qualifications where candidates meet the required standards. The regulatory authorities, in partnership with the awarding bodies, are in charge of quality assurance of the system. They collaborate with the Scottish Qualifications Authority (SQA) to ensure that NVQs and their Scottish equivalent, Scottish Vocational Qualifications (SVQs), are based on national occupational standards and remain aligned with each other. The full list of accredited qualifications in England, Wales and Northern Ireland can be found on the new National Database of Accredited Qualifications (www.accreditedqualifications.org.uk).

The Office of the Qualifications and Examinations Regulator (Ofqual)
Spring Place
Coventry Business Park
Herald Avenue
Coventry
CV5 6UB
Tel: 0300 303 3344
Fax: 0300 303 3348
E-mail: info@ofqual.gov.uk
Website: www.ofqual.gov.uk

Ofqual Northern Ireland
2nd Floor
Glendinning House
6 Murray Street
Belfast
BT16 6DN
Tel: 028 9033 0706
Fax: 028 9023 1621
E-mail: infoni@ofqual.gov.uk

Department for Children, Education, Lifelong Learning and Skills (DCELLS), Qualifications and Curriculum Group
Castle Buildings
Womanby Street
Cardiff CF10 1SX
Tel: 0300 060330
E-mail: dcells.enquiries@wales.gsi.gov.uk
Website: www.wales.gov.uk

Council for the Curriculum, Examinations and Assessment (CCEA)
29 Clarendon Road
Clarendon Dock
Belfast BT1 3BG
Tel: 02890 261200
Fax: 02890 261234
E-mail: info@ccea.org.uk
Website: www.ccea.org.uk

Scottish Qualifications Authority (SQA)
The Optima Building
58 Robertson Street
Glasgow G2 8DQ
Tel: 0845 279 1000
Fax: 0845 213 5000
or
Ironmills Road
Dalkeith
Midlothian EH22 1LE
Tel: 0845 279 1000
Fax: 0845 213 5000
E-mail: customer@sqa.org.uk
Website: www.sqa.org.uk

Awarding bodies

Awarding bodies are responsible for the design and assessment of vocational education and training qualifications. The awarding bodies work with the regulatory authorities to develop qualifications and to ensure that standards are met. They manage the assessment, verification and awarding of qualifications and oversee quality assurance. They award certificates for assessed units and for full vocational qualifications, including NVQs.

There are 117 awarding bodies (see p 339 for a full list). Many of these are sector-based and provide specific qualifications for their particular industry. However, there are also a number of key awarding bodies that provide a wide range of vocational qualifications across sectors and subjects. These include:

- Edexcel (offers BTEC qualifications);
- City & Guilds (includes Pitman qualifications);
- Cambridge International Examinations (CIE qualifications are mainly available outside of the UK and not within the national framework);
- OCR;
- AQA;
- EDI.

QUALIFICATIONS

The NQF levels span from Entry Level to Level 8 setting out the levels at which qualifications are recognized. A sector and subject classification has also been introduced to sit alongside the Framework.

The National Qualifications Framework (NQF) for England, Wales and Northern Ireland sets out the levels at which qualifications are recognized

The National Qualifications Framework (NQF) helps learners to make informed decisions about the qualifications they need and allows them to select at a glance the full picture of the structure of qualifications in England, Wales and Northern Ireland. They can also compare the levels of different qualifications and identify clear progression routes for their chosen career. Only qualifications that have been accredited by the regulatory authorities are included in the NQF. To find out more visit the National Database of Accredited Qualifications website: www.accreditedqualifications.org.uk and the Qualifications and Curriculum Development Agency website: www.qcda.gov.uk.

Basic Skills

In September 2001 national qualifications in adult literacy and numeracy became available for the first time. The accreditation of these qualifications assures users that they are based on the national standards and ensures consistency in terms of level, demand, content and outcomes. The qualifications are available at entry level and at Levels 1 and 2. The tests for these certificates match the key skills Level 1 and 2 tests used for communication and application of number. The adult literacy qualifications are approved for use pre-16. Students on post-16 full-time programmes are more likely to work towards key skills qualifications.

All adult literacy and adult numeracy qualifications must be based on the national standards. At entry level, fifty per cent of each award must be made up of tasks or assessments which are independently or externally set or validated, externally marked or moderated, and are conducted under supervised and specified conditions. At levels 1 and 2 the assessment of these qualifications is via the shared adult literacy/adult numeracy/key skill test.

Entry Level

Entry level is the first level in the National Qualifications Framework. All Entry level qualifications (known as Entry level certificates) are pitched below an NVQ or Vocationally Related Qualification at Level 1 and below grade G of a GCSE. So that small steps of achievement can be recognized, Entry level is sub-divided into three further sub-levels: Entry 1, Entry 2 and Entry 3, with Entry 3 being the highest. Each sub-level provides progression to the next sub-level while Entry 3 qualifications are specifically designed to help learners progress to related Level 1 qualifications. Qualifications can cover one or more of the Entry sub-levels. They may address any area of learning from, for example, life skills to literacy, religious studies to retail.

Key Skills

Key skills qualifications are available at Levels 1 to 4 in each of the key skills of application of number, communication, ICT, working with others, improving own learning and performance and problem solving. They are offered by a wide range of awarding bodies. In England the first three of these key skills are assessed by an internally assessed portfolio of evidence and an externally set and marked test. Both parts have to be passed; there is no prescribed weighting for each. For the last three, the assessment is portfolio based.

Apprenticeships

Apprenticeships have been designed and developed in partnership with employers and Sector Skills Councils to provide an effective, high-quality, work-based route to the skills employers are looking for.

Thousands of employers in the United Kingdom now recruit apprentices. These employers welcome this opportunity to develop the skills, flexibility, loyalty and confidence that their organizations need – in effect, to grow their own workforce.

Work based learning, in the form of apprenticeships, gives young people the opportunity to gain recognized, career-building qualifications while working in a real job. All apprentice frameworks must comprise:

- a competence based element;
- a knowledge based element;
- transferable or Key Skills;
- employment rights and responsibilities.

The apprenticeship is not a qualification in its own right. Instead, it is described by the Learning and Skills Council as 'the achievement of a collection of qualification components, each requiring differing assessment methods and requiring registration and associated costs'. The training itself is a mix of practical, on-the-job instruction, with elements of off-the-job learning (for example, day release to college).

Introduction

There are 250,000 apprentices enrolled nationwide in more than 180 different apprenticeships frameworks across 80 different industry sectors. It is possible to take an Apprenticeship or an Advanced Apprenticeship, at levels 2 and 3 (and beyond) respectively. Most apprenticeships are completed in one to three years (the higher the level pursued the longer it takes).

The different occupational areas covered by apprenticeships are as follows. Each of these areas contains several specific occupations shown, and details of each can be found on the website www.apprenticeships.org.uk and individual website addresses in the types of apprenticeship directory.

Agriculture, Horticulture and Animal Care

Agriculture, Crops and Livestock; Amenity Horticulture; Animal Care; Dry Stone Walling; Environmental Conservation; Equine; Farriery; Fencing; Floristry; Game and Wildlife Management; Land-based Service Engineering; Production Horticulture; Trees and Timber; Veterinary Nursing.

Arts, Media and Publishing

Creative; Design; Information and Library Services; Photo Imaging for Staff Photographers; QA Game Testing

Business, Administration and Law

Accounting; Advising on Financial Products; Business and Administration; Contact Centres; Customer Service; Marketing and Communications; Payroll; Providing Financial Services; Retail Motor Industry: Vehicle Sales; Sales and Telesales; Team Leading and Management

Construction, Planning and the Built Environment

Building Services Engineers; Construction; Electrical and Electronic Servicing; Electrotechnical; Heating, Ventilating, Air Conditioning and Refrigeration; Plumbing; Set Crafts; Surveying

Education and Training

Supporting Teaching and Learning in Schools; Learning and Development/Direct Training and Support

Engineering and Manufacturing Technologies

Apparel; Building Products Occupations; Carry and Deliver Goods; Ceramics; Coating Operations; Driving Goods Vehicles; Electricity Industry; Engineering; Engineering Construction; Engineering Technology; Extractive and Mineral Processing Operations; Food Manufacture; Footwear and Leather Goods; Furniture, Furnishings and Interiors Industry; Gas Industry; Gas Network Operations; Glass Industry Occupations; Industrial Applications; Marine Industry; Metal Processing; Nuclear Decommissioning; Passenger Carrying Vehicle Driving, Bus and Coach; Polymer Processing Operations; Print and Printed Packaging; Process Technology; Rail Transport Engineering; Rail Transport Operations; Retail Motor Industry: Roadside Assistance and Recovery; Retail Motor Industry: Vehicle Body and Paint Operations; Retail Motor Industry: Vehicle Fitting; Retail Motor Industry: Vehicle Maintenance and Repair; Retail Motor Industry: Vehicle Parts Operations; Saddlery; Sea Fishing; Signmaking; Specialised Process Operations (Nuclear); Textiles; Traffic Office; Transport Engineering and Maintenance; Water Industry

Health, Public Services and Care

Advice and Guidance; Children's Care, Learning and Development; Community Development; Community Justice; Dental Nursing; Emergency Fire Service Operations; Health and Social Care; Housing; Laboratory Technicians; Optical; Pharmacy Technicians and Assistants; Security; Youth Work

Information and Communications Technology

IT and Telecoms Professionals; IT Users; ICT Professional

Leisure, Travel and Tourism

Active Leisure and Learning; Aviation Operations on the Ground; Cabin Crew; Sorting Excellence; Travel and Tourism Services

Retail and Commercial Enterprise
Barbering; Beauty Therapy; Cleaning and Support Services; Hairdressing; Hospitality and Catering; Logistics Operations Management; Mail Services; Nail Services; Property Services; Purchasing and Supply Management; Retail; Spa Therapy; Warehousing and Storage

Apprenticeships and NVQs

During the course of employment, workplace training will enable the apprentice to obtain an NVQ. The learning provider or local college will provide training for Key Skills and also a relevant technical certificate. Completion of an apprenticeship will qualify for an NVQ at level 2, an Advanced Apprenticeship at level 3 and 4 (and in theory the highest level you can go to for an Advanced Apprenticeship is Foundation Degree level at level 5). Find out more at www.apprenticeships.org.uk.

The National Apprenticeship Service

The National Apprenticeship Service was launched in April 2009 and has responsibilities for driving forward the Government's ambitions for Apprenticeships. It also has responsibility for employer services, learner services, and a web-based vacancy matching system, alongside accountability for the national delivery of targets for apprenticeships and the coordination of funding for places. Find out more at www.apprenticeships.org.uk.

National Vocational Qualifications (NVQs)

NVQs are available for study throughout England, Wales and Northern Ireland. Based on national occupational standards set and developed by industry lead bodies, employers and employees in each field, they are practical and relevant to work. They are designed to cover various aspects of a job or area of work, assessing the skills actually used in the workplace. The standards set define the skills or competences needed by people working in particular occupations.

These qualifications can be completed unit by unit, enabling an individual to build up to a qualification as conveniently as possible. A mix of mandatory and optional units can enable a candidate to tailor the qualification to their particular role.

NVQs can be included in the Qualifications and Credit Framework (see below) and the National Qualifications Framework. The NVQ Framework covers the first five levels, from routine work at Level 1 through to senior management at Level 5. There are no barriers to access, such as age limits or entry requirements. NVQs are open to anyone who can demonstrate they reach the required standard.

Vocational Qualifications (VQs)

A wide range of vocational qualifications (VQs) is accredited into the National Qualifications Framework (NQF). These qualifications cover almost every industry sector, and every level of the NQF. VQs are offered by a large number of awarding bodies. They range from broad-based VQs to specialist qualifications designed for a particular sector. In many cases, suites of qualifications are available, offering progression through the levels of the NQF.

Scottish Vocational Qualifications (SVQs)

Scottish Vocational Qualifications (SVQs) Scottish Vocational Qualifications (SVQs) are work-based qualifications which record the 'skills, knowledge and understanding' of an individual in relation to their work. They are based on National Occupational Standards developed by National Training Organizations Sector Skills Councils (SSCs).

National Occupational Standards identify the level of competence expected of people in particular job roles. SSCs work with employers to develop National Occupational Standards for each industry sector. Competence means the ability to perform tasks, and this is assessed on the job. This may be as an employee, through a Modern Apprenticeship, or as a school or college student through a work placement.

Qualifications and Credit Framework

The Qualifications and Credit Framework is a new way of recognizing and accrediting qualifications. It applies in England, Wales and Northern Ireland and works by awarding credit for qualifications and units which enable people to go at their own pace to gain qualifications. The QCF ensures that every unit and qualification in the framework has a credit value, with one credit representing 10 hours of work, and a level between Entry level and level 8. The three sizes of qualification in the QCF are:

- Awards (1 to 12 credits)
- Certificates (13 to 36 credits)
- Diplomas (37 credits or more)

This makes it possible to have an award at level 1 or at level 8 because the type of qualification (award, certificate, diploma) represents the size, not the level of difficulty.

For further information on the Qualifications and Credit Framework and a timetable for implementation, visit the Qualifications and Curriculum Development Agency (QCDA) website: www.qcda.gov.uk or the Office of the Qualifications and Examinations Regulator (Ofqual) website: www.ofqual.gov.uk.

The NQF and the QCF

The NQF sets out the levels against which a qualification can be recognised (in England, Wales and Northern Ireland) and the QCF is a way of recognising skills and qualifications by awarding credit for qualifications and units.

Employers' benefits and obligations

The employer benefits from the development of a fully trained skilled workforce at a time of national skills shortages, with the increased expectation of retention of such staff, but are obliged to provide facilities for workplace training and for attendance at day-time courses, as well as financial obligations. Specific rates apply to the occupations covered.

Employee benefits

Vocational qualifications can be obtained as a result of satisfactory completion of work-based learning, combined with courses conducted at colleges listed in Part 4. Some secondary schools also offer facilities for such courses.

Apart from the great benefit of earning whilst learning, the acquisition of vocational qualifications can have the effect of opening up routes to higher professional or academic qualifications, for those who have not obtained exemptions or entry qualifications through academic studies.

BTEC qualifications (National Certificates and Diplomas) can provide entrance credentials for some university degrees. NVQs and SVQs can provide entrance credentials for entry to various professional bodies; level 3 NVQs/SVQs are acceptable for entry into graduate grades of some professional bodies, leading to higher qualifications.

National Skills Academies

National Skills Academies are employer-led centres of excellence which deliver the skills required by each sector of the economy. They are focused on vocational education and skills training, delivering to young people and adults. There are currently eleven active sectors:

- Construction
- Creative and cultural
- Financial services
- Food and drink manufacturing
- Hospitality
- Manufacturing
- Materials, production and supply
- Nuclear
- Process industries
- Retail
- Sport and active leisure

At the time of writing there are five sectors in the business planning stage:

- Enterprise
- Fashion, textiles and jewellery
- IT
- Power
- Social care

Find out more at the National Skills Academy website, www. nationalskillsacademy. gov.uk.

Part 2

Directory of Vocational Qualifications and Apprenticeships

Agriculture, Horticulture and Animal Care

Agriculture

Advanced Diploma

Environmental and Land Based Studies – Level 3
Awarding body:
 AQA
 City & Guilds
 EDEXCEL
 OCR

Advanced National Certificate

Agriculture – Level 3
Awarding body:
 NPTC

Award

Care of Farm Animals – Entry Level
Awarding body:
 EDEXCEL

Controlling Risks to Health and Safety in Agriculture and Production Horticulture – Level 3
Awarding body:
 Lantra Awards

Land-based Studies – Level 1
Awarding body:
 NPTC

Preparation and Operation of a Tractor – Level 1
Awarding body:
 EDEXCEL

Safe Use of Pesticides – Level 2
Awarding body:
 NPTC

Safe Use of Veterinary Medicines – Level 2
Awarding body:
 NPTC

Safe Working in Agriculture and Production Horticulture – Level 2
Awarding body:
 Lantra Awards

the Planning and Supervising the Safe use of Veterinary Medicines – Level 3
Awarding body:
 NPTC

Wild Game Meat Hygiene – Level 2
Awarding body:
 Lantra Awards

Work-based Agriculture – Level 2
Awarding body:
 NPTC

Work-based Agriculture – Level 3
Awarding body:
 NPTC

BTEC First Certificate

Agriculture – Level 2
Awarding body:
 EDEXCEL

Land-based Technology – Level 2
Awarding body:
 EDEXCEL

BTEC First Diploma

Agriculture – Level 2
Awarding body:
   EDEXCEL

Land-based Technology – Level 2
Awarding body:
   EDEXCEL

BTEC Higher National Certificate

Equine Management – Level 5
Awarding body:
   EDEXCEL

BTEC Higher National Diploma

Equine Management – Level 5
Awarding body:
   EDEXCEL

BTEC National Award

Agriculture – Level 3
Awarding body:
   EDEXCEL

Fish Management – Level 3
Awarding body:
   EDEXCEL

Land-based Technology – Level 3
Awarding body:
   EDEXCEL

BTEC National Certificate

Agriculture – Level 3
Awarding body:
   EDEXCEL

Fish Management – Level 3
Awarding body:
   EDEXCEL

Land-based Technology – Level 3
Awarding body:
   EDEXCEL

BTEC National Diploma

Agriculture – Level 3
Awarding body:
   EDEXCEL

Fish Management – Level 3
Awarding body:
   EDEXCEL

Land-based Technology – Level 3
Awarding body:
   EDEXCEL

Certificate

All Terrain Vehicle Handling – Level 2
Awarding body:
   NPTC

Basic Stockmanship and Welfare – Level 2
Awarding body:
   NPTC

Cattle Foot Trimming – Level 3
Awarding body:
   NPTC

Controlling Risks to Health and Safety in Agriculture/ Horticulture – Level 3
Awarding body:
   Lantra Awards
   NPTC

Forklift Truck Operations – Level 2
Awarding body:
   NPTC

Granular Fertiliser Application – Level 2
Awarding body:
   NPTC

Health and Safety for those Working in the Equine Industry – Level 2
Awarding body:
   NPTC

Introductory Floristry – Level 1
Awarding body:
   Lantra Awards

**Land Based Machine Maintenance –
Level 2**
Awarding body:
  NPTC

Land Studies – Entry Level
Awarding body:
  WJEC

Land-Based Activities – Level 2
Awarding body:
  Lantra Awards

Land-based Studies – Level 1
Awarding body:
  NPTC

Livestock Husbandry – Level 2
Awarding body:
  NPTC

**Long Distance Transport of Animals by
Road – Level 2**
Awarding body:
  NPTC

**Managing Health and Safety in
Agriculture/Horticulture – Level 4**
Awarding body:
  Lantra Awards
  NPTC

**Manual Handling Operations – Risk
Assessment – Level 2**
Awarding body:
  NPTC

Milking and Dairy Hygiene – Level 3
Awarding body:
  NPTC

Off Road Driving – Level 2
Awarding body:
  NPTC

Pig Husbandry Skills – Level 2
Awarding body:
  NPTC

**Pig Husbandry Skills – Breeding Herd
Operations – Level 2**
Awarding body:
  NPTC

**Pig Husbandry Skills – Weaner, Grower
and Finishing Operations – Level 2**
Awarding body:
  NPTC

**Pig Unit Supervision and Operation –
Level 3**
Awarding body:
  NPTC

**Protection of Water, Environment and
Recommendations – Level 3**
Awarding body:
  NPTC

Rural Business Administration – Level 3
Awarding body:
  NPTC

**Safe Manual Handling Operator –
Level 1**
Awarding body:
  NPTC

Safe Use of Pesticides – Level 2
Awarding body:
  NPTC

Safe Use of Sheep Dips – Level 2
Awarding body:
  NPTC

**The Welfare of Animals During
Transport – Level 2**
Awarding body:
  Lantra Awards

**Tractor Driving and Related Operations
– Level 2**
Awarding body:
  NPTC

**Transport of Animals by Road (Short
Journeys) – Level 2**
Awarding body:
  NPTC

Vertebrate Pest Control – Level 2
Awarding body:
  NPTC

Work-based Agriculture – Level 2
Awarding body:
  NPTC

Work-based Agriculture – Level 3
Awarding body:
  NPTC

Working Safely in Agriculture/ Horticulture – Level 2
Awarding body:
  Lantra Awards
  NPTC

Diploma

Land-based Studies – Level 1
Awarding body:
  NPTC

Work-based Agriculture – Level 2
Awarding body:
  NPTC

Work-based Agriculture – Level 3
Awarding body:
  NPTC

Foundation Diploma

Environmental and Land Based Studies – Level 1
Awarding body:
  AQA
  City & Guilds
  EDEXCEL
  OCR

Higher Diploma

Environmental and Land Based Studies – Level 2
Awarding body:
  AQA
  City & Guilds
  EDEXCEL
  OCR

Introductory Certificate

Land and Environment – Level 1
Awarding body:
  EDEXCEL

Introductory Diploma

Land and Environment – Level 1
Awarding body:
  EDEXCEL

National Certificate

Agriculture – Level 2
Awarding body:
  NPTC

National Vocational Qualification

Agricultural Management – Level 4
Awarding body:
  NPTC

Livestock Markets (Droving Livestock) – Level 2
Awarding body:
  NPTC

Principal Learning

Environmental and Land Based Studies – Level 1
Awarding body:
  AQA
  City & Guilds

Environmental and Land-based Studies – Level 1
Awarding body:
  EDEXCEL

Environmental and Land-based studies – Level 2
Awarding body:
  AQA
  City & Guilds
  EDEXCEL

Environmental and Land-based studies – Level 3
Awarding body:
  AQA
  City & Guilds
  EDEXCEL

Progression Diploma

**Environmental and Land Based Studies –
Level 3**
Awarding body:
AQA
City & Guilds
EDEXCEL
OCR

Animal Care and Veterinary Science

Advanced Certificate

Dog Grooming – Level 3
Awarding body:
NPTC

Pet Store Management – Level 3
Awarding body:
NPTC

Advanced National Certificate

Animal Management – Level 3
Awarding body:
NPTC

Horse Management – Level 3
Awarding body:
NPTC

Management of Zoo Animals – Level 3
Awarding body:
NPTC

Advanced National Diploma

Animal Management – Level 3
Awarding body:
NPTC

Horse Management – Level 3
Awarding body:
NPTC

Award

**Hydrotherapy for Small Animals –
Level 2**
Awarding body:
ABC

**Hydrotherapy for Small Animals –
Level 3**
Awarding body:
ABC

Small Animal Care – Level 3
Awarding body:
ABC

Work-based Animal Care – Level 2
Awarding body:
NPTC

Work-based Animal Care – Level 3
Awarding body:
NPTC

BTEC First Certificate

Animal Care – Level 2
Awarding body:
EDEXCEL

Fish Husbandry – Level 2
Awarding body:
EDEXCEL

Horse Care – Level 2
Awarding body:
EDEXCEL

BTEC First Diploma

Animal Care – Level 2
Awarding body:
EDEXCEL

Fish Husbandry – Level 2
Awarding body:
EDEXCEL

Horse Care – Level 2
Awarding body:
EDEXCEL

BTEC Higher National Certificate

Animal Management – Level 5
Awarding body:
EDEXCEL

BTEC Higher National Diploma

Animal Management – Level 5
Awarding body:
EDEXCEL

BTEC National Award

Animal Management – Level 3
Awarding body:
EDEXCEL

Horse Management – Level 3
Awarding body:
EDEXCEL

BTEC National Certificate

Animal Management – Level 3
Awarding body:
EDEXCEL

Horse Management – Level 3
Awarding body:
EDEXCEL

BTEC National Diploma

Animal Management – Level 3
Awarding body:
EDEXCEL

Horse Management – Level 3
Awarding body:
EDEXCEL

Certificate

Animal Nursing Assistants – Level 2
Awarding body:
ABC

Assistant Ride Leaders in Equestrian Tourism – Level 2
Awarding body:
EQL

BHS Stage 3 Horse Knowledge and Care – Level 3
Awarding body:
EQL

Equine Skills – Level 1
Awarding body:
NPTC

Equine Transport – Level 3
Awarding body:
BHEST

Forgework – Level 2
Awarding body:
NPTC

Horse Care – Level 3
Awarding body:
BHEST

Horse Management – Level 3
Awarding body:
NPTC

Hydrotherapy for Small Animals – Level 3
Awarding body:
ABC

Operational Principles of Kennels and Catteries – Level 3
Awarding body:
NPTC

Planning and Supervising the Safe Use of Veterinary Medicines – Level 3
Awarding body:
NPTC

Principles of Animal Management within a Pet Store – Level 3
Awarding body:
NPTC

Ride Leaders in Equestrian Tourism – Level 3
Awarding body:
EQL

Riding & Road Safety – Level 2
Awarding body:
EQL

Safe Use of Veterinary Medicines – Level 2
Awarding body:
NPTC

Safe Working in the Equine Industry – Level 2
Awarding body:
NPTC

Small Animal Care – Level 2
Awarding body:
ABC

Small Animal Care – Level 3
Awarding body:
ABC

Stage 1 Horse Knowledge, Care and Riding – Level 1
Awarding body:
EQL

Stage 2 Horse Knowledge and Care – Level 2
Awarding body:
EQL

Stage 2 Horse Knowledge, Care and Riding – Level 2
Awarding body:
EQL

Stage 3 Horse Knowledge, Care and Riding – Level 3
Awarding body:
EQL

The Welfare of Animals (Equines) in Transport – Level 3
Awarding body:
BDS

The Welfare of Animals (Equines) in Transport (Attendant/Driver) – Level 3
Awarding body:
BDS

Veterinary Nursing Theory – Level 2
Awarding body:
RCVS

Veterinary Nursing Theory – Level 3
Awarding body:
RCVS

Veterinary Practice Receptionists – Level 2
Awarding body:
NPTC

Work-based Animal Care – Level 2
Awarding body:
NPTC

Work-based Animal Care – Level 3
Awarding body:
NPTC

Diploma

Farriery – Level 3
Awarding body:
WCF

Work-Based Animal Care – Level 2
Awarding body:
ABC
NPTC

Work-Based Animal Care – Level 3
Awarding body:
ABC
NPTC

Intermediate Certificate

Dog Grooming – Level 2
Awarding body:
NPTC

Horse Care – Level 2
Awarding body:
    BHEST

Intermediate Instructor Certificate

The Equine Coach – Level 5
Awarding body:
    EQL

National Certificate

Animal Care – Level 2
Awarding body:
    NPTC

Horse Care – Level 2
Awarding body:
    NPTC

Veterinary Care Assistants – Level 2
Awarding body:
    NPTC

National Vocational Qualification

Animal Care and Management – Level 4
Awarding body:
    NPTC

Equine Management – Level 4
Awarding body:
    NPTC

Farriery – Level 3
Awarding body:
    BHEST

Horse Care – Level 1
Awarding body:
    BHEST
    EQL
    NPTC

Horse Care – Level 2
Awarding body:
    EQL
    NPTC

Horse Care and Management – Level 3
Awarding body:
    EQL
    NPTC

Introductory Racehorse Care – Level 1
Awarding body:
    BHEST

Racehorse Care – Level 2
Awarding body:
    BHEST

Racehorse Care and Management – Level 3
Awarding body:
    BHEST

Veterinary Nursing – Level 2
Awarding body:
    RCVS

Veterinary Nursing – Level 3
Awarding body:
    RCVS

Environmental Conservation

Award

Converting Biomass into Fuel and Energy – Level 2
Awarding body:
    ABC

Converting Wind into Energy – Level 2
Awarding body:
    ABC

Practical Environmental and Conservation Skills – Level 1
Awarding body:
ABC

Sustainability and the Renewables Industry – Level 2
Awarding body:
ABC

Sustainable Energy – Level 3
Awarding body:
ABC

Waste Treatment Technologies – Level 4
Awarding body:
WAMITAB

BTEC First Certificate

Countryside and Environment – Level 2
Awarding body:
EDEXCEL

BTEC First Diploma

Countryside and Environment – Level 2
Awarding body:
EDEXCEL

BTEC Higher National Certificate

Environmental Conservation – Level 5
Awarding body:
EDEXCEL

BTEC Higher National Diploma

Environmental Conservation – Level 5
Awarding body:
EDEXCEL

Certificate

Environmental Sustainability – Level 1
Awarding body:
ASCENTIS

Environmental Sustainability – Level 2
Awarding body:
ASCENTIS

Land Based Operations – Level 1
Awarding body:
ABC

Practical Environmental and Conservation Skills – Level 1
Awarding body:
ABC

Practical Environmental Studies – Level 2
Awarding body:
ABC

Sustainable Energy – Level 2
Awarding body:
ABC

Sustainable Energy – Level 3
Awarding body:
ABC

The Principles of Live Quarry Shooting – Level 2
Awarding body:
NPTC

Waste and Resource Management – Level 3
Awarding body:
WAMITAB

Diploma

Environmental Management – Level 6
Awarding body:
NEBOSH

Work-Based Environmental Conservation – Level 1
Awarding body:
ABC

National Certificate

Environmental Conservation – Level 2
Awarding body:
NPTC

National Vocational Qualification

Cleaning and Support Services – Level 1
Awarding body:
    WAMITAB

Cleaning and Support Services – Level 2
Awarding body:
    WAMITAB

Environmental Conservation – Level 2
Awarding body:
    EDEXCEL
    NPTC

Environmental Conservation – Level 3
Awarding body:
    EDEXCEL
    NPTC

Facilities Management – Level 3
Awarding body:
    WAMITAB

Gamekeeping and Wildlife Management – Level 2
Awarding body:
    NPTC

Gamekeeping and Wildlife Management – Level 3
Awarding body:
    NPTC

Managing Waste Collections Operations – Level 4
Awarding body:
    WAMITAB

Recycling Operations – Level 1
Awarding body:
    City & Guilds
    WAMITAB

Recycling Operations – Level 2
Awarding body:
    City & Guilds
    WAMITAB

Removal of Hazardous and Non-hazardous Waste (Construction) – Level 2
Awarding body:
    WAMITAB

The Management of Recycling Operations – Level 3
Awarding body:
    City & Guilds
    WAMITAB

The Management of Recycling Operations – Level 4
Awarding body:
    City & Guilds
    WAMITAB

The Management of Recycling Operations: Small Scale Operations – Level 4
Awarding body:
    City & Guilds
    WAMITAB

Waste Management Operations – Level 1
Awarding body:
    City & Guilds
    WAMITAB

Waste Management Operations – Level 2
Awarding body:
    City & Guilds
    NCFE
    WAMITAB

Waste Management Operations: Civic Amenity Site – Level 3
Awarding body:
    City & Guilds
    WAMITAB

Waste Management Operations: Closed Landfill – Level 3
Awarding body:
    City & Guilds
    WAMITAB

Waste Management Operations: Inert Waste – Level 3
Awarding body:
    City & Guilds
    WAMITAB

Waste Management Operations: Managing Incineration – Level 4
Awarding body:
City & Guilds
WAMITAB

Waste Management Operations: Managing Landfill Hazardous Waste – Level 4
Awarding body:
City & Guilds
WAMITAB

Waste Management Operations: Managing Landfill Non-Hazardous Waste – Level 4
Awarding body:
City & Guilds
WAMITAB

Waste Management Operations: Managing Transfer Hazardous Waste – Level 4
Awarding body:
City & Guilds
WAMITAB

Waste Management Operations: Managing Transfer Non-Hazardous Waste – Level 4
Awarding body:
City & Guilds
WAMITAB

Waste Management Operations: Managing Treatment Hazardous Waste – Level 4
Awarding body:
City & Guilds
WAMITAB

Waste Management Operations: Managing Treatment Non-Hazardous Waste – Level 4
Awarding body:
City & Guilds
WAMITAB

Waste Management Supervision – Level 3
Awarding body:
City & Guilds
WAMITAB

Weighbridge Operations – Level 2
Awarding body:
WAMITAB

Horticulture and Forestry

Advanced Certificate

Horticulture – Level 3
Awarding body:
RHS

Advanced National Certificate

Countryside Management – Level 3
Awarding body:
NPTC

Horticulture – Level 3
Awarding body:
NPTC

Sports and Amenity Turf Management – Level 3
Awarding body:
NPTC

Advanced National Diploma

Horticulture – Level 3
Awarding body:
NPTC

Award

Amenity Horticulture – Level 3
Awarding body:
  NPTC

Computer Aided Drawing for Garden Design – Level 2
Awarding body:
  NOCN

Drawing and Graphics for Garden Design – Level 2
Awarding body:
  NOCN

Floristry – Level 2
Awarding body:
  NPTC

Floristry – Level 3
Awarding body:
  NPTC

Garden Design – Level 2
Awarding body:
  NOCN

Maintaining drainage and irrigation systems – Level 3
Awarding body:
  NPTC

Managing planted areas for their amenity value – Level 3
Awarding body:
  NPTC

Managing Sports Turf Areas – Level 3
Awarding body:
  NPTC

Practical Horticulture Skills – Level 1
Awarding body:
  NPTC

Specifying and Monitoring Landscape Maintenance – Level 3
Awarding body:
  NPTC

Work-Based Agriculture – Level 1
Awarding body:
  NPTC

Work-Based Animal Care – Level 1
Awarding body:
  NPTC

Work-Based Horticulture – Level 1
Awarding body:
  NPTC

Work-based Horticulture – Level 2
Awarding body:
  NPTC

Work-based Horticulture – Level 3
Awarding body:
  NPTC

Work-Based Land-based Operations – Level 1
Awarding body:
  NPTC

BTEC First Certificate

Floristry – Level 2
Awarding body:
  EDEXCEL

Horticulture – Level 2
Awarding body:
  EDEXCEL

BTEC First Diploma

Floristry – Level 2
Awarding body:
  EDEXCEL

Horticulture – Level 2
Awarding body:
  EDEXCEL

BTEC Higher National Certificate

Horticulture – Level 5
Awarding body:
  EDEXCEL

BTEC Higher National Diploma

Horticulture – Level 5
Awarding body:
  EDEXCEL

BTEC National Award

Countryside Management – Level 3
Awarding body:
  EDEXCEL

Floristry – Level 3
Awarding body:
  EDEXCEL

Forestry and Arboriculture – Level 3
Awarding body:
  EDEXCEL

Horticulture – Level 3
Awarding body:
  EDEXCEL

BTEC National Certificate

Countryside Management – Level 3
Awarding body:
  EDEXCEL

Floristry – Level 3
Awarding body:
  EDEXCEL

Forestry and Arboriculture – Level 3
Awarding body:
  EDEXCEL

Horticulture – Level 3
Awarding body:
  EDEXCEL

BTEC National Diploma

Countryside Management – Level 3
Awarding body:
  EDEXCEL

Floristry – Level 3
Awarding body:
  EDEXCEL

Forestry and Arboriculture – Level 3
Awarding body:
  EDEXCEL

Horticulture – Level 3
Awarding body:
  EDEXCEL

Certificate

Amenity Horticulture – Level 3
Awarding body:
  NPTC

Ancillary Operations for Sports and Amenity Turf Operators – Level 2
Awarding body:
  NPTC

Arboriculture (Theory) – Level 2
Awarding body:
  ABC

Brushcutting Operations – Level 2
Awarding body:
  NPTC

Chainsaw and Related Operations – Level 2
Awarding body:
  NPTC

Climb Trees and Perform Aerial Rescue – Level 2
Awarding body:
  NPTC

Floristry – Level 2
Awarding body:
  NPTC

Floristry – Level 3
Awarding body:
  NPTC

Forest Machine Operations – Level 2
Awarding body:
  NPTC

Garden and Planting Design – Level 3
Awarding body:
  NOCN

Garden Design – Level 2
Awarding body:
 NOCN

Gardening – Level 2
Awarding body:
 NPTC

Grassed and Planted Areas – Level 3
Awarding body:
 NPTC

Horticulture – Level 2
Awarding body:
 NPTC
 RHS

Landscape operations for front-line staff – Level 3
Awarding body:
 NPTC

Manually Fed Wood Chippers – Level 2
Awarding body:
 NPTC

Practical Horticulture Skills – Level 1
Awarding body:
 NPTC

Safe Operation of Dumper Trucks – Level 2
Awarding body:
 NPTC

Safe Use and Operation of Mobile Elevated Work Platforms – Level 2
Awarding body:
 NPTC

Safe Use of Abrasive Wheel Machines – Level 2
Awarding body:
 NPTC

Safe Use of Hedge Trimmers – Level 2
Awarding body:
 NPTC

Safe Use of Mowers – Level 2
Awarding body:
 NPTC

Safe Use of Pedestrian Controlled Power Driven Cultivators – Level 2
Awarding body:
 NPTC

Safe Use of Plant Machinery – Level 2
Awarding body:
 NPTC

Safe Use of Turf Maintenance Equipment – Level 2
Awarding body:
 NPTC

Stump Grinding Operations – Level 2
Awarding body:
 NPTC

Work-based Agriculture – Level 1
Awarding body:
 NPTC

Work-based Animal Care – Level 1
Awarding body:
 NPTC

Work-based Horticulture – Level 1
Awarding body:
 NPTC

Work-based Horticulture – Level 2
Awarding body:
 NPTC

Work-based Horticulture – Level 3
Awarding body:
 NPTC

Work-based Land-Based Operations – Level 1
Awarding body:
 NPTC

Diploma

Amenity Horticulture – Level 3
Awarding body:
 NPTC

Floristry – Level 2
Awarding body:
 NPTC

Floristry – Level 3
Awarding body:
  NPTC

Garden and Planting Design – Level 3
Awarding body:
  NOCN

Golf Course Supervision/Deputy Head Groundsman – Level 3
Awarding body:
  NPTC

Horticulture – Level 3
Awarding body:
  RHS

Landscape Management/Supervision – Level 3
Awarding body:
  NPTC

Landscape operations for front-line staff – Level 3
Awarding body:
  NPTC

Practical Horticulture Skills – Level 1
Awarding body:
  NPTC

Work-based Agriculture – Level 1
Awarding body:
  NPTC

Work-based Animal Care – Level 1
Awarding body:
  NPTC

Work-based Horticulture – Level 1
Awarding body:
  NPTC

Work-based Horticulture – Level 2
Awarding body:
  ABC
  NPTC

Work-based Horticulture – Level 3
Awarding body:
  ABC
  NPTC

Work-based Land-based Operations – Level 1
Awarding body:
  NPTC

Higher Diploma

Floristry(ICSF) – Level 4
Awarding body:
  NPTC

Master Diploma

Professional Floristry (NDSF) – Level 5
Awarding body:
  NPTC

National Certificate

Horticulture – Level 2
Awarding body:
  NPTC

Sports and Amenity Turf Maintenance – Level 2
Awarding body:
  NPTC

National Vocational Qualification

Amenity Horticulture Management – Level 4
Awarding body:
  NPTC

Arboriculture – Level 2
Awarding body:
  NPTC

Floristry – Level 2
Awarding body:
  NPTC

Floristry – Level 3
Awarding body:
  NPTC

Floristry Business Management – Level 4
Awarding body:
  NPTC

Forestry – Level 2
Awarding body:
   NPTC

Treework – Level 3
Awarding body:
   NPTC

Professional Diploma

Arboriculture – Level 6
Awarding body:
   ABC

Technicians Certificate

Arboriculture – Level 3
Awarding body:
   ABC

Arts, Media and Publishing

Crafts, Creative Arts and Design

Advanced Diploma

Creative and Media – Level 3
Awarding body:
AQA
City & Guilds
EDEXCEL
OCR
RSL

Award

3D Design – Level 1
Awarding body:
EDEXCEL

3D Materials Exploration – Level 3
Awarding body:
ABC

3D Visual Thinking – Level 3
Awarding body:
ABC

Application of Visual Thinking – Level 3
Awarding body:
ABC

Art and Design – Entry Level
Awarding body:
EDEXCEL

Art and Design – Level 1
Awarding body:
EDEXCEL
NOCN

Art and Design – Level 2
Awarding body:
NOCN

Art and Design – Level 3
Awarding body:
NOCN

Bookbinding Conservation – Level 3
Awarding body:
ABC

CAD Skills for Interior Design – Level 3
Awarding body:
ABC

Calligraphy Skills – Level 3
Awarding body:
ABC

Colour Theory and Practice – Level 3
Awarding body:
ABC

Communication Drawing – Level 3
Awarding body:
ABC

Copy Writing – Level 3
Awarding body:
ABC

Craft Bookbinding – Level 3
Awarding body:
ABC

Creative Book Structures – Level 3
Awarding body:
ABC

Creative Craft using Art and Design – Level 1
Awarding body:
NCFE

Creative Craft using Art and Design – Level 2
Awarding body:
NCFE

**Creative Craft using Balloon Crafts –
Level 1**
Awarding body:
  NCFE

**Creative Craft using Balloon Crafts –
Level 2**
Awarding body:
  NCFE

**Creative Craft using Beauty Crafts –
Level 1**
Awarding body:
  NCFE

**Creative Craft using Beauty Crafts –
Level 2**
Awarding body:
  NCFE

Creative Craft using Body Art – Level 1
Awarding body:
  NCFE

Creative Craft using Body Art – Level 2
Awarding body:
  NCFE

**Creative Craft using Bookbinding –
Level 1**
Awarding body:
  NCFE

**Creative Craft using Bookbinding –
Level 2**
Awarding body:
  NCFE

**Creative Craft using Cake Decoration –
Level 1**
Awarding body:
  NCFE

**Creative Craft using Cake Decoration –
Level 2**
Awarding body:
  NCFE

**Creative Craft using Carnival Crafts –
Level 1**
Awarding body:
  NCFE

**Creative Craft using Carnival Crafts –
Level 2**
Awarding body:
  NCFE

Creative Craft using Ceramics – Level 1
Awarding body:
  NCFE

Creative Craft using Ceramics – Level 2
Awarding body:
  NCFE

**Creative Craft using Construction Crafts
– Level 1**
Awarding body:
  NCFE

**Creative Craft using Construction Crafts
– Level 2**
Awarding body:
  NCFE

Creative Craft using Cookery – Level 1
Awarding body:
  NCFE

Creative Craft using Cookery – Level 2
Awarding body:
  NCFE

**Creative Craft using Creative Cards –
Level 1**
Awarding body:
  NCFE

**Creative Craft using Creative Cards –
Level 2**
Awarding body:
  NCFE

**Creative Craft using Digital Imaging –
Level 1**
Awarding body:
  NCFE

**Creative Craft using Digital Imaging –
Level 2**
Awarding body:
  NCFE

**Creative Craft using Drawing and
Painting – Level 1**
Awarding body:
  NCFE

Creative Craft using Drawing and Painting – Level 2
Awarding body:
  NCFE

Creative Craft using Dressmaking – Level 1
Awarding body:
  NCFE

Creative Craft using Dressmaking – Level 2
Awarding body:
  NCFE

Creative Craft using Embroidery – Level 1
Awarding body:
  NCFE

Creative Craft using Embroidery – Level 2
Awarding body:
  NCFE

Creative Craft using Environmental and Land-based Crafts – Level 1
Awarding body:
  NCFE

Creative Craft using Environmental and Land-based Crafts – Level 2
Awarding body:
  NCFE

Creative Craft using Fashion – Level 1
Awarding body:
  NCFE

Creative Craft using Fashion – Level 2
Awarding body:
  NCFE

Creative Craft using Fibre Crafts – Level 1
Awarding body:
  NCFE

Creative Craft using Fibre Crafts – Level 2
Awarding body:
  NCFE

Creative Craft using Floral Crafts – Level 1
Awarding body:
  NCFE

Creative Craft using Floral Crafts – Level 2
Awarding body:
  NCFE

Creative Craft using Floristry – Level 1
Awarding body:
  NCFE

Creative Craft using Floristry – Level 2
Awarding body:
  NCFE

Creative Craft using Furniture Crafts – Level 1
Awarding body:
  NCFE

Creative Craft using Furniture Crafts – Level 2
Awarding body:
  NCFE

Creative Craft using Garden Design – Level 1
Awarding body:
  NCFE

Creative Craft using Garden Design – Level 2
Awarding body:
  NCFE

Creative Craft using Glass Crafts – Level 1
Awarding body:
  NCFE

Creative Craft using Glass Crafts – Level 2
Awarding body:
  NCFE

Creative Craft using Graphic Crafts – Level 1
Awarding body:
  NCFE

**Creative Craft using Graphic Crafts –
Level 2**
Awarding body:
   NCFE

**Creative Craft using Hairdressing –
Level 1**
Awarding body:
   NCFE

**Creative Craft using Hairdressing –
Level 2**
Awarding body:
   NCFE

**Creative Craft using Illustration –
Level 1**
Awarding body:
   NCFE

**Creative Craft using Illustration –
Level 2**
Awarding body:
   NCFE

**Creative Craft using Interior Design –
Level 1**
Awarding body:
   NCFE

**Creative Craft using Interior Design –
Level 2**
Awarding body:
   NCFE

**Creative Craft using International
Cookery – Level 1**
Awarding body:
   NCFE

**Creative Craft using International
Cookery – Level 2**
Awarding body:
   NCFE

Creative Craft using Jewellery – Level 1
Awarding body:
   NCFE

Creative Craft using Jewellery – Level 2
Awarding body:
   NCFE

**Creative Craft using Life Drawing –
Level 1**
Awarding body:
   NCFE

**Creative Craft using Life Drawing –
Level 2**
Awarding body:
   NCFE

Creative Craft using Make-Up – Level 1
Awarding body:
   NCFE

Creative Craft using Make-Up – Level 2
Awarding body:
   NCFE

**Creative Craft using Metalwork –
Level 1**
Awarding body:
   NCFE

**Creative Craft using Metalwork –
Level 2**
Awarding body:
   NCFE

**Creative Craft using Mixed Crafts –
Level 1**
Awarding body:
   NCFE

**Creative Craft using Mixed Crafts –
Level 2**
Awarding body:
   NCFE

**Creative Craft using Model Making –
Level 1**
Awarding body:
   NCFE

**Creative Craft using Model Making –
Level 2**
Awarding body:
   NCFE

**Creative Craft using Music Composition
– Level 1**
Awarding body:
   NCFE

Creative Craft using Music Composition – Level 2
Awarding body:
NCFE

Creative Craft using Nail Art – Level 1
Awarding body:
NCFE

Creative Craft using Nail Art – Level 2
Awarding body:
NCFE

Creative Craft using Nursery Art – Level 1
Awarding body:
NCFE

Creative Craft using Nursery Art – Level 2
Awarding body:
NCFE

Creative Craft using Paper Crafts – Level 1
Awarding body:
NCFE

Creative Craft using Paper Crafts – Level 2
Awarding body:
NCFE

Creative Craft using Patisserie and Confectionery – Level 1
Awarding body:
NCFE

Creative Craft using Patisserie and Confectionery – Level 2
Awarding body:
NCFE

Creative Craft using Pattern Cutting – Level 1
Awarding body:
NCFE

Creative Craft using Pattern Cutting – Level 2
Awarding body:
NCFE

Creative Craft using Photography – Level 1
Awarding body:
NCFE

Creative Craft using Photography – Level 2
Awarding body:
NCFE

Creative Craft using Pottery – Level 1
Awarding body:
NCFE

Creative Craft using Pottery – Level 2
Awarding body:
NCFE

Creative Craft using Printing – Level 1
Awarding body:
NCFE

Creative Craft using Printing – Level 2
Awarding body:
NCFE

Creative Craft using Sculpture – Level 1
Awarding body:
NCFE

Creative Craft using Sculpture – Level 2
Awarding body:
NCFE

Creative Craft using Seasonal Crafts – Level 1
Awarding body:
NCFE

Creative Craft using Seasonal Crafts – Level 2
Awarding body:
NCFE

Creative Craft using Silversmithing – Level 1
Awarding body:
NCFE

Creative Craft using Silversmithing – Level 2
Awarding body:
NCFE

**Creative Craft using Soft Furnishings –
Level 1**
Awarding body:
   NCFE

**Creative Craft using Soft Furnishings –
Level 2**
Awarding body:
   NCFE

**Creative Craft using Stage Crafts –
Level 1**
Awarding body:
   NCFE

**Creative Craft using Stage Crafts –
Level 2**
Awarding body:
   NCFE

**Creative Craft using Stained Glass –
Level 1**
Awarding body:
   NCFE

**Creative Craft using Stained Glass –
Level 2**
Awarding body:
   NCFE

**Creative Craft using Sugar Decorative
Crafts – Level 1**
Awarding body:
   NCFE

**Creative Craft using Sugar Decorative
Crafts – Level 2**
Awarding body:
   NCFE

**Creative Craft using Technical Drawing
– Level 1**
Awarding body:
   NCFE

**Creative Craft using Technical Drawing
– Level 2**
Awarding body:
   NCFE

Creative Craft using Textiles – Level 1
Awarding body:
   NCFE

Creative Craft using Textiles – Level 2
Awarding body:
   NCFE

**Creative Craft using Time-based Studies
– Level 1**
Awarding body:
   NCFE

**Creative Craft using Time-based Studies
– Level 2**
Awarding body:
   NCFE

**Creative Craft using Toy Making –
Level 1**
Awarding body:
   NCFE

**Creative Craft using Toy Making –
Level 2**
Awarding body:
   NCFE

**Creative Craft using Upholstery –
Level 1**
Awarding body:
   NCFE

**Creative Craft using Upholstery –
Level 2**
Awarding body:
   NCFE

**Creative Craft using Watercolour
Painting – Level 1**
Awarding body:
   NCFE

**Creative Craft using Watercolour
Painting – Level 2**
Awarding body:
   NCFE

**Creative Craft using Wax Crafts –
Level 1**
Awarding body:
   NCFE

**Creative Craft using Wax Crafts –
Level 2**
Awarding body:
   NCFE

**Creative Craft using Window Dressing –
Level 1**
Awarding body:
  NCFE

**Creative Craft using Window Dressing –
Level 2**
Awarding body:
  NCFE

**Creative Craft using Wood Crafts –
Level 1**
Awarding body:
  NCFE

**Creative Craft using Wood Crafts –
Level 2**
Awarding body:
  NCFE

Creative Skills – Level 2
Awarding body:
  NOCN

Creative Skills – Level 3
Awarding body:
  NOCN

Creative Skills Development – Level 1
Awarding body:
  NOCN

**Creative Techiques in Textiles – Hand
Woven Functional Item – Level 3**
Awarding body:
  City & Guilds

**Creative Techniques in Balloon Artistry
– Aerial Balloon Displays – Level 2**
Awarding body:
  City & Guilds

**Creative Techniques in Balloon Artistry
– Aerial Balloons – Level 1**
Awarding body:
  City & Guilds

**Creative Techniques in Balloon Artistry
– Aerial Designs – Level 3**
Awarding body:
  City & Guilds

**Creative Techniques in Balloon Artistry
– Balloon Arrangements – Level 1**
Awarding body:
  City & Guilds

**Creative Techniques in Balloon Artistry
– Balloon Arrangements, Special
Occasions – Level 2**
Awarding body:
  City & Guilds

**Creative Techniques in Balloon Artistry
– Classic Balloon Décor – Level 1**
Awarding body:
  City & Guilds

**Creative Techniques in Balloon Artistry
– Classic Balloon Décor – Level 2**
Awarding body:
  City & Guilds

**Creative Techniques in Balloon Artistry
– Classic Balloon Décor – Level 3**
Awarding body:
  City & Guilds

**Creative Techniques in Balloon Artistry
– Corporate Balloon Arrangements –
Level 3**
Awarding body:
  City & Guilds

**Creative Techniques in Balloon Artistry
– Festive Balloon Design and Event
Décor – Level 2**
Awarding body:
  City & Guilds

**Creative Techniques in Balloon Artistry
– Festive Designs and Event Décor –
Level 3**
Awarding body:
  City & Guilds

**Creative Techniques in Balloon Artistry
– Festive Occasions and Event Décor –
Level 1**
Awarding body:
  City & Guilds

**Creative Techniques in Building
Business Knowledge – Analysing
Creative Businesses – Level 2**
Awarding body:
  City & Guilds

Creative Techniques in Building Business Knowledge – Handbook for a Creative Business – Level 3
Awarding body:
    City & Guilds

Creative Techniques in Building Business Knowledge – Local Creative Businesses – Level 1
Awarding body:
    City & Guilds

Creative Techniques in Ceramic Pathway Press Moulding – Level 2
Awarding body:
    City & Guilds

Creative Techniques in Ceramics -Thrown Containers with Lids – Level 3
Awarding body:
    City & Guilds

Creative Techniques in Ceramics – Coiled Clay Form – Level 2
Awarding body:
    City & Guilds

Creative Techniques in Ceramics – Coiled Form – Level 1
Awarding body:
    City & Guilds

Creative Techniques in Ceramics – Glaze Developments – Level 3
Awarding body:
    City & Guilds

Creative Techniques in Ceramics – Glazes – Level 2
Awarding body:
    City & Guilds

Creative Techniques in Ceramics – Large Coiled Form – Level 3
Awarding body:
    City & Guilds

Creative Techniques in Ceramics – Low Relief Tile Panel – Level 3
Awarding body:
    City & Guilds

Creative Techniques in Ceramics – Open and Decorated Thrown Form – Level 2
Awarding body:
    City & Guilds

Creative Techniques in Ceramics – Pinched Forms – Level 2
Awarding body:
    City & Guilds

Creative Techniques in Ceramics – Pinched Forms – Level 3
Awarding body:
    City & Guilds

Creative Techniques in Ceramics – Slab Built Form – Level 1
Awarding body:
    City & Guilds

Creative Techniques in Ceramics – Slab Built Form – Level 2
Awarding body:
    City & Guilds

Creative Techniques in Ceramics – Slab Form with Lid – Level 3
Awarding body:
    City & Guilds

Creative Techniques in Ceramics – Slip Cast Modular Form – Level 3
Awarding body:
    City & Guilds

Creative Techniques in Ceramics – Surface Decoration – Level 2
Awarding body:
    City & Guilds

Creative Techniques in Ceramics – Surface Decoration – Level 3
Awarding body:
    City & Guilds

Creative Techniques in Ceramics – Thrown Open Form – Level 1
Awarding body:
    City & Guilds

Creative Techniques in Ceramics – Tile Making – Level 2
Awarding body:
    City & Guilds

Creative Techniques in Create, Store and Use Data for a Creative Business – Level 3
Awarding body:
City & Guilds

Creative Techniques in Creating Promotional Material for a Product and Creative Business – Level 3
Awarding body:
City & Guilds

Creative Techniques in Creating Promotional Material for Corporate Business – Level 2
Awarding body:
City & Guilds

Creative Techniques in Creative Computing – 2D Digital Drawing – Level 1
Awarding body:
City & Guilds

Creative Techniques in Creative Computing – 2D Digital Drawing and Text – Level 3
Awarding body:
City & Guilds

Creative Techniques in Creative Computing – 2D Narrative – Level 1
Awarding body:
City & Guilds

Creative Techniques in Creative Computing – 2D/3D Narrative – Level 3
Awarding body:
City & Guilds

Creative Techniques in Creative Computing – Advanced 2D Narrative – Level 2
Awarding body:
City & Guilds

Creative Techniques in Creative Computing – Captioned 2D Digital Drawing – Level 2
Awarding body:
City & Guilds

Creative Techniques in Creative Computing – Character Concept Art – Level 1
Awarding body:
City & Guilds

Creative Techniques in Creative Computing – Commercial Website Design – Level 3
Awarding body:
City & Guilds

Creative Techniques in Creative Computing – Concept Art, Digital Gallery – Level 3
Awarding body:
City & Guilds

Creative Techniques in Creative Computing – Concept Art, Portfolio – Level 2
Awarding body:
City & Guilds

Creative Techniques in Creative Computing – Digital Collage and Montage – Level 1
Awarding body:
City & Guilds

Creative Techniques in Creative Computing – DVD Portfolio of Digital Composite Imagery – Level 2
Awarding body:
City & Guilds

Creative Techniques in Creative Computing – Exploring Typography – Level 1
Awarding body:
City & Guilds

Creative Techniques in Creative Computing – Folding Package – Level 1
Awarding body:
City & Guilds

Creative Techniques in Creative Computing – Homepage Design – Level 1
Awarding body:
City & Guilds

Creative Techniques in Creative Computing – Illustrated Publication – Level 3
Awarding body:
   City & Guilds

Creative Techniques in Creative Computing – Interactive Portfolio of Digital Composite Imagery – Level 3
Awarding body:
   City & Guilds

Creative Techniques in Creative Computing – Letter Form in an Environment – Level 2
Awarding body:
   City & Guilds

Creative Techniques in Creative Computing – Package Design – Level 2
Awarding body:
   City & Guilds

Creative Techniques in Creative Computing – Promotional Video – Level 1
Awarding body:
   City & Guilds

Creative Techniques in Creative Computing – Theatrical Trailer – Level 3
Awarding body:
   City & Guilds

Creative Techniques in Creative Computing – Type Design – Level 3
Awarding body:
   City & Guilds

Creative Techniques in Creative Computing – Video Diary – Level 2
Awarding body:
   City & Guilds

Creative Techniques in Creative Computing – Website Design – Level 2
Awarding body:
   City & Guilds

Creative Techniques in Creative Sketchbooks – Level 1
Awarding body:
   City & Guilds

Creative Techniques in Creative Sketchbooks – Level 2
Awarding body:
   City & Guilds

Creative Techniques in Creative Sketchbooks – Level 3
Awarding body:
   City & Guilds

Creative Techniques in Decorated Interior Textiles – Colour – Level 2
Awarding body:
   City & Guilds

Creative Techniques in Decorated Interior Textiles – Pattern – Level 2
Awarding body:
   City & Guilds

Creative Techniques in Decorative Effects – A Set of Full Sized Stained and Polished Stool or Chair Legs – Level 2
Awarding body:
   City & Guilds

Creative Techniques in Decorative Effects – Advanced Broken Colour Paint Effects – Level 3
Awarding body:
   City & Guilds

Creative Techniques in Decorative Effects – Advanced Marbling Effects – Level 3
Awarding body:
   City & Guilds

Creative Techniques in Decorative Effects – Advanced Stencilling Effects – Level 3
Awarding body:
   City & Guilds

Creative Techniques in Decorative Effects – Advanced Wood Graining Effects – Level 3
Awarding body:
   City & Guilds

Creative Techniques in Decorative Effects – Application of Metal Leaf – Level 2
Awarding body:
   City & Guilds

Creative Techniques in Decorative Effects – Decorative Painting of Wall and Door Surfaces – Level 3
Awarding body:
  City & Guilds

Creative Techniques in Decorative Effects – Distressing and Ageing Paint Effects – Level 3
Awarding body:
  City & Guilds

Creative Techniques in Decorative Effects – Experimental Collection of Decorative, Painted Samples – Level 3
Awarding body:
  City & Guilds

Creative Techniques in Decorative Effects – Marbling – Level 2
Awarding body:
  City & Guilds

Creative Techniques in Decorative Effects – Stained and Polished Box or Display Case – Level 2
Awarding body:
  City & Guilds

Creative Techniques in Decorative Effects – Wood Graining – Level 2
Awarding body:
  City & Guilds

Creative Techniques in Design – Level 1
Awarding body:
  City & Guilds

Creative Techniques in Design – Level 2
Awarding body:
  City & Guilds

Creative Techniques in Design for Interior Décor – Studio Apartment – Level 3
Awarding body:
  City & Guilds

Creative Techniques in Design for Interiors – Interior Décor, Broken Colour Effects – Level 2
Awarding body:
  City & Guilds

Creative Techniques in Design for Interiors – Interior Design Bedroom and Bathroom – Level 1
Awarding body:
  City & Guilds

Creative Techniques in Design for Interiors – Interior Design Living Room and Kitchen – Level 1
Awarding body:
  City & Guilds

Creative Techniques in Design for Interiors – Interior Design, Bedroom with En Suite Shower Room – Level 2
Awarding body:
  City & Guilds

Creative Techniques in Design for Interiors – Interior Design, Home Based Office – Level 2
Awarding body:
  City & Guilds

Creative Techniques in Design for Interiors – Interior Design, Loft Space – Level 2
Awarding body:
  City & Guilds

Creative Techniques in Design for Interiors – Paint Effects – Level 1
Awarding body:
  City & Guilds

Creative Techniques in Design for Interiors – Textile Decoration – Level 1
Awarding body:
  City & Guilds

Creative Techniques in Drawing and Painting – Colour Study – Level 2
Awarding body:
  City & Guilds

Creative Techniques in Drawing and Painting – Facial Expressions – Level 3
Awarding body:
  City & Guilds

Creative Techniques in Drawing and Painting – Full Length Figure – Level 2
Awarding body:
  City & Guilds

Creative Techniques in Drawing and Painting – Human Figure, Colour – Level 1
Awarding body:
City & Guilds

Creative Techniques in Drawing and Painting – Interior – Level 3
Awarding body:
City & Guilds

Creative Techniques in Drawing and Painting – Landscape – Level 3
Awarding body:
City & Guilds

Creative Techniques in Drawing and Painting – Landscape, Garden or Woodland Scene – Level 2
Awarding body:
City & Guilds

Creative Techniques in Drawing and Painting – Natural Form – Level 2
Awarding body:
City & Guilds

Creative Techniques in Drawing and Painting – Natural Form – Level 3
Awarding body:
City & Guilds

Creative Techniques in Drawing and Painting – Oils and Acrylics – Level 1
Awarding body:
City & Guilds

Creative Techniques in Drawing and Painting – Reflective Surfaces – Level 3
Awarding body:
City & Guilds

Creative Techniques in Drawing and Painting – Still Life – Level 2
Awarding body:
City & Guilds

Creative Techniques in Drawing and Painting – Still Life with Background – Level 3
Awarding body:
City & Guilds

Creative Techniques in Drawing and Painting – Townscape or Building Study – Level 2
Awarding body:
City & Guilds

Creative Techniques in Drawing and Painting – Townscape with Buildings and Figures – Level 3
Awarding body:
City & Guilds

Creative Techniques in Drawing and Painting – Watercolour and Inks – Level 1
Awarding body:
City & Guilds

Creative Techniques in Drawing and Painting – Waterscape – Level 2
Awarding body:
City & Guilds

Creative Techniques in Drawing and Painting – Waterscape – Level 3
Awarding body:
City & Guilds

Creative Techniques in Drawing Skills – Perspective – Level 2
Awarding body:
City & Guilds

Creative Techniques in Drawing Skills – Portfolio – Level 1
Awarding body:
City & Guilds

Creative Techniques in Drawing Systems – Perspective – Level 3
Awarding body:
City & Guilds

Creative Techniques in Drawings Systems – Form – Level 3
Awarding body:
City & Guilds

Creative Techniques in Fashion – A Blouse or Shirt with Advanced Styling – Level 3
Awarding body:
City & Guilds

Creative Techniques in Fashion – A Blouse, Shirt or Jacket – Level 2
Awarding body:
    City & Guilds

Creative Techniques in Fashion – A Panelled Skirt – Level 2
Awarding body:
    City & Guilds

Creative Techniques in Fashion – A Tailored Jacket – Level 2
Awarding body:
    City & Guilds

Creative Techniques in Fashion – A Tailored Skirt – Level 2
Awarding body:
    City & Guilds

Creative Techniques in Fashion – A Victorian Style Corset – Level 2
Awarding body:
    City & Guilds

Creative Techniques in Fashion – Advanced Fabric Decoration – Level 3
Awarding body:
    City & Guilds

Creative Techniques in Fashion – Advanced Millinery, Blocked Felt Hat with Decorative Join – Level 3
Awarding body:
    City & Guilds

Creative Techniques in Fashion – Advanced Millinery, Bridal Headwear – Level 3
Awarding body:
    City & Guilds

Creative Techniques in Fashion – Advanced Millinery, Pile Fabric Soft Hat – Level 3
Awarding body:
    City & Guilds

Creative Techniques in Fashion – Advanced Style Cullotte, Trousers or Shorts – Level 3
Awarding body:
    City & Guilds

Creative Techniques in Fashion – Advanced Style Dress – Level 3
Awarding body:
    City & Guilds

Creative Techniques in Fashion – Advanced Style, Lined Jacket – Level 3
Awarding body:
    City & Guilds

Creative Techniques in Fashion – An Advanced Style Skirt – Level 3
Awarding body:
    City & Guilds

Creative Techniques in Fashion – Casual Trousers – Level 1
Awarding body:
    City & Guilds

Creative Techniques in Fashion – Computer Pattern Grading, Blouse or Shirt – Level 2
Awarding body:
    City & Guilds

Creative Techniques in Fashion – Computer Pattern Grading, Skirt and Trousers or Shorts – Level 2
Awarding body:
    City & Guilds

Creative Techniques in Fashion – Computer Pattern Grading, Waistcoat and Jacket – Level 2
Awarding body:
    City & Guilds

Creative Techniques in Fashion – Corsetry Bra – Level 2
Awarding body:
    City & Guilds

Creative Techniques in Fashion – Embellished Bag with a Handle – Level 1
Awarding body:
    City & Guilds

Creative Techniques in Fashion – Fabric Decoration – Level 1
Awarding body:
    City & Guilds

Creative Techniques in Fashion – Fabric Decoration, Added Colour – Level 2
Awarding body:
  City & Guilds

Creative Techniques in Fashion – Fabric Decoration, Added Pattern – Level 2
Awarding body:
  City & Guilds

Creative Techniques in Fashion – Fabric Hat – Level 1
Awarding body:
  City & Guilds

Creative Techniques in Fashion – Fitted, Unlined Trousers – Level 2
Awarding body:
  City & Guilds

Creative Techniques in Fashion – Illustration – Level 1
Awarding body:
  City & Guilds

Creative Techniques in Fashion – Illustration, Children's Wear – Level 2
Awarding body:
  City & Guilds

Creative Techniques in Fashion – Illustration, Women's and Men's Wear Collection – Level 2
Awarding body:
  City & Guilds

Creative Techniques in Fashion – Illustration, Women's Wear – Level 2
Awarding body:
  City & Guilds

Creative Techniques in Fashion – Lingerie – Level 2
Awarding body:
  City & Guilds

Creative Techniques in Fashion – Millinery, Blocked Felt Hat – Level 2
Awarding body:
  City & Guilds

Creative Techniques in Fashion – Millinery, Blocked Straw Hat with a Brim – Level 2
Awarding body:
  City & Guilds

Creative Techniques in Fashion – Millinery, Soft Hat with Textured Sideband – Level 2
Awarding body:
  City & Guilds

Creative Techniques in Fashion – Pattern Cutting and Modelling – Level 3
Awarding body:
  City & Guilds

Creative Techniques in Fashion – Pattern Cutting, Adapting a Bodice Block to a Design – Level 2
Awarding body:
  City & Guilds

Creative Techniques in Fashion – Pattern Cutting, Bodice and Sleeve Blocks and Toiles – Level 2
Awarding body:
  City & Guilds

Creative Techniques in Fashion – Pattern Cutting, Dress Blocks and Adaptations – Level 2
Awarding body:
  City & Guilds

Creative Techniques in Fashion – Pattern Cutting, Skirt and Trouser Blocks and Toiles – Level 2
Awarding body:
  City & Guilds

Creative Techniques in Fashion – Sewing Machine Skills – Level 1
Awarding body:
  City & Guilds

Creative Techniques in Fashion – Sleeveless Blouse or Top – Level 1
Awarding body:
  City & Guilds

Creative Techniques in Fashion – Theatre Costume for a Named Character – Level 2
Awarding body:
    City & Guilds

Creative Techniques in Fashion – Theatre Costume from Found Objects – Level 1
Awarding body:
    City & Guilds

Creative Techniques in Fashion – Theatre Costume from Paper – Level 1
Awarding body:
    City & Guilds

Creative Techniques in Fashion – Theatre Costume with Supports – Level 3
Awarding body:
    City & Guilds

Creative Techniques in Fashion – Theatre Costume, Advanced Historical Costume – Level 3
Awarding body:
    City & Guilds

Creative Techniques in Fashion – Theatre Costume, Body Extensions for Character Performance – Level 3
Awarding body:
    City & Guilds

Creative Techniques in Fashion – Theatre Costume, Historical and Accessory – Level 2
Awarding body:
    City & Guilds

Creative Techniques in Fashion – Unlined Skirt – Level 1
Awarding body:
    City & Guilds

Creative Techniques in Fashion – Waspie Corset – Level 2
Awarding body:
    City & Guilds

Creative Techniques in Fashion Accessory – Structured, Lined Handbag – Level 2
Awarding body:
    City & Guilds

Creative Techniques in Fashion, Theatre Costume, An Advanced Accessory – Level 3
Awarding body:
    City & Guilds

Creative Techniques in Floral Design – Accurate Botanical Illustrations – Level 3
Awarding body:
    City & Guilds

Creative Techniques in Floral Design – Bespoke Tributes – Level 3
Awarding body:
    City & Guilds

Creative Techniques in Floral Design – Botanical Drawings – Level 1
Awarding body:
    City & Guilds

Creative Techniques in Floral Design – Botanical Illustrations – Level 2
Awarding body:
    City & Guilds

Creative Techniques in Floral Design – Boutonnieres and Corsages – Level 1
Awarding body:
    City & Guilds

Creative Techniques in Floral Design – Co-ordinated Wedding Items – Level 2
Awarding body:
    City & Guilds

Creative Techniques in Floral Design – Complex Hand Tied Designs – Level 3
Awarding body:
    City & Guilds

Creative Techniques in Floral Design – Contemporary Floral Designs; Colour, Line and Texture – Level 1
Awarding body:
    City & Guilds

Creative Techniques in Floral Design – Contemporary Floral Designs; Material Manipulation and Collage – Level 2
Awarding body:
City & Guilds

Creative Techniques in Floral Design – Contemporary Floral Designs; Shape and Form – Level 3
Awarding body:
City & Guilds

Creative Techniques in Floral Design – Decorative Table Arrangements – Level 2
Awarding body:
City & Guilds

Creative Techniques in Floral Design – Hand Tied Bouquets – Level 2
Awarding body:
City & Guilds

Creative Techniques in Floral Design – Hanging Decorative Items – Level 2
Awarding body:
City & Guilds

Creative Techniques in Floral Design – Hanging Floral Displays for Special Occasions – Level 3
Awarding body:
City & Guilds

Creative Techniques in Floral Design – Hung Items and Garlands – Level 1
Awarding body:
City & Guilds

Creative Techniques in Floral Design – Large Decorative Arrangements – Level 3
Awarding body:
City & Guilds

Creative techniques in Floral Design – Small Hand Tied Items – Level 1
Awarding body:
City & Guilds

Creative Techniques in Floral Design – Small Tributes – Level 1
Awarding body:
City & Guilds

Creative Techniques in Floral Design – Specialist Wedding Designs – Level 3
Awarding body:
City & Guilds

Creative Techniques in Floral Design – Traditional Floral Arrangements – Level 1
Awarding body:
City & Guilds

Creative Techniques in Floral Design – Tributes with Bases – Level 2
Awarding body:
City & Guilds

Creative Techniques in Floral Design – Wedding Items – Level 1
Awarding body:
City & Guilds

Creative Techniques in Floral Design – Wired Bridal Bouquets – Level 3
Awarding body:
City & Guilds

Creative Techniques in Floral Design – Wired Items – Level 2
Awarding body:
City & Guilds

Creative Techniques in Garden Design – Country Garden – Level 1
Awarding body:
City & Guilds

Creative Techniques in Garden Design – Low Maintenance Garden – Level 2
Awarding body:
City & Guilds

Creative Techniques in Garden Design – Urban Garden – Level 2
Awarding body:
City & Guilds

Creative Techniques in Glasswork – 2D Copper Foil Item – Level 1
Awarding body:
City & Guilds

Creative Techniques in Glasswork – 3D Copper Foil Item – Level 2
Awarding body:
City & Guilds

Creative Techniques in Glasswork – Cast Glass, Item – Level 2
Awarding body:
    City & Guilds

Creative Techniques in Glasswork – Cast Glass, Panel – Level 1
Awarding body:
    City & Guilds

Creative Techniques in Glasswork – Cast Glass, Sculpture – Level 3
Awarding body:
    City & Guilds

Creative Techniques in Glasswork – Fused Glass Jewellery Item – Level 1
Awarding body:
    City & Guilds

Creative Techniques in Glasswork – Fused Glass Jewellery, Range – Level 3
Awarding body:
    City & Guilds

Creative Techniques in Glasswork – Fused Glass Jewellery, Set – Level 2
Awarding body:
    City & Guilds

Creative Techniques in Glasswork – Leaded Panel – Level 1
Awarding body:
    City & Guilds

Creative Techniques in Glasswork – Leaded Panel, Architectural – Level 3
Awarding body:
    City & Guilds

Creative Techniques in Glasswork – Leaded Panel, Decorative – Level 2
Awarding body:
    City & Guilds

Creative Techniques in Glasswork – Pate de Verre, One Mould Sculpture or Vessel – Level 2
Awarding body:
    City & Guilds

Creative Techniques in Glasswork – Pate de Verre, Textured Sheet – Level 1
Awarding body:
    City & Guilds

Creative Techniques in Glasswork – Pate de Verre, Two Mould Item – Level 3
Awarding body:
    City & Guilds

Creative Techniques in Glasswork – Sandblasted Architectural Panel – Level 3
Awarding body:
    City & Guilds

Creative Techniques in Glasswork – Sandblasted Panel – Level 2
Awarding body:
    City & Guilds

Creative Techniques in Glasswork – Sandblasting – Level 1
Awarding body:
    City & Guilds

Creative Techniques in Glasswork – Sculptural Copper Foil Form – Level 3
Awarding body:
    City & Guilds

Creative Techniques in Glasswork – Slumped Glass Item – Level 1
Awarding body:
    City & Guilds

Creative Techniques in Glasswork – Slumped Glass Vessel – Level 2
Awarding body:
    City & Guilds

Creative Techniques in Glasswork – Slumped Glass, Set of Vessels – Level 3
Awarding body:
    City & Guilds

Creative Techniques in Glasswork – Warm Glass Panel – Level 1
Awarding body:
    City & Guilds

Creative Techniques in Glasswork – Warm Glass Panel – Level 2
Awarding body:
    City & Guilds

Creative Techniques in Glasswork – Warm Glass, Installation – Level 3
Awarding body:
    City & Guilds

Creative Techniques in Interior Décor – Kitchen and Utility Room – Level 3
Awarding body:
City & Guilds

Creative Techniques in Interior Décor – Master Bedroom Suite with Integral Wet Room and Walk-In Wardrobe Facilities – Level 3
Awarding body:
City & Guilds

Creative Techniques in Interior Décor – Outdoor Room – Level 3
Awarding body:
City & Guilds

Creative Techniques in Interior Décor – Sitting Room with French Doors leading to a Conservatory – Level 3
Awarding body:
City & Guilds

Creative Techniques in Interior Décor – Study and Hobby Room – Level 3
Awarding body:
City & Guilds

Creative Techniques in Introduction to Creating Promotional Materials – Level 1
Awarding body:
City & Guilds

Creative Techniques in Jewellery – Assembly Device – Level 3
Awarding body:
City & Guilds

Creative Techniques in Jewellery – Box Snap – Level 3
Awarding body:
City & Guilds

Creative Techniques in Jewellery – Bracelet Joints – Level 3
Awarding body:
City & Guilds

Creative Techniques in Jewellery – Brooch – Level 1
Awarding body:
City & Guilds

Creative Techniques in Jewellery – Brooch – Level 2
Awarding body:
City & Guilds

Creative Techniques in Jewellery – Brooch Findings – Level 2
Awarding body:
City & Guilds

Creative Techniques in Jewellery – Chain – Level 2
Awarding body:
City & Guilds

Creative Techniques in Jewellery – Clasp Device – Level 2
Awarding body:
City & Guilds

Creative Techniques in Jewellery – Cluster Ring – Level 2
Awarding body:
City & Guilds

Creative Techniques in Jewellery – Cuff-links – Level 1
Awarding body:
City & Guilds

Creative Techniques in Jewellery – Decorated Buttons – Level 2
Awarding body:
City & Guilds

Creative Techniques in Jewellery – Decorative Band Ring – Level 1
Awarding body:
City & Guilds

Creative Techniques in Jewellery – Dress Ring – Level 2
Awarding body:
City & Guilds

Creative Techniques in Jewellery – Fretwork Brooch – Level 3
Awarding body:
City & Guilds

Creative Techniques in Jewellery – Hollow Bead Pendant – Level 2
Awarding body:
City & Guilds

**Creative Techniques in Jewellery –
Master Pattern – Level 3**
Awarding body:
City & Guilds

**Creative Techniques in Jewellery – Pair
of Earrings – Level 1**
Awarding body:
City & Guilds

**Creative Techniques in Jewellery –
Pendant – Level 1**
Awarding body:
City & Guilds

**Creative Techniques in Jewellery –
Pendant of Stone Settings – Level 3**
Awarding body:
City & Guilds

**Creative Techniques in Jewellery –
Personalised Key Fob – Level 1**
Awarding body:
City & Guilds

**Creative Techniques in Jewellery – Ring
with a Cabochon Stone – Level 1**
Awarding body:
City & Guilds

**Creative Techniques in Jewellery –
Tri-coloured Ring – Level 3**
Awarding body:
City & Guilds

**Creative Techniques in Jewellery –
Unusual Setting – Level 3**
Awarding body:
City & Guilds

**Creative Techniques in Jewellery – Wrist
Chain – Level 1**
Awarding body:
City & Guilds

**Creative Techniques in Life Drawing –
Anatomical Illustrations – Level 3**
Awarding body:
City & Guilds

**Creative Techniques in Life Drawing –
Anatomy – Level 2**
Awarding body:
City & Guilds

**Creative Techniques in Life Drawing –
Figure, Colour – Level 3**
Awarding body:
City & Guilds

**Creative Techniques in Life Drawing –
Full Human Figure, Linear – Level 2**
Awarding body:
City & Guilds

**Creative Techniques in Life Drawing –
Full Human Figure, Tonal – Level 2**
Awarding body:
City & Guilds

**Creative Techniques in Life Drawing –
Full Length Pose, Linear – Level 3**
Awarding body:
City & Guilds

**Creative Techniques in Life Drawing –
Full Length Pose, Tonal – Level 3**
Awarding body:
City & Guilds

**Creative Techniques in Life Drawing –
Gesture Drawings – Level 2**
Awarding body:
City & Guilds

**Creative Techniques in Life Drawing –
Hands and Feet – Level 1**
Awarding body:
City & Guilds

**Creative Techniques in Life Drawing –
Heads, Hands and Feet – Level 2**
Awarding body:
City & Guilds

**Creative Techniques in Life Drawing –
Human Figure, Linear – Level 1**
Awarding body:
City & Guilds

**Creative Techniques in Life Drawing –
Human Figure, Tonal – Level 1**
Awarding body:
City & Guilds

**Creative Techniques in Life Drawing –
Movement – Level 3**
Awarding body:
City & Guilds

**Creative Techniques in Life Drawing –
Portraiture – Level 2**
Awarding body:
City & Guilds

**Creative Techniques in Life Drawing –
Realistic Portrait – Level 3**
Awarding body:
City & Guilds

**Creative Techniques in Mark Making –
Images from Photographs – Level 2**
Awarding body:
City & Guilds

**Creative Techniques in Mark Making –
Individual Studies – Level 3**
Awarding body:
City & Guilds

**Creative Techniques in Mark Making –
Low Relief – Level 2**
Awarding body:
City & Guilds

**Creative Techniques in Mark Making –
Portfolio of Work – Level 2**
Awarding body:
City & Guilds

**Creative Techniques in Mixed Media –
Abstract Artwork – Level 3**
Awarding body:
City & Guilds

**Creative Techniques in Mixed Media –
Black and White Studies – Level 2**
Awarding body:
City & Guilds

**Creative Techniques in Mixed Media –
Collage – Level 1**
Awarding body:
City & Guilds

**Creative Techniques in Mixed Media –
Developed Piece – Level 2**
Awarding body:
City & Guilds

**Creative Techniques in Mixed Media –
Low Relief Compositions – Level 2**
Awarding body:
City & Guilds

**Creative Techniques in Passementerie –
Level 1**
Awarding body:
City & Guilds

**Creative Techniques in Passementerie –
a Functional Item – Level 3**
Awarding body:
City & Guilds

**Creative Techniques in Passementerie –
Accessory – Level 3**
Awarding body:
City & Guilds

**Creative Techniques in Passementerie –
Matching Set of a Tassel, Cord and
Woven Braid – Level 2**
Awarding body:
City & Guilds

**Creative Techniques in Passementerie –
Sample Collection – Level 3**
Awarding body:
City & Guilds

**Creative Techniques in Passementerie –
Traditional Tassel Tie Back with
Trimmings – Level 2**
Awarding body:
City & Guilds

**Creative Techniques in Passementerie –
Wall Hanging – Level 3**
Awarding body:
City & Guilds

**Creative Techniques in Printmaking –
Block Prints – Level 2**
Awarding body:
City & Guilds

**Creative Techniques in Printmaking –
Collagraph Prints – Level 2**
Awarding body:
City & Guilds

**Creative Techniques in Printmaking –
Drypoint Printing – Level 3**
Awarding body:
City & Guilds

**Creative Techniques in Printmaking –
Glue Prints – Level 1**
Awarding body:
   City & Guilds

**Creative Techniques in Printmaking –
Lino Prints – Level 2**
Awarding body:
   City & Guilds

**Creative Techniques in Printmaking –
Monoprinting – Level 2**
Awarding body:
   City & Guilds

**Creative Techniques in Printmaking –
Monoprinting – Level 3**
Awarding body:
   City & Guilds

**Creative Techniques in Printmaking –
Monotype Printing – Level 3**
Awarding body:
   City & Guilds

**Creative Techniques in Printmaking –
Multiple Block Lino Printing – Level 3**
Awarding body:
   City & Guilds

**Creative Techniques in Printmaking –
Printing with Found Materials – Level 1**
Awarding body:
   City & Guilds

**Creative Techniques in Printmaking –
Relief Printing – Level 2**
Awarding body:
   City & Guilds

**Creative Techniques in Printmaking –
Resist Prints – Level 2**
Awarding body:
   City & Guilds

**Creative Techniques in Printmaking –
Screen Printing – Level 2**
Awarding body:
   City & Guilds

**Creative Techniques in Printmaking –
Silk Screen Printing – Level 3**
Awarding body:
   City & Guilds

**Creative Techniques in Printmaking –
Stencil Printing – Level 2**
Awarding body:
   City & Guilds

**Creative Techniques in Printmaking –
Stencil Printing – Level 3**
Awarding body:
   City & Guilds

**Creative Techniques in Producing
Documents for a Creative Business –
Level 1**
Awarding body:
   City & Guilds

**Creative Techniques in Producing
Documents for a Creative Business –
Level 2**
Awarding body:
   City & Guilds

**Creative Techniques in Professional
Practice associated with the Creative
Industries – Level 1**
Awarding body:
   City & Guilds

**Creative Techniques in Professional
Practice associated with the Creative
Industries – Level 2**
Awarding body:
   City & Guilds

**Creative Techniques in Professional
Practice associated with the Creative
Industries – Level 3**
Awarding body:
   City & Guilds

**Creative Techniques in Research for
Design – Level 3**
Awarding body:
   City & Guilds

**Creative Techniques in Sampling –
Design Ideas – Level 1**
Awarding body:
   City & Guilds

**Creative Techniques in Sampling –
Develop, Refine and Innovate Ideas –
Level 3**
Awarding body:
   City & Guilds

**Creative Techniques in Sampling –
Exploring Potential of Ideas and
Materials – Level 2**
Awarding body:
City & Guilds

**Creative Techniques in Soft Furnishings
– Advanced Shaped Window Treatments
– Level 3**
Awarding body:
City & Guilds

**Creative Techniques in Soft Furnishings
– Co-ordinated Bed Furnishings –
Level 3**
Awarding body:
City & Guilds

**Creative Techniques in Soft Furnishings
– Co-ordinated Cushions – Level 3**
Awarding body:
City & Guilds

**Creative Techniques in Soft Furnishings
– Collection of Rug Samples – Level 2**
Awarding body:
City & Guilds

**Creative Techniques in Soft Furnishings
– Decorative Cushion – Level 2**
Awarding body:
City & Guilds

**Creative Techniques in Soft Furnishings
– Decorative Duvet Cover – Level 2**
Awarding body:
City & Guilds

**Creative Techniques in Soft Furnishings
– Experimental Collection of Samples –
Level 3**
Awarding body:
City & Guilds

**Creative Techniques in Soft Furnishings
– Firm Lampshade – Level 2**
Awarding body:
City & Guilds

**Creative Techniques in Soft Furnishings
– Interlined Curtains – Level 2**
Awarding body:
City & Guilds

**Creative Techniques in Soft Furnishings
– Lined Curtain Valance and Pair of Tie
Backs – Level 2**
Awarding body:
City & Guilds

**Creative Techniques in Soft Furnishings
– Loose Cover for an Arm Chair –
Level 3**
Awarding body:
City & Guilds

**Creative Techniques in Soft Furnishings
– Loose Cover for an Easy Chair –
Level 2**
Awarding body:
City & Guilds

**Creative Techniques in Soft Furnishings
– Making Lined Curtains – Level 1**
Awarding body:
City & Guilds

**Creative Techniques in Soft Furnishings
– Pair of Interlined Draw Curtains with
an Advanced Heading, Swags and Tails –
Level 3**
Awarding body:
City & Guilds

**Creative Techniques in Soft Furnishings
– Sewing Machine Skills – Level 1**
Awarding body:
City & Guilds

**Creative Techniques in Soft Furnishings
– Simple Decorated Cushion – Level 1**
Awarding body:
City & Guilds

**Creative Techniques in Soft Furnishings
– Tailored Lampshade – Level 2**
Awarding body:
City & Guilds

**Creative Techniques in Soft Furnishings
– Window Blind – Level 2**
Awarding body:
City & Guilds

**Creative Techniques in Start-up Business
Skills – Business Plan for a Creative
Business – Level 3**
Awarding body:
City & Guilds

Creative Techniques in Start-up Business Skills – Promoting a Creative Product – Level 2
Awarding body:
City & Guilds

Creative Techniques in Start-up Business Skills – Promotion for an Item – Level 1
Awarding body:
City & Guilds

Creative Techniques in Sugar Decoration – Bar Gateau – Level 1
Awarding body:
City & Guilds

Creative Techniques in Sugar Decoration – Botanical Study – Level 1
Awarding body:
City & Guilds

Creative Techniques in Sugar Decoration – Botanical Study – Level 2
Awarding body:
City & Guilds

Creative Techniques in Sugar Decoration – Botanical Study – Level 3
Awarding body:
City & Guilds

Creative Techniques in Sugar Decoration – Displays using chocolate couverture – Level 3
Awarding body:
City & Guilds

Creative Techniques in Sugar Decoration – Fantasy Flower Display – Level 3
Awarding body:
City & Guilds

Creative Techniques in Sugar Decoration – Fantasy Flowers – Level 1
Awarding body:
City & Guilds

Creative Techniques in Sugar Decoration – Fantasy Flowers – Level 2
Awarding body:
City & Guilds

Creative Techniques in Sugar Decoration – Floral Sugar Display for Table Ware – Level 2
Awarding body:
City & Guilds

Creative Techniques in Sugar Decoration – Floral Sugar Display for Tableware – Level 1
Awarding body:
City & Guilds

Creative Techniques in Sugar Decoration – Marzipan Centre Piece – Level 3
Awarding body:
City & Guilds

Creative Techniques in Sugar Decoration – Marzipan Modelling – Level 2
Awarding body:
City & Guilds

Creative Techniques in Sugar Decoration – Novelty Cake – Level 3
Awarding body:
City & Guilds

Creative Techniques in Sugar Decoration – Pastillage – Level 1
Awarding body:
City & Guilds

Creative Techniques in Sugar Decoration – Pastillage – Level 2
Awarding body:
City & Guilds

Creative Techniques in Sugar Decoration – Pastillage Box – Level 3
Awarding body:
City & Guilds

Creative Techniques in Sugar Decoration – Royal Icing – Level 1
Awarding body:
City & Guilds

Creative Techniques in Sugar Decoration – Royal Icing – Level 2
Awarding body:
City & Guilds

Creative Techniques in Sugar Decoration – Royal Icing – Level 3
Awarding body:
City & Guilds

Creative Techniques in Sugar Decoration – Sugar Flower Wired Double Ended Spray – Level 3
Awarding body:
City & Guilds

Creative Techniques in Sugar Decoration – Sugar Foliage Table Centre Piece – Level 3
Awarding body:
City & Guilds

Creative Techniques in Sugar Decoration – Sugar Paste Cake – Level 1
Awarding body:
City & Guilds

Creative Techniques in Sugar Decoration – Sugar Paste Cake – Level 2
Awarding body:
City & Guilds

Creative Techniques in Sugar Decoration – Sugar Paste Cake – Level 3
Awarding body:
City & Guilds

Creative Techniques in Sugar Decoration – Table Styling – Level 1
Awarding body:
City & Guilds

Creative Techniques in Sugar Decoration – Table Styling – Level 2
Awarding body:
City & Guilds

Creative Techniques in Sugar Decoration – Tea Fancies – Level 2
Awarding body:
City & Guilds

Creative Techniques in Sugar Decoration – Wired Floral Corsage – Level 1
Awarding body:
City & Guilds

Creative Techniques in Sugar Decoration – Wired Floral Double Ended Spray – Level 2
Awarding body:
City & Guilds

Creative Techniques in Sugar Decoration – Working with Marzipan – Level 1
Awarding body:
City & Guilds

Creative Techniques in Sugar Decoration – Works using Chocolate Couverture – Level 2
Awarding body:
City & Guilds

Creative Techniques in Sugar Decoration – Works using Chocolate Coverings – Level 1
Awarding body:
City & Guilds

Creative Techniques in Textiles – Advanced Textile Decoration – Level 3
Awarding body:
City & Guilds

Creative Techniques in Textiles – Basket using Coiling Techniques – Level 3
Awarding body:
City & Guilds

Creative Techniques in Textiles – Basket using Plaiting Techniques – Level 3
Awarding body:
City & Guilds

Creative Techniques in Textiles – Basket using Rush, Cane, or Willow Techniques – Level 3
Awarding body:
City & Guilds

Creative Techniques in Textiles – Basket using Twining Techniques – Level 3
Awarding body:
City & Guilds

Creative Techniques in Textiles – Basket Weaving, Oval Basket with Side Handles – Level 2
Awarding body:
City & Guilds

Creative Techniques in Textiles – Basket Weaving, Round Basket with Cross Handle – Level 2
Awarding body:
City & Guilds

Creative Techniques in Textiles – Collection of Co-ordinated Hand Knit Items for an Interior – Level 3
Awarding body:
City & Guilds

Creative Techniques in Textiles – Collection of Co-ordinated Knitweave Items for an Interior – Level 3
Awarding body:
City & Guilds

Creative Techniques in Textiles – Collection of Hand Embroidered Textiles – Level 2
Awarding body:
City & Guilds

Creative Techniques in Textiles – Collection of Hand Knit Textiles – Level 2
Awarding body:
City & Guilds

Creative Techniques in Textiles – Collection of Hand Made Felt – Level 2
Awarding body:
City & Guilds

Creative Techniques in Textiles – Collection of Machine Embroidered Textiles – Level 2
Awarding body:
City & Guilds

Creative Techniques in Textiles – Collection of Machine Knit Textiles – Level 2
Awarding body:
City & Guilds

Creative Techniques in Textiles – Collection of Quilting, Patchwork and Appliqué Textiles – Level 2
Awarding body:
City & Guilds

Creative Techniques in Textiles – Collection of Woven Textiles – Level 2
Awarding body:
City & Guilds

Creative Techniques in Textiles – Crocheted Textiles – Level 1
Awarding body:
City & Guilds

Creative Techniques in Textiles – Experimental Collection of Basketry Techniques – Level 3
Awarding body:
City & Guilds

Creative Techniques in Textiles – Experimental Collection of Hand Embroidery – Level 3
Awarding body:
City & Guilds

Creative Techniques in Textiles – Experimental Collection of Hand Knit Textiles – Level 3
Awarding body:
City & Guilds

Creative Techniques in Textiles – Experimental Collection of Hand Made Felt – Level 3
Awarding body:
City & Guilds

Creative Techniques in Textiles – Experimental Collection of Hand Woven Textiles – Level 3
Awarding body:
City & Guilds

Creative Techniques in Textiles – Experimental Collection of Machine Embroidery – Level 3
Awarding body:
City & Guilds

Creative Techniques in Textiles – Experimental Collection of Machine Knit Textiles – Level 3
Awarding body:
City & Guilds

Creative Techniques in Textiles – Experimental Collection of Quilting, Patchwork and Appliqué – Level 3
Awarding body:
City & Guilds

Creative Techniques in Textiles – Fashion Garment Created from an Open Machine Knit Fabric – Level 3
Awarding body:
City & Guilds

Creative Techniques in Textiles – Felt Making – Level 1
Awarding body:
City & Guilds

Creative Techniques in Textiles – Hand Embroidered Accessory or Set of Accessories – Level 3
Awarding body:
City & Guilds

Creative Techniques in Textiles – Hand Embroidered Functional Item – Level 3
Awarding body:
City & Guilds

Creative Techniques in Textiles – Hand Embroidered Panel or Hanging – Level 3
Awarding body:
City & Guilds

Creative Techniques in Textiles – Hand Embroidery – Level 1
Awarding body:
City & Guilds

Creative Techniques in Textiles – Hand Knit Fashion Garment – Level 3
Awarding body:
City & Guilds

Creative Techniques in Textiles – Hand Knit Textiles – Level 1
Awarding body:
City & Guilds

Creative Techniques in Textiles – Hand Made Felt Accessory or Set of Accessories – Level 3
Awarding body:
City & Guilds

Creative Techniques in Textiles – Hand Made Felt Functional Item – Level 3
Awarding body:
City & Guilds

Creative Techniques in Textiles – Hand Made Felt Panel or Hanging – Level 3
Awarding body:
City & Guilds

Creative Techniques in Textiles – Hand Weaving – Level 1
Awarding body:
City & Guilds

Creative Techniques in Textiles – Hand Woven Accessory or Set of Accessories – Level 3
Awarding body:
City & Guilds

Creative Techniques in Textiles – Hand Woven Baskets – Level 1
Awarding body:
City & Guilds

Creative Techniques in Textiles – Innovative Hand Embroidery – Level 2
Awarding body:
City & Guilds

Creative Techniques in Textiles – Innovative Hand Made Felt – Level 2
Awarding body:
City & Guilds

Creative Techniques in Textiles – Innovative Hand Woven Textile – Level 2
Awarding body:
City & Guilds

Creative Techniques in Textiles – Innovative Machine Embroidery – Level 2
Awarding body:
City & Guilds

Creative Techniques in Textiles – Innovative Machine Knit Garment – Level 2
Awarding body:
City & Guilds

Creative Techniques in Textiles – Item of Appliqué with Quilting – Level 2
Awarding body:
City & Guilds

Creative Techniques in Textiles – Item of Patchwork with Quilting – Level 2
Awarding body:
City & Guilds

Creative Techniques in Textiles – Machine Embroidered Accessory or Set of Accessories – Level 3
Awarding body:
City & Guilds

Creative Techniques in Textiles – Machine Embroidered Functional Item – Level 3
Awarding body:
City & Guilds

Creative Techniques in Textiles – Machine Embroidered Hanging – Level 3
Awarding body:
City & Guilds

Creative Techniques in Textiles – Machine Embroidery – Level 1
Awarding body:
City & Guilds

Creative Techniques in Textiles – Machine Knit Textiles – Level 1
Awarding body:
City & Guilds

Creative Techniques in Textiles – Patchwork and Quilting – Level 1
Awarding body:
City & Guilds

Creative Techniques in Textiles – Quilted Patchwork Panel or Hanging – Level 3
Awarding body:
City & Guilds

Creative Techniques in Textiles – Quilting, Patchwork and Appliqué, Container or Box – Level 3
Awarding body:
City & Guilds

Creative Techniques in Textiles – Set of Hand Knit Fashion Accessories – Level 3
Awarding body:
City & Guilds

Creative Techniques in Textiles – Sewing Machine Skills – Level 1
Awarding body:
City & Guilds

Creative Techniques in Textiles – Textile Decoration, Added Colour – Level 2
Awarding body:
City & Guilds

Creative Techniques in Textiles – Textile Decoration, Added Pattern – Level 2
Awarding body:
City & Guilds

Creative Techniques in Textiles – Traditional Hand Embroidery – Level 2
Awarding body:
City & Guilds

Creative Techniques in Textiles – Traditional Hand Knit Garment – Level 2
Awarding body:
City & Guilds

Creative Techniques in Textiles – Traditional Hand Made Felt – Level 2
Awarding body:
City & Guilds

Creative Techniques in Textiles – Traditional Hand Woven Textile – Level 2
Awarding body:
City & Guilds

Creative Techniques in Textiles – Traditional Machine Embroidery – Level 2
Awarding body:
City & Guilds

Creative Techniques in Textiles – Traditional Machine Knit Garment – Level 2
Awarding body:
City & Guilds

**Creative Techniques in Textiles –
Wholecloth Quilt – Level 3**
Awarding body:
City & Guilds

**Creative Techniques in Textiles – Textile
Decoration – Level 1**
Awarding body:
City & Guilds

**Creative Techniques in Upholstery – A
Chair with Deep Buttoned Back and/or
Seat – Level 3**
Awarding body:
City & Guilds

**Creative Techniques in Upholstery – a
Drop-in Seat – Level 1**
Awarding body:
City & Guilds

**Creative Techniques in Upholstery – An
Upholstered Easy Chair with Arms –
Level 3**
Awarding body:
City & Guilds

**Creative Techniques in Upholstery –
Chair with a Sprung Arm and/or
Independent Sprung Edge – Level 3**
Awarding body:
City & Guilds

**Creative Techniques in Upholstery –
Chair with a Sprung Seat – Level 3**
Awarding body:
City & Guilds

**Creative Techniques in Upholstery –
Modern Upholstered Stool – Level 1**
Awarding body:
City & Guilds

**Creative Techniques in Upholstery –
Small Ottoman or Box with a Lid –
Level 2**
Awarding body:
City & Guilds

**Creative Techniques in Upholstery –
Stuff Over Seat – Level 2**
Awarding body:
City & Guilds

**Creative Techniques in Upholstery –
Traditional Upholstered Stool – Level 2**
Awarding body:
City & Guilds

**Creative Techniques in Upholstery –
Upholstered Decorative Headboard –
Level 3**
Awarding body:
City & Guilds

**Creative Techniques in Upholstery –
Upholstered Headboard – Level 2**
Awarding body:
City & Guilds

Darkroom Printing – Level 1
Awarding body:
City & Guilds

**Data Management for Web Design –
Level 3**
Awarding body:
ABC

Design and Layout Skills – Level 3
Awarding body:
ABC

Design Visualisation – Level 3
Awarding body:
ABC

Designing Book Structures – Level 3
Awarding body:
ABC

Desktop Publishing Skills – Level 3
Awarding body:
ABC

Digital Illustration – Level 3
Awarding body:
ABC

Digital Image Modification – Level 1
Awarding body:
City & Guilds

**Digital Modelling for Architectural
Environments – Level 3**
Awarding body:
ABC

Digital Photo-Imaging – Level 3
Awarding body:
　ABC

Digital Typography – Level 3
Awarding body:
　ABC

Employment in the Fashion Industries – Level 3
Awarding body:
　NOCN

Experimental Letterpress – Level 3
Awarding body:
　ABC

Experimental Web Design – Level 3
Awarding body:
　ABC

Fashion – Advanced Millinery, Blocked Straw Hat with Double Brim – Level 3
Awarding body:
　City & Guilds

Fashion – Advanced Millinery, Draped Hat – Level 3
Awarding body:
　City & Guilds

Fashion and Clothing – Level 1
Awarding body:
　EDEXCEL

Fashion Display and Presentation – Level 3
Awarding body:
　ABC

Graphics – Level 1
Awarding body:
　EDEXCEL

Illustration Skills – Level 3
Awarding body:
　ABC

Image Capture – Level 1
Awarding body:
　City & Guilds

Interactive Use of Media – Level 1
Awarding body:
　EDEXCEL

Large Format Photography – Level 3
Awarding body:
　ABC

Letterpress Skills – Level 3
Awarding body:
　ABC

Life Drawing – Level 3
Awarding body:
　ABC

Lithographic Print Processes – Level 3
Awarding body:
　ABC

Making it in Fashion – Level 1
Awarding body:
　NOCN

Merchandising Display and Presentation – Level 3
Awarding body:
　ABC

Model Making and Presentation – Level 3
Awarding body:
　ABC

Multi-Colour Lithographic Printing – Level 3
Awarding body:
　ABC

Multi-media Software Skills – Level 3
Awarding body:
　ABC

Narrative Structures – Level 3
Awarding body:
　ABC

Photo Image Presentation – Level 1
Awarding body:
　City & Guilds

Photographic Colour Printing – Level 3
Awarding body:
　ABC

Photographic Darkroom Skills – Level 3
Awarding body:
　ABC

Photography – Level 1
Awarding body:
EDEXCEL

Photography Skills – Level 3
Awarding body:
ABC

Photojournalism – Level 3
Awarding body:
ABC

**Pixel-Based Image Manipulation –
Level 3**
Awarding body:
ABC

Print Buying – Level 3
Awarding body:
ABC

**Print Finishing and Paper Purchasing –
Level 3**
Awarding body:
ABC

**Print Production and Workflow
Management – Level 3**
Awarding body:
ABC

**Print Specification and Production for
Designers – Level 3**
Awarding body:
ABC

Printmaking Skills – Level 3
Awarding body:
ABC

Screen Printing – Level 3
Awarding body:
ABC

Screen Printing Skills – Level 3
Awarding body:
ABC

Skills for the Fashion Industries – Level 2
Awarding body:
NOCN

**Software Skills for 3D Modelling –
Level 3**
Awarding body:
ABC

Street Fashion Photography – Level 3
Awarding body:
ABC

Studio Photography Practice – Level 3
Awarding body:
ABC

Textiles – Level 1
Awarding body:
EDEXCEL

Time-Based Web Design – Level 3
Awarding body:
ABC

**Understanding Printing Technology
Processes – Level 3**
Awarding body:
ABC

**Vector-Based Image Generation –
Level 3**
Awarding body:
ABC

Visual Arts – Level 1
Awarding body:
EDEXCEL

Visual Thinking – Level 3
Awarding body:
ABC

Web Production Skills – Level 3
Awarding body:
ABC

BTEC Award

3D Design – Level 2
Awarding body:
EDEXCEL

3D Design – Level 3
Awarding body:
EDEXCEL

Design Crafts – Level 3
Awarding body:
EDEXCEL

Fashion and Clothing – Level 2
Awarding body:
EDEXCEL

Fashion and Clothing – Level 3
Awarding body:
EDEXCEL

Graphics – Level 2
Awarding body:
EDEXCEL

Graphics – Level 3
Awarding body:
EDEXCEL

Interactive Use of Media – Level 2
Awarding body:
EDEXCEL

Interactive use of Media – Level 3
Awarding body:
EDEXCEL

Photography – Level 2
Awarding body:
EDEXCEL

Photography – Level 3
Awarding body:
EDEXCEL

Textiles – Level 2
Awarding body:
EDEXCEL

Textiles – Level 3
Awarding body:
EDEXCEL

Visual Arts – Level 2
Awarding body:
EDEXCEL

Visual Arts – Level 3
Awarding body:
EDEXCEL

BTEC Certificate

3D Design – Level 2
Awarding body:
EDEXCEL

3D Design – Level 3
Awarding body:
EDEXCEL

Art and Design – Level 2
Awarding body:
EDEXCEL

Art and Design – Level 3
Awarding body:
EDEXCEL

Design Crafts – Level 3
Awarding body:
EDEXCEL

Fashion and Clothing – Level 2
Awarding body:
EDEXCEL

Fashion and Clothing – Level 3
Awarding body:
EDEXCEL

Graphics – Level 2
Awarding body:
EDEXCEL

Graphics – Level 3
Awarding body:
EDEXCEL

Interactive Use of Media – Level 2
Awarding body:
EDEXCEL

Interactive use of Media – Level 3
Awarding body:
EDEXCEL

Photography – Level 2
Awarding body:
EDEXCEL

Photography – Level 3
Awarding body:
EDEXCEL

Textiles – Level 2
Awarding body:
EDEXCEL

Textiles – Level 3
Awarding body:
EDEXCEL

Visual Arts – Level 2
Awarding body:
EDEXCEL

Visual Arts – Level 3
Awarding body:
  EDEXCEL

BTEC Diploma

3D Design – Level 2
Awarding body:
  EDEXCEL

3D Design – Level 3
Awarding body:
  EDEXCEL

Art and Design – Level 2
Awarding body:
  EDEXCEL

Art and Design – Level 3
Awarding body:
  EDEXCEL

Design Crafts – Level 3
Awarding body:
  EDEXCEL

Fashion and Clothing – Level 2
Awarding body:
  EDEXCEL

Fashion and Clothing – Level 3
Awarding body:
  EDEXCEL

Graphics – Level 2
Awarding body:
  EDEXCEL

Graphics – Level 3
Awarding body:
  EDEXCEL

Interactive Use of Media – Level 2
Awarding body:
  EDEXCEL

Interactive use of Media – Level 3
Awarding body:
  EDEXCEL

Photography – Level 2
Awarding body:
  EDEXCEL

Photography – Level 3
Awarding body:
  EDEXCEL

Textiles – Level 2
Awarding body:
  EDEXCEL

Textiles – Level 3
Awarding body:
  EDEXCEL

Visual Arts – Level 2
Awarding body:
  EDEXCEL

Visual Arts – Level 3
Awarding body:
  EDEXCEL

BTEC Extended Certificate

Art and Design – Level 2
Awarding body:
  EDEXCEL

BTEC Extended Diploma

Art and Design – Level 3
Awarding body:
  EDEXCEL

BTEC First Certificate

Art and Design – Level 2
Awarding body:
  EDEXCEL

BTEC First Diploma

Art and Design – Level 2
Awarding body:
  EDEXCEL

BTEC Foundation Diploma

Art and Design – Level 3
Awarding body:
  EDEXCEL

BTEC Higher National Certificate

3D Design – Level 5
Awarding body:
EDEXCEL

Fine Arts – Level 5
Awarding body:
EDEXCEL

Graphic Design – Level 5
Awarding body:
EDEXCEL

Photography – Level 5
Awarding body:
EDEXCEL

BTEC Higher National Diploma

3D Design – Level 5
Awarding body:
EDEXCEL

Fine Arts – Level 5
Awarding body:
EDEXCEL

Graphic Design – Level 5
Awarding body:
EDEXCEL

Photography – Level 5
Awarding body:
EDEXCEL

Specialist Makeup (Film and Television) – Level 5
Awarding body:
EDEXCEL

BTEC National Award

Art and Design – Level 3
Awarding body:
EDEXCEL

BTEC National Certificate

Art and Design – Level 3
Awarding body:
EDEXCEL

BTEC National Diploma

Art and Design – Level 3
Awarding body:
EDEXCEL

BTEC Subsidiary Diploma

Art and Design – Level 3
Awarding body:
EDEXCEL

Certificate

3D Design – Level 1
Awarding body:
EDEXCEL

Advertising and Promotion – Level 3
Awarding body:
ABC

Animation – Level 2
Awarding body:
NCFE

Applied Graphics Skills – Level 3
Awarding body:
ABC

Art – Entry Level
Awarding body:
ASCENTIS
WJEC

Art – Level 1
Awarding body:
ASCENTIS

Art – Level 2
Awarding body:
ASCENTIS

Art and Design – Entry Level
Awarding body:
AQA
CCEA
OCR

Art and Design – Level 1
Awarding body:
EDEXCEL
NOCN

Art and Design – Level 1,2
Awarding body:
Cambridge International

Art and Design – Level 2
Awarding body:
NCFE
NOCN

Art and Design – Level 3
Awarding body:
NCFE
NOCN

Art, Design and Creative Studies – Level 1
Awarding body:
ABC

Art, Design and Creative Studies – Level 2
Awarding body:
ABC

Black and White Photography – Level 3
Awarding body:
ABC

Close-up Image Capture – Level 1
Awarding body:
City & Guilds

Close-up Photo Imaging – Level 1
Awarding body:
City & Guilds

Corporate Identity and Branding – Level 3
Awarding body:
ABC

Craft and Design – Entry Level
Awarding body:
ASCENTIS

Craft and Design – Level 1
Awarding body:
ASCENTIS

Craft and Design – Level 2
Awarding body:
ASCENTIS

Creative and Cultural Practice – Level 2
Awarding body:
EDI

Creative and Cultural Practice – Level 3
Awarding body:
EDI

Creative Craft – Level 1
Awarding body:
CCEA
NCFE

Creative Craft – Level 2
Awarding body:
CCEA
NCFE

Creative Craft – Level 3
Awarding body:
CCEA
NCFE

Creative Craft using Art and Design – Level 3
Awarding body:
NCFE

Creative Craft using Balloon Crafts – Level 3
Awarding body:
NCFE

Creative Craft using Beauty Crafts – Level 3
Awarding body:
NCFE

Creative Craft using Bookbinding – Level 3
Awarding body:
NCFE

Creative Craft using Cake Decoration – Level 3
Awarding body:
NCFE

Creative Craft using Carnival Crafts – Level 3
Awarding body:
  NCFE

Creative Craft using Ceramics – Level 3
Awarding body:
  NCFE

Creative Craft using Construction Crafts – Level 3
Awarding body:
  NCFE

Creative Craft using Cookery – Level 3
Awarding body:
  NCFE

Creative Craft using Creative Cards – Level 3
Awarding body:
  NCFE

Creative Craft using Digital Imaging – Level 3
Awarding body:
  NCFE

Creative Craft using Drawing and Painting – Level 3
Awarding body:
  NCFE

Creative Craft using Dressmaking – Level 3
Awarding body:
  NCFE

Creative Craft using Embroidery – Level 3
Awarding body:
  NCFE

Creative Craft using Environmental and Land-Based Crafts – Level 3
Awarding body:
  NCFE

Creative Craft using Fashion – Level 3
Awarding body:
  NCFE

Creative Craft using Fibre Crafts – Level 3
Awarding body:
  NCFE

Creative Craft using Floral Crafts – Level 3
Awarding body:
  NCFE

Creative Craft using Floristry – Level 3
Awarding body:
  NCFE

Creative Craft using Furniture Crafts – Level 3
Awarding body:
  NCFE

Creative Craft using Garden Design – Level 3
Awarding body:
  NCFE

Creative Craft using Glass Crafts – Level 3
Awarding body:
  NCFE

Creative Craft using Graphic Crafts – Level 3
Awarding body:
  NCFE

Creative Craft using Illustration – Level 3
Awarding body:
  NCFE

Creative Craft using Interior Design – Level 3
Awarding body:
  NCFE

Creative Craft using International Cookery – Level 3
Awarding body:
  NCFE

Creative Craft using Jewellery – Level 3
Awarding body:
  NCFE

Creative Craft using Life Drawing – Level 3
Awarding body:
  NCFE

Creative Craft using Make-Up – Level 3
Awarding body:
  NCFE

**Creative Craft using Metalwork –
Level 3**
Awarding body:
NCFE

**Creative Craft using Mixed Crafts –
Level 3**
Awarding body:
NCFE

**Creative Craft using Model Making –
Level 3**
Awarding body:
NCFE

**Creative Craft using Music Composition
– Level 3**
Awarding body:
NCFE

Creative Craft using Nail Art – Level 3
Awarding body:
NCFE

**Creative Craft using Nursery Art –
Level 3**
Awarding body:
NCFE

**Creative Craft using Paper Crafts –
Level 3**
Awarding body:
NCFE

**Creative Craft using Patisserie and
Confectionery – Level 3**
Awarding body:
NCFE

**Creative Craft using Pattern Cutting –
Level 3**
Awarding body:
NCFE

**Creative Craft using Photography –
Level 3**
Awarding body:
NCFE

Creative Craft using Pottery – Level 3
Awarding body:
NCFE

Creative Craft using Printing – Level 3
Awarding body:
NCFE

Creative Craft using Sculpture – Level 3
Awarding body:
NCFE

**Creative Craft using Seasonal Crafts –
Level 3**
Awarding body:
NCFE

**Creative Craft using Silversmithing –
Level 3**
Awarding body:
NCFE

**Creative Craft using Soft Furnishings –
Level 3**
Awarding body:
NCFE

**Creative Craft using Stage Crafts –
Level 3**
Awarding body:
NCFE

**Creative Craft using Stained Glass –
Level 3**
Awarding body:
NCFE

**Creative Craft using Sugar Decorative
Crafts – Level 3**
Awarding body:
NCFE

**Creative Craft using Technical Drawing
– Level 3**
Awarding body:
NCFE

Creative Craft using Textiles – Level 3
Awarding body:
NCFE

**Creative Craft using Time-Based Studies
– Level 3**
Awarding body:
NCFE

**Creative Craft using Toy Making –
Level 3**
Awarding body:
NCFE

**Creative Craft using Upholstery –
Level 3**
Awarding body:
  NCFE

**Creative Craft using Watercolour
Painting – Level 3**
Awarding body:
  NCFE

**Creative Craft using Wax Crafts –
Level 3**
Awarding body:
  NCFE

**Creative Craft using Window Dressing –
Level 3**
Awarding body:
  NCFE

**Creative Craft using Wood Crafts –
Level 3**
Awarding body:
  NCFE

Creative Techniques in 2D – Level 1
Awarding body:
  City & Guilds

Creative Techniques in 2D – Level 2
Awarding body:
  City & Guilds

Creative Techniques in 2D – Level 3
Awarding body:
  City & Guilds

Creative Techniques in 3D – Level 1
Awarding body:
  City & Guilds

Creative Techniques in 3D – Level 2
Awarding body:
  City & Guilds

Creative Techniques in 3D – Level 3
Awarding body:
  City & Guilds

**Creative Techniques in Employability
Skills – Level 1**
Awarding body:
  City & Guilds

**Creative Techniques in Employability
Skills – Level 2**
Awarding body:
  City & Guilds

**Creative Techniques in Employability
Skills – Level 3**
Awarding body:
  City & Guilds

Creative Techniques in Fashion – Level 1
Awarding body:
  City & Guilds

Creative Techniques in Fashion – Level 2
Awarding body:
  City & Guilds

Creative Techniques in Fashion – Level 3
Awarding body:
  City & Guilds

Creative Techniques in Floral – Level 1
Awarding body:
  City & Guilds

Creative Techniques in Floral – Level 2
Awarding body:
  City & Guilds

Creative Techniques in Floral – Level 3
Awarding body:
  City & Guilds

**Creative Techniques in Interiors –
Level 1**
Awarding body:
  City & Guilds

**Creative Techniques in Interiors –
Level 2**
Awarding body:
  City & Guilds

**Creative Techniques in Sugarcraft –
Level 1**
Awarding body:
  City & Guilds

**Creative Techniques in Sugarcraft –
Level 2**
Awarding body:
  City & Guilds

**Creative Techniques in Sugarcraft –
Level 3**
Awarding body:
City & Guilds

Creative Techniques in Textiles – Level 1
Awarding body:
City & Guilds

Creative Techniques in Textiles – Level 2
Awarding body:
City & Guilds

Creative Techniques in Textiles – Level 3
Awarding body:
City & Guilds

Digital Graphics – Level 3
Awarding body:
ABC

**Employment in the Fashion Industries –
Level 3**
Awarding body:
NOCN

Experimental Illustration – Level 3
Awarding body:
ABC

Experimental Printmaking – Level 3
Awarding body:
ABC

Fashion and Clothing – Level 1
Awarding body:
EDEXCEL

Graphic Design – Level 1
Awarding body:
NCFE

Graphic Design – Level 2
Awarding body:
NCFE

Graphic Printmaking – Level 3
Awarding body:
ABC

**Graphical and Material Studies –
Entry Level**
Awarding body:
CCEA
WJEC

Graphics – Level 1
Awarding body:
EDEXCEL

Illustration – Level 3
Awarding body:
ABC

Image Capture of Buildings – Level 1
Awarding body:
City & Guilds

Image Capture of Events – Level 1
Awarding body:
City & Guilds

Image Capture of Landscapes – Level 1
Awarding body:
City & Guilds

Image Capture of People – Level 1
Awarding body:
City & Guilds

iMedia Users – Level 1
Awarding body:
OCR

iMedia Users – Level 2
Awarding body:
OCR

iMedia Users – Level 3
Awarding body:
OCR

Information Design – Level 3
Awarding body:
ABC

Interactive Media – Level 1
Awarding body:
NCFE

Interactive Media – Level 2
Awarding body:
NCFE

Interactive Media – Level 3
Awarding body:
NCFE

Interactive Use of Media – Level 1
Awarding body:
EDEXCEL

Interior Design Modelling and Visualising – Level 3
Awarding body:
ABC

International Fashion Studies – Level 2
Awarding body:
ABC

Magazine and Publishing Design – Level 3
Awarding body:
ABC

Making it in Fashion – Level 1
Awarding body:
NOCN

Narrative Illustration – Level 3
Awarding body:
ABC

Photo Image Capture – Level 1
Awarding body:
City & Guilds

Photo Imaging of Buildings – Level 1
Awarding body:
City & Guilds

Photo Imaging of Events – Level 1
Awarding body:
City & Guilds

Photo Imaging of Landscapes – Level 1
Awarding body:
City & Guilds

Photo Imaging of People – Level 1
Awarding body:
City & Guilds

Photography – Level 1
Awarding body:
City & Guilds
EDEXCEL
NCFE

Photography – Level 2
Awarding body:
NCFE

Photography (Buildings) – Level 1
Awarding body:
City & Guilds

Photography (Close-up) – Level 1
Awarding body:
City & Guilds

Photography (Events) – Level 1
Awarding body:
City & Guilds

Photography (Landscape) – Level 1
Awarding body:
City & Guilds

Photography (People) – Level 1
Awarding body:
City & Guilds

Skills for the Fashion Industries – Level 2
Awarding body:
NOCN

Studio and Location Photography – Level 3
Awarding body:
ABC

Technical Theatre – Level 1
Awarding body:
NCFE

Textiles – Level 1
Awarding body:
EDEXCEL

Typographic Design – Level 3
Awarding body:
ABC

Visual Arts – Level 1
Awarding body:
EDEXCEL

Diploma

3D Design – Level 1
Awarding body:
EDEXCEL

3D Modelling and Animation – Level 3
Awarding body:
ABC

Art and Design – Level 1
Awarding body:
EDEXCEL
NOCN

Art and Design – Level 2
Awarding body:
    NOCN

Art and Design – Level 3
Awarding body:
    NOCN

Business for Creative Practitioners – Level 4
Awarding body:
    ABC

Creative Techniques in 2D – Level 1
Awarding body:
    City & Guilds

Creative Techniques in 2D – Level 2
Awarding body:
    City & Guilds

Creative Techniques in 2D – Level 3
Awarding body:
    City & Guilds

Creative Techniques in 3D – Level 1
Awarding body:
    City & Guilds

Creative Techniques in 3D – Level 2
Awarding body:
    City & Guilds

Creative Techniques in 3D – Level 3
Awarding body:
    City & Guilds

Creative Techniques in Fashion – Level 1
Awarding body:
    City & Guilds

Creative Techniques in Fashion – Level 2
Awarding body:
    City & Guilds

Creative Techniques in Fashion – Level 3
Awarding body:
    City & Guilds

Creative Techniques in Floral – Level 1
Awarding body:
    City & Guilds

Creative Techniques in Floral – Level 2
Awarding body:
    City & Guilds

Creative Techniques in Floral – Level 3
Awarding body:
    City & Guilds

Creative Techniques in Interiors – Level 1
Awarding body:
    City & Guilds

Creative Techniques in Interiors – Level 2
Awarding body:
    City & Guilds

Creative Techniques in Interiors – Level 3
Awarding body:
    City & Guilds

Creative Techniques in Sugarcraft – Level 1
Awarding body:
    City & Guilds

Creative Techniques in Sugarcraft – Level 2
Awarding body:
    City & Guilds

Creative Techniques in Sugarcraft – Level 3
Awarding body:
    City & Guilds

Creative Techniques in Textiles – Level 1
Awarding body:
    City & Guilds

Creative Techniques in Textiles – Level 2
Awarding body:
    City & Guilds

Creative Techniques in Textiles – Level 3
Awarding body:
    City & Guilds

Digital Design – Level 3
Awarding body:
    ABC

Digital Media – Level 3
Awarding body:
    ABC

Digital Origination – Level 3
Awarding body:
ABC

Display Design – Level 3
Awarding body:
ABC

Employment in the Fashion Industries – Level 3
Awarding body:
NOCN

Fashion and Clothing – Level 1
Awarding body:
EDEXCEL

Flower Design – Level 3
Awarding body:
ABC

Foundation Studies (Art, Design and Media) – Level 3
Awarding body:
WJEC

Foundation Studies in Art, Design and Media – Level 3
Awarding body:
ABC

Foundation Studies in Art, Design and Media – Level 4
Awarding body:
ABC

Graphic Design – Level 3
Awarding body:
ABC

Graphics – Level 1
Awarding body:
EDEXCEL

iMedia Users – Level 1
Awarding body:
OCR

iMedia Users – Level 2
Awarding body:
OCR

iMedia Users – Level 3
Awarding body:
OCR

Interactive Media and Animation – Level 2
Awarding body:
NCFE

Interactive Use of Media – Level 1
Awarding body:
EDEXCEL

Interior Design – Level 3
Awarding body:
ABC

Photography – Level 1
Awarding body:
EDEXCEL

Photography – Level 3
Awarding body:
ABC

Print Media – Level 3
Awarding body:
ABC

Skills for the Fashion Industries – Level 2
Awarding body:
NOCN

Textiles – Level 1
Awarding body:
EDEXCEL

V&A Assistant Curator Programme – Level 4
Awarding body:
EDI

Visual Arts – Level 1
Awarding body:
EDEXCEL

Double Award

Advertising – Level 3
Awarding body:
ABC

Animation Skills – Level 3
Awarding body:
ABC

Experimental Digital Media – Level 3
Awarding body:
ABC

Experimental Typography – Level 3
Awarding body:
 ABC

Graphics Skills – Level 3
Awarding body:
 ABC

Photography for Designers – Level 3
Awarding body:
 ABC

Printmaking – Level 3
Awarding body:
 ABC

Prop Making – Level 3
Awarding body:
 ABC

Publications Design – Level 3
Awarding body:
 ABC

Reportage Portraiture – Level 3
Awarding body:
 ABC

Extended Certificate

Creative Craft – Level 2
Awarding body:
 NCFE

Foundation Diploma

Art and Design – Level 3
Awarding body:
 UAL

Art and Design – Level 4
Awarding body:
 UAL

Creative and Media – Level 1
Awarding body:
 AQA
 City & Guilds
 EDEXCEL
 OCR
 RSL

Higher Diploma

Creative and Media – Level 2
Awarding body:
 AQA
 City & Guilds
 EDEXCEL
 OCR
 RSL

Higher Professional Diploma

Creative Arts – Level 4
Awarding body:
 City & Guilds

Intermediate Certificate

Clock and Watch Servicing – Level 2
Awarding body:
 EAL

Introductory Certificate

Art, Design and Media – Level 1
Awarding body:
 EDEXCEL

Introductory Diploma

Art, Design and Media – Level 1
Awarding body:
 EDEXCEL

National Award

Applied Art, Design and Media – Level 1
Awarding body:
 OCR

Art and Design – Level 2
Awarding body:
 OCR

Community Arts Management – Level 2
Awarding body:
 EDI

Community Arts Management – Level 3
Awarding body:
  EDI

Cultural and Heritage Venue Operations – Level 2
Awarding body:
  EDI

Cultural and Heritage Venue Operations – Level 3
Awarding body:
  EDI

Live Events and Promotion – Level 2
Awarding body:
  EDI

Live Events and Promotion – Level 3
Awarding body:
  EDI

Music Business (Recording Industry) – Level 2
Awarding body:
  EDI

Music Business (Recording Industry) – Level 3
Awarding body:
  EDI

Technical Theatre (Costume and Wardrobe) – Level 2
Awarding body:
  EDI

Technical Theatre (Costume and Wardrobe) – Level 3
Awarding body:
  EDI

Technical Theatre (Rigging, Lighting and Sound) – Level 2
Awarding body:
  EDI

Technical Theatre (Rigging, Lighting and Sound) – Level 3
Awarding body:
  EDI

National Certificate

Applied Art, Design and Media – Level 1
Awarding body:
  OCR

Art and Design – Level 2
Awarding body:
  OCR

Art and Design – Level 3
Awarding body:
  OCR

National Diploma

Art and Design – Level 3
Awarding body:
  OCR

Professional Production Skills – Level 6
Awarding body:
  TCL

National Extended Diploma

Art and Design – Level 3
Awarding body:
  OCR

National First Award

Applied Art, Design and Media – Level 1
Awarding body:
  OCR

National Vocational Qualification

Design – Level 3
Awarding body:
  EDEXCEL

Design Management – Level 4
Awarding body:
  EDEXCEL

Design Support – Level 2
Awarding body:
  EDEXCEL

Digital Print Production – Level 2
Awarding body:
City & Guilds

Digital Print Production – Level 3
Awarding body:
City & Guilds

Engineering Woodworking, Pattern and Model Making – Level 3
Awarding body:
EAL

Photo Imaging – Level 2
Awarding body:
City & Guilds

Photo Imaging – Level 3
Awarding body:
City & Guilds

Photo Imaging – Level 4
Awarding body:
City & Guilds

Pre-U Certificate

Art and Design: 3D Design (Principal) – Level 3
Awarding body:
Cambridge International

Art and Design: Fine Art (Principal) – Level 3
Awarding body:
Cambridge International

Art and Design: Graphic Communication (Principal) – Level 3
Awarding body:
Cambridge International

Art and Design: Lens Based Imagery (Principal) – Level 3
Awarding body:
Cambridge International

Art and Design: Textile Design (Principal) – Level 3
Awarding body:
Cambridge International

Art and Design: Unendorsed (Principal) – Level 3
Awarding body:
Cambridge International

Art History (Principal) – Level 3
Awarding body:
Cambridge International

Principal Learning

Creative and Media – Level 1
Awarding body:
AQA
City & Guilds
EDEXCEL
OCR

Creative and Media – Level 2
Awarding body:
AQA
City & Guilds
EDEXCEL
OCR

Creative and Media – Level 3
Awarding body:
AQA
City & Guilds
EDEXCEL
OCR

Creative and Media (Wales) – Level 1
Awarding body:
OCR

Creative and Media (Wales) – Level 2
Awarding body:
OCR

Creative and Media (Wales) – Level 3
Awarding body:
OCR

Progression Diploma

Creative and Media – Level 3
Awarding body:
AQA
City & Guilds
EDEXCEL
OCR
RSL

Media and Communication

Award

3D Digital Animation Techniques – Level 3
Awarding body:
  ABC

Darkroom Printing – Level 1
Awarding body:
  City & Guilds

Digital Image Manipulation – Level 1
Awarding body:
  City & Guilds

Digital Image Manipulation – Level 2
Awarding body:
  City & Guilds

Digital Video Editing – Level 3
Awarding body:
  ABC

Image Capture – Level 1
Awarding body:
  City & Guilds

Operational Photography – Level 2
Awarding body:
  City & Guilds

Photo Image Capture – Level 2
Awarding body:
  City & Guilds

Photo Image Capture – Level 3
Awarding body:
  City & Guilds

Photo Image Capture and Manipulation – Level 1
Awarding body:
  City & Guilds

Photo Image Management & Storage – Level 2
Awarding body:
  City & Guilds

Photo Image Output – Level 2
Awarding body:
  City & Guilds

Photo Image Output – Level 3
Awarding body:
  City & Guilds

Photo Image Presentation – Level 1
Awarding body:
  City & Guilds

Photo Image Presentation – Level 2
Awarding body:
  City & Guilds

Photography – Level 1
Awarding body:
  City & Guilds

Planning and Developing Games Design – Level 3
Awarding body:
  ABC

Podcasting – Level 1
Awarding body:
  NCFE

Radio Production – Level 1
Awarding body:
  NCFE

Radio Production – Level 2
Awarding body:
  NCFE

Radio Production Skills – Level 3
Awarding body:
  ABC

Single Camera Programme Making – Level 3
Awarding body:
  ABC

Sound Editing – Level 3
Awarding body:
  ABC

Specialist Image Capture – Level 1
Awarding body:
   City & Guilds

Talk Radio Broadcast Skills – Level 3
Awarding body:
   ABC

BTEC Diploma

Computer Games Production – Level 3
Awarding body:
   EDEXCEL

Quality Assurance for Computer Games Development – Level 3
Awarding body:
   EDEXCEL

BTEC First Certificate

Media – Level 2
Awarding body:
   EDEXCEL

BTEC First Diploma

Media – Level 2
Awarding body:
   EDEXCEL

BTEC Higher National Certificate

Interactive Media – Level 5
Awarding body:
   EDEXCEL

Media – Level 5
Awarding body:
   EDEXCEL

BTEC Higher National Diploma

Interactive Media – Level 5
Awarding body:
   EDEXCEL

Media – Level 5
Awarding body:
   EDEXCEL

BTEC National Award

Media Production – Level 3
Awarding body:
   EDEXCEL

BTEC National Certificate

Media Production – Level 3
Awarding body:
   EDEXCEL

BTEC National Diploma

Media Production – Level 3
Awarding body:
   EDEXCEL

Certificate

Audio Electronics and Connectivity – Level 3
Awarding body:
   City & Guilds

Audio Mastering, Restoration and Editing – Level 3
Awarding body:
   City & Guilds

Audio Visual Industries Induction – Level 2
Awarding body:
   City & Guilds

Business skills for the Photo Imaging Industry – Level 3
Awarding body:
   City & Guilds

Business skills for the Photo Imaging Industry – Level 3
Awarding body:
   City & Guilds

Cinematography Skills – Level 3
Awarding body:
ABC

Digital Broadcast and Composition – Level 3
Awarding body:
City & Guilds

Digital Image Manipulation – Level 2
Awarding body:
City & Guilds

Image Management and Storage – Level 3
Awarding body:
City & Guilds

Live Sound and Performance Technology – Level 3
Awarding body:
City & Guilds

Location Photography – Level 2
Awarding body:
City & Guilds

Location Photography – Level 3
Awarding body:
City & Guilds

Location Photography and Image Printing – Level 2
Awarding body:
City & Guilds

Location Photography and Image Printing – Level 3
Awarding body:
City & Guilds

Location Photography, Image Printing and Presentation – Level 2
Awarding body:
City & Guilds

Location Photography, Image Printing and Presentation – Level 3
Awarding body:
City & Guilds

Media Studies – Entry Level
Awarding body:
WJEC

Multi Track Recording and Automation – Level 3
Awarding body:
City & Guilds

Multi Track Recording and Composition – Level 3
Awarding body:
City & Guilds

Multi Track Recording and Microphone Techniques – Level 3
Awarding body:
City & Guilds

Multi Track Recording and Mixing – Level 3
Awarding body:
City & Guilds

Music and Sound Composition – Level 3
Awarding body:
City & Guilds

Operational Photography – Level 2
Awarding body:
City & Guilds

Photo Image Capture – Level 2
Awarding body:
City & Guilds

Photo Image Capture – Level 3
Awarding body:
City & Guilds

Photo Image Capture and Manipulation – Level 3
Awarding body:
City & Guilds

Photo Image Capture and Output – Level 3
Awarding body:
City & Guilds

Photo Image Capture and Presentation – Level 3
Awarding body:
City & Guilds

Photo Image Capture and Printing – Level 2
Awarding body:
City & Guilds

**Photo Image Capture and Printing –
Level 3**
Awarding body:
  City & Guilds

**Photo Image Capture, Printing and
Presentation – Level 2**
Awarding body:
  City & Guilds

**Photo Image Capture, Printing and
Presentation – Level 3**
Awarding body:
  City & Guilds

**Photo Image Management and Storage –
Level 2**
Awarding body:
  City & Guilds

**Photo Image Management and Storage –
Level 3**
Awarding body:
  City & Guilds

**Photo Image Manipulation and
Management – Level 3**
Awarding body:
  City & Guilds

**Photo Image Output, Management and
Storage – Level 3**
Awarding body:
  City & Guilds

**Photo Image Printing, Management and
Storage – Level 2**
Awarding body:
  City & Guilds

**Photo Image Printing, Management and
Storage – Level 3**
Awarding body:
  City & Guilds

Photo Imaging – Level 2
Awarding body:
  City & Guilds

Photo Imaging – Level 3
Awarding body:
  City & Guilds

Photo Journalism – Level 3
Awarding body:
  City & Guilds

**Photography and Photo Imaging –
Level 2**
Awarding body:
  City & Guilds

**Photography and Photo Imaging –
Level 3**
Awarding body:
  City & Guilds

**Principles of Crime Scene Investigation
Photography – Level 3**
Awarding body:
  City & Guilds

Print and Photo Journalism – Level 3
Awarding body:
  City & Guilds

**Printing and Graphic Communications –
Level 2**
Awarding body:
  City & Guilds

**Printing and Graphic Communications –
Level 3**
Awarding body:
  City & Guilds

Printing Photo Images – Level 2
Awarding body:
  City & Guilds

Printing Photo Images – Level 3
Awarding body:
  City & Guilds

Radio Production – Level 1
Awarding body:
  NCFE

Radio Production – Level 2
Awarding body:
  NCFE

**Software Sound Manipulation and
Composition – Level 3**
Awarding body:
  City & Guilds

Sound and Music Technology – Level 1
Awarding body:
  City & Guilds

Sound and Music Technology – Level 3
Awarding body:
    City & Guilds

Sound Facility Design – Level 3
Awarding body:
    City & Guilds

**Specialist Photography (Buildings) –
Level 1**
Awarding body:
    City & Guilds

**Specialist Photography (Close Up) –
Level 1**
Awarding body:
    City & Guilds

**Specialist Photography (Events) –
Level 1**
Awarding body:
    City & Guilds

**Specialist Photography (Landscape) –
Level 1**
Awarding body:
    City & Guilds

**Specialist Photography (People) –
Level 1**
Awarding body:
    City & Guilds

**Specialist Photography and Image
Output – Level 2**
Awarding body:
    City & Guilds

**Specialist Photography and Image
Output – Level 3**
Awarding body:
    City & Guilds

**Specialist Photography and Presentation
– Level 2**
Awarding body:
    City & Guilds

**Specialist Photography and Presentation
– Level 3**
Awarding body:
    City & Guilds

**Specialist Photography, image output
and presentation – Level 3**
Awarding body:
    City & Guilds

Studio Photography – Level 2
Awarding body:
    City & Guilds

Studio Photography – Level 3
Awarding body:
    City & Guilds

**Studio Photography and Image Printing
– Level 2**
Awarding body:
    City & Guilds

**Studio Photography and Image Printing
– Level 3**
Awarding body:
    City & Guilds

**Studio Photography, Image Printing and
Presentation – Level 2**
Awarding body:
    City & Guilds

**Studio Photography, Image Printing and
Presentation – Level 3**
Awarding body:
    City & Guilds

**Surround Sound and Composition –
Level 3**
Awarding body:
    City & Guilds

Surround Sound and Film – Level 3
Awarding body:
    City & Guilds

Video Production – Level 2
Awarding body:
    NCFE

**Working in the Photo Imaging Industry
– Level 2**
Awarding body:
    City & Guilds

Diploma

Advanced Media Techniques – Level 3
Awarding body:
 City & Guilds

Animation – Level 3
Awarding body:
 ABC

Clapper Loaders – Level 2
Awarding body:
 UAL

Focus Pullers – Level 3
Awarding body:
 UAL

Foundation Studies (Media Production) – Level 3
Awarding body:
 ABC

Media Techniques – Level 3
Awarding body:
 City & Guilds

Music Technology and Sound Engineering – Level 3
Awarding body:
 City & Guilds

Music Technology and Sound Production – Level 3
Awarding body:
 City & Guilds

Photo Imaging – Level 2
Awarding body:
 City & Guilds

Photography and Photo Imaging – Level 2
Awarding body:
 City & Guilds

Photography and Photo Imaging – Level 3
Awarding body:
 City & Guilds

Professional Photo Imaging – Level 3
Awarding body:
 City & Guilds

Radio Production – Level 1
Awarding body:
 NCFE

Radio Production – Level 2
Awarding body:
 NCFE

Sound and Music Technology – Level 2
Awarding body:
 City & Guilds

Sound and Music Technology – Level 3
Awarding body:
 City & Guilds

Sound Design and Music Technology – Level 3
Awarding body:
 ABC

Sound Engineering – Level 3
Awarding body:
 City & Guilds

Double Award

Film and Television Screenwriting – Level 3
Awarding body:
 ABC

Film and Video Production – Level 3
Awarding body:
 ABC

Music Broadcast Skills – Level 3
Awarding body:
 ABC

Extended Certificate

Radio Production – Level 1
Awarding body:
 NCFE

Radio Production – Level 2
Awarding body:
 NCFE

Extended Diploma

Radio Production – Level 1
Awarding body:
  NCFE

Radio Production – Level 2
Awarding body:
  NCFE

Graded Examination

Communication Skills – Level 1
Awarding body:
  TCL

Communication Skills – Level 2
Awarding body:
  TCL

Communication Skills – Level 3
Awarding body:
  TCL

Introductory Award

Radio Production – Level 1
Awarding body:
  NCFE

Radio Production – Level 2
Awarding body:
  NCFE

National Award

Media – Level 2
Awarding body:
  OCR

National Certificate

Media – Level 2
Awarding body:
  OCR

Media – Level 3
Awarding body:
  OCR

National Diploma

Media – Level 3
Awarding body:
  OCR

National Extended Diploma

Media – Level 3
Awarding body:
  OCR

National Vocational Qualification

Computer Games Testing – Level 2
Awarding body:
  City & Guilds

Crane Technicians (Audio Visual Industries) – Level 2
Awarding body:
  City & Guilds

Film and Television Lighting (Best Boy) – Level 3
Awarding body:
  City & Guilds

Film and Television Lighting (Console Operator) – Level 3
Awarding body:
  City & Guilds

Film and Television Lighting (Gaffer) – Level 4
Awarding body:
  City & Guilds

Film and Television Lighting (Generator Operator) – Level 3
Awarding body:
  City & Guilds

Film and Television Lighting (Lighting Technician) – Level 3
Awarding body:
  City & Guilds

Grip for the Audio Visual Industries – Level 2
Awarding body:
  City & Guilds

**Grip for the Audio Visual Industries –
Level 3**
Awarding body:
    City & Guilds

**Grip for the Creative Industries –
Level 2**
Awarding body:
    City & Guilds

**Grip for the Creative Media Industries –
Level 3**
Awarding body:
    City & Guilds

Production for Television – Level 3
Awarding body:
    City & Guilds

**Stagehands in Film and Television –
Level 2**
Awarding body:
    City & Guilds

**Stagehands in Film and Television
(Supervising Stagehand, Chargehand
and Head of Department) – Level 3**
Awarding body:
    City & Guilds

Performing Arts

Advanced Graded Examination

Dance – Level 3
Awarding body:
    BBO
    ISTD
    RAD

Music Literacy – Level 3
Awarding body:
    ABRSM

Music Performance – Level 3
Awarding body:
    ABRSM

Music Theory/Literacy – Level 3
Awarding body:
    TCL

Theatre Dance – Level 3
Awarding body:
    GQAL

Advanced Vocational Graded Examination

Dance – Level 3
Awarding body:
    BBO
    ISTD
    RAD

Theatre Dance – Level 3
Awarding body:
    GQAL

Associate

Music Performance (ALCM) – Level 5
Awarding body:
    TVU

Music Teaching (ALCM) – Level 5
Awarding body:
    TVU

Associate Diploma

**Communication Skills (ATCL) (Public
Speaking) – Level 4**
Awarding body:
    TCL

Music Literacy (AMusTCL) – Level 4
Awarding body:
  TCL

Music Performance (ATCL Recital) – Level 4
Awarding body:
  TCL

Performing (ATCL) – Level 4
Awarding body:
  TCL

Principles of Instrumental/Vocal Teaching (ATCL) – Level 4
Awarding body:
  TCL

Pro-Music Performance (ATCL) – Level 4
Awarding body:
  TCL

Award

Business for the Creative Industries – Level 3
Awarding body:
  NCFE

Communication – Level 1
Awarding body:
  LAMDA

Communication – Level 2
Awarding body:
  LAMDA

Copy-Editing – Level 3
Awarding body:
  ABC

Creative Practitioners – Level 4
Awarding body:
  RSL

Features Journalism Skills – Level 3
Awarding body:
  ABC

Internet Safety – Level 1
Awarding body:
  SQA

Music Business – Level 2
Awarding body:
  NCFE

Music Educators – Level 3
Awarding body:
  RSL

Music Practitioners – Level 1
Awarding body:
  RSL

Music Practitioners – Level 2
Awarding body:
  RSL

Music Practitioners – Level 3
Awarding body:
  RSL

Music Technology – Level 1
Awarding body:
  NCFE

Music Technology – Level 2
Awarding body:
  NCFE

Performance – Level 1
Awarding body:
  LAMDA

Performance – Level 2
Awarding body:
  LAMDA

Performing Arts – Entry Level
Awarding body:
  EDEXCEL

Performing Arts – Level 1
Awarding body:
  EDEXCEL

The Arts – Level 1
Awarding body:
  TCL

The Arts – Level 2
Awarding body:
  TCL

The Arts – Level 3
Awarding body:
  TCL

Writing Skills for Journalism – Level 3
Awarding body:
ABC

BTEC Certificate

Performing Arts – Level 2
Awarding body:
EDEXCEL

Performing Arts – Level 3
Awarding body:
EDEXCEL

Production Arts – Level 3
Awarding body:
EDEXCEL

BTEC Diploma

Performing Arts – Level 2
Awarding body:
EDEXCEL

Performing Arts – Level 3
Awarding body:
EDEXCEL

Production Arts – Level 3
Awarding body:
EDEXCEL

BTEC Extended Certificate

Performing Arts – Level 2
Awarding body:
EDEXCEL

BTEC Extended Diploma

Performing Arts – Level 3
Awarding body:
EDEXCEL

Production Arts – Level 3
Awarding body:
EDEXCEL

BTEC First Certificate

Music – Level 2
Awarding body:
EDEXCEL

Performing Arts – Level 2
Awarding body:
EDEXCEL

BTEC First Diploma

Music – Level 2
Awarding body:
EDEXCEL

Performing Arts – Level 2
Awarding body:
EDEXCEL

BTEC Higher National Certificate

Music Performance – Level 5
Awarding body:
EDEXCEL

Music Production – Level 5
Awarding body:
EDEXCEL

Performing Arts – Level 5
Awarding body:
EDEXCEL

BTEC Higher National Diploma

Music Performance – Level 5
Awarding body:
EDEXCEL

Music Production – Level 5
Awarding body:
EDEXCEL

Performing Arts – Level 5
Awarding body:
EDEXCEL

BTEC National Award

Music – Level 3
Awarding body:
  EDEXCEL

Music Technology – Level 3
Awarding body:
  EDEXCEL

Performing Arts – Level 3
Awarding body:
  EDEXCEL

Production Arts – Level 3
Awarding body:
  EDEXCEL

BTEC National Certificate

Music – Level 3
Awarding body:
  EDEXCEL

Music Technology – Level 3
Awarding body:
  EDEXCEL

Performing Arts – Level 3
Awarding body:
  EDEXCEL

Production Arts – Level 3
Awarding body:
  EDEXCEL

BTEC National Diploma

Music – Level 3
Awarding body:
  EDEXCEL

Music Technology – Level 3
Awarding body:
  EDEXCEL

Performing Arts – Level 3
Awarding body:
  EDEXCEL

Production Arts – Level 3
Awarding body:
  EDEXCEL

BTEC Subsidiary Diploma

Performing Arts – Level 3
Awarding body:
  EDEXCEL

Production Arts – Level 3
Awarding body:
  EDEXCEL

Certificate

An Introduction to Dance Teaching – Level 3
Awarding body:
  BBO

Business for the Creative Industries – Level 3
Awarding body:
  NCFE

Carnival Skills – Level 2
Awarding body:
  ABC

Classical Musical Instrument Technology – Level 2
Awarding body:
  EDI

Classical Musical Instrument Technology – Level 3
Awarding body:
  EDI

Communication – Level 3
Awarding body:
  LAMDA

Community Arts – Level 2
Awarding body:
  ABC

Creative Practitioners – Level 4
Awarding body:
  RSL

Dance Education – Level 4
Awarding body:
  ISTD

Dance Teaching – Level 4
Awarding body:
  GQAL

Dance Teaching Assistant – Level 3
Awarding body:
GQAL

Digital Literacy – Entry Level
Awarding body:
SQA

Drama – Entry Level
Awarding body:
OCR
WJEC

Foundation Dance Practice – Level 3
Awarding body:
ISTD

Journalism – Level 3
Awarding body:
NCTJ

Lifespan Development and Learning in Dance – Level 3
Awarding body:
ISTD

Music – Entry Level
Awarding body:
WJEC

Music – Level 1,2
Awarding body:
Cambridge International

Music Business – Level 2
Awarding body:
NCFE

Music Educators – Level 3
Awarding body:
RSL

Music Literacy – Level 2
Awarding body:
ABRSM

Music Performance – Entry Level 3
Awarding body:
ABRSM

Music Performance – Level 1
Awarding body:
ABRSM

Music Practitioners – Level 1
Awarding body:
RSL

Music Practitioners – Level 2
Awarding body:
RSL

Music Practitioners – Level 3
Awarding body:
RSL

Music Technology – Level 1
Awarding body:
NCFE

Music Technology – Level 2
Awarding body:
NCFE

Observation and Understanding of Learning Techniques in Dance – Level 3
Awarding body:
ISTD

Oral Communication Skills – Entry Level
Awarding body:
ESB

Performance – Level 3
Awarding body:
LAMDA

Performance Skills – Level 1
Awarding body:
CCEA
NCFE

Performance Skills – Level 2
Awarding body:
CCEA
NCFE

Performing Arts – Level 1
Awarding body:
EDEXCEL

Practical Performance Skills (Dance) – Level 1
Awarding body:
TCL

Promotion of Health and Safety in Dance – Level 3
Awarding body:
ISTD

**Safe and Effective Dance Practice –
Level 5**
Awarding body:
TCL

**Speech and Drama (Performance
Studies) – Level 3**
Awarding body:
LAMDA

**Steel Stringed Fretted Instrument
Construction – Level 2**
Awarding body:
EDI

**Tamil Listening (Breakthrough) (Asset
Languages) – Entry Level**
Awarding body:
OCR

Combined Diploma

Music Practitioners – Level 3
Awarding body:
RSL

Diploma

**Applications for ICT in Libraries –
Level 4**
Awarding body:
SQA

**Business for the Creative Industries –
Level 3**
Awarding body:
NCFE

Creative Practitioners – Level 4
Awarding body:
RSL

Dance – Level 4
Awarding body:
GQAL

Dance Teaching – Level 4
Awarding body:
BBO
GQAL

Foundation Studies (Dance) – Level 3
Awarding body:
ABC

**Foundation Studies (Performance) –
Level 3**
Awarding body:
ABC

Image Styling for Performance – Level 3
Awarding body:
ABC

Music Business – Level 2
Awarding body:
NCFE

Music Direction – Level 4
Awarding body:
ABRSM

Music Educators – Level 3
Awarding body:
RSL

Music Performance – Level 4
Awarding body:
ABRSM
RSL
TVU

Music Performance (LRSL Perf) – Level 6
Awarding body:
RSL

Music Practitioners – Level 1
Awarding body:
RSL

Music Practitioners – Level 2
Awarding body:
RSL

Music Practitioners – Level 3
Awarding body:
RSL

Music Teaching (DipLCM) – Level 4
Awarding body:
TVU

Music Teaching (DipRSL) – Level 4
Awarding body:
RSL

Music Teaching (LRSL) – Level 6
Awarding body:
RSL

Music Technology – Level 1
Awarding body:
NCFE

Music Technology – Level 2
Awarding body:
NCFE

Performing Arts – Level 1
Awarding body:
EDEXCEL

Principles of Instrumental/Vocal Teaching – Level 4
Awarding body:
ABRSM

Double Award

News Journalism – Level 3
Awarding body:
ABC

Extended Certificate

Business for the Creative Industries – Level 3
Awarding body:
NCFE

Music Business – Level 2
Awarding body:
NCFE

Music Technology – Level 1
Awarding body:
NCFE

Music Technology – Level 2
Awarding body:
NCFE

Extended Diploma

Business for the Creative Industries – Level 3
Awarding body:
NCFE

Music Business – Level 2
Awarding body:
NCFE

Music Technology – Level 1
Awarding body:
NCFE

Music Technology – Level 2
Awarding body:
NCFE

Fellowship

Music Direction – Level 7
Awarding body:
ABRSM

Music Education – Level 7
Awarding body:
ABRSM

Music Performance – Level 7
Awarding body:
ABRSM

Music Performance (FLCM) – Level 7
Awarding body:
TVU

Fellowship Diploma

Directing (FTCL) – Level 7
Awarding body:
TCL

Music Composition (FTCL) – Level 7
Awarding body:
TCL

Music Education (FTCL) – Level 7
Awarding body:
TCL

Music Literacy (FMusTCL) – Level 7
Awarding body:
TCL

Music Performance (FTCL Recital) – Level 7
Awarding body:
TCL

Performing (FTCL) – Level 7
Awarding body:
TCL

Foundation

Dance Instruction – Level 3
Awarding body:
ISTD

Foundation Graded Examination

Dance – Level 1
Awarding body:
BBO
ISTD
RAD

Music Literacy – Level 1
Awarding body:
ABRSM

Music Performance – Level 1
Awarding body:
ABRSM

Theatre Dance – Level 1
Awarding body:
GQAL

Graded Examination

Drama – Level 1
Awarding body:
TCL
TVU

Drama – Level 2
Awarding body:
TCL
TVU

Drama – Level 3
Awarding body:
TCL
TVU

Music Literacy – Level 1
Awarding body:
TVU

Music Literacy – Level 2
Awarding body:
TVU

Music Literacy – Level 3
Awarding body:
TVU

Music Performance – Entry Level
Awarding body:
RSL

Music Performance – Level 1
Awarding body:
RSL
TCL
TVU

Music Performance – Level 2
Awarding body:
RSL
TCL
TVU

Music Performance – Level 3
Awarding body:
RSL
TCL
TVU

Music Theatre – Level 1
Awarding body:
TVU

Music Theatre – Level 2
Awarding body:
TVU

Music Theatre – Level 3
Awarding body:
TVU

Music Theory/Literacy – Level 1
Awarding body:
TCL

Music Theory/Literacy – Level 2
Awarding body:
TCL

Musical Theatre For The Actor/Singer – Level 1
Awarding body:
LAMDA

Musical Theatre For The Actor/Singer – Level 2
Awarding body:
LAMDA

Musical Theatre For The Actor/Singer – Level 3
Awarding body:
LAMDA

Spanish Dance – Level 1
Awarding body:
TCL

Spanish Dance – Level 2
Awarding body:
TCL

Speech – Level 1
Awarding body:
ESB
TCL
TVU

Speech – Level 2
Awarding body:
ESB
TVU

Speech – Level 3
Awarding body:
ESB
TCL
TVU

Speech and Drama – Level 1
Awarding body:
TCL
TVU

Speech and Drama – Level 2
Awarding body:
TCL
TVU

Speech and Drama – Level 3
Awarding body:
TCL
TVU

Intermediate Certificate

Dance – Level 2
Awarding body:
ISTD

Intermediate Graded Examination

Dance – Level 2
Awarding body:
BBO
ISTD
RAD

Music Performance – Level 2
Awarding body:
ABRSM

Theatre Dance – Level 2
Awarding body:
GQAL

Intermediate Level Certificate

Music Performance – Level 2
Awarding body:
ABRSM

Intermediate Vocational Graded Examination

Dance – Level 2
Awarding body:
BBO
RAD

Introductory Award

Business for the Creative Industries – Level 3
Awarding body:
NCFE

Music Business – Level 2
Awarding body:
NCFE

Music Technology – Level 1
Awarding body:
NCFE

Music Technology – Level 2
Awarding body:
NCFE

Introductory Certificate

Performing Arts – Level 1
Awarding body:
EDEXCEL

Introductory Diploma

Performing Arts – Level 1
Awarding body:
EDEXCEL

Licentiate

Instrumental/Vocal Teaching – Level 6
Awarding body:
ABRSM

Music Direction – Level 6
Awarding body:
ABRSM

Music Performance – Level 6
Awarding body:
ABRSM

Music Performance (LLCM) – Level 6
Awarding body:
TVU

Music Teaching (LLCM) – Level 6
Awarding body:
TVU

Licentiate Diploma

Communication Skills (LTCL/LGSMD) (Public Speaking) – Level 6
Awarding body:
TCL

Instrumental/Vocal Teaching (LTCL) – Level 6
Awarding body:
TCL

Music Composition (LTCL) – Level 6
Awarding body:
TCL

Music Literacy (LMusTCL) – Level 6
Awarding body:
TCL

Music Performance (LTCL/LGSMD Recital) – Level 6
Awarding body:
TCL

Music Teaching (LTCL) – Level 6
Awarding body:
TCL

Performing (LTCL/LGSMD) – Level 6
Awarding body:
TCL

Pro-Music Performance (LTCL) – Level 6
Awarding body:
TCL

National Certificate

Professional Acting – Level 5
Awarding body:
TCL

Professional Dance (Classical Ballet) (Contemporary Dance) – Level 5
Awarding body:
TCL

National Diploma

Professional Acting – Level 6
Awarding body:
TCL

Professional Dance – Level 6
Awarding body:
TCL

Professional Musical Theatre – Level 6
Awarding body:
TCL

National Vocational Qualification

Information and Library Services – Level 2
Awarding body:
  City & Guilds
  EDI

Information and Library Services – Level 3
Awarding body:
  City & Guilds
  EDI

Newspaper Writing – Level 4
Awarding body:
  EDI

Pre-U Certificate

Music (Principal) – Level 3
Awarding body:
  Cambridge International

Professional Diploma

Audio Recording – Level 5
Awarding body:
  EDEXCEL

Business and Management for the Arts: Music Production – Level 5
Awarding body:
  EDEXCEL

Community Music Management – Level 5
Awarding body:
  EDEXCEL

Concert Lighting – Level 5
Awarding body:
  EDEXCEL

Costume Management – Level 5
Awarding body:
  EDEXCEL

Creative Music Technology – Level 5
Awarding body:
  EDEXCEL

Front of House Management – Level 5
Awarding body:
  EDEXCEL

Light and Sound: Technical Theatre Management – Level 5
Awarding body:
  EDEXCEL

Live Sound – Level 5
Awarding body:
  EDEXCEL

Music Composition – Level 5
Awarding body:
  EDEXCEL

Music Management – Level 5
Awarding body:
  EDEXCEL

Music Performance – Level 5
Awarding body:
  EDEXCEL

Music Science and Acoustics – Level 5
Awarding body:
  EDEXCEL

Performance and Making – Level 5
Awarding body:
  EDEXCEL

Performance: Acting – Level 5
Awarding body:
  EDEXCEL

Set Design Management – Level 5
Awarding body:
  EDEXCEL

Songwriting – Level 5
Awarding body:
  EDEXCEL

Sound for the Media – Level 5
Awarding body:
  EDEXCEL

Sound Studio Management – Level 5
Awarding body:
  EDEXCEL

Stage Sound – Level 5
Awarding body:
  EDEXCEL

Progression Award

**Library and Information Services –
Level 3**
Awarding body:
   City & Guilds

Vocational Graded Examination

Spanish Dance – Level 3
Awarding body:
   TCL

Theatre Dance – Level 2
Awarding body:
   GQAL

Business, Administration and Law

Accounting and Finance

Advanced Diploma

Financial Planning – Level 6
Awarding body:
  CII

Award

Accounting and Book-keeping – Level 3
Awarding body:
  City & Guilds

Book-Keeping and Accounts – Level 1
Awarding body:
  City & Guilds

Book-Keeping and Accounts – Level 2
Awarding body:
  City & Guilds

Book-keeping – Level 2
Awarding body:
  AAT

Business Finance – Level 1
Awarding body:
  City & Guilds

Business Finance – Level 2
Awarding body:
  City & Guilds

Business Finance – Level 3
Awarding body:
  City & Guilds

Computerised Accounts – Level 1
Awarding body:
  City & Guilds

Computerised Accounts – Level 2
Awarding body:
  City & Guilds

Computerised Accounts – Level 3
Awarding body:
  City & Guilds

Insurance, legal and regulatory – Level 2
Awarding body:
  CII

Introduction to Financial Services – Level 3
Awarding body:
  CCN

Introduction to Investment – Level 3
Awarding body:
  SII

Introduction to the Financial Services Industry – Level 2
Awarding body:
  CCN

Providing Financial Advice – Level 3
Awarding body:
  EDEXCEL

Tax Professionals – Level 3
Awarding body:
  AAT

BTEC National Award

Personal and Business Finance – Level 3
Awarding body:
  EDEXCEL

Certificate

Accounting – Level 2
Awarding body:
  ACCA
  OCR

Accounting – Level 3
Awarding body:
ACCA
EDI
OCR

Accounting – Level 4
Awarding body:
ACCA

Accounting (IAS) – Level 3
Awarding body:
EDI

Accounting Technicians – Level 2
Awarding body:
AAT

Advised Sales for Motor Industry Insurance Products – Level 2
Awarding body:
City & Guilds

Basic Book-keeping – Level 1
Awarding body:
ABC

Book-keeping – Level 1
Awarding body:
EDI
IAB

Book-keeping – Level 2
Awarding body:
IAB

Book-keeping and Accounts – Level 2
Awarding body:
EDI

Book-keeping – Level 1
Awarding body:
OCR

Computerised Book-keeping – Level 1
Awarding body:
IAB

Computerised Book-keeping – Level 2
Awarding body:
ABC
IAB

Computerised Payroll – Level 2
Awarding body:
IAB

Corporate Finance – Level 3
Awarding body:
SII

Equity Release – Level 3
Awarding body:
CII

Finance for Non Financial Managers – Level 3
Awarding body:
IAB

Financial Administration – Level 3
Awarding body:
CII

Financial Advisers – Level 3
Awarding body:
IFS

Financial Management – Level 3
Awarding body:
ABE

Financial Planning – Level 3
Awarding body:
CII

Financial Planning and Long Term Care Insurance – Level 3
Awarding body:
CII

Financial Studies – Level 3
Awarding body:
IFS

Insurance – Level 3
Awarding body:
CII

Introduction to Securities & Investment – Level 3
Awarding body:
SII

Investment Administration (IAQ) – Level 3
Awarding body:
SII

Investment Management – Level 3
Awarding body:
CFA UK

Investments – Level 3
Awarding body:
  SII

Islamic Finance (IFQ) – Level 3
Awarding body:
  SII

IT in Investment Operations – Level 3
Awarding body:
  SII

Local Taxation and Benefits – Level 3
Awarding body:
  IRRV

Mortgage Advice – Level 3
Awarding body:
  CII

Mortgage Advice and Practice – Level 3
Awarding body:
  IFS

Payroll – Level 1
Awarding body:
  IAB

Payroll – Level 2
Awarding body:
  IAB

Payroll Administration – Level 2
Awarding body:
  AAT

Payroll Administration – Level 3
Awarding body:
  AAT

Private Client Investment Advice & Management – Level 6
Awarding body:
  SII

Regulated Equity Release – Level 3
Awarding body:
  IFS

Diploma

Accounting – Level 2
Awarding body:
  OCR

Accounting – Level 3
Awarding body:
  OCR

Accounting and Advanced Book-keeping – Level 3
Awarding body:
  IAB

Accounting Technicians – Level 3
Awarding body:
  AAT

Accounting Technicians – Level 4
Awarding body:
  AAT

Accounting to International Standards – Level 4
Awarding body:
  IAB

Book-keeping – Level 1
Awarding body:
  OCR

Computerised Accounting – Level 3
Awarding body:
  IAB

Computerised Payroll – Level 3
Awarding body:
  IAB

Cost and Management Accounting – Level 3
Awarding body:
  IAB

Credit Management – Level 2
Awarding body:
  ICM

Credit Management – Level 3
Awarding body:
  ICM

Credit Management – Level 5
Awarding body:
  ICM

Financial Administration – Level 3
Awarding body:
  IAB

Financial Advisers – Level 4
Awarding body:
IFS

Financial Information for Managers – Level 4
Awarding body:
IAB

Financial Management – Level 4
Awarding body:
IAB

Financial Management – Level 5
Awarding body:
ABE

Financial Planning – Level 4
Awarding body:
CII

Financial Studies – Level 3
Awarding body:
IFS

Introduction to Financial Services – Level 2
Awarding body:
IFS

Payroll – Level 3
Awarding body:
IAB

Personal and Business Tax – Level 4
Awarding body:
IAB

Personal Finance – Level 2
Awarding body:
IAB

Small Business Financial Management – Level 3
Awarding body:
IAB

Wealth Management – Level 6
Awarding body:
SII

Foundation Certificate

Personal Finance – Level 1
Awarding body:
IFS

Intermediate Certificate

Personal Finance – Level 2
Awarding body:
IFS

National Vocational Qualification

Accounting – Level 2
Awarding body:
AAT
City & Guilds
EDEXCEL

Accounting – Level 3
Awarding body:
AAT
City & Guilds
EDEXCEL

Accounting – Level 4
Awarding body:
AAT

Housing and Council Tax Benefits – Level 3
Awarding body:
IRRV

Local Taxation – Level 3
Awarding body:
IRRV

Providing Financial Advice – Level 3
Awarding body:
EDEXCEL

Retail Financial Services – Level 2
Awarding body:
City & Guilds
EDEXCEL
EDI

Retail Financial Services – Level 3
Awarding body:
 City & Guilds
 EDEXCEL
 EDI

Administration

Advanced Diploma

Administrative Management – Level 5
Awarding body:
 IAM

Award

Administration – Level 2
Awarding body:
 OCR

Administration – Level 3
Awarding body:
 OCR

Administration (Business Professional) – Level 1
Awarding body:
 OCR

Administration (Business Professional) – Level 2
Awarding body:
 OCR

Administration (Business Professional) – Level 3
Awarding body:
 OCR

Administration (Business Professional) – Level 4
Awarding body:
 OCR

Advanced Legal Information Processing – Level 3
Awarding body:
 City & Guilds

Business Administration – Entry Level
Awarding body:
 EDEXCEL

Business Administration – Level 1
Awarding body:
 EDEXCEL

Business Administration and Practice – Level 1
Awarding body:
 EDI

Business Administration and Practice – Level 2
Awarding body:
 EDI

Business Administration and Practice – Level 3
Awarding body:
 EDI

Business Skills – Level 2
Awarding body:
 City & Guilds
 EDI
 OCR

Business Skills – Level 3
Awarding body:
 City & Guilds
 EDI
 OCR

Business Studies – Level 2
Awarding body:
 City & Guilds

Customer Service – Level 1
Awarding body:
City & Guilds
EDEXCEL

Customer Service – Level 2
Awarding body:
City & Guilds

Customer Service – Level 3
Awarding body:
City & Guilds

Legal Information Processing – Level 2
Awarding body:
City & Guilds

Legal Information Processing – Level 3
Awarding body:
City & Guilds

Medical Terminology – Level 2
Awarding body:
City & Guilds

Office Procedures – Level 1
Awarding body:
City & Guilds

Office Procedures – Level 2
Awarding body:
City & Guilds

Pension Trusteeship (Defined Contribution and Defined Benefit Schemes) – Level 3
Awarding body:
PMI

Pension Trusteeship (Defined Contribution Schemes) – Level 3
Awarding body:
PMI

Proof-reading in the Legal Environment – Level 2
Awarding body:
City & Guilds

Proof-reading in the Legal Environment – Level 3
Awarding body:
City & Guilds

Public Sector Pensions Administration – Level 3
Awarding body:
PMI

Teeline Shorthand for Journalists – Level 3
Awarding body:
ABC

Touch-Typing (e-type) – Level 1
Awarding body:
BCS

Touch-Typing (e-type) – Level 2
Awarding body:
BCS

BTEC Award

Administering Examinations – Level 3
Awarding body:
EDEXCEL

Business Administration – Level 2
Awarding body:
EDEXCEL

Business Administration – Level 3
Awarding body:
EDEXCEL

Clerks to Governors – Level 3
Awarding body:
EDEXCEL

Customer Service – Level 2
Awarding body:
EDEXCEL

Customer Service – Level 3
Awarding body:
EDEXCEL

Introduction to Administering Examinations – Level 2
Awarding body:
EDEXCEL

BTEC Certificate

Business Administration – Level 2
Awarding body:
EDEXCEL

Business Administration – Level 3
Awarding body:
  EDEXCEL

Customer Service – Level 2
Awarding body:
  EDEXCEL

Customer Service – Level 3
Awarding body:
  EDEXCEL

BTEC Diploma

Business Administration – Level 2
Awarding body:
  EDEXCEL

Business Administration – Level 3
Awarding body:
  EDEXCEL

BTEC Professional Certificate

Managing Examinations – Level 4
Awarding body:
  EDEXCEL

Certificate

Administration (Business Professional) – Level 1
Awarding body:
  OCR

Administration (Business Professional) – Level 2
Awarding body:
  OCR

Administration (Business Professional) – Level 3
Awarding body:
  OCR

Administration (Business Professional) – Level 4
Awarding body:
  OCR

Administrative Management – Level 3
Awarding body:
  IAM

Business Administration – Level 1
Awarding body:
  EDEXCEL

Business Administration and Practice – Level 1
Awarding body:
  EDI

Business Administration and Practice – Level 2
Awarding body:
  EDI

Business Administration and Practice – Level 3
Awarding body:
  EDI

Business and Administration – Level 2
Awarding body:
  City & Guilds
  IMIAL

Business and Administration – Level 3
Awarding body:
  City & Guilds

Business and Administration (Organisations and People) – Level 2
Awarding body:
  EDI

Business and Administration (Organisations and People) – Level 3
Awarding body:
  EDI

Business Skills – Level 2
Awarding body:
  City & Guilds
  EDI
  OCR

Business Skills – Level 3
Awarding body:
  City & Guilds
  EDI
  OCR

City & Guilds Level 1 Certificate for Introduction to the Contact Centre Industry – Level 1
Awarding body:
City & Guilds

Conflict Handling and Prevention – Level 2
Awarding body:
City & Guilds

Customer Service – Level 2
Awarding body:
City & Guilds
EDI
OCR
VTCT

Customer Service – Level 3
Awarding body:
City & Guilds
EDI
OCR

Customer Service for the Motor Industry – Level 2
Awarding body:
IMIAL

Customer Service for the Motor Industry – Level 3
Awarding body:
IMIAL

Legal Secretaries – Level 2
Awarding body:
City & Guilds

Legal Secretaries – Level 3
Awarding body:
City & Guilds

Medical Administration – Level 2
Awarding body:
City & Guilds

Medical Administration – Level 3
Awarding body:
City & Guilds

Medical Terminology – Level 3
Awarding body:
City & Guilds

Primary Care Management – Level 5
Awarding body:
City & Guilds

Diploma

Administration (Business Professional) – Level 1
Awarding body:
OCR

Administration (Business Professional) – Level 2
Awarding body:
OCR

Administration (Business Professional) – Level 3
Awarding body:
OCR

Administration (Business Professional) – Level 4
Awarding body:
OCR

Administrative Management – Level 4
Awarding body:
IAM

Business Administration – Level 1
Awarding body:
EDEXCEL

Business Administration – Level 3
Awarding body:
IMIAL

Business Administration and Practice – Level 2
Awarding body:
EDI

Business Administration and Practice – Level 3
Awarding body:
EDI

Business and Administration – Level 2
Awarding body:
City & Guilds

Business and Administration – Level 3
Awarding body:
City & Guilds

Business Skills – Level 2
Awarding body:
    City & Guilds
    EDI
    OCR

Business Skills – Level 3
Awarding body:
    City & Guilds
    EDI
    OCR

Legal Secretaries – Level 2
Awarding body:
    City & Guilds

Legal Secretaries – Level 3
Awarding body:
    City & Guilds

Medical Administration – Level 2
Awarding body:
    City & Guilds

Medical Secretaries – Level 3
Awarding body:
    City & Guilds

Member Directed Pension Scheme Administration – Level 3
Awarding body:
    PMI

Primary Care Management – Level 5
Awarding body:
    City & Guilds

Higher Professional Diploma

Business Administration – Level 4
Awarding body:
    City & Guilds

Introductory Award

Administrative Management – Level 2
Awarding body:
    IAM

Introductory Certificate

Conflict Handling – Level 1
Awarding body:
    City & Guilds

Customer Service – Level 1
Awarding body:
    City & Guilds

Hospitality Customer Service – Level 1
Awarding body:
    City & Guilds

National Vocational Qualification

Business and Administration – Level 1
Awarding body:
    City & Guilds
    EDI
    NCFE
    OCR

Business and Administration – Level 2
Awarding body:
    City & Guilds
    EAL
    EDI
    IMIAL
    NCFE
    OCR
    OU
    SQA

Business and Administration – Level 3
Awarding body:
    City & Guilds
    EAL
    EDI
    IMIAL
    NCFE
    OCR
    OU
    SQA

Business and Administration – Level 4

Awarding body:
City & Guilds
EDI
NCFE
OCR
OU

Customer Service – Level 1

Awarding body:
City & Guilds
EDEXCEL
EDI
NCFE
OCR
SQA
VTCT

Customer Service – Level 2

Awarding body:
Active IQ
City & Guilds
EDEXCEL
EDI
IMIAL
NCFE
OCR
OU
SQA
VTCT

Customer Service – Level 3

Awarding body:
Active IQ
City & Guilds
EDEXCEL
EDI
IMIAL
NCFE
OCR
OU
SQA
VTCT

Customer Service – Level 4

Awarding body:
City & Guilds
EDEXCEL
OCR
OU

Business Management

Advanced Diploma

Accounting and Finance – Level 6

Awarding body:
IOCM

Business Management – Level 6

Awarding body:
ABE

Business Studies – Level 6

Awarding body:
IOCM

Business, Administration and Finance – Level 3

Awarding body:
AQA
City & Guilds
EDEXCEL
EDI
OCR

Commercial Management – Level 6

Awarding body:
IOCM

Human Resource Development – Level 6
Awarding body:
  IOCM

Human Resource Management – Level 6
Awarding body:
  ABE

Maritime Management – Level 6
Awarding body:
  IOCM

Marketing Management – Level 6
Awarding body:
  IOCM

Marketing, Advertising and Public Relations – Level 6
Awarding body:
  IOCM

Professional Selling – Level 6
Awarding body:
  IOCM

Purchasing and Supply – Level 5
Awarding body:
  CIPS

Tourism and Business – Level 6
Awarding body:
  IOCM

Travel, Tourism and Hospitality Management – Level 6
Awarding body:
  ABE

Award

Business Awareness – Level 3
Awarding body:
  ILM

Business Enterprise – Level 2
Awarding body:
  OCR

Business Enterprise – Level 3
Awarding body:
  OCR

Business Practices – Level 2
Awarding body:
  ABC

Business Start Up – Level 2
Awarding body:
  VTCT

Business Start-Up – Level 3
Awarding body:
  VTCT

Customer Awareness – Level 2
Awarding body:
  ILM

Developing Peer Reviewers – Level 5
Awarding body:
  CCN

Developing Social Enterprises – Level 5
Awarding body:
  ILM

Effective Team Member Skills – Level 2
Awarding body:
  ILM

Enterprise Awareness – Level 2
Awarding body:
  ILM

Executive Management – Level 7
Awarding body:
  ILM

Exploring Business Enterprise – Level 2
Awarding body:
  ILM

Facilities Management – Level 3
Awarding body:
  ILM

First Line Management – Level 3
Awarding body:
  ILM

Initial Text Processing – Entry Level
Awarding body:
  OCR

Introduction to Business Improvement – Level 2
Awarding body:
  ILM

Leadership – Level 3
Awarding body:
   ILM

Leadership – Level 4
Awarding body:
   ILM

Leadership – Level 5
Awarding body:
   ILM

**Leadership and Management Skills –
Level 3**
Awarding body:
   ILM

**Leadership and Management Skills –
Level 5**
Awarding body:
   ILM

**Leadership Coaching and Mentoring –
Level 7**
Awarding body:
   CMI

Management – Level 4
Awarding body:
   ILM

Management – Level 5
Awarding body:
   ILM

Management – Level 6
Awarding body:
   ILM

Management and Leadership – Level 4
Awarding body:
   CMI

Management and Leadership – Level 5
Awarding body:
   CMI

Management and Leadership – Level 6
Awarding body:
   CMI

**Management Coaching and Mentoring –
Level 5**
Awarding body:
   CMI

**Managing Equality and Diversity in an
Organisation – Level 4**
Awarding body:
   ILM

Managing Operations – Level 3
Awarding body:
   ILM

**Managing Voluntary and Community
Organisations – Level 3**
Awarding body:
   NOCN

Managing Volunteers – Level 3
Awarding body:
   NOCN

Mentoring for Young Learners – Level 2
Awarding body:
   ILM

Personal Development – Level 2
Awarding body:
   ILM

**Personal Professional Development –
Level 5**
Awarding body:
   ILM

**Preparing for a Business Venture –
Level 2**
Awarding body:
   OCR

**Preparing for Business Enterprise –
Level 2**
Awarding body:
   ILM

Promoting Social Enterprise – Level 5
Awarding body:
   ILM

Self Employment & Enterprise – Level 2
Awarding body:
   NOCN

**Self Employment and Enterprise –
Level 3**
Awarding body:
   NOCN

Service Improvement – Level 3
Awarding body:
ILM

Site Waste Management Awareness – Level 2
Awarding body:
ILM

Skills for Business – Level 1
Awarding body:
ABC

Skills for Business – Level 2
Awarding body:
ABC

Skills for Business – Level 3
Awarding body:
ABC

Social Impact Assessment – Level 5
Awarding body:
ILM

Speed Keying – Entry Level
Awarding body:
OCR

Starting a Business Venture – Level 3
Awarding body:
OCR

Starting Your Enterprise – Level 3
Awarding body:
ILM

Strategic Direction and Leadership – Level 8
Awarding body:
CMI

Strategic Leadership – Level 7
Awarding body:
ILM

Strategic Management and Leadership – Level 7
Awarding body:
CMI

Sustaining Social Enterprises – Level 5
Awarding body:
ILM

Team Leading – Level 2
Awarding body:
CMI
ILM

Text Processing (Business Professional) – Level 1
Awarding body:
OCR

Text Processing (Business Professional) – Level 2
Awarding body:
OCR

Text Processing (Business Professional) – Level 3
Awarding body:
OCR

Trade Union Health and Safety Representatives – Level 1
Awarding body:
NOCN

Trade Union Health and Safety Representatives – Level 2
Awarding body:
NOCN

Trade Union Health and Safety Representatives – Level 3
Awarding body:
NOCN

Trade Union Learning Representatives – Level 2
Awarding body:
NOCN

Trade Union Learning Representatives – Level 3
Awarding body:
NOCN

Trade Union Representatives – Level 1
Awarding body:
NOCN

Trade Union Representatives – Level 2
Awarding body:
NOCN

Trade Union Representatives – Level 3
Awarding body:
NOCN

Trade Unions Today – Level 1
Awarding body:
  NOCN

Trade Unions Today – Level 2
Awarding body:
  NOCN

Trade Unions Today – Level 3
Awarding body:
  NOCN

Understanding Business Enterprise Activities – Level 1
Awarding body:
  OCR

Understanding Business Enterprise Activities – Level 2
Awarding body:
  OCR

Understanding Business Enterprise Activities – Level 3
Awarding body:
  OCR

Understanding Social Enterprise – Level 5
Awarding body:
  ILM

Vocational Assessment of Leadership and Management – Level 4
Awarding body:
  ILM

Volunteer Management – Level 3
Awarding body:
  Lantra Awards

Workplace Learning Champions – Level 2
Awarding body:
  NOCN

Workplace Learning Champions – Level 3
Awarding body:
  NOCN

Workplace Coaching for Team Leaders and First Line Managers – Level 3
Awarding body:
  ILM

Workplace Mentoring – Level 3
Awarding body:
  ILM

BTEC Advanced Professional Award

Management Studies – Level 7
Awarding body:
  EDEXCEL

BTEC Advanced Professional Certificate

Management Studies – Level 7
Awarding body:
  EDEXCEL

BTEC Advanced Professional Diploma

Management Studies – Level 7
Awarding body:
  EDEXCEL

BTEC Award

Introducing Management – Level 3
Awarding body:
  EDEXCEL

Introducing Team Leading – Level 2
Awarding body:
  EDEXCEL

Management – Level 3
Awarding body:
  EDEXCEL

Sales – Level 2
Awarding body:
  EDEXCEL

Team Leading – Level 2
Awarding body:
  EDEXCEL

Understanding Enterprise – Level 2
Awarding body:
  EDEXCEL

BTEC Certificate

Business – Level 2
Awarding body:
EDEXCEL

Business – Level 3
Awarding body:
EDEXCEL

**Lean Organisation Management
Techniques – Level 2**
Awarding body:
EDEXCEL

Management – Level 3
Awarding body:
EDEXCEL

Sales – Level 3
Awarding body:
EDEXCEL

**Understanding Enterprise and
Entrepreneurship – Level 2**
Awarding body:
EDEXCEL

BTEC Diploma

Business – Level 2
Awarding body:
EDEXCEL

Business – Level 3
Awarding body:
EDEXCEL

**Enterprise and Entrepreneurship –
Level 3**
Awarding body:
EDEXCEL

**Training and Operational Management –
Level 3**
Awarding body:
EDEXCEL

**Understanding Enterprise and
Entrepreneurship – Level 2**
Awarding body:
EDEXCEL

BTEC Extended Certificate

Business – Level 2
Awarding body:
EDEXCEL

BTEC Extended Diploma

Business – Level 3
Awarding body:
EDEXCEL

BTEC First Certificate

Business – Level 2
Awarding body:
EDEXCEL

BTEC First Diploma

Business – Level 2
Awarding body:
EDEXCEL

BTEC Higher National Certificate

Business – Level 5
Awarding body:
EDEXCEL

BTEC Higher National Diploma

Business – Level 5
Awarding body:
EDEXCEL

BTEC National Award

Business – Level 3
Awarding body:
EDEXCEL

BTEC National Certificate

Business – Level 3
Awarding body:
   EDEXCEL

BTEC National Diploma

Business – Level 3
Awarding body:
   EDEXCEL

BTEC Subsidiary Diploma

Business – Level 3
Awarding body:
   EDEXCEL

Understanding Enterprise and Entrepreneurship – Level 3
Awarding body:
   EDEXCEL

Certificate

Accounting and Finance – Level 4
Awarding body:
   IOCM

Automotive Management – Level 3
Awarding body:
   IMIAL

Business Awareness and Advanced Professional Study – Level 6
Awarding body:
   CIPD

Business Enterprise – Level 2
Awarding body:
   CCEA
   IAB

Business Enterprise – Level 3
Awarding body:
   CCEA

Business Information Systems – Level 3
Awarding body:
   ABE

Business Management – Level 3
Awarding body:
   ABE

Business Practices – Level 2
Awarding body:
   ABC

Business Start-Up – Level 2
Awarding body:
   VTCT

Business Start-Up – Level 3
Awarding body:
   VTCT

Business Studies – Entry Level
Awarding body:
   CCEA
   OCR
   WJEC

Business Studies – Level 4
Awarding body:
   IOCM

Business Support – Level 5
Awarding body:
   ILM

Business Improvement Techniques – Level 2
Awarding body:
   EAL

Coaching and Mentoring – Level 3
Awarding body:
   CMI

Coaching and Mentoring in Management – Level 5
Awarding body:
   ILM

Conflict Management – Level 2
Awarding body:
   ASCENTIS

Contributing to a Project – Level 2
Awarding body:
   EDI

Effective Team Member Skills – Level 2
Awarding body:
   ILM

Enterprise (Young Enterprise Team Programme) – Entry Level
Awarding body:
OCR

Enterprise (Young Enterprise) – Level 1
Awarding body:
OCR

Enterprise (Young Enterprise) – Level 2
Awarding body:
OCR

Executive Coaching and Leadership Mentoring – Level 7
Awarding body:
ILM

Executive Management – Level 7
Awarding body:
ILM

Facilities Management – Level 3
Awarding body:
ILM

First Line Management – Level 3
Awarding body:
CMI
ILM

Human Resource Management – Level 3
Awarding body:
ABE

Innovation in the workplace – Level 2
Awarding body:
ILM

Journalism – Level 4
Awarding body:
IOCM

Leadership – Level 3
Awarding body:
ILM

Leadership – Level 5
Awarding body:
ILM

Leadership and Management Skills – Level 3
Awarding body:
ILM

Leadership and Management Skills – Level 4
Awarding body:
ILM

Leadership and Management Skills – Level 5
Awarding body:
ILM

Leadership Coaching and Mentoring – Level 7
Awarding body:
CMI

Leading and Managing (Peer Review) – Level 7
Awarding body:
CCN

Leading Quality Improvement – Level 5
Awarding body:
ILM

Leading Quality Improvement – Level 7
Awarding body:
ILM

Management – Level 3
Awarding body:
EDI

Management – Level 4
Awarding body:
ILM

Management – Level 5
Awarding body:
ILM

Management and Leadership – Level 4
Awarding body:
CMI

Management and Leadership – Level 5
Awarding body:
CMI

Management and Leadership – Level 6
Awarding body:
CMI

Management Coaching and Mentoring – Level 5
Awarding body:
CMI

Managing Voluntary and Community Organisations – Level 2
Awarding body:
   NOCN

Managing Voluntary and Community Organisations – Level 3
Awarding body:
   NOCN

Operations Management – Level 3
Awarding body:
   IOM

Preparing for a Business Venture – Level 2
Awarding body:
   OCR

Preparing for Business Enterprise – Level 2
Awarding body:
   ILM

Professional Workplace Coaches – Level 3
Awarding body:
   ILM

Project Management – Level 3
Awarding body:
   EDI

Public Policy Making – Level 7
Awarding body:
   ILM

Purchasing and Supply – Level 3
Awarding body:
   CIPS

Quality Assurance – Level 3
Awarding body:
   CQI

Sales Management – Level 2
Awarding body:
   ILM

Self Employment and Enterprise – Level 2
Awarding body:
   NOCN

Self Employment and Enterprise – Level 3
Awarding body:
   NOCN

Service Improvement – Level 5
Awarding body:
   ILM

Site Waste Management Planning and Implementation – Level 3
Awarding body:
   ILM

Skills for Business – Level 1
Awarding body:
   ABC

Skills for Business – Level 2
Awarding body:
   ABC

Skills for Business – Level 3
Awarding body:
   ABC

Social Enterprise Support – Level 5
Awarding body:
   ILM

Starting a Business Venture – Level 3
Awarding body:
   OCR

Starting Your Enterprise – Level 3
Awarding body:
   ILM

Strategic Direction and Leadership – Level 8
Awarding body:
   CMI

Strategic Leadership – Level 7
Awarding body:
   ILM

Strategic Management and Leadership – Level 7
Awarding body:
   CMI

Stress Management – Level 2
Awarding body:
   ASCENTIS

Team Leading – Level 2
Awarding body:
CMI
EDI
ILM

Text Processing (Business Professional) – Level 1
Awarding body:
OCR

Text Processing (Business Professional) – Level 2
Awarding body:
OCR

Text Processing (Business Professional) – Level 3
Awarding body:
OCR

Trade Union Health and Safety Representatives – Level 1
Awarding body:
NOCN

Trade Union Health and Safety Representatives – Level 2
Awarding body:
NOCN

Trade Union Health and Safety Representatives (Next Steps) – Level 2
Awarding body:
NOCN

Trade Union Health and Safety Representatives (Next Steps) – Level 3
Awarding body:
NOCN

Trade Union Learning Representatives – Level 2
Awarding body:
NOCN

Trade Union Learning Representatives – Level 3
Awarding body:
NOCN

Trade Union Organising Academy – Level 3
Awarding body:
NOCN

Trade Union Representatives (Stage 1) – Level 1
Awarding body:
NOCN

Trade Union Representatives (Stage 1) – Level 2
Awarding body:
NOCN

Trade Union Representatives (Stepping Up) – Level 2
Awarding body:
NOCN

Trade Union Representatives (Stepping Up) – Level 3
Awarding body:
NOCN

Trade Union Tutor Training – Level 3
Awarding body:
NOCN

Trade Unions Today – Level 2
Awarding body:
NOCN

Trade Unions Today – Level 3
Awarding body:
NOCN

Travel and Tourism – Level 4
Awarding body:
IOCM

Travel, Tourism and Hospitality Management – Level 3
Awarding body:
ABE

Workplace Coaching and Mentoring – Level 3
Awarding body:
ILM

Workplace Mentoring – Level 3
Awarding body:
ILM

Diploma

Accounting and Finance – Level 5
Awarding body:
IOCM

Business – Level 4
Awarding body:
  NCC

Business – Level 5
Awarding body:
  NCC

Business Management – Level 5
Awarding body:
  ABE

Business Practices – Level 2
Awarding body:
  ABC

Business Studies – Level 5
Awarding body:
  IOCM

Business, Administration and Finance – Level 2
Awarding body:
  EDI

Coaching and Mentoring – Level 3
Awarding body:
  CMI

Commercial Management – Level 5
Awarding body:
  IOCM

Executive Management – Level 7
Awarding body:
  ILM

Facilities Management – Level 3
Awarding body:
  ILM

First Line Management – Level 3
Awarding body:
  CMI
  ILM

Human Resource Development – Level 5
Awarding body:
  IOCM

Human Resource Management – Level 5
Awarding body:
  ABE

Journalism – Level 5
Awarding body:
  IOCM

Leadership and Management – Level 3
Awarding body:
  ILM

Leadership and Management – Level 4
Awarding body:
  ILM

Leadership and Management – Level 5
Awarding body:
  ILM

Leadership Coaching and Mentoring – Level 7
Awarding body:
  CMI

Management – Level 4
Awarding body:
  ILM

Management – Level 5
Awarding body:
  ILM

Management and Leadership – Level 4
Awarding body:
  CMI

Management and Leadership – Level 5
Awarding body:
  CMI

Management and Leadership – Level 6
Awarding body:
  CMI

Management Coaching and Mentoring – Level 5
Awarding body:
  CMI

Maritime Management – Level 5
Awarding body:
  IOCM

Marketing Management – Level 5
Awarding body:
  IOCM

Operations Management – Level 5
Awarding body:
  IOM

Professional Executive Coaches and Leadership Mentors – Level 7
Awarding body:
ILM

Professional Management Coaches and Mentors – Level 5
Awarding body:
ILM

Professional Selling – Level 5
Awarding body:
IOCM

Public Service Leadership – Level 6
Awarding body:
CMI

Purchasing and Supply – Level 4
Awarding body:
CIPS

Social Enterprise Support – Level 5
Awarding body:
ILM

Strategic Direction and Leadership – Level 8
Awarding body:
CMI

Strategic Leadership – Level 7
Awarding body:
ILM

Strategic Leadership and Executive Management – Level 7
Awarding body:
ILM

Strategic Management and Leadership – Level 7
Awarding body:
CMI

Team Leading – Level 2
Awarding body:
CMI

Text Processing (Business Professional) – Level 1
Awarding body:
OCR

Text Processing (Business Professional) – Level 2
Awarding body:
OCR

Text Processing (Business Professional) – Level 3
Awarding body:
OCR

Tourism and Business – Level 5
Awarding body:
IOCM

Trade Union Health and Safety Representatives – Occupational Health and Safety – Level 2
Awarding body:
NOCN

Trade Union Health and Safety Representatives – Occupational Health and Safety – Level 3
Awarding body:
NOCN

Trade Union Organising Academy – Level 3
Awarding body:
NOCN

Trade Union Representatives – Contemporary Trade Unionism – Level 2
Awarding body:
NOCN

Trade Union Representatives – Contemporary Trade Unionism – Level 3
Awarding body:
NOCN

Trade Union Representatives – Employment Law – Level 2
Awarding body:
NOCN

Trade Union Representatives – Employment Law – Level 3
Awarding body:
NOCN

Trade Union Tutor Training – Level 3
Awarding body:
NOCN

Travel, Tourism and Hospitality Management – Level 5
Awarding body:
ABE

Extended Diploma

Leadership and Management – Level 4
Awarding body:
ILM

Leadership and Management – Level 5
Awarding body:
ILM

Management – Level 4
Awarding body:
ILM

Management – Level 5
Awarding body:
ILM

Foundation Diploma

Business, Administration and Finance – Level 1
Awarding body:
AQA
City & Guilds
EDEXCEL
EDI
OCR

Graduate Diploma

Commercial Management – Level 6
Awarding body:
IOCM

Management Studies – Level 6
Awarding body:
IOCM

Maritime Management – Level 6
Awarding body:
IOCM

Marketing Management – Level 6
Awarding body:
IOCM

Purchasing and Supply – Level 6
Awarding body:
CIPS

Sales Coaching – Level 6
Awarding body:
IOCM

Tourism Management – Level 6
Awarding body:
IOCM

Higher Diploma

Business, Administration and Finance – Level 2
Awarding body:
AQA
City & Guilds
EDEXCEL
OCR

Introductory Certificate

Business, Retail and Administration – Level 1
Awarding body:
EDEXCEL

Management – Level 3
Awarding body:
CMI

Purchasing and Supply – Level 2
Awarding body:
CIPS

Team Leading – Level 2
Awarding body:
CMI

Introductory Diploma

Business, Retail and Administration – Level 1
Awarding body:
EDEXCEL

Management – Level 4
Awarding body:
CMI

Introductory Executive Diploma

Management – Level 7
Awarding body:
CMI

Master Professional Diploma

Strategy and Development – Level 7
Awarding body:
City & Guilds

National Award

Business – Level 2
Awarding body:
OCR

Business and ICT – Level 1
Awarding body:
OCR

National Certificate

Business – Level 2
Awarding body:
OCR

Business – Level 3
Awarding body:
OCR

Business and ICT – Level 1
Awarding body:
OCR

National Diploma

Business – Level 3
Awarding body:
OCR

National Extended Diploma

Business – Level 3
Awarding body:
OCR

National First Award

Business and ICT – Level 1
Awarding body:
OCR

National Vocational Qualification

Business and Administration – Level 1
Awarding body:
EDEXCEL

Business and Administration – Level 2
Awarding body:
EDEXCEL

Business and Administration – Level 3
Awarding body:
EDEXCEL

Business and Administration – Level 4
Awarding body:
EDEXCEL

Business Support – Level 4
Awarding body:
OCR

Business-Improvement Techniques – Level 2
Awarding body:
City & Guilds
EAL
EDEXCEL
EDI
ETCAL
PAA\VQSET
SQA

Business-Improvement Techniques – Level 3
Awarding body:
City & Guilds
EAL
EDEXCEL
EDI
ETCAL
PAA\VQSET
SQA

**Business-Improvement Techniques –
Level 4**
Awarding body:
City & Guilds
EAL
EDEXCEL
EDI
ETCAL
PAA\VQSET

**Business-Improvement Techniques –
Lean Leadership – Level 5**
Awarding body:
City & Guilds
EDEXCEL

Coaching and Mentoring – Level 3
Awarding body:
CMI

**Developing an Established Business
Enterprise – Level 4**
Awarding body:
OCR

Environmental Management – Level 4
Awarding body:
ILM

Facilities Management – Level 3
Awarding body:
City & Guilds
EDEXCEL

First Line Management – Level 3
Awarding body:
CMI

Management – Level 3
Awarding body:
CIPD
CMI
EAL
ECITB
EDEXCEL
EDI
ILM
OCR
OU
SQA

Management – Level 4
Awarding body:
CIPD
CMI
EAL
EDEXCEL
EDI
ILM
OCR
OU
SQA

Management – Level 5
Awarding body:
CIPD
CMI
EDEXCEL
EDI
ILM
OCR
OU
SQA

Personnel Management – Level 4
Awarding body:
CIPD
ILM

Personnel Strategy – Level 5
Awarding body:
CIPD
ILM

Personnel Support – Level 3
Awarding body:
CIPD
ILM

Project Management – Level 4
Awarding body:
OU

Project Management – Level 5
Awarding body:
OU

Revenue Protection – Level 3
Awarding body:
City & Guilds

**Starting a New Business Enterprise –
Level 3**
Awarding body:
    EDI
    ILM
    OCR

Supply Chain Management – Level 2
Awarding body:
    EDEXCEL

Supply Chain Management – Level 3
Awarding body:
    EDEXCEL

Supply Chain Management – Level 4
Awarding body:
    EDEXCEL

Supply Chain Management – Level 5
Awarding body:
    EDEXCEL

Team Leading – Level 2
Awarding body:
    CIPD
    CMI
    EDEXCEL
    EDI
    ILM
    NCFE
    OCR
    OU
    SQA

**The Management of Volunteers –
Level 3**
Awarding body:
    ILM

**The Management of Volunteers –
Level 4**
Awarding body:
    ILM

**The Management of Volunteers –
Level 5**
Awarding body:
    ILM

Postgraduate Certificate

Personnel and Development – Level 7
Awarding body:
    CIPD

Postgraduate Diploma

Business Management – Level 7
Awarding body:
    ABE

Personnel and Development – Level 7
Awarding body:
    CIPD

Pre-U Certificate

**Business and Management (Principal) –
Level 3**
Awarding body:
    Cambridge International

Principal Learning

**Business, Administration and Finance –
Level 1**
Awarding body:
    AQA
    City & Guilds
    EDEXCEL
    EDI
    OCR

**Business, Administration and Finance –
Level 2**
Awarding body:
    AQA
    City & Guilds
    EDEXCEL
    EDI
    OCR

**Business, Administration and Finance –
Level 3**
Awarding body:
    AQA
    City & Guilds
    EDEXCEL
    EDI
    OCR

Professional Award

Management Studies – Level 5
Awarding body:
EDEXCEL

Professional Certificate

Management Studies – Level 5
Awarding body:
EDEXCEL

Professional Diploma

Management Studies – Level 5
Awarding body:
EDEXCEL

Progression Diploma

Business, Administration and Finance – Level 3
Awarding body:
AQA
City & Guilds
EDEXCEL
EDI
OCR

Law and Legal Services

Award

Legal Studies – Level 2
Awarding body:
City & Guilds

BTEC Award

Law and Legal Work – Level 2
Awarding body:
EDEXCEL

Law and Legal Work – Level 3
Awarding body:
EDEXCEL

BTEC National Award

Applied Law – Level 3
Awarding body:
EDEXCEL

Certificate

Incident, Fraud and Claims Investigation – Level 4
Awarding body:
DnAA

Law – Level 6
Awarding body:
ILEX

Law and Practice – Level 3
Awarding body:
ILEX

Legal Studies – Level 2
Awarding body:
City & Guilds

Diploma

Business Law – Level 3
Awarding body:
IAB

Law and Practice – Level 3
Awarding body:
ILEX

Law and Practice – Level 6
Awarding body:
ILEX

Legal Practice – Level 6
Awarding body:
ILEX

Legal Studies – Level 2
Awarding body:
City & Guilds

Vocational Paralegal Studies – Level 3
Awarding body:
City & Guilds

Extended Diploma

Law and Practice – Level 3
Awarding body:
ILEX

Higher Diploma

Law – Level 6
Awarding body:
ILEX

National Vocational Qualification

Court Operations – Level 2
Awarding body:
SQA

Professional Diploma

Law – Level 3
Awarding body:
ILEX

Professional Higher Diploma

Law – Level 6
Awarding body:
ILEX

Marketing and Sales

Advanced Certificate

Market and Social Research Practice – Level 5
Awarding body:
MRS

Advanced Diploma

Marketing – Level 6
Awarding body:
ABE

Award

Account Management – Level 5
Awarding body:
ISMM

Advanced Sales and Marketing – Level 3
Awarding body:
ISMM

Basic Sales Skills – Level 1
Awarding body:
ISMM

Operational Sales and Marketing Management – Level 4
Awarding body:
ISMM

Sales and Marketing – Level 2
Awarding body:
  ISMM

Sales Management – Level 5
Awarding body:
  ISMM

Strategic Sales and Account Management – Level 6
Awarding body:
  ISMM

Certificate

Account Management – Level 5
Awarding body:
  ISMM

Advanced Sales and Marketing – Level 3
Awarding body:
  ISMM

Market and Social Research – Level 2
Awarding body:
  City & Guilds

Marketing – Level 3
Awarding body:
  ABE
  EDI

Operational Sales and Marketing Management – Level 4
Awarding body:
  ISMM

Sales – Level 3
Awarding body:
  City & Guilds

Sales and Marketing – Level 2
Awarding body:
  ISMM

Sales Management – Level 5
Awarding body:
  ISMM

Strategic Sales and Account Management – Level 6
Awarding body:
  ISMM

Vehicle Sales – Level 2
Awarding body:
  IMIAL

Diploma

Account Management – Level 5
Awarding body:
  ISMM

Advanced Sales and Marketing – Level 3
Awarding body:
  ISMM

Market and Social Research Practice – Level 7
Awarding body:
  MRS

Marketing – Level 5
Awarding body:
  ABE

Operational Sales and Marketing Management – Level 4
Awarding body:
  ISMM

Sales and Account Management – Level 5
Awarding body:
  ISMM

Sales Management – Level 5
Awarding body:
  ISMM

Strategic Sales – Level 5
Awarding body:
  ISMM

Strategic Sales and Account Management – Level 6
Awarding body:
  ISMM

Vehicle Sales – Level 3
Awarding body:
  IMIAL

Foundation Award

Public Relations – Level 3
Awarding body:
  City & Guilds

Introductory Certificate

Hospitality Selling – Level 1
Awarding body:
  City & Guilds

Marketing – Level 2
Awarding body:
  CIM

Marketing – Level 3
Awarding body:
  CIM

Selling – Level 1
Awarding body:
  City & Guilds

National Vocational Qualification

Marketing – Level 2
Awarding body:
  City & Guilds

Marketing – Level 3
Awarding body:
  City & Guilds

Marketing – Level 4
Awarding body:
  City & Guilds

Sales – Level 2
Awarding body:
  Active IQ
  City & Guilds
  EDEXCEL
  Skillsfirst
  VTCT

Sales – Level 3
Awarding body:
  Active IQ
  City & Guilds
  EDEXCEL
  Skillsfirst
  VTCT

Sales – Level 4
Awarding body:
  City & Guilds

Telesales – Level 2
Awarding body:
  City & Guilds

Telesales – Level 3
Awarding body:
  City & Guilds

Vehicle Sales – Level 2
Awarding body:
  IMIAL

Vehicle Sales – Level 3
Awarding body:
  IMIAL

Professional Certificate

Marketing – Level 3
Awarding body:
  CIM

Marketing – Level 4
Awarding body:
  CIM

Professional Diploma

Marketing – Level 6
Awarding body:
  CIM

Construction, Planning and the Built Environment

Architecture

Certificate

The Inspection and Testing of Electrical Equipment (Code of Practice for In-Service Inspection) – Level 3
Awarding body:
City & Guilds

Building and Construction

Advanced Award

Construction – Level 3
Awarding body:
CSkills Awards

Advanced Diploma

Construction and the Built Environment – Level 3
Awarding body:
AQA
City & Guilds
EDEXCEL
OCR

Award

Adjudication in the Construction Industry – Level 3
Awarding body:
RSPH

Basic Landscaping – Level 1
Awarding body:
ABC

Building Crafts (Fixtures and Fittings) – Level 1
Awarding body:
CSkills Awards

Building Crafts (Materials) – Level 1
Awarding body:
CSkills Awards

Building Heritage – Level 2
Awarding body:
ABC

Building Services Engineering – Level 1
Awarding body:
ABC

Building Services Engineering – Level 2
Awarding body:
ABC

**Building Services Engineering
(Electrical) – Level 3**
Awarding body:
  ABC

**Building Services Engineering
Mechanical – Level 3**
Awarding body:
  ABC

Construction – Entry Level
Awarding body:
  EDEXCEL

Construction – Level 1
Awarding body:
  EDEXCEL

**Construction (Design and Management)
Regulations – Level 3**
Awarding body:
  OU

**Construction and the Built Environment
– Level 1**
Awarding body:
  EDEXCEL

Construction Trades – Level 2
Awarding body:
  CCEA

Creating Interiors – Level 1
Awarding body:
  ABC

Creating Interiors – Level 2
Awarding body:
  ABC

Design and Landscape Skills – Level 3
Awarding body:
  ABC

Domestic Energy Assessment – Level 3
Awarding body:
  NFOPP

**Emergency Rescue and Recovery of
Casualties from Confined Spaces in the
Water Industry – Level 3**
Awarding body:
  City & Guilds

**Ensuring Buildings and Amenities are
Inclusive Environments – Level 4**
Awarding body:
  RSPH

Hard Landscaping – Level 2
Awarding body:
  ABC

**Overseeing Work in Confined Spaces in
the Water Industry – Level 4**
Awarding body:
  City & Guilds

**Performing Electrical Installation
Operations – Level 2**
Awarding body:
  ABC

**Performing Heating and Ventilation
Operations – Level 2**
Awarding body:
  ABC

**Performing Plumbing Operations –
Level 2**
Awarding body:
  ABC

**Performing Refrigeration and Air
Conditioning Operations – Level 2**
Awarding body:
  ABC

**Plant Operations (Agricultural Tractor)
– Level 2**
Awarding body:
  CSkills Awards

**Plant Operations (Compact Crane) –
Level 2**
Awarding body:
  CSkills Awards

**Plant Operations (Concrete Pump –
Trailer Mounted) – Level 2**
Awarding body:
  CSkills Awards

**Plant Operations (Concrete Pump –
Truck Mounted Boom) – Level 2**
Awarding body:
  CSkills Awards

Plant Operations (Construction Plant Attachments) – Level 2
Awarding body:
CSkills Awards

Plant Operations (Crawler – Tractor/Dozer) – Level 2
Awarding body:
CSkills Awards

Plant Operations (Crawler – Tractor/Side Boom) – Level 2
Awarding body:
CSkills Awards

Plant Operations (Crawler Crane) – Level 2
Awarding body:
CSkills Awards

Plant Operations (Crusher) – Level 2
Awarding body:
CSkills Awards

Plant Operations (Demolition Plant – 360 Demolition-based Excavator) – Level 2
Awarding body:
CSkills Awards

Plant Operations (Dragline) – Level 2
Awarding body:
CSkills Awards

Plant Operations (Dump Truck – Articulated Chassis) – Level 2
Awarding body:
CSkills Awards

Plant Operations (Dump Truck – Rigid Chassis) – Level 2
Awarding body:
CSkills Awards

Plant Operations (Excavator 180 above 5 tonnes) – Level 2
Awarding body:
CSkills Awards

Plant Operations (Excavator 180 below 5 tonnes) – Level 2
Awarding body:
CSkills Awards

Plant Operations (Excavator 360 above 10 tonnes) – Level 2
Awarding body:
CSkills Awards

Plant Operations (Excavator 360 below 10 tonnes) – Level 2
Awarding body:
CSkills Awards

Plant Operations (Forklift Side-Loader) – Level 2
Awarding body:
CSkills Awards

Plant Operations (Forward Tipping Dumper) – Level 2
Awarding body:
CSkills Awards

Plant Operations (Grader) – Level 2
Awarding body:
CSkills Awards

Plant Operations (Hoist) – Level 2
Awarding body:
CSkills Awards

Plant Operations (Industrial Forklift Truck) – Level 2
Awarding body:
CSkills Awards

Plant Operations (Loader Compressor) – Level 2
Awarding body:
CSkills Awards

Plant Operations (Lorry Loader) – Level 2
Awarding body:
CSkills Awards

Plant Operations (Mobile Crane) – Level 2
Awarding body:
CSkills Awards

Plant Operations (Mobile Elevating Work Platform – Boom) – Level 2
Awarding body:
CSkills Awards

Plant Operations (Mobile Elevating Work Platform – Mast Climber) – Level 2
Awarding body:
    CSkills Awards

Plant Operations (Mobile Elevating Work Platform – Scissor) – Level 2
Awarding body:
    CSkills Awards

Plant Operations (Motorised Scraper) – Level 2
Awarding body:
    CSkills Awards

Plant Operations (Pedestrian Operated Tower Crane) – Level 2
Awarding body:
    CSkills Awards

Plant Operations (Piling Rig – Bored above 15 tonnes) – Level 2
Awarding body:
    CSkills Awards

Plant Operations (Piling Rig – Bored below 15 tonnes) – Level 2
Awarding body:
    CSkills Awards

Plant Operations (Piling Rig – Driven above 15 tonnes) – Level 2
Awarding body:
    CSkills Awards

Plant Operations (Piling Rig – Driven below 15 tonnes) – Level 2
Awarding body:
    CSkills Awards

Plant Operations (Piling Rig – Tripod) – Level 2
Awarding body:
    CSkills Awards

Plant Operations (Reach Truck) – Level 2
Awarding body:
    CSkills Awards

Plant Operations (Ride-on Roller) – Level 2
Awarding body:
    CSkills Awards

Plant Operations (Rough Terrain Masted Forklift) – Level 2
Awarding body:
    CSkills Awards

Plant Operations (Screener) – Level 2
Awarding body:
    CSkills Awards

Plant Operations (Skid Steer Loader) – Level 2
Awarding body:
    CSkills Awards

Plant Operations (Skip Handler) – Level 2
Awarding body:
    CSkills Awards

Plant Operations (Slinger/Signaller) – Level 2
Awarding body:
    CSkills Awards

Plant Operations (Soil/Landfill Compactor) – Level 2
Awarding body:
    CSkills Awards

Plant Operations (Telescopic Handler) – Level 2
Awarding body:
    CSkills Awards

Plant Operations (Tower Crane) – Level 2
Awarding body:
    CSkills Awards

Plant Operations (Tracked Loading Shovel) – Level 2
Awarding body:
    CSkills Awards

Plant Operations (Transporter Loader/Securer – Non-STGO) – Level 2
Awarding body:
    CSkills Awards

Plant Operations (Transporter Loader/Securer – STGO) – Level 2
Awarding body:
    CSkills Awards

Plant Operations (Trencher) – Level 2
Awarding body:
   CSkills Awards

Plant Operations (Wheeled Loading Shovel) – Level 2
Awarding body:
   CSkills Awards

Plumbing Industrial and Commercial Installation – Level 3
Awarding body:
   City & Guilds

Preservation of Heritage Buildings and Sites – Level 3
Awarding body:
   ABC

The Principles and Practices of Sustainable Waste Management – Level 3
Awarding body:
   WAMITAB

Working in High Risk Confined Spaces in the Water Industry – Level 2
Awarding body:
   City & Guilds

Working in Low Risk Confined Spaces in the Water Industry – Level 2
Awarding body:
   City & Guilds

Working in Medium Risk Confined Spaces in the Water Industry – Level 2
Awarding body:
   City & Guilds

BTEC Award

Construction and the Built Environment – Level 3
Awarding body:
   EDEXCEL

Construction and the Built Environment (Craft) – Level 2
Awarding body:
   EDEXCEL

Construction and the Built Environment (Technician) – Level 2
Awarding body:
   EDEXCEL

BTEC Certificate

Construction – Level 2
Awarding body:
   EDEXCEL

Construction and the Built Environment – Level 3
Awarding body:
   EDEXCEL

Construction and the Built Environment (Craft) – Level 2
Awarding body:
   EDEXCEL

Construction and the Built Environment (Technician) – Level 2
Awarding body:
   EDEXCEL

BTEC Diploma

Construction – Level 2
Awarding body:
   EDEXCEL

Construction and the Built Environment – Level 3
Awarding body:
   EDEXCEL

BTEC Extended Certificate

Construction – Level 2
Awarding body:
   EDEXCEL

Construction and the Built Environment – Level 3
Awarding body:
   EDEXCEL

Construction and the Built Environment (Craft) – Level 2
Awarding body:
   EDEXCEL

Construction and the Built Environment (Technician) – Level 2
Awarding body:
  EDEXCEL

BTEC Extended Diploma

Construction and the Built Environment – Level 3
Awarding body:
  EDEXCEL

BTEC First Certificate

Construction – Level 2
Awarding body:
  EDEXCEL

BTEC First Diploma

Construction – Level 2
Awarding body:
  EDEXCEL

BTEC Higher National Certificate

Building Services Engineering – Level 5
Awarding body:
  EDEXCEL

Civil Engineering – Level 5
Awarding body:
  EDEXCEL

Construction – Level 5
Awarding body:
  EDEXCEL

BTEC Higher National Diploma

Building Services Engineering – Level 5
Awarding body:
  EDEXCEL

Civil Engineering – Level 5
Awarding body:
  EDEXCEL

Construction – Level 5
Awarding body:
  EDEXCEL

BTEC National Award

Construction – Level 3
Awarding body:
  EDEXCEL

BTEC National Certificate

Building Services Engineering – Level 3
Awarding body:
  EDEXCEL

Civil Engineering – Level 3
Awarding body:
  EDEXCEL

Construction – Level 3
Awarding body:
  EDEXCEL

BTEC National Diploma

Building Services Engineering – Level 3
Awarding body:
  EDEXCEL

Civil Engineering – Level 3
Awarding body:
  EDEXCEL

Construction – Level 3
Awarding body:
  EDEXCEL

BTEC Subsidiary Diploma

Construction and the Built Environment – Level 3
Awarding body:
  EDEXCEL

Certificate

Adjudication in the Construction Industry – Level 5
Awarding body:
  RSPH

Asbestos Inspection Procedures – Level 3
Awarding body:
  RSPH

Basic Construction Skills – Level 1
Awarding body:
  City & Guilds

Basic Plumbing Studies – Level 2
Awarding body:
  City & Guilds

Building Craft Occupations – Level 1
Awarding body:
  CSkills Awards

Building Crafts (Construction) – Level 1
Awarding body:
  CSkills Awards

Building Crafts (Finishing) – Level 1
Awarding body:
  CSkills Awards

Building Services Engineering (Electrical) – Level 3
Awarding body:
  ABC

Building Services Engineering (Mechanical) – Level 3
Awarding body:
  ABC

CAA Plant Maintenance – Level 3
Awarding body:
  CSkills Awards

Complex Commercial Refrigeration and Air Conditioning Systems – Level 3
Awarding body:
  City & Guilds

Complex Domestic Natural Gas Installation and Maintenance – Level 3
Awarding body:
  City & Guilds

Construction – Level 1
Awarding body:
  EDEXCEL

Construction and the Built Environment – Level 1
Awarding body:
  EDEXCEL

Creating Interiors – Level 2
Awarding body:
  ABC

Defence Engineering (Bricklaying and Concreting) – Level 2
Awarding body:
  CSkills Awards

Defence Engineering (Carpentry and Joinery) – Level 1
Awarding body:
  CSkills Awards

Defence Engineering (Plant Supervision) – Level 3
Awarding body:
  CSkills Awards

Domestic Natural Gas Installation and Maintenance – Level 2
Awarding body:
  City & Guilds

Dry Stone Walling – Level 1
Awarding body:
  Lantra Awards

Dry Stone Walling – Level 2
Awarding body:
  Lantra Awards

Dry Stone Walling – Level 3
Awarding body:
  Lantra Awards

Energy Efficiency for Domestic Heating – Level 3
Awarding body:
  City & Guilds

Gas Emergency Service Operations – Level 3
Awarding body:
  City & Guilds

Heating and Ventilating – Maintenance of System Components – Level 2
Awarding body:
City & Guilds

Heating and Ventilating – Rectification of Systems – Level 3
Awarding body:
City & Guilds

Heating and Ventilating Installation – Level 2
Awarding body:
City & Guilds

Heating and Ventilating Installation – Level 3
Awarding body:
City & Guilds

Highway Electrical Work – Public Lighting – Level 2
Awarding body:
Lantra Awards

Highway Electrical Work – Public Lighting – Level 3
Awarding body:
Lantra Awards

Highway Electrical Work – Traffic Signals – Level 2
Awarding body:
Lantra Awards

Highway Electrical Work – Traffic Signals – Level 3
Awarding body:
Lantra Awards

Highways Maintenance – Level 2
Awarding body:
SQA

Management of Electrical Equipment Maintenance (Code of Practice for In-Service Inspection) – Level 3
Awarding body:
City & Guilds

Plant Operations (Building/Construction) – Level 2
Awarding body:
CSkills Awards

Plant Operations (Cranes/Lifting) – Level 2
Awarding body:
CSkills Awards

Plant Operations (Demolition) – Level 2
Awarding body:
CSkills Awards

Plant Operations (Earthmoving/Civils) – Level 2
Awarding body:
CSkills Awards

Plant Operations (Groundworks) – Level 2
Awarding body:
CSkills Awards

Plant Operations (Land Based) – Level 2
Awarding body:
CSkills Awards

Plant Operations (Materials Handling) – Level 2
Awarding body:
CSkills Awards

Plant Operations (Piling) – Level 2
Awarding body:
CSkills Awards

Plant Operations (Road Maintenance) – Level 2
Awarding body:
CSkills Awards

Plant Operations (Waste/Recycling) – Level 2
Awarding body:
CSkills Awards

Plumbing Studies – Level 3
Awarding body:
City & Guilds

Site Management – Level 4
Awarding body:
CIOB

Site Supervisory Studies – Level 3
Awarding body:
CIOB

Small Commercial Refrigeration and Air Conditioning Systems – Level 2
Awarding body:
City & Guilds

Thermal Insulation – Level 2
Awarding body:
City & Guilds

Valuation of Residential Property for Secured Lending – Level 4
Awarding body:
ABBE

Diploma

Adjudication in the Construction Industry – Level 5
Awarding body:
RSPH

Bench Joinery – Level 2
Awarding body:
CSkills Awards

Bench Joinery – Level 3
Awarding body:
CSkills Awards

Bricklaying – Level 1
Awarding body:
CSkills Awards

Bricklaying – Level 2
Awarding body:
CSkills Awards

Bricklaying – Level 3
Awarding body:
CSkills Awards

Built-up Felt Roofing – Level 2
Awarding body:
CSkills Awards

Carpentry and Joinery – Level 1
Awarding body:
CSkills Awards

Civil Engineering – Level 3
Awarding body:
CSkills Awards

Construction – Level 1
Awarding body:
EDEXCEL

Construction and Civil Engineering Services – Level 1
Awarding body:
CSkills Awards

Construction Operations – General Construction – Level 2
Awarding body:
CSkills Awards

Craft Masonry – Level 2
Awarding body:
CSkills Awards

Defence Engineering (Bricklaying and Concreting) – Level 2
Awarding body:
CSkills Awards

Defence Engineering (Bricklaying and Concreting) – Level 3
Awarding body:
CSkills Awards

Defence Engineering (Building Finisher) – Level 2
Awarding body:
CSkills Awards

Defence Engineering (Building Finisher) – Level 3
Awarding body:
CSkills Awards

Defence Engineering (Carpentry and Joinery) – Level 2
Awarding body:
CSkills Awards

Defence Engineering (Carpentry and Joinery) – Level 3
Awarding body:
CSkills Awards

Display Energy Certificates – Level 3
Awarding body:
ABBE
City & Guilds

Domestic Energy Assessment – Level 3
Awarding body:
ABBE

Domestic Energy Assessors – Level 3
Awarding body:
City & Guilds

Dry Lining – Level 2
Awarding body:
CSkills Awards

Fencing – Level 2
Awarding body:
Lantra Awards

Fencing – Level 3
Awarding body:
Lantra Awards

Fitted Interiors – Level 2
Awarding body:
CSkills Awards

Floor Covering – Textile and Impervious – Level 2
Awarding body:
CSkills Awards

Formworking – Level 2
Awarding body:
CSkills Awards

Highways Maintenance – Excavation Operations – Level 2
Awarding body:
CSkills Awards

Home Inspection – Level 4
Awarding body:
ABBE

Home Inspectors – Level 4
Awarding body:
City & Guilds

Interior Systems – Level 2
Awarding body:
CSkills Awards

Maintenance Operations – Level 2
Awarding body:
CSkills Awards

Mastic Asphalting – Level 2
Awarding body:
CSkills Awards

Non Domestic Energy Assessment – Level 3
Awarding body:
ABBE

Non Domestic Energy Assessment – Level 4
Awarding body:
ABBE

Non-Domestic Energy Assessors – Level 3
Awarding body:
City & Guilds

Non-Domestic Energy Assessors – Level 4
Awarding body:
City & Guilds

On Construction Energy Assessment – Level 3
Awarding body:
ABBE

Painting and Decorating – Level 1
Awarding body:
CSkills Awards

Painting and Decorating – Level 2
Awarding body:
CSkills Awards

Painting and Decorating – Level 3
Awarding body:
CSkills Awards

Plastering – Level 1
Awarding body:
CSkills Awards

Plastering – Level 2
Awarding body:
CSkills Awards

Plastering – Fibrous – Level 3
Awarding body:
CSkills Awards

Plastering – Solid – Level 3
Awarding body:
CSkills Awards

Roof Sheeting and Cladding – Level 2
Awarding body:
CSkills Awards

Roof Slating and Tiling – Level 2
Awarding body:
CSkills Awards

Roof Slating and Tiling – Level 3
Awarding body:
CSkills Awards

Scaffolding – Level 2
Awarding body:
CSkills Awards

Shopfitting Bench Joinery – Level 2
Awarding body:
CSkills Awards

Shopfitting Bench Joinery – Level 3
Awarding body:
CSkills Awards

Site Carpentry – Level 2
Awarding body:
CSkills Awards

Site Carpentry – Level 3
Awarding body:
CSkills Awards

Site Management – Level 4
Awarding body:
CIOB

Spatial Data Management – Level 3
Awarding body:
ABBE

Stonemasonry – Banker – Level 2
Awarding body:
CSkills Awards

Stonemasonry – Banker – Level 3
Awarding body:
CSkills Awards

Surveying, Property and Maintenance – Level 3
Awarding body:
ABBE

Thatching – Level 2
Awarding body:
CSkills Awards

Wall and Floor Tiling – Level 2
Awarding body:
CSkills Awards

Wall and Floor Tiling – Level 3
Awarding body:
CSkills Awards

Woodmachining – Level 2
Awarding body:
CSkills Awards

Woodmachining – Level 3
Awarding body:
CSkills Awards

Extended Certificate

Construction and the Built Environment – Level 1
Awarding body:
EDEXCEL

Foundation Award

Construction – Level 1
Awarding body:
CSkills Awards

Foundation Certificate

Plant Maintenance – Level 1
Awarding body:
CSkills Awards

Foundation Diploma

Construction and the Built Environment – Level 1
Awarding body:
AQA
City & Guilds
EDEXCEL
OCR

Higher Diploma

Construction and the Built Environment – Level 2
Awarding body:
AQA
City & Guilds
EDEXCEL
OCR

Higher Professional Diploma

Building Services Engineering – Level 4
Awarding body:
City & Guilds

Intermediate Award

Construction – Level 2
Awarding body:
CSkills Awards

Intermediate Certificate

Plant Maintenance – Level 2
Awarding body:
CSkills Awards

Introductory Certificate

Basic Construction Skills – Level 1
Awarding body:
City & Guilds

Construction – Level 1
Awarding body:
EDEXCEL

Introductory Diploma

Construction – Level 1
Awarding body:
EDEXCEL

IVQ Advanced Diploma

Electrical Installation – Level 3
Awarding body:
City & Guilds

Painting and Decorating – Level 3
Awarding body:
City & Guilds

Plumbing – Level 3
Awarding body:
City & Guilds

Refrigeration and Air Conditioning – Level 3
Awarding body:
City & Guilds

Timber Vocations – Level 3
Awarding body:
City & Guilds

Trowel Vocations – Level 3
Awarding body:
City & Guilds

IVQ Advanced Technician Diploma

Construction – Level 5
Awarding body:
City & Guilds

IVQ Certificate

Electrical Installation – Level 1
Awarding body:
City & Guilds

Painting and Decorating – Level 1
Awarding body:
City & Guilds

Plumbing – Level 1
Awarding body:
City & Guilds

Preservation Skills – Level 1
Awarding body:
City & Guilds

**Refrigeration and Air Conditioning –
Level 1**
Awarding body:
City & Guilds

Timber Vocations – Level 1
Awarding body:
City & Guilds

Trowel Vocations – Level 1
Awarding body:
City & Guilds

IVQ Diploma

Electrical Installation – Level 2
Awarding body:
City & Guilds

Painting and Decorating – Level 2
Awarding body:
City & Guilds

Plumbing – Level 2
Awarding body:
City & Guilds

**Refrigeration and Air Conditioning –
Level 2**
Awarding body:
City & Guilds

Timber Vocations – Level 2
Awarding body:
City & Guilds

Trowel Vocations – Level 2
Awarding body:
City & Guilds

IVQ Technician Certificate

Construction – Level 2
Awarding body:
City & Guilds

IVQ Technician Diploma

Construction – Level 3
Awarding body:
City & Guilds

National Vocational Qualification

**Accessing Operations and Rigging –
Level 1**
Awarding body:
CSkills Awards

**Accessing Operations and Rigging –
Level 2**
Awarding body:
CSkills Awards

**Accessing Operations and Rigging –
Level 3**
Awarding body:
CSkills Awards

**Applied Waterproof Membranes –
Level 2**
Awarding body:
CSkills Awards

**Associated Industrial Services
Occupations – Level 2**
Awarding body:
CSkills Awards

**Building Maintenance and Estate Service
– Level 3**
Awarding body:
City & Guilds

**Building Maintenance and Estate Service
– Level 4**
Awarding body:
City & Guilds

Built Environment Design – Level 3
Awarding body:
EDEXCEL

Built Environment Design – Level 4
Awarding body:
EDEXCEL

**Built Environment Design and
Consultancy – Level 5**
Awarding body:
EDEXCEL

**CAA Level 3 NVQ for Heritage Skills
(Construction) – Level 3**
Awarding body:
CSkills Awards

**Chimney Engineering/Cleaning. –
Level 2**
Awarding body:
CSkills Awards

**Cladding Occupations (Construction) –
Level 2**
Awarding body:
CSkills Awards

**Cladding Occupations (Construction) –
Level 3**
Awarding body:
CSkills Awards

**Construction & Civil Engineering
Services (Public Utilities) – Level 2**
Awarding body:
CSkills Awards

**Construction and Civil Engineering
Services – Level 1**
Awarding body:
CSkills Awards
EDEXCEL

**Construction Contracting Operations –
Level 3**
Awarding body:
ABBE
CSkills Awards
EDEXCEL

**Construction Contracting Operations –
Level 4**
Awarding body:
ABBE
CSkills Awards
EDEXCEL

Construction Management – Level 5
Awarding body:
EDEXCEL

Construction Operations – Level 2
Awarding body:
CSkills Awards
EDEXCEL
SQA

**Construction Senior Management –
Level 5**
Awarding body:
CSkills Awards
EDEXCEL

Construction Site Management – Level 4
Awarding body:
CSkills Awards
EDEXCEL

**Construction Site Management
(Highways Maintenance) – Level 4**
Awarding body:
MPQC

Construction Site Supervision – Level 3
Awarding body:
CSkills Awards
EDEXCEL
MPQC

Controlling Lifting Operations – Level 3
Awarding body:
CSkills Awards
EDEXCEL

**Decorative Finishing and Industrial
Painting Occupations – Level 1**
Awarding body:
CSkills Awards

**Decorative Finishing and Industrial
Painting Occupations – Level 2**
Awarding body:
CSkills Awards
EDEXCEL
SQA

**Decorative Finishing and Industrial
Painting Occupations – Level 3**
Awarding body:
CSkills Awards

Demolition – Level 2
Awarding body:
CSkills Awards
EDEXCEL

**Directional Drilling Operations
(Construction) – Level 2**
Awarding body:
CSkills Awards

**Domestic Natural Gas Installation –
Level 2**
Awarding body:
City & Guilds

**Domestic Natural Gas Installation –
Level 3**
Awarding body:
City & Guilds

**Domestic Natural Gas Installation and
Maintenance (ACS) – Level 2**
Awarding body:
City & Guilds

**Domestic Natural Gas Installation and
Maintenance (ACS) – Level 3**
Awarding body:
City & Guilds

**Domestic Natural Gas Maintenance –
Level 2**
Awarding body:
City & Guilds

**Domestic Natural Gas Maintenance –
Level 3**
Awarding body:
City & Guilds

Electrotechnical Services – Level 3
Awarding body:
Lantra Awards

**Erection of Precast Concrete
(Construction) – Level 2**
Awarding body:
CSkills Awards

Fencing – Level 2
Awarding body:
Lantra Awards

Fencing Business Management – Level 4
Awarding body:
Lantra Awards

Fenestration Installation – Level 2
Awarding body:
GQA

**Fenestration Installation and Surveying –
Level 3**
Awarding body:
GQA

Fitted Interiors – Level 2
Awarding body:
CSkills Awards

Floorcovering – Level 1
Awarding body:
CSkills Awards

Floorcovering – Level 2
Awarding body:
CSkills Awards

Floorcovering – Level 3
Awarding body:
CSkills Awards

Formwork (Construction) – Level 2
Awarding body:
CSkills Awards
EDEXCEL

Formwork (Construction) – Level 3
Awarding body:
CSkills Awards
EDEXCEL

**Gas Emergency Service Operations
(ACS) – Level 3**
Awarding body:
City & Guilds

Glazing – Level 2
Awarding body:
GQA

Glazing – Level 3
Awarding body:
GQA

Highways Maintenance – Level 2
Awarding body:
CSkills Awards
MPQC

Hire and Rental Operations – Level 2
Awarding body:
CSkills Awards

**Industrial and Commercial Gas
Installation and Maintenance – Level 2**
Awarding body:
City & Guilds

**Industrial and Commercial Gas
Installation and Maintenance – Level 3**
Awarding body:
City & Guilds

Industrial Building Systems – Level 2
Awarding body:
    CSkills Awards

Installing Domestic Fascias, Soffits and Bargeboards – Level 2
Awarding body:
    GQA

Installing Highway Electrical Systems – Level 2
Awarding body:
    Lantra Awards

Insulation and Building Treatments (Construction) – Level 2
Awarding body:
    City & Guilds

Interior Systems – Level 2
Awarding body:
    CSkills Awards
    EDEXCEL
    SQA

Land Drilling Operations (Construction) – Level 2
Awarding body:
    CSkills Awards

Liquid Petroleum Gas Installation and Maintenance – Level 2
Awarding body:
    City & Guilds

Liquid Petroleum Gas Installation and Maintenance – Level 3
Awarding body:
    City & Guilds

Maintenance Operations – Level 2
Awarding body:
    EDEXCEL

Maintenance Operations (Construction) – Level 2
Awarding body:
    CSkills Awards

Mastic Asphalt – Level 2
Awarding body:
    CSkills Awards

Mastic Asphalt – Level 3
Awarding body:
    CSkills Awards

Mechanical Engineering Services – Heating and Ventilating (Maintenance of Systems Components) – Level 2
Awarding body:
    City & Guilds

Mechanical Engineering Services – Heating and Ventilating (Rectification of Systems) – Level 3
Awarding body:
    City & Guilds

Mechanical Engineering Services – Heating and Ventilating Installation – Level 2
Awarding body:
    City & Guilds

Mechanical Engineering Services – Heating and Ventilating Installation – Level 3
Awarding body:
    City & Guilds

Mechanical Engineering Services – Plumbing – Level 2
Awarding body:
    City & Guilds

Mechanical Engineering Services – Plumbing – Level 3
Awarding body:
    City & Guilds

Mechanical Engineering Services – Plumbing (Domestic) – Level 3
Awarding body:
    City & Guilds

Mechanical Engineering Services – Refrigeration and Air Conditioning – Level 2
Awarding body:
    City & Guilds

Mechanical Engineering Services – Refrigeration and Air Conditioning – Level 3
Awarding body:
    City & Guilds

Network Construction Operations: Mainlaying (Water) – Level 2
Awarding body:
    EDEXCEL

Network Construction Operations: Servicelaying (Water) – Level 2
Awarding body:
EDEXCEL

Occupational Work Supervision – Level 3
Awarding body:
CSkills Awards
EDEXCEL

Piling Operations – Level 2
Awarding body:
CSkills Awards
EDEXCEL

Plant Installations (Construction) – Level 2
Awarding body:
CSkills Awards

Plant Installations (Construction) – Level 3
Awarding body:
CSkills Awards

Plant Maintenance – Level 1
Awarding body:
CSkills Awards

Plant Maintenance – Level 2
Awarding body:
CSkills Awards
EDEXCEL

Plant Maintenance – Level 3
Awarding body:
CSkills Awards

Plant Operations – Level 2
Awarding body:
CSkills Awards
EDEXCEL
Lantra Awards
MPQC
OCR
SQA

Plastering – Level 1
Awarding body:
CSkills Awards

Plastering – Level 2
Awarding body:
EDEXCEL

Plastering – Level 3
Awarding body:
CSkills Awards

Plastering (Construction) – Level 2
Awarding body:
CSkills Awards
SQA

Post-Tensioning Operations – Level 2
Awarding body:
CSkills Awards

Property and Caretaking Supervision – Level 3
Awarding body:
ABBE

Provide Energy Efficiency Services – Level 3
Awarding body:
City & Guilds

Providing Security, Emergency and Alarm Systems – Level 2
Awarding body:
City & Guilds

Providing Security, Emergency and Alarm Systems – Level 3
Awarding body:
City & Guilds

Quantity Surveying Practice – Level 4
Awarding body:
ABBE

Refractory Installations – Level 2
Awarding body:
CSkills Awards

Removal of Hazardous and Non-Hazardous Waste (Construction) – Level 2
Awarding body:
CSkills Awards

Roadbuilding (Construction) – Level 1
Awarding body:
CSkills Awards

Roadbuilding (Construction) – Level 2
Awarding body:
CSkills Awards
MPQC

Roofing Occupations – Level 2
Awarding body:
  CSkills Awards

Roofing Occupations – Level 3
Awarding body:
  CSkills Awards

Set Crafts – Level 3
Awarding body:
  CSkills Awards

Site Inspection – Level 3
Awarding body:
  ABBE

Site Inspection – Level 4
Awarding body:
  ABBE
  EDEXCEL

Site Logistics Operations – Level 2
Awarding body:
  EDEXCEL

Site Logistics Operations (Construction) – Level 2
Awarding body:
  CSkills Awards

Spatial Data Management – Level 3
Awarding body:
  ABBE

Spatial Data Management – Level 4
Awarding body:
  ABBE

Specialist Concrete Occupations – Level 2
Awarding body:
  CSkills Awards
  EDEXCEL

Specialist Installation Occupations – Level 3
Awarding body:
  CSkills Awards

Specialist Installation Occupations (Construction) – Level 2
Awarding body:
  CSkills Awards
  EDEXCEL

Steelfixing Occupations – Level 2
Awarding body:
  CSkills Awards
  EDEXCEL

Stonemasonry – Level 3
Awarding body:
  CSkills Awards

Stonemasonry (Construction) – Level 1
Awarding body:
  CSkills Awards

Stonemasonry (Construction) – Level 2
Awarding body:
  CSkills Awards

Sub-Structure Work Occupations – Level 2
Awarding body:
  CSkills Awards

Sub-Structure Work Occupations – Level 3
Awarding body:
  CSkills Awards

Super-Structure Work Occupations (Construction) – Level 2
Awarding body:
  CSkills Awards

Supervising Hire and Rental Operations (Equipment, Plant and Tools) – Level 3
Awarding body:
  CSkills Awards

Surveying, Property and Maintenance – Level 3
Awarding body:
  ABBE

Surveying, Property and Maintenance – Level 4
Awarding body:
  ABBE

Temporary Traffic Management – Level 2
Awarding body:
  CSkills Awards

Thermal Insulation – Level 2
Awarding body:
  City & Guilds

Thermal Insulation (Construction) – Level 2
Awarding body:
    City & Guilds

Trowel Occupations – Level 1
Awarding body:
    CSkills Awards
    EDEXCEL

Trowel Occupations – Level 2
Awarding body:
    CSkills Awards
    EDEXCEL

Trowel Occupations – Level 3
Awarding body:
    CSkills Awards
    EDEXCEL

Tunnelling Operations – Level 2
Awarding body:
    CSkills Awards

Wall and Floor Tiling – Level 2
Awarding body:
    CSkills Awards

Wall and Floor Tiling – Level 3
Awarding body:
    CSkills Awards

Wood Occupations – Level 1
Awarding body:
    CSkills Awards

Wood Occupations – Level 2
Awarding body:
    CSkills Awards
    EDEXCEL

Wood Occupations – Level 3
Awarding body:
    CSkills Awards

Wood Preserving – Industrial Pre-Treatment – Level 2
Awarding body:
    CSkills Awards

Woodmachining (Construction/Sawmilling Extrusion) – Level 2
Awarding body:
    CSkills Awards

Woodmachining (Construction/Sawmilling Extrusion) – Level 3
Awarding body:
    CSkills Awards

Woodmachining (Furniture) – Level 2
Awarding body:
    CSkills Awards

Woodmachining (Furniture) – Level 3
Awarding body:
    CSkills Awards

Principal Learning

Construction and the Built Environment – Level 1
Awarding body:
    AQA
    City & Guilds
    EDEXCEL

Construction and the Built Environment – Level 2
Awarding body:
    AQA
    City & Guilds
    EDEXCEL

Construction and the Built Environment – Level 3
Awarding body:
    AQA
    City & Guilds
    EDEXCEL

Construction and the Built Environment (Wales) – Level 1
Awarding body:
    WJEC-EDEXCEL

Construction and the Built Environment (Wales) – Level 2
Awarding body:
    WJEC-EDEXCEL

Construction and the Built Environment (Wales) – Level 3
Awarding body:
    WJEC-EDEXCEL

Progression Diploma

**Construction and the Built Environment
– Level 3**
Awarding body:
　AQA
　City & Guilds
　EDEXCEL
　OCR

Urban, Rural and Regional Planning

Diploma

Commercial Property Agency – Level 5
Awarding body:
　NFOPP

Residential Estate Agency – Level 5
Awarding body:
　NFOPP

**Residential Letting & Management –
Level 5**
Awarding body:
　NFOPP

National Vocational Qualification

**Built Environment Development and
Control – Level 3**
Awarding body:
　ABBE

**Built Environment Development and
Control – Level 4**
Awarding body:
　ABBE

Education and Training

Direct Learning Support

Award

Developing Skills for Supporting Teaching and Learning in Schools – Level 2
Awarding body:
NCFE

Disability Awareness – Level 1
Awarding body:
EDI

Equality and Diversity – Level 2
Awarding body:
EDI

Preparing to Support Learning – Level 2
Awarding body:
ASCENTIS
CACHE
City & Guilds
NCFE

Preparing to Support Learning – Level 3
Awarding body:
ASCENTIS
CACHE
City & Guilds
NCFE

Support Work in Schools – Level 2
Awarding body:
CACHE
City & Guilds
EDEXCEL
OCR

Support Work in Schools – Level 3
Awarding body:
CACHE
City & Guilds
EDEXCEL
OCR

Work with Parents – Level 2
Awarding body:
City & Guilds

Work with Parents – Level 3
Awarding body:
City & Guilds

Work with Parents – Level 4
Awarding body:
City & Guilds

BTEC Certificate

Introduction to Life Coaching Skills – Level 2
Awarding body:
EDEXCEL

Life Coaching Skills and Practice – Level 3
Awarding body:
EDEXCEL

Supporting Teaching and Learning in Schools – Level 2
Awarding body:
EDEXCEL

Supporting Teaching and Learning in Schools – Level 3
Awarding body:
EDEXCEL

Certificate

Adult Literacy Subject Support – Level 3
Awarding body:
ASCENTIS
City & Guilds

Adult Numeracy Subject Support – Level 3
Awarding body:
ASCENTIS
City & Guilds

Delivering Learning Using a VLE – Level 3
Awarding body:
EDI

Employability Skills – Level 2
Awarding body:
EDI

ESOL Subject Support – Level 3
Awarding body:
City & Guilds

Learning Support – Level 3
Awarding body:
ASCENTIS
CACHE
City & Guilds

Learning Support (Literacy, Numeracy and ESOL) – Level 2
Awarding body:
ASCENTIS

Literacy, Language, Numeracy and ICT Awareness – Level 2
Awarding body:
ASCENTIS

Personnel Practice – Level 3
Awarding body:
CIPD

Recruitment and Selection – Level 3
Awarding body:
CIPD

Support Work in Schools – Level 2
Awarding body:
CACHE
City & Guilds
EDEXCEL
OCR

Support Work in Schools – Level 3
Awarding body:
CACHE
City & Guilds
EDEXCEL
OCR

Supporting Learning in Primary Schools – Level 4
Awarding body:
OU

Supporting Teaching and Learning in Schools – Level 2
Awarding body:
CACHE
NCFE
OCR

Supporting Teaching and Learning in Schools – Level 3
Awarding body:
CACHE
NCFE
OCR

Supporting, Teaching and Learning in Schools – Level 2
Awarding body:
City & Guilds

Teaching Assistants – Level 2
Awarding body:
CCEA

Teaching Assistants – Level 3
Awarding body:
CCEA

Training Practice – Level 3
Awarding body:
CIPD

Work with Parents – Level 3
Awarding body:
City & Guilds

Diploma

Learning Coach – Level 3
Awarding body:
NOCN

Support Work in Schools – Level 3
Awarding body:
 CACHE
 City & Guilds
 EDEXCEL
 OCR

Extended Certificate

Supporting Teaching and Learning in Schools – Level 2
Awarding body:
 NCFE

National Vocational Qualification

Co-ordination of Learning and Development Provision – Level 4
Awarding body:
 CIPD
 City & Guilds
 EAL
 EDEXCEL
 EDI
 OCR
 PAA\VQSET

Direct Training and Support – Level 3
Awarding body:
 CIPD
 City & Guilds
 EAL
 EDEXCEL
 EDI
 OCR
 PAA\VQSET

Learning and Development – Level 3
Awarding body:
 CIPD
 City & Guilds
 EAL
 EDEXCEL
 EDI
 OCR
 OU
 PAA\VQSET
 SQA

Learning and Development – Level 4
Awarding body:
 CIPD
 City & Guilds
 EAL
 EDEXCEL
 EDI
 OCR
 OU
 PAA\VQSET
 SQA

Learning and Development – Level 5
Awarding body:
 CIPD
 City & Guilds
 EDEXCEL
 OCR

Management of Learning and Development Provision – Level 4
Awarding body:
 CIPD
 City & Guilds
 EAL
 EDEXCEL
 EDI
 OCR
 PAA\VQSET

Supporting Teaching and Learning in Schools – Level 2
Awarding body:
 CACHE
 City & Guilds
 EDEXCEL
 OCR

Supporting Teaching and Learning in Schools – Level 3
Awarding body:
 CACHE
 City & Guilds
 EDEXCEL
 OCR

Teaching and Lecturing

Additional Diploma

Teaching English (ESOL) in the Lifelong Learning Sector – Level 5
Awarding body:
    ASCENTIS
    Cambridge ESOL
    City & Guilds

Teaching English (Literacy) in the Lifelong Learning Sector – Level 5
Awarding body:
    ASCENTIS
    City & Guilds
    OCR

Teaching for Literacy in the Lifelong Learning Sector – Level 5
Awarding body:
    EDEXCEL

Teaching Mathematics (Numeracy) in the Lifelong Learning Sector – Level 5
Awarding body:
    City & Guilds
    OCR

Advanced Diploma

Assessing Candidates Using a Range of Methods – Level 3
Awarding body:
    BHEST

Assessing Candidates' Performance through Observation – Level 3
Awarding body:
    BHEST

Associate Diploma

Teaching (ATCL) – Level 4
Awarding body:
    TCL

Award

Assessing Candidates Performance Through Observation – Level 3
Awarding body:
    ETCAL
    IMIAL
    PAA\VQSET
    VTCT

Assessing Candidates Using a Range of Methods – Level 3
Awarding body:
    CACHE
    CIPD
    City & Guilds
    CMI
    EAL
    EDEXCEL
    EDI
    ETCAL
    GQA
    HAB
    IMIAL
    NCFE
    OCR
    OU
    PAA\VQSET
    VTCT

Assessing Candidates' Performance through Observation – Level 3
Awarding body:
    CACHE
    CIPD
    City & Guilds
    CMI
    EAL
    EDEXCEL
    EDI
    GQA
    HAB
    NCFE
    OCR
    OU

Conducting External Quality Assurance of the Assessment Process – Level 4
Awarding body:
BHEST
CACHE
CIPD
City & Guilds
CMI
EAL
EDEXCEL
EDI
GQA
HAB
IMIAL
NCFE
OCR
OU
PAA\VQSET
VTCT

Conducting Internal Quality Assurance of the Assessment Process – Level 4
Awarding body:
BHEST
CACHE
CIPD
City & Guilds
CMI
EAL
EDEXCEL
EDI
ETCAL
GQA
HAB
IMIAL
NCFE
OCR
OU
PAA\VQSET
VTCT

Delivering e-Testing – Level 3
Awarding body:
EDI

Literacy, Numeracy and ICT Awareness – Level 2
Awarding body:
City & Guilds

Preparing to Teach in the Lifelong Learning Sector – Level 3
Awarding body:
ASCENTIS
CIPD
City & Guilds
CYQ
EDI
FAQ
NCFE
OCR

Preparing to Teach in the Lifelong Learning Sector – Level 4
Awarding body:
ASCENTIS
Cambridge ESOL
CIPD
City & Guilds
EDI
FAQ
NCFE
OCR
TCL

Teaching in the Lifelong Learning Sector – Level 5
Awarding body:
City & Guilds

BTEC Award

Preparing to Teach in the Lifelong Learning Sector – Level 3
Awarding body:
EDEXCEL

Preparing to Teach in the Lifelong Learning Sector – Level 4
Awarding body:
EDEXCEL

BTEC Certificate

14-19 Diploma Practitioners – Level 5
Awarding body:
EDEXCEL

Teaching in the Lifelong Learning Sector – Level 3
Awarding body:
EDEXCEL

Teaching in the Lifelong Learning Sector – Level 4
Awarding body:
EDEXCEL

BTEC Professional Award

Teaching Employability Skills (Pilot) – Level 4
Awarding body:
EDEXCEL

Teaching Vocational Learning (Pilot) – Level 4
Awarding body:
EDEXCEL

BTEC Professional Certificate

Teaching Employability Skills and Vocational Learning (Pilot) – Level 4
Awarding body:
EDEXCEL

Certificate

Adult Literacy Subject Specialists – Level 4
Awarding body:
City & Guilds

Adult Numeracy Subject Specialists – Level 4
Awarding body:
City & Guilds

Aquatic Teaching – Level 2
Awarding body:
STA

Assessing and Teaching Learners with Specific Learning Difficulties (Dyslexia) – Level 7
Awarding body:
OCR

Assistant Instructor's Certificate (Equine Coach) – Level 3
Awarding body:
EQL

BHS Level 3 Preliminary Teacher's Certificate (Equine Coach) – Level 3
Awarding body:
EQL

Delivering Basic Skills to Adults – Level 3
Awarding body:
City & Guilds

Delivering Learning: An Introduction – Level 3
Awarding body:
City & Guilds

Education Practice: ICT Advanced – Level 3
Awarding body:
EDI

Education Practice: ICT Skills – Level 3
Awarding body:
EDI

Education Principles and Practice – Level 3
Awarding body:
EDI

Educational Use of ICT – Level 3
Awarding body:
EDI

ESOL Subject Specialists – Level 4
Awarding body:
City & Guilds

FE Teaching Stage 1 – Level 4
Awarding body:
City & Guilds

FE Teaching Stage 2 – Level 4
Awarding body:
City & Guilds

FE Teaching Stage 3 – Level 5
Awarding body:
City & Guilds

Higher Level Study Skills – Level 4
Awarding body:
   City & Guilds

Internal Verification Practice in Sport – Level 3
Awarding body:
   1st4sport

Introduction to Assessment Practice in Sport – Level 3
Awarding body:
   1st4sport

Learning Support – Level 2
Awarding body:
   City & Guilds

Teaching English to Speakers of Other Languages (CELTA) – Level 5
Awarding body:
   Cambridge ESOL

Teaching English to Speakers of Other Languages (Cert TESOL) – Level 4
Awarding body:
   TCL

Teaching in the Lifelong Learning Sector – Level 3
Awarding body:
   ASCENTIS
   CIPD
   City & Guilds
   EDI
   OCR

Teaching in the Lifelong Learning Sector – Level 4
Awarding body:
   ASCENTIS
   CIPD
   City & Guilds
   EDI
   OCR

Teaching Learners with Specific Learning Difficulties (Dyslexia) – Level 5
Awarding body:
   OCR

Tutoring in Sport – Level 3
Awarding body:
   1st4sport

Diploma

Assessing and Teaching Learners with Specific Learning Difficulties (Dyslexia) – Level 7
Awarding body:
   OCR

Education Practice: ICT Advanced – Level 4
Awarding body:
   EDI

Speech and Drama Education – Level 5
Awarding body:
   LAMDA

Teaching English (ESOL) in the Lifelong Learning Sector – Level 5
Awarding body:
   Cambridge ESOL
   City & Guilds
   TCL

Teaching English (Literacy) in the Lifelong Learning Sector – Level 5
Awarding body:
   City & Guilds
   OCR

Teaching English to Speakers of Other Languages (Delta) – Level 7
Awarding body:
   Cambridge ESOL

Teaching in the Lifelong Learning Sector – Level 5
Awarding body:
   ASCENTIS
   City & Guilds
   EDEXCEL
   OCR

Teaching in the Lifelong Learning Sector English (ESOL) – Level 5
Awarding body:
   TCL

Teaching Mathematics (Numeracy) in the Lifelong Learning Sector – Level 5
Awarding body:
   ASCENTIS
   City & Guilds
   OCR

Fellowship Diploma

Education Studies (FTCL) – Level 7
Awarding body:
   TCL

TESOL Education Studies (FTCL) – Level 7
Awarding body:
   TCL

Higher Professional Diploma

Community Development – Level 4
Awarding body:
   City & Guilds

IVQ Advanced Diploma

Teaching, Training and Assessing Learning – Level 3
Awarding body:
   City & Guilds

IVQ Diploma

Training Skills – Level 2
Awarding body:
   City & Guilds

IVQ Specialist Advanced Diploma

Teaching, Training and Assessing Learning – Level 3
Awarding body:
   City & Guilds

Licentiate Diploma

Teaching (LTCL/LGSMD) – Level 6
Awarding body:
   TCL

Teaching English to Speakers of Other Languages (LTCL) – Level 7
Awarding body:
   TCL

Engineering and Manufacturing Technologies

Engineering

Advanced Diploma

Engineering – Level 3
Awarding body:
AQA
City & Guilds
EDEXCEL
OCR

Award

Advanced Welding Skills – Level 3
Awarding body:
City & Guilds

Computer Aided Design and Manufacturing – Level 2
Awarding body:
City & Guilds

Computer Aided Design and Manufacturing – Level 3
Awarding body:
City & Guilds

Computer Aided Design Parametric Modelling – Level 1
Awarding body:
City & Guilds

Engineering Practice – Level 2
Awarding body:
City & Guilds

Engineering Practice – Level 3
Awarding body:
City & Guilds

F-Gas and ODS Regulations: Category III – Level 2
Awarding body:
City & Guilds

F-Gas and ODS Regulations: Category I – Level 2
Awarding body:
City & Guilds

F-Gas and ODS Regulations: Category II – Level 2
Awarding body:
City & Guilds

F-Gas and ODS Regulations: Category IV – Level 2
Awarding body:
City & Guilds

Industrial Environment Awareness – Level 2
Awarding body:
EAL

Introductory Welding Skills – Level 1
Awarding body:
City & Guilds

Maritime Studies – Level 2
Awarding body:
EAL

Personal Site Safety Responsibilities – Level 3
Awarding body:
ECITB

Water Engineering (Sludge Works) – Level 2
Awarding body:
City & Guilds

Water Engineering (Waste Water – Simple Works) – Level 2
Awarding body:
  City & Guilds

Water Engineering (Water – Medium Works) – Level 2
Awarding body:
  City & Guilds

Welding Skills – Level 2
Awarding body:
  City & Guilds

BTEC Award

Engineering (Aerospace) – Level 3
Awarding body:
  EDEXCEL

Engineering (Applied Science) – Level 2
Awarding body:
  EDEXCEL

Engineering (Applied Science) – Level 3
Awarding body:
  EDEXCEL

Engineering (Automotive) – Level 2
Awarding body:
  EDEXCEL

Engineering (Automotive) – Level 3
Awarding body:
  EDEXCEL

Engineering (Electrical/Mechanical) – Level 3
Awarding body:
  EDEXCEL

Engineering (Manufacturing) – Level 3
Awarding body:
  EDEXCEL

Engineering (Operations and Maintenance) – Level 3
Awarding body:
  EDEXCEL

Engineering (Specialist) – Level 2
Awarding body:
  EDEXCEL

BTEC Certificate

Engineering – Level 2
Awarding body:
  EDEXCEL

Engineering (Applied Science) – Level 2
Awarding body:
  EDEXCEL

Engineering (Automotive) – Level 2
Awarding body:
  EDEXCEL

Engineering (Specialist) – Level 2
Awarding body:
  EDEXCEL

BTEC Diploma

Aircraft Avionic Maintenance Engineering – Level 3
Awarding body:
  EDEXCEL

Aircraft Mechanical Maintenance Engineering – Level 3
Awarding body:
  EDEXCEL

Engineering – Level 2
Awarding body:
  EDEXCEL

Engineering (Aerospace) – Level 3
Awarding body:
  EDEXCEL

Engineering (Applied Science) – Level 3
Awarding body:
  EDEXCEL

Engineering (Automotive) – Level 3
Awarding body:
  EDEXCEL

Engineering (Electrical/Mechanical) – Level 3
Awarding body:
  EDEXCEL

Engineering (Manufacturing) – Level 3
Awarding body:
  EDEXCEL

Engineering (Operations and Maintenance) – Level 3
Awarding body:
  EDEXCEL

Manufacturing Engineering – Level 3
Awarding body:
  EDEXCEL

Mechanical Engineering – Level 3
Awarding body:
  EDEXCEL

Operations and Maintenance Engineering – Level 3
Awarding body:
  EDEXCEL

BTEC Extended Certificate

Engineering – Level 2
Awarding body:
  EDEXCEL

Engineering (Aerospace) – Level 3
Awarding body:
  EDEXCEL

Engineering (Applied Science) – Level 2
Awarding body:
  EDEXCEL

Engineering (Applied Science) – Level 3
Awarding body:
  EDEXCEL

Engineering (Automotive) – Level 2
Awarding body:
  EDEXCEL

Engineering (Automotive) – Level 3
Awarding body:
  EDEXCEL

Engineering (Electrical/Mechanical) – Level 3
Awarding body:
  EDEXCEL

Engineering (Manufacturing) – Level 3
Awarding body:
  EDEXCEL

Engineering (Operations and Maintenance) – Level 3
Awarding body:
  EDEXCEL

Engineering (Specialist) – Level 2
Awarding body:
  EDEXCEL

BTEC Extended Diploma

Manufacturing Engineering – Level 3
Awarding body:
  EDEXCEL

Mechanical Engineering – Level 3
Awarding body:
  EDEXCEL

Operations and Maintenance Engineering – Level 3
Awarding body:
  EDEXCEL

BTEC First Certificate

Engineering – Level 2
Awarding body:
  EDEXCEL

BTEC First Diploma

Engineering – Level 2
Awarding body:
  EDEXCEL

BTEC Higher National Certificate

Aerospace Engineering – Level 5
Awarding body:
  EDEXCEL

Electrical/Electronic Engineering – Level 5
Awarding body:
  EDEXCEL

Marine Engineering – Level 5
Awarding body:
  EDEXCEL

Mechanical Engineering – Level 5
Awarding body:
EDEXCEL

Operations Engineering – Level 5
Awarding body:
EDEXCEL

BTEC Higher National Diploma

Aerospace Engineering – Level 5
Awarding body:
EDEXCEL

Electrical/Electronic Engineering – Level 5
Awarding body:
EDEXCEL

Marine Engineering – Level 5
Awarding body:
EDEXCEL

Mechanical Engineering – Level 5
Awarding body:
EDEXCEL

Operations Engineering – Level 5
Awarding body:
EDEXCEL

BTEC National Award

Blacksmithing and Metalworking – Level 3
Awarding body:
EDEXCEL

Engineering – Level 3
Awarding body:
EDEXCEL

BTEC National Certificate

Aerospace Engineering – Level 3
Awarding body:
EDEXCEL

Blacksmithing and Metalworking – Level 3
Awarding body:
EDEXCEL

Electrical/Electronic Engineering – Level 3
Awarding body:
EDEXCEL

Engineering – Level 3
Awarding body:
EDEXCEL

Manufacturing Engineering – Level 3
Awarding body:
EDEXCEL

Mechanical Engineering – Level 3
Awarding body:
EDEXCEL

Operations and Maintenance Engineering – Level 3
Awarding body:
EDEXCEL

BTEC National Diploma

Aerospace Engineering – Level 3
Awarding body:
EDEXCEL

Blacksmithing and Metalworking – Level 3
Awarding body:
EDEXCEL

Electrical/Electronic Engineering – Level 3
Awarding body:
EDEXCEL

Engineering – Level 3
Awarding body:
EDEXCEL

Manufacturing Engineering – Level 3
Awarding body:
EDEXCEL

Mechanical Engineering – Level 3
Awarding body:
EDEXCEL

Operations and Maintenance Engineering – Level 3
Awarding body:
EDEXCEL

Certificate

2D Computer Aided Design – Level 2
Awarding body:
City & Guilds

Aeronautical Engineering – Level 2
Awarding body:
City & Guilds

Aeronautical Engineering – Level 3
Awarding body:
City & Guilds

Arc Welding – Level 1
Awarding body:
EAL

Boat Building, Maintenance and Support – Level 2
Awarding body:
City & Guilds

Boat Building, Maintenance and Support – Level 3
Awarding body:
City & Guilds

Chemical and Pharmaceutical Based Process Maintenance – Level 2
Awarding body:
PAA\VQSET

Computer Aided Design – Level 3
Awarding body:
City & Guilds

Computer Aided Design (CAD) Parametric Modelling – Level 1
Awarding body:
City & Guilds

Computer Aided Design (CAD) Parametric Modelling – Level 2
Awarding body:
City & Guilds

Computer Aided Design (CAD) Parametric Modelling – Level 3
Awarding body:
City & Guilds

Computer Aided Design and Manufacturing (2D) – Level 2
Awarding body:
City & Guilds

Computer Aided Design and Manufacturing (2D) – Level 3
Awarding body:
City & Guilds

Computer Aided Design and Manufacturing (3D) – Level 3
Awarding body:
City & Guilds

Cycle Maintenance – Level 2
Awarding body:
EAL

Digital Television Aerial Installation – Level 2
Awarding body:
City & Guilds

Domestic Electrical Installers – Level 2
Awarding body:
EAL

Electrical Technology Engineering – Level 3
Awarding body:
City & Guilds

Electronics – Level 1
Awarding body:
EAL

Electrotechnical Technology – Level 2
Awarding body:
City & Guilds

Electrotechnical Technology – Level 3
Awarding body:
City & Guilds

Engineering – Level 1
Awarding body:
City & Guilds

Engineering – Level 2
Awarding body:
City & Guilds

Engineering – Level 3
Awarding body:
City & Guilds

Engineering and Technology – Level 1
Awarding body:
EAL

Engineering and Technology – Level 2
Awarding body:
 EAL

Engineering Construction – Level 3
Awarding body:
 City & Guilds

Engineering Practice – Level 2
Awarding body:
 City & Guilds

Engineering Practice – Level 3
Awarding body:
 City & Guilds

Fundamental Inspection, Testing and Initial Verification – Level 2
Awarding body:
 City & Guilds

In-Service Inspection and Testing of Electrical Equipment (PAT) – Level 3
Awarding body:
 EAL

Land-based Service Engineering – Level 2
Awarding body:
 NPTC

Land-based Service Engineering – Level 3
Awarding body:
 NPTC

Oil Fired Services – Level 2
Awarding body:
 City & Guilds

Oil Fired Services – Level 3
Awarding body:
 City & Guilds

Performing Testing Operations in the Lift and Escalator Industry – Level 4
Awarding body:
 EAL

Plumbing – Level 2
Awarding body:
 EAL

Positional Welding – Level 2
Awarding body:
 EAL

Process Industries Maintenance – Level 2
Awarding body:
 PAA\VQSET

Repair, Restoration and Conservation of Clocks and Watches – Level 3
Awarding body:
 EAL

The Certification of Electrical Installations – Level 3
Awarding body:
 City & Guilds

The Requirements for Electrical Installations (16 to 17th edition update BS7671 June 2008) – Level 3
Awarding body:
 City & Guilds

The Requirements for Electrical Installations (BS 7671 June 2008) – Level 3
Awarding body:
 City & Guilds

Water Engineering – Level 2
Awarding body:
 City & Guilds

Water Engineering – Complex Works – Level 2
Awarding body:
 City & Guilds

Water Engineering – Medium Works – Level 2
Awarding body:
 City & Guilds

Water Sector Competent Operator – Sludge Complex Works – Level 2
Awarding body:
 City & Guilds

Water Sector Competent Operator – Sludge Simple Works – Level 2
Awarding body:
 City & Guilds

Water Sector Competent Operator – Water Complex Works – Level 2
Awarding body:
 City & Guilds

**Water Sector Competent Operator –
Water Medium Works – Level 2**
Awarding body:
City & Guilds

**Water Sector Competent Operator –
Water Simple Works – Level 2**
Awarding body:
City & Guilds

Diploma

**Advanced Electrical and Electronic
Principles – Level 3**
Awarding body:
EAL

**Advanced Fabrication and Welding
Principles – Level 3**
Awarding body:
EAL

**Advanced Maintenance Engineering
Principles – Level 3**
Awarding body:
EAL

**Advanced Manufacture Techniques –
Computer Numerical Control (CNC) –
Level 3**
Awarding body:
EAL

**Advanced Mechanical Engineering
Principles – Level 3**
Awarding body:
EAL

**Advanced Personal Computer (PC)
Maintenance – Level 3**
Awarding body:
EAL

Analogue Electronics – Level 3
Awarding body:
EAL

Automated Welding Processes – Level 3
Awarding body:
EAL

**Building Electrical Maintenance –
Level 3**
Awarding body:
EAL

**Building Mechanical Maintenance
Systems & Services – Level 3**
Awarding body:
EAL

**Computer Numerical Control (CNC)
Programming/machining – Level 3**
Awarding body:
EAL

Cycle Maintenance – Level 3
Awarding body:
EAL

Digital Electronics – Level 3
Awarding body:
EAL

Domestic Plumbing – Level 3
Awarding body:
EAL

**Electrical Power Engineering – Current
Transformer/Voltage Transformer
Metering – Level 3**
Awarding body:
City & Guilds

**Electrical Power Engineering –
Overhead Lines – Level 2**
Awarding body:
City & Guilds

**Electrical Power Engineering –
Overhead Lines – Level 3**
Awarding body:
City & Guilds

**Electrical Power Engineering – Single
and Three Phase Metering (Whole
Current) – Level 2**
Awarding body:
City & Guilds

**Electrical Power Engineering –
Substation Plant – Level 2**
Awarding body:
City & Guilds

**Electrical Power Engineering –
Substation Plant – Level 3**
Awarding body:
City & Guilds

**Electrical Power Engineering –
Underground Cables – Level 2**
Awarding body:
City & Guilds

**Electrical Power Engineering –
Underground Cables – Level 3**
Awarding body:
City & Guilds

**Electrical Testing and Commissioning –
Level 3**
Awarding body:
EAL

Electrotechnical Services – Level 3
Awarding body:
EAL

Engineering and Technology – Level 2
Awarding body:
EAL

Engineering and Technology – Level 3
Awarding body:
EAL

**Engineering and Technology
(Progressive) – Level 3**
Awarding body:
EAL

**Engineering Inspection and Quality
Control – Level 3**
Awarding body:
EAL

**Engineering Pattern Development
Methods – Level 3**
Awarding body:
EAL

Engineering Practice – Level 3
Awarding body:
City & Guilds

**General Engineering Maintenance
Techniques – Level 3**
Awarding body:
EAL

**Inspecting and Testing Electrotechnical
Systems and Equipment – Level 3**
Awarding body:
EAL

**Installation of Electrical Equipment –
Level 3**
Awarding body:
EAL

**Maintenance of Fluid Power Systems
and Components – Level 3**
Awarding body:
EAL

**Maintenance of Hydraulic Systems and
Components – Level 3**
Awarding body:
EAL

**Maintenance of Mechanical Systems –
Level 3**
Awarding body:
EAL

**Maintenance of Pneumatic Systems and
Components – Level 3**
Awarding body:
EAL

**Maintenance of Refrigeration Systems –
Level 3**
Awarding body:
EAL

**Managing Engineering Fabrication
Activities – Level 3**
Awarding body:
EAL

**Manual Metal-Arc (MMA) Welding
Process – Level 3**
Awarding body:
EAL

Mechanised Welding Processes – Level 3
Awarding body:
EAL

**Metal Inert Gas/Metal Active Gas
(MIG/MAG) Welding Process – Level 3**
Awarding body:
EAL

Microelectronics – Level 3
Awarding body:
EAL

Nuclear Decommissioning (NVQ) – Level 2
Awarding body:
PAA\VQSET

Producing Pipework Fabrications – Level 3
Awarding body:
EAL

Producing Plate Fabrications – Level 3
Awarding body:
EAL

Producing Sheetmetal Fabrications – Level 3
Awarding body:
EAL

Programmable Logic Controllers (PLCs) – Level 3
Awarding body:
EAL

Radiation Protection (NVQ) – Level 2
Awarding body:
PAA\VQSET

Radiation Protection (NVQ) – Level 3
Awarding body:
PAA\VQSET

Radiation Protection (NVQ) – Level 4
Awarding body:
PAA\VQSET

Requirements for Electrical Installations (BS 7671: January 2008) – Level 3
Awarding body:
EAL

Requirements for Electrical Installations (BS 7671: January 2008) Update – Level 3
Awarding body:
EAL

Toolmaking, Presswork and Extrusion – Level 3
Awarding body:
EAL

Tungsten Inert Gas (TIG) Welding Process – Level 3
Awarding body:
EAL

Water Engineering – Level 3
Awarding body:
City & Guilds

Water Sector Competent Operator – Sludge Complex Works – Level 2
Awarding body:
City & Guilds

Water Sector Competent Operator – Waste Water Complex Works – Level 2
Awarding body:
City & Guilds

Water Sector Competent Operator – Waste Water Simple Works – Level 2
Awarding body:
City & Guilds

Water Sector Competent Operator – Water Complex Works – Level 2
Awarding body:
City & Guilds

Water Sector Competent Operator – Water Medium Works – Level 2
Awarding body:
City & Guilds

Extended Certificate

Engineering Practice – Level 2
Awarding body:
City & Guilds

Foundation Diploma

Engineering – Level 1
Awarding body:
AQA
City & Guilds
EDEXCEL
OCR

Higher Diploma

Engineering – Level 2
Awarding body:
 AQA
 City & Guilds
 EDEXCEL
 OCR

Introductory Certificate

Engineering – Level 1
Awarding body:
 EDEXCEL

Introductory Diploma

Engineering – Level 1
Awarding body:
 EDEXCEL

IVQ Advanced Diploma

Oil and Gas Operations – Level 3
Awarding body:
 City & Guilds

IVQ Advanced Technician Diploma

Electrical and Electronic Engineering – Level 5
Awarding body:
 City & Guilds

Engineering – Level 5
Awarding body:
 City & Guilds

IVQ Certificate

Engineering Skills – Level 1
Awarding body:
 City & Guilds

IVQ Diploma

Engineering Skills – Level 2
Awarding body:
 City & Guilds

IVQ Technician Certificate

Electrical and Electronic Engineering – Level 2
Awarding body:
 City & Guilds

Engineering – Level 2
Awarding body:
 City & Guilds

IVQ Technician Diploma

Electrical and Electronic Engineering – Level 3
Awarding body:
 City & Guilds

Engineering – Level 3
Awarding body:
 City & Guilds

National Vocational Qualification

Aeronautical Engineering – Level 2
Awarding body:
 EAL

Aeronautical Engineering – Level 3
Awarding body:
 City & Guilds
 EAL
 ETCAL

Automotive Engineering – Level 3
Awarding body:
 EAL

Building Services Engineering Technology and Project Management – Level 3
Awarding body:
 EAL

Building Services Engineering Technology and Project Management – Level 4
Awarding body:
EAL

Business Improvement Techniques – Level 2
Awarding body:
EAL

Business Improvement Techniques – Level 2
Awarding body:
City & Guilds

Chemical, Pharmaceutical and Petro-Chemical Operations – Level 1
Awarding body:
City & Guilds
PAA\VQSET

Chemical, Pharmaceutical and Petro-Chemical Operations – Level 2
Awarding body:
City & Guilds
PAA\VQSET

Chemical, Pharmaceutical and Petro-Chemical Operations – Level 3
Awarding body:
City & Guilds
PAA\VQSET

Chemical, Pharmaceutical and Petro-Chemical Operations – Level 4
Awarding body:
City & Guilds
PAA\VQSET

Constructing Capital Plant Steel Structures (Erecting) – Level 3
Awarding body:
ECITB

Constructional Steelwork Site Operations – Level 2
Awarding body:
ECITB

Controlling Process Operations – Level 3
Awarding body:
CABWI

Design and Draughting – Level 3
Awarding body:
ECITB

Designing Water Networks – Level 3
Awarding body:
CABWI

Distribution Control – Level 2
Awarding body:
CABWI

Electrical and Electronic Engineering – Level 3
Awarding body:
EAL
ETCAL

Electrical and Electronic Servicing – Level 2
Awarding body:
City & Guilds
EAL

Electrical and Electronic Servicing – Level 3
Awarding body:
City & Guilds
EAL

Electrical Machine Repair and Rewind – Level 3
Awarding body:
City & Guilds

Electrical Panel Building – Level 3
Awarding body:
City & Guilds

Electricity System Technology Engineering – Level 3
Awarding body:
City & Guilds

Electricity System Technology Engineering Support – Level 2
Awarding body:
City & Guilds

Electrotechnical Services – Level 3
Awarding body:
City & Guilds
EAL

Engineering Leadership – Level 3
Awarding body:
   EAL

Engineering Leadership – Level 4
Awarding body:
   EAL

Engineering Maintenance – Level 3
Awarding body:
   City & Guilds
   EAL
   ETCAL

Engineering Maintenance and Installation – Level 2
Awarding body:
   City & Guilds
   EAL

Engineering Surveying, Systems or Services – Level 4
Awarding body:
   OU

Engineering Technical Support – Level 2
Awarding body:
   City & Guilds
   EAL

Engineering Technical Support – Level 3
Awarding body:
   City & Guilds
   EAL
   ETCAL

Engineering Technology Maintenance – Level 3
Awarding body:
   City & Guilds

Engineering Technology Maintenance Support – Level 2
Awarding body:
   City & Guilds

Engineering Technology Operations – Level 3
Awarding body:
   City & Guilds

Engineering Technology Operations Foundation – Level 1
Awarding body:
   City & Guilds

Engineering Technology Operations Support – Level 2
Awarding body:
   City & Guilds

Engineering Toolmaking – Level 3
Awarding body:
   EAL

Environmental Improvements Techniques – Level 2
Awarding body:
   EAL

Fabricating of Steel Structures (Plating) – Level 3
Awarding body:
   ECITB

Fabrication and Welding – Level 3
Awarding body:
   EAL

Fabrication and Welding Engineering – Level 2
Awarding body:
   City & Guilds
   EAL
   ETCAL

Fabrication and Welding Engineering – Level 3
Awarding body:
   City & Guilds
   ETCAL

Gas Network Engineering Management – Level 4
Awarding body:
   OU

Gas Network Operations – Level 1
Awarding body:
   City & Guilds

Gas Network Operations – Craft – Level 3
Awarding body:
   City & Guilds

Gas Network Operations – Mainlaying – Level 2
Awarding body:
   City & Guilds

Gas Network Operations – Servicelaying – Level 2
Awarding body:
   City & Guilds

Hybrid Vehicle Introduction and Environmental Improvements – Level 2
Awarding body:
   EAL

Installation and Commissioning – Level 3
Awarding body:
   City & Guilds
   EAL

Installing and Commissioning Electrotechnical Systems and Equipment (Plant) – Level 3
Awarding body:
   ECITB

Installing Plant and Systems – Instrument Pipefitting – Level 3
Awarding body:
   ECITB

Installing Plant and Systems – Mechanical – Level 3
Awarding body:
   ECITB

Installing Plant and Systems – Pipefitting – Level 3
Awarding body:
   ECITB

Installing Structured Cabling Systems – Level 2
Awarding body:
   EAL

Land-based Service Engineering – Level 2
Awarding body:
   NPTC

Land-based Service Engineering – Level 3
Awarding body:
   NPTC

Leakage Control – Level 3
Awarding body:
   CABWI

Leakage Detection – Level 2
Awarding body:
   CABWI

Maintain Water Supply (Network) – Level 3
Awarding body:
   CABWI

Maintaining Plant and Systems – Electrical – Level 3
Awarding body:
   ECITB

Maintaining Plant and Systems – Instrument and Control – Level 3
Awarding body:
   ECITB

Maintaining Plant and Systems – Mechanical – Level 3
Awarding body:
   ECITB

Managing and Controlling Process Operations – Level 3
Awarding body:
   CABWI

Managing Waste Collection Operations – Level 4
Awarding body:
   City & Guilds

Marine Engineering – Level 2
Awarding body:
   EAL

Marine Engineering – Level 3
Awarding body:
   EAL

Materials Processing and Finishing – Level 2
Awarding body:
   City & Guilds
   EAL

Materials Processing and Finishing – Level 3
Awarding body:
   EAL

Mechanical Engineering Services – Heating and Ventilating Installation – Level 2
Awarding body:
    EAL

Mechanical Engineering Services – Heating and Ventilating Installation – Level 3
Awarding body:
    EAL

Mechanical Engineering Services – Plumbing – Level 2
Awarding body:
    EAL

Mechanical Engineering Services – Plumbing (Domestic) – Level 3
Awarding body:
    EAL

Mechanical Manufacturing Engineering – Level 2
Awarding body:
    City & Guilds
    EAL
    ETCAL

Mechanical Manufacturing Engineering – Level 3
Awarding body:
    City & Guilds
    EAL
    ETCAL

Monitoring the Water Environment – Level 2
Awarding body:
    CABWI

Moving Loads – Level 3
Awarding body:
    ECITB

Network Construction Operations (Water) – Level 1
Awarding body:
    CABWI

Network Construction Operations (Water) – Level 3
Awarding body:
    CABWI

Network Construction Operations: Mainlaying (Water) – Level 2
Awarding body:
    CABWI

Network Construction Operations: Servicelaying (Water) – Level 2
Awarding body:
    CABWI

Non Destructive Testing – Level 3
Awarding body:
    ECITB

Nuclear Decommissioning – Level 2
Awarding body:
    City & Guilds

Nuclear Decommissioning – Level 3
Awarding body:
    City & Guilds

Operating Process Plant: Sludge – Level 2
Awarding body:
    CABWI

Operating Process Plant: Waste Water – Level 2
Awarding body:
    CABWI

Operating Process Plant: Water – Level 2
Awarding body:
    CABWI

Performing Engineering Operations – Level 1
Awarding body:
    City & Guilds
    EAL
    EDEXCEL
    ETCAL
    PAA\VQSET

Performing Engineering Operations – Level 2
Awarding body:
    City & Guilds
    EAL
    EDEXCEL
    ETCAL
    PAA\VQSET

Plant Operations – Level 2
Awarding body:
    EAL

**Process Engineering Maintenance –
Level 2**
Awarding body:
    PAA\VQSET

**Process Engineering Maintenance –
Level 3**
Awarding body:
    PAA\VQSET

Project Control – Level 3
Awarding body:
    ECITB

Project Control – Level 4
Awarding body:
    ECITB

Project Control Support – Level 2
Awarding body:
    ECITB

Radiation Protection – Level 2
Awarding body:
    City & Guilds

Radiation Protection – Level 3
Awarding body:
    City & Guilds

Radiation Protection – Level 4
Awarding body:
    City & Guilds

Sewerage Maintenance – Level 1
Awarding body:
    CABWI

Sewerage Maintenance – Level 2
Awarding body:
    CABWI

**Supporting Engineering Activities –
Level 2**
Awarding body:
    ECITB

**Utilities Control Centre Operations –
Level 2**
Awarding body:
    CABWI

Utilities Metering Operations – Level 2
Awarding body:
    CABWI

**Utilities Network Planning and
Management – Level 4**
Awarding body:
    CABWI

**Water Fittings Regulations Enforcement
– Level 3**
Awarding body:
    CABWI

Welding – Pipework – Level 3
Awarding body:
    ECITB

Welding – Plate – Level 3
Awarding body:
    ECITB

Principal Learning

Engineering – Level 1
Awarding body:
    AQA
    City & Guilds
    EDEXCEL
    OCR

Engineering – Level 2
Awarding body:
    AQA
    City & Guilds
    EDEXCEL
    OCR

Engineering – Level 3
Awarding body:
    AQA
    City & Guilds
    EDEXCEL
    OCR

Engineering (Wales) – Level 1
Awarding body:
    OCR
    WJEC-EDEXCEL

Engineering (Wales) – Level 2
Awarding body:
    OCR
    WJEC-EDEXCEL

Engineering (Wales) – Level 3
Awarding body:
  OCR
  WJEC-EDEXCEL

Progression Award

**Electrical and Electronics Servicing –
Level 3**
Awarding body:
  City & Guilds

**Electrical Electronics Servicing:
Consumer/Commercial Electronics –
Level 2**
Awarding body:
  City & Guilds

Progression Diploma

Engineering – Level 3
Awarding body:
  AQA
  City & Guilds
  EDEXCEL
  OCR

Manufacturing Technologies

Advanced Diploma

**Manufacturing and Product Design –
Level 3**
Awarding body:
  AQA
  City & Guilds
  EDEXCEL
  OCR

Award

**An introduction to Extraction and
Mineral Processing – Level 2**
Awarding body:
  MPQC

Apparel Product Development – Level 2
Awarding body:
  PAA\VQSET

**Chemical and Pharmaceutical Based
Process Support (Clean and Prepare
Complex Items of Plant and Equipment)
– Level 2**
Awarding body:
  PAA\VQSET

**Chemical and Pharmaceutical Based
Process Support (Prepare Process
Materials) – Level 2**
Awarding body:
  PAA\VQSET

**Chemical and Pharmaceutical Based
Process Support (Transfer Materials) –
Level 2**
Awarding body:
  PAA\VQSET

**Distribution Services in the Textile
Industry Professional Skills
Development – Level 3**
Awarding body:
  ABC

**Distribution Services in the Textile
Industry Vocational Skills Development
– Level 2**
Awarding body:
  ABC

**Distribution Services in the Textile
Industry Working Practices – Level 2**
Awarding body:
  ABC

**Fabrication and Welding Practice –
Level 2**
Awarding body:
　ABC

**Fabrication and Welding Practice –
Level 3**
Awarding body:
　ABC

**Fabrication and Welding Practices –
Level 2**
Awarding body:
　ABC

Fashion and Textiles – Level 1
Awarding body:
　ABC

Fashion and Textiles – Level 2
Awarding body:
　ABC

Fashion and Textiles – Level 3
Awarding body:
　ABC

Food Manufacture – Level 2
Awarding body:
　City & Guilds

Food Manufacture – Level 3
Awarding body:
　City & Guilds

Food Safety for Manufacturing – Level 2
Awarding body:
　CIEH
　EDI
　FDQ
　HABC
　RSPH

**Food Safety for Manufacturing (Meat
and Poultry) – Level 2**
Awarding body:
　FDQ

**Food Safety Management for
Manufacturing – Level 4**
Awarding body:
　CIEH
　HABC
　RSPH

**Food Safety Supervision for
Manufacturing – Level 3**
Awarding body:
　CIEH
　HABC
　RSPH

**HACCP for Food Manufacturing –
Level 3**
Awarding body:
　CIEH
　EDI
　HABC
　RSPH

**HACCP Management for Food
Manufacturing – Level 4**
Awarding body:
　RSPH

Manufacturing Textiles – Level 1
Awarding body:
　City & Guilds

Manufacturing Textiles – Level 2
Awarding body:
　City & Guilds

**Operating Safely and Effectively in
Polymer Processing and Related
Operations – Level 2**
Awarding body:
　PAA\VQSET

**Packaging Support (Sampling and
Testing) – Level 2**
Awarding body:
　PAA\VQSET

**Polymer and Composites Based Process
Support (Contribute to the Provision of
Ancillary Systems) – Level 2**
Awarding body:
　PAA\VQSET

**Polymer and Composites Based Process
Support (Maintain Process Equipment) –
Level 2**
Awarding body:
　PAA\VQSET

Polymer and Composites Based Process Support (Pick Polymer Stock and Make Up Orders) – Level 2
Awarding body:
    PAA\VQSET

Polymer and Composites Based Process Support (Provide Technical Services) – Level 4
Awarding body:
    PAA\VQSET

Polymer and Composites Based Process Support (Rectify Process Problems) – Level 3
Awarding body:
    PAA\VQSET

Polymer and Composites Based Process Support (Routine Servicing – Plant and Equipment) – Level 3
Awarding body:
    PAA\VQSET

Polymer Based Process Support (Inspect and Finish Products) – Level 2
Awarding body:
    PAA\VQSET

Principles of Working in Food Manufacture – Level 2
Awarding body:
    FDQ

Proficiency in Poultry Meat Inspection – Level 2
Awarding body:
    FDQ
    RSPH

Shoe Repair, Key Cutting and Associated Multi Services – Level 2
Awarding body:
    ABC

The Principles of Managing Health and Safety in the Extractive and Mineral Processing Industries – Level 3
Awarding body:
    MPQC

BTEC Higher National Certificate

Fashion and Textiles – Level 5
Awarding body:
    EDEXCEL

Manufacturing Engineering – Level 5
Awarding body:
    EDEXCEL

BTEC Higher National Diploma

Fashion and Textiles – Level 5
Awarding body:
    EDEXCEL

Manufacturing Engineering – Level 5
Awarding body:
    EDEXCEL

Certificate

Advanced Packaging Operations – Level 2
Awarding body:
    PAA\VQSET

Apparel Manufacturing Technology (NVQ) – Level 3
Awarding body:
    ABC

Apparel Product Development – Level 2
Awarding body:
    PAA\VQSET

Apparel Product Development – Level 3
Awarding body:
    PAA\VQSET

Apparel, Footwear, Leather or Textile Production – Level 2
Awarding body:
    ABC

Cake Decoration – Level 1
Awarding body:
    ABC

Cake Decoration – Level 2
Awarding body:
    ABC

Cake Decoration – Level 3
Awarding body:
ABC

Ceramics Manufacturing – Level 2
Awarding body:
PAA\VQSET

Chemical and Pharmaceutical Based Process Operations – Level 2
Awarding body:
PAA\VQSET

Chemical and Pharmaceutical Based Process Operations – Level 3
Awarding body:
PAA\VQSET

Clay Building Products – Level 2
Awarding body:
PAA\VQSET

Clay Building Products – Level 3
Awarding body:
PAA\VQSET

Composite Based Process Operations – Level 2
Awarding body:
PAA\VQSET

Composite Based Process Operations – Level 3
Awarding body:
PAA\VQSET

Design and Technology – Entry Level
Awarding body:
AQA
EDEXCEL
OCR
WJEC

Distribution Services in the Textile Industry Working Practices – Level 2
Awarding body:
ABC

Emergency Response in Chemical, Pharmaceutical & Petro-chemical Industries – Level 4
Awarding body:
PAA\VQSET

Extraction and Mineral Processing – Level 2
Awarding body:
MPQC

Extraction and Mineral Processing – Level 3
Awarding body:
MPQC

Extractives and Mineral Processing Industries – Level 3
Awarding body:
MPQC

Fabrication and Welding Practice – Level 1
Awarding body:
ABC

Fabrication and Welding Practice – Level 2
Awarding body:
ABC

Fabrication and Welding Practice – Level 3
Awarding body:
ABC

Fabrication and Welding Practices – Level 1
Awarding body:
ABC

Fashion and Textiles – Level 1
Awarding body:
ABC

Fashion and Textiles – Level 2
Awarding body:
ABC

Fashion and Textiles – Level 3
Awarding body:
ABC

Food Manufacture – Level 2
Awarding body:
City & Guilds

Food Manufacture – Level 3
Awarding body:
City & Guilds

Footwear and Leather (NVQ) – Level 2
Awarding body:
  ABC

Footwear and Leather (NVQ) – Level 3
Awarding body:
  ABC

Furniture Production – Level 1
Awarding body:
  City & Guilds

Furniture Production – Level 2
Awarding body:
  City & Guilds

Furniture Production – Level 3
Awarding body:
  City & Guilds

Glass Related Operations – Level 2
Awarding body:
  GQA

Glass Related Operations – Level 3
Awarding body:
  GQA

Knife Skills for the meat and poultry industry – Level 1
Awarding body:
  FDQ

Level 4 Certificate for Optical Technicians – Level 4
Awarding body:
  WCSM

Management – Level 2
Awarding body:
  FDQ

Management – Level 3
Awarding body:
  FDQ

Management – Level 4
Awarding body:
  FDQ

Manufacturing Sewn Products (NVQ) – Level 2
Awarding body:
  ABC

Manufacturing Textiles – Level 2
Awarding body:
  City & Guilds

Meat and Poultry – Level 2
Awarding body:
  FDQ

Meat and Poultry – Level 3
Awarding body:
  FDQ

Meat Hygiene and Inspection – Level 3
Awarding body:
  RSPH

Operating Safely and Effectively in Polymer Processing and Related Operations – Level 2
Awarding body:
  PAA\VQSET

Optical Production Processes – Level 2
Awarding body:
  WCSM

Optical Production Processes – Level 3
Awarding body:
  WCSM

Packaging Operations – Level 2
Awarding body:
  PAA\VQSET

Packaging Technology – Level 3
Awarding body:
  PIABC

Paper Technology – Level 2
Awarding body:
  PAA\VQSET

Paper Technology – Level 3
Awarding body:
  PAA\VQSET

Polymer Based Process Operations – Level 2
Awarding body:
  PAA\VQSET

Polymer Based Process Operations – Level 3
Awarding body:
  PAA\VQSET

**Poultry Meat Hygiene and Inspection –
Level 3**
Awarding body:
RSPH

Process Technology – Level 2
Awarding body:
City & Guilds

Process Technology – Level 3
Awarding body:
City & Guilds

Saddlery – Level 1
Awarding body:
NPTC

Saddlery – Level 2
Awarding body:
NPTC

Saddlery – Level 3
Awarding body:
NPTC

**Shoe Repair, Key Cutting and Associated
Multi Services – Level 2**
Awarding body:
ABC

Signmaking – Level 3
Awarding body:
PAA\VQSET

Technology and Design – Entry Level
Awarding body:
CCEA

Textile Technology – Level 3
Awarding body:
ABC

Wired Sugar Flowers – Level 1
Awarding body:
ABC

Wired Sugar Flowers – Level 2
Awarding body:
ABC

Diploma

Apparel Product Development – Level 2
Awarding body:
PAA\VQSET

Apparel Product Development – Level 3
Awarding body:
PAA\VQSET

Apparel/Footwear Production – Level 3
Awarding body:
ABC

**Downstream Control Room Operations
– Level 3**
Awarding body:
PAA\VQSET

Downstream Field Operations – Level 3
Awarding body:
PAA\VQSET

**Extractives and Mineral Processing
Industries – Level 3**
Awarding body:
MPQC

**Fabrication and Welding Practice –
Level 3**
Awarding body:
ABC

Fashion and Textiles – Level 1
Awarding body:
ABC

Fashion and Textiles – Level 2
Awarding body:
ABC

Fashion and Textiles – Level 3
Awarding body:
ABC

Food Manufacture – Level 2
Awarding body:
City & Guilds

Food Manufacture – Level 3
Awarding body:
City & Guilds

Meat Hygiene and Inspection – Level 3
Awarding body:
RSPH

Packaging Technology – Level 4
Awarding body:
PIABC

Shoe Repair, Key Cutting and Associated Multi Services – Level 2
Awarding body:
  ABC

Supervisory Management in Fabrication and Welding Studies – Level 4
Awarding body:
  ABC

Foundation Diploma

Manufacturing and Product Design – Level 1
Awarding body:
  AQA
  City & Guilds
  EDEXCEL
  OCR

Higher Diploma

Manufacturing and Product Design – Level 2
Awarding body:
  AQA
  City & Guilds
  EDEXCEL
  OCR

Introductory Certificate

FDQ Level 4 Introductory Certificate in Management – Level 4
Awarding body:
  FDQ

Management – Level 2
Awarding body:
  FDQ

Management – Level 3
Awarding body:
  FDQ

National Vocational Qualification

Automotive Glazing – Level 2
Awarding body:
  GQA

Automotive Glazing – Level 3
Awarding body:
  GQA

Bespoke Cutting and Tailoring – Level 3
Awarding body:
  ABC

Blasting Operations – Level 3
Awarding body:
  MPQC

Bulk Explosive Truck Operations – Level 3
Awarding body:
  MPQC

Carton Manufacture – Level 3
Awarding body:
  City & Guilds

Combined Working Practices – Level 2
Awarding body:
  PAA\VQSET

Combined Working Practices – Level 3
Awarding body:
  PAA\VQSET

Drilling Operations (Extractives) – Level 2
Awarding body:
  MPQC

Dry Cleaning Service Support – Level 2
Awarding body:
  PAA\VQSET

Dry Cleaning: Operations – Level 2
Awarding body:
  PAA\VQSET

Envelope Manufacture – Level 2
Awarding body:
  City & Guilds

Envelope Manufacture – Level 3
Awarding body:
  City & Guilds

Fibreboard Operations – Level 2
Awarding body:
PAA\VQSET

Fibreboard Operations – Level 3
Awarding body:
PAA\VQSET

Food Manufacture – Level 1
Awarding body:
City & Guilds
EDEXCEL
FDQ
SQA

Food Manufacture – Level 2
Awarding body:
City & Guilds
EDEXCEL
FDQ
SQA

Food Manufacture – Level 3
Awarding body:
City & Guilds
EDEXCEL
FDQ
SQA

Glass Manufacturing – Level 2
Awarding body:
GQA

Glass Manufacturing – Level 3
Awarding body:
GQA

Glass Processing – Level 2
Awarding body:
GQA

Glass Processing – Level 3
Awarding body:
GQA

Hand Binding – Level 3
Awarding body:
City & Guilds

Health, Safety and Environmental Management in the Extractive and Minerals Processing Industries – Level 3
Awarding body:
MPQC

Health, Safety and Environmental Management in the Extractive and Minerals Processing Industries – Level 4
Awarding body:
MPQC

Health, Safety and Environmental Management in the Extractive and Minerals Processing Industries – Level 5
Awarding body:
MPQC

Jewellery Manufacture – Level 2
Awarding body:
SQA

Laboratory and Associated Technical Activities – Level 1
Awarding body:
City & Guilds
PAA\VQSET

Laboratory and Associated Technical Activities – Level 2
Awarding body:
City & Guilds
PAA\VQSET

Laboratory and Associated Technical Activities – Level 3
Awarding body:
City & Guilds
PAA\VQSET

Laboratory and Associated Technical Activities – Level 4
Awarding body:
City & Guilds
PAA\VQSET

Laundry Operations – Level 2
Awarding body:
PAA\VQSET

Laundry Operations: Batch Washing – Level 2
Awarding body:
PAA\VQSET

Laundry Service Support – Level 2
Awarding body:
PAA\VQSET

Machine Printing – Level 2
Awarding body:
    City & Guilds

Machine Printing – Level 3
Awarding body:
    City & Guilds

Making and Installing Furniture – Level 2
Awarding body:
    City & Guilds

Making and Installing Production Furniture – Level 3
Awarding body:
    City & Guilds

Making and Repairing Hand-Crafted Furniture and Furnishings – Level 3
Awarding body:
    City & Guilds

Manufacturing Ceramic and Associated Products – Level 1
Awarding body:
    PAA\VQSET

Manufacturing Ceramic and Associated Products – Level 2
Awarding body:
    PAA\VQSET

Manufacturing Sewn Products – Level 2
Awarding body:
    ABC

Manufacturing Textiles – Level 3
Awarding body:
    City & Guilds

Mechanised Print Finishing and Binding – Level 2
Awarding body:
    City & Guilds

Mechanised Print Finishing and Binding – Level 3
Awarding body:
    City & Guilds

Metal Processing and Allied Operations – Level 2
Awarding body:
    EAL

Metal Processing and Allied Operations – Level 3
Awarding body:
    EAL

Mining Operations – Level 2
Awarding body:
    MPQC

Mining Operations – Level 3
Awarding body:
    MPQC

Optical Manufacturing – Level 2
Awarding body:
    City & Guilds

Optical Manufacturing – Level 3
Awarding body:
    City & Guilds

Packaging Operators – Level 1
Awarding body:
    FDQ
    PAA\VQSET

Packaging Operators – Level 2
Awarding body:
    FDQ
    PAA\VQSET
    PIABC

Performing Manufacturing Operations – Level 1
Awarding body:
    City & Guilds
    EAL
    EDEXCEL
    EDI
    PAA\VQSET

Performing Manufacturing Operations – Level 2
Awarding body:
    City & Guilds
    EAL
    EDEXCEL
    EDI
    ETCAL
    PAA\VQSET

Plant Operations (Extractives) – Level 2
Awarding body:
    MPQC

Polymer Processing and Related Operations – Level 1
Awarding body:
PAA\VQSET

Polymer Processing and Related Operations – Level 2
Awarding body:
PAA\VQSET

Polymer Processing and Related Operations – Level 3
Awarding body:
PAA\VQSET

Print Administration – Level 3
Awarding body:
City & Guilds

Process Engineering Maintenance – Level 2
Awarding body:
City & Guilds

Process Engineering Maintenance – Level 3
Awarding body:
City & Guilds

Process Operations: Hydrocarbons (Control Room) – Level 3
Awarding body:
City & Guilds

Processing Operations for the Extractive and Minerals Processing Industries – Level 1
Awarding body:
MPQC

Processing Operations for the Extractive and Minerals Processing Industries – Level 2
Awarding body:
MPQC

Processing Operations for the Extractive and Minerals Processing Industries – Level 3
Awarding body:
MPQC

Processing Operations: Hydrocarbons – Level 1
Awarding body:
City & Guilds
PAA\VQSET

Processing Operations: Hydrocarbons – Level 2
Awarding body:
City & Guilds
PAA\VQSET

Processing Operations: Hydrocarbons – Level 3
Awarding body:
City & Guilds
PAA\VQSET

Processing Operations: Hydrocarbons (Control Room) – Level 3
Awarding body:
PAA\VQSET

Producing Surface Coatings – Level 2
Awarding body:
City & Guilds

Production of Glass Supporting Fabrications – Level 2
Awarding body:
GQA

Production of Glass Supporting Fabrications – Level 3
Awarding body:
GQA

Refinery Control Room Operations – Level 3
Awarding body:
PAA\VQSET

Refinery Field Operations – Level 3
Awarding body:
City & Guilds
PAA\VQSET

Signmaking – Level 2
Awarding body:
PAA\VQSET

Signmaking – Level 3
Awarding body:
PAA\VQSET

Supervision of Underground Mining Operations – Level 3
Awarding body:
   MPQC

Supporting the Production of Furniture and Furnishings – Level 1
Awarding body:
   City & Guilds

Woodmachining – Level 2
Awarding body:
   City & Guilds

Woodmachining – Level 3
Awarding body:
   City & Guilds

Principal Learning

Manufacturing and Product Design – Level 1
Awarding body:
   EDEXCEL
   OCR

Manufacturing and Product Design – Level 2
Awarding body:
   EDEXCEL
   OCR

Manufacturing and Product Design – Level 3
Awarding body:
   EDEXCEL
   OCR

Progression Diploma

Manufacturing and Product Design – Level 3
Awarding body:
   AQA
   City & Guilds
   EDEXCEL
   OCR

Transportation Operations and Maintenance

Award

Advanced Vehicle Maintenance and Repair – Level 3
Awarding body:
   City & Guilds

Air Cabin Crew (New Entrant) – Level 2
Awarding body:
   City & Guilds

Aircraft Boarding and Arrival Services – Level 2
Awarding body:
   City & Guilds

Aircraft Dispatch Process – Level 2
Awarding body:
   City & Guilds

Aircraft Load Instruction Reports – Level 2
Awarding body:
   City & Guilds

Aircraft Marshalling – Level 2
Awarding body:
   City & Guilds

Airport Baggage Facilities – Level 2
Awarding body:
   City & Guilds

Airport Baggage Processing – Level 2
Awarding body:
   City & Guilds

Airport Check In Services – Level 2
Awarding body:
   City & Guilds

**Airport Special Status Passengers –
Level 2**
Awarding body:
 City & Guilds

**Automotive Pre-Vocational Learning –
Level 1**
Awarding body:
 IMIAL

**Automotive Refrigerant Handling
(EC842-2006) – Level 3**
Awarding body:
 IMIAL

Basic Mobile Air Conditioning – Level 3
Awarding body:
 City & Guilds

Commercial Moving – Level 1
Awarding body:
 EDEXCEL

**Diagnosis and Repair of Mobile Air
Conditioning/Climate Control Systems –
Level 3**
Awarding body:
 City & Guilds

**Hybrid Electric Vehicle Operation and
Maintenance – Level 2**
Awarding body:
 IMIAL

**Hybrid Electric Vehicle Repair and
Replacement – Level 3**
Awarding body:
 IMIAL

**Introduction to Travel Planning –
Level 4**
Awarding body:
 OU

**Introduction to Vehicle Maintenance
and Repair – Level 1**
Awarding body:
 City & Guilds

**Introduction to Vehicle Technology –
Entry Level**
Awarding body:
 IMIAL

**Loading and Unloading of Aircraft –
Level 2**
Awarding body:
 City & Guilds

Motor Vehicle Studies – Level 1
Awarding body:
 ABC

Rail Services – Level 2
Awarding body:
 City & Guilds

**Rail Track Engineering Maintenance –
Level 2**
Awarding body:
 Network Rail

Support Flight Operations – Level 2
Awarding body:
 City & Guilds

**Vehicle Body and Paint Operations –
Level 1**
Awarding body:
 IMIAL

Vehicle Fitting Operations – Level 1
Awarding body:
 IMIAL

Vehicle Maintenance – Level 1
Awarding body:
 IMIAL

**Vehicle Maintenance and Repair –
Level 1**
Awarding body:
 IMIAL

**Vehicle Maintenance and Repair –
Level 2**
Awarding body:
 City & Guilds

**Vehicle Systems and Body and Paint
Maintenance – Entry Level**
Awarding body:
 City & Guilds

**Welcome Host (Customer Service) –
Level 2**
Awarding body:
 City & Guilds

BTEC Award

Transporting Passengers by Taxi and Private Hire – Level 2
Awarding body:
EDEXCEL

Vehicle Immobilisation – Level 2
Awarding body:
EDEXCEL

BTEC Certificate

Road Freight Logistics – Level 3
Awarding body:
EDEXCEL

BTEC First Certificate

Vehicle Technology – Level 2
Awarding body:
EDEXCEL

BTEC First Diploma

Vehicle Technology – Level 2
Awarding body:
EDEXCEL

BTEC Higher National Certificate

Vehicle Operations Management – Level 5
Awarding body:
EDEXCEL

BTEC Higher National Diploma

Vehicle Operations Management – Level 5
Awarding body:
EDEXCEL

BTEC National Award

Vehicle Technology – Level 3
Awarding body:
EDEXCEL

BTEC National Certificate

Vehicle Technology – Level 3
Awarding body:
EDEXCEL

BTEC National Diploma

Vehicle Technology – Level 3
Awarding body:
EDEXCEL

Certificate

Advanced Automotive Diagnostic Techniques – Level 4
Awarding body:
City & Guilds

Air Cabin Crew (New Entrant) – Level 2
Awarding body:
City & Guilds

Automotive Air Conditioning and Climate Control (EC842-2006) – Level 3
Awarding body:
IMIAL

Automotive Pre-Vocational Learning – Level 2
Awarding body:
IMIAL

Aviation Operations on the Ground – Level 2
Awarding body:
City & Guilds

Commercial Moving – Level 2
Awarding body:
EDEXCEL

De-icing aircraft – Level 2
Awarding body:
City & Guilds

Defensive Driving – Level 2
Awarding body:
EDI

**International Passenger Transport –
Level 3**
Awarding body:
OCR

International Road Haulage – Level 3
Awarding body:
OCR

**Introduction to Vehicle Technology –
Entry Level**
Awarding body:
IMIAL

**Marine Vessel Support For Seagoing
Deckhands – Level 2**
Awarding body:
EDEXCEL

**Mobile Air Conditioning Systems –
Level 3**
Awarding body:
City & Guilds

**Motor Vehicle and Road User Studies –
Entry Level**
Awarding body:
WJEC

Motor Vehicle Studies – Level 1
Awarding body:
ABC

National Passenger Transport – Level 3
Awarding body:
OCR

National Road Haulage – Level 3
Awarding body:
OCR

Road Passenger Transport – Level 2
Awarding body:
EDI

**Roadside Assistance and Recovery –
Level 2**
Awarding body:
City & Guilds
IMIAL

**Roadside Assistance and Recovery –
Level 3**
Awarding body:
City & Guilds

**Specialised Plant and Machinery
Operations – Level 1**
Awarding body:
CSkills Awards

The Aviation Environment – Level 2
Awarding body:
City & Guilds

**Transport Engineering and Maintenance
– Level 2**
Awarding body:
EDI

**Transport Engineering and Maintenance
– Level 3**
Awarding body:
EDI

**Transport Engineering Maintenance for
Passenger Carrying Vehicles – Level 2**
Awarding body:
IMIAL

**Transportation of Petrochemicals by
Road – Level 2**
Awarding body:
PAA\VQSET

**Travel and Tourism Communication
Skills – Ground and Cabin Crew
Pathway – Level 2**
Awarding body:
ESB

**Travel and Tourism Communication
Skills – Ground and Cabin Crew
Pathway – Level 3**
Awarding body:
ESB

Travel Planning – Level 5
Awarding body:
OU

**Vehicle Body and Paint Operations –
Level 1**
Awarding body:
City & Guilds

**Vehicle Body and Paint Operations –
Level 2**
Awarding body:
   City & Guilds
   IMIAL

**Vehicle Body and Paint Operations –
Level 3**
Awarding body:
   City & Guilds

Vehicle Fitting Operations – Level 1
Awarding body:
   City & Guilds

Vehicle Fitting Operations – Level 2
Awarding body:
   City & Guilds
   IMIAL

Vehicle Fitting Operations – Level 3
Awarding body:
   City & Guilds

Vehicle Maintenance – Level 1
Awarding body:
   City & Guilds
   IMIAL

**Vehicle Maintenance and Repair –
Level 2**
Awarding body:
   City & Guilds
   IMIAL

**Vehicle Maintenance and Repair –
Level 3**
Awarding body:
   City & Guilds

Vehicle Parts Operations – Level 2
Awarding body:
   City & Guilds
   IMIAL

Vehicle Parts Operations – Level 3
Awarding body:
   City & Guilds

Diploma

Air Cabin Crew (New Entrant) – Level 2
Awarding body:
   City & Guilds

**Automotive Maintenance and Repair –
Level 2**
Awarding body:
   City & Guilds
   IMIAL

**Automotive Master Technicians –
Level 4**
Awarding body:
   IMIAL

**Introduction to Vehicle Technology –
Entry Level**
Awarding body:
   IMIAL

Motor Vehicle Studies – Level 1
Awarding body:
   ABC

**Roadside Assistance and Recovery –
Level 2**
Awarding body:
   City & Guilds

**Roadside Assistance and Recovery –
Level 3**
Awarding body:
   City & Guilds
   IMIAL

The Aviation Environment – Level 2
Awarding body:
   City & Guilds

**Transport Engineering Maintenance for
Passenger Carrying Vehicles – Level 3**
Awarding body:
   IMIAL

**Vehicle Body and Paint Operations –
Level 1**
Awarding body:
   City & Guilds

**Vehicle Body and Paint Operations –
Level 2**
Awarding body:
   City & Guilds

**Vehicle Body and Paint Operations –
Level 3**
Awarding body:
   City & Guilds
   IMIAL

Vehicle Fitting Operations – Level 1
Awarding body:
    City & Guilds

Vehicle Fitting Operations – Level 2
Awarding body:
    City & Guilds

Vehicle Fitting Operations – Level 3
Awarding body:
    City & Guilds
    IMIAL

Vehicle Maintenance – Level 1
Awarding body:
    City & Guilds
    IMIAL

Vehicle Maintenance and Repair – Level 2
Awarding body:
    City & Guilds

Vehicle Maintenance and Repair – Level 3
Awarding body:
    City & Guilds
    IMIAL

Vehicle Parts Operations – Level 3
Awarding body:
    IMIAL

Intermediate Certificate

Specialised Plant and Machinery Operations – Level 2
Awarding body:
    CSkills Awards
    Lantra Awards

IVQ Advanced Diploma

Diagnostic Techniques – Level 3
Awarding body:
    City & Guilds

Vehicle Maintenance and Repair – Level 3
Awarding body:
    City & Guilds

IVQ Advanced Technician Diploma

Diagnostic Techniques – Level 5
Awarding body:
    City & Guilds

Motor Vehicle Engineering – Level 5
Awarding body:
    City & Guilds

Motor Vehicle Management – Level 5
Awarding body:
    City & Guilds

IVQ Certificate

Motor Vehicle Systems – Level 1
Awarding body:
    City & Guilds

Vehicle Maintenance and Repair – Level 1
Awarding body:
    City & Guilds

IVQ Diploma

Motor Vehicle Systems – Level 2
Awarding body:
    City & Guilds

Vehicle Maintenance and Repair – Level 2
Awarding body:
    City & Guilds

IVQ Specialist Advanced Diploma

Vehicle Maintenance and Repair – Level 3
Awarding body:
    City & Guilds

IVQ Specialist Certificate

Vehicle Maintenance and Repair – Level 1
Awarding body:
  City & Guilds

IVQ Specialist Diploma

Vehicle Maintenance and Repair – Level 2
Awarding body:
  City & Guilds

IVQ Technician Certificate

Motor Vehicle Systems – Level 2
Awarding body:
  City & Guilds

IVQ Technician Diploma

Motor Vehicle Systems – Level 3
Awarding body:
  City & Guilds

National Award

Vehicle Maintenance and Repair – Level 1
Awarding body:
  IMIAL

National Certificate

Vehicle Maintenance and Repair – Level 2
Awarding body:
  IMIAL

National Diploma

Vehicle Maintenance and Repair – Level 3
Awarding body:
  IMIAL

National Vocational Qualification

Aviation Operations in the Air – Cabin Crew – Level 2
Awarding body:
  City & Guilds
  EAL

Aviation Operations in the Air – Cabin Crew – Level 3
Awarding body:
  City & Guilds
  EAL

Carry and Deliver Goods – Level 2
Awarding body:
  CSkills Awards

Co-ordinating Aviation Operations on the Ground – Level 3
Awarding body:
  City & Guilds
  EAL

Driving Goods Vehicles – Level 2
Awarding body:
  CSkills Awards

Driving Instruction – Level 3
Awarding body:
  EDEXCEL
  EDI

Managing in Road Passenger Transport – Level 3
Awarding body:
  EDEXCEL

Managing in Road Passenger Transport – Level 4
Awarding body:
  EDEXCEL

Marine Engineering Operations – Level 3
Awarding body:
  EDEXCEL

Marine Engineering Operations – Level 4
Awarding body:
  EDEXCEL

Marine Vessel Operations – Level 3
Awarding body:
EDEXCEL

Marine Vessel Operations – Level 4
Awarding body:
EDEXCEL

Marine Vessel Support – Level 2
Awarding body:
EDEXCEL

Passenger Carrying Vehicle Driving (Bus and Coach) – Level 2
Awarding body:
City & Guilds
EDEXCEL
EDI
SQA

Plant Operations – Level 2
Awarding body:
EDI

Port Operations – Level 2
Awarding body:
EAL

Providing Aviation Operations on the Ground – Level 2
Awarding body:
City & Guilds
EAL

Rail Operations Supervisory – Level 3
Awarding body:
City & Guilds

Rail Transport Operations (Control Room Operations) – Level 2
Awarding body:
City & Guilds

Rail Transport Operations (Driving) – Level 2
Awarding body:
City & Guilds

Rail Transport Operations (Passenger Services) – Level 2
Awarding body:
City & Guilds

Rail Transport Operations (Shunting) – Level 2
Awarding body:
City & Guilds

Rail Transport Operations (Signal Operations) – Level 2
Awarding body:
City & Guilds

Railway Engineering – Level 1
Awarding body:
City & Guilds

Railway Engineering – Level 2
Awarding body:
City & Guilds

Railway Engineering – Level 3
Awarding body:
City & Guilds

Road Passenger Transport Operations – Level 2
Awarding body:
EDEXCEL
EDI

Road Passenger Transport Operations – Level 3
Awarding body:
EDEXCEL
EDI

Road Passenger Vehicle Driving – Level 2
Awarding body:
City & Guilds
EDEXCEL
EDI
NCFE
SQA

Roadside Assistance and Recovery – Level 2
Awarding body:
City & Guilds
IMIAL

Roadside Assistance and Recovery – Level 3
Awarding body:
City & Guilds
IMIAL

Specialised Plant and Machinery Operations (Lifting and Transferring) – Level 2
Awarding body:
City & Guilds
EDEXCEL

Supervision of Port Operations – Level 3
Awarding body:
EAL

Traffic Office – Level 2
Awarding body:
EDEXCEL
SQA

Traffic Office – Level 3
Awarding body:
EDEXCEL
SQA

Transport Engineering and Maintenance – Level 1
Awarding body:
EDI

Transport Engineering and Maintenance – Level 2
Awarding body:
EDI
IMIAL

Transport Engineering and Maintenance – Level 3
Awarding body:
EDI
IMIAL

Vehicle Body and Paint Operations – Level 2
Awarding body:
City & Guilds
IMIAL

Vehicle Body and Paint Operations – Level 3
Awarding body:
City & Guilds
IMIAL

Vehicle Fitting Operations – Level 1
Awarding body:
City & Guilds
IMIAL

Vehicle Fitting Operations – Level 2
Awarding body:
City & Guilds
IMIAL

Vehicle Fitting Operations – Level 3
Awarding body:
City & Guilds
IMIAL

Vehicle Maintenance and Repair – Level 2
Awarding body:
City & Guilds
EAL
IMIAL

Vehicle Maintenance and Repair – Level 3
Awarding body:
City & Guilds
IMIAL

Vehicle Parts Operations – Level 2
Awarding body:
City & Guilds
IMIAL

Vehicle Parts Operations – Level 3
Awarding body:
City & Guilds
IMIAL

Weighbridge Operations – Level 2
Awarding body:
MPQC
PAA\VQSET

Health, Public Services and Care

Child Development and Well Being

Award

Caring for Children – Entry Level
Awarding body:
   City & Guilds
   EDEXCEL

Caring for Children – Level 1
Awarding body:
   EDEXCEL

Child Care and Education – Level 2
Awarding body:
   CACHE

Child Care and Education – Level 3
Awarding body:
   CACHE

Early Years and Child Care for Playworkers – Level 3
Awarding body:
   CACHE
   City & Guilds

Getting Started in a Pre-school Setting – Level 1
Awarding body:
   CACHE

Health and Social Care – Entry Level
Awarding body:
   City & Guilds

Playwork – Level 2
Awarding body:
   CACHE

Playwork – Level 3
Awarding body:
   CACHE

Playwork for Early Years and Child Care Workers – Level 3
Awarding body:
   CACHE
   City & Guilds

Playwork Principles into Practice – Level 2
Awarding body:
   SQA

Safeguarding Children and Young People – Level 2
Awarding body:
   NCFE

Safeguarding Children and Young People – Level 3
Awarding body:
   City & Guilds

BTEC Certificate

Children's Care, Learning and Development – Level 2
Awarding body:
   EDEXCEL

Children's Care, Learning and Development – Level 3
Awarding body:
   EDEXCEL

BTEC First Certificate

Children's Care, Learning and Development – Level 2
Awarding body:
   EDEXCEL

BTEC First Diploma

Children's Care, Learning and Development – Level 2
Awarding body:
 EDEXCEL

BTEC Higher National Certificate

Advanced Practice in Work with Children and Families – Level 5
Awarding body:
 EDEXCEL

BTEC Higher National Diploma

Advanced Practice in Work with Children and Families – Level 5
Awarding body:
 EDEXCEL

BTEC National Award

Children's Care, Learning and Development – Level 3
Awarding body:
 EDEXCEL

BTEC National Certificate

Children's Care, Learning and Development – Level 3
Awarding body:
 EDEXCEL

BTEC National Diploma

Children's Care, Learning and Development – Level 3
Awarding body:
 EDEXCEL

BTEC Professional Diploma

Specialised Play for Sick Children and Young People – Level 4
Awarding body:
 EDEXCEL

Certificate

Caring for Children – Level 1
Awarding body:
 City & Guilds
 EDEXCEL

Child Care and Education – Level 2
Awarding body:
 CACHE

Child Care and Education – Level 3
Awarding body:
 CACHE

Child Development – Entry Level
Awarding body:
 OCR

Childcare – Entry Level
Awarding body:
 WJEC

Children's Care, Learning and Development – Level 2
Awarding body:
 CACHE
 City & Guilds
 EDI

Children's Care, Learning and Development – Level 3
Awarding body:
 CACHE
 City & Guilds
 EDI

Developing Skills for Early Years Practice – Level 2
Awarding body:
 NCFE

Developing Skills for Working with Children and Young People – Level 2
Awarding body:
 NCFE

Early Years Care and Education (Welsh Medium) – Level 2
Awarding body:
   CACHE

Early Years Foundation Stage Practice – Level 3
Awarding body:
   CACHE
   City & Guilds
   NCFE

Early Years Practice – Level 4
Awarding body:
   OU

First Aid for those Caring for Children – Level 2
Awarding body:
   EDI

Home Economics: Child Development – Entry Level
Awarding body:
   AQA

Management of Quality Standards in Children's Services – Level 4
Awarding body:
   CACHE

Playwork – Level 2
Awarding body:
   CACHE
   City & Guilds

Playwork – Level 3
Awarding body:
   CACHE
   City & Guilds

Playwork Principles into Practice – Level 2
Awarding body:
   SQA

Pre-School Practice – Level 2
Awarding body:
   CACHE

Preparation for Childcare – Entry Level
Awarding body:
   CACHE

Professional Development in Work with Children and Young People – Level 3
Awarding body:
   CACHE

Safeguarding Children and Young People – Level 3
Awarding body:
   City & Guilds

Specialist Leaders of Behaviour and Attendance of Children and Young People – Level 3
Awarding body:
   City & Guilds

Supporting Playwork Practice – Level 2
Awarding body:
   CACHE

Work with Children – Level 3
Awarding body:
   City & Guilds

Diploma

Caring for Children – Level 1
Awarding body:
   EDEXCEL

Child Care and Education – Level 2
Awarding body:
   CACHE

Child Care and Education – Level 3
Awarding body:
   CACHE

Early Years Care and Education (Welsh Medium) – Level 3
Awarding body:
   CACHE

Home-based Childcare – Level 3
Awarding body:
   CACHE

Playgroup Practice in Wales (DPPW) – Level 3
Awarding body:
   CACHE

Playwork – Level 2
Awarding body:
CACHE
City & Guilds

Playwork – Level 3
Awarding body:
CACHE
City & Guilds

Playwork Principles into Practice – Level 2
Awarding body:
SQA

Pre-school Practice – Level 3
Awarding body:
CACHE

Specialist Leaders of Behaviour and Attendance of Children and Young People – Level 4
Awarding body:
City & Guilds

Foundation Award

Caring for Children – Level 1
Awarding body:
CACHE

Higher Professional Diploma

Early Years – Level 4
Awarding body:
City & Guilds

National Vocational Qualification

Children's Care, Learning and Development – Level 2
Awarding body:
CACHE
City & Guilds
EDEXCEL
EDI

Children's Care, Learning and Development – Level 3
Awarding body:
CACHE
City & Guilds
EDEXCEL
EDI

Children's Care, Learning and Development – Level 4
Awarding body:
CACHE
City & Guilds
EDEXCEL
EDI

Playwork – Level 2
Awarding body:
CACHE
City & Guilds
EDEXCEL
EDI

Playwork – Level 3
Awarding body:
CACHE
City & Guilds
EDEXCEL
EDI

Playwork – Level 4
Awarding body:
City & Guilds
EDEXCEL
EDI

Health and Social Care

Advanced Diploma

Society, Health and Development – Level 3
Awarding body:
AQA
City & Guilds
EDEXCEL
OCR

The Theory and Practice of Counselling (Therapeutic Work) – Level 4
Awarding body:
ABC

Award

An Introduction to the Hair and Beauty Sector – Entry Level
Awarding body:
ITEC

An Introduction to the Hair and Beauty Sector – Level 1
Awarding body:
ITEC

Business Practice for Complementary Therapies – Level 3
Awarding body:
VTCT

Buying or Renting a Home – Level 1
Awarding body:
EDI

Community Development – Level 1
Awarding body:
NOCN

Conflict Resolution and Personal Safety – Level 2
Awarding body:
CIEH

Counselling Skills and Theory – Level 3
Awarding body:
NCFE

Defusing Difficult Situations in the Workplace – Level 2
Awarding body:
ABC

Developing Information, Advice or Guidance – Level 2
Awarding body:
NOCN

Effective Augmentative and Alternative Communication – Entry Level
Awarding body:
City & Guilds

Effective Listening Skills – Level 2
Awarding body:
CPCAB

Emergency First Aid at Work – Level 2
Awarding body:
CIEH
EDI
FAQ
HABC
ITC
Lantra Awards
STA

Emergency First Aid for Sport – Level 2
Awarding body:
STA

Face, Neck and Chest Massage for Complementary Therapies – Level 2
Awarding body:
VTCT

Faith Community Development – Level 1
Awarding body:
NOCN

Faith Community Development – Level 2
Awarding body:
NOCN

First Steps in Childcare – Entry Level
Awarding body:
    EDEXCEL

Hazard Awareness – Level 1
Awarding body:
    RSPH

Head and Scalp Massage for Complementary Therapies – Level 2
Awarding body:
    VTCT

Health and Safety – Level 1
Awarding body:
    ASCENTIS

Health and Safety for Complementary Therapies – Level 3
Awarding body:
    VTCT

Health and Safety for Supervisors in the Workplace – Level 3
Awarding body:
    RSPH

Health and Safety for the Workplace – Level 2
Awarding body:
    City & Guilds

Health and Safety in Health and Social Care – Level 2
Awarding body:
    CIEH

Health and Safety in the Workplace – Level 2
Awarding body:
    CIEH
    EDI
    HABC
    RSPH

Health and Safety in the Workplace – Level 3
Awarding body:
    CIEH

Health and Safety in the Workplace – Level 4
Awarding body:
    CIEH

Health and Social Care – Entry Level
Awarding body:
    EDEXCEL

Health and Social Care – Level 1
Awarding body:
    EDEXCEL

Health Promotion – Level 2
Awarding body:
    RSPH

Healthy Eating – Level 1
Awarding body:
    EDEXCEL

Healthy Eating and Well Being for the Complementary Therapy Client – Level 3
Awarding body:
    ITEC

Healthy Eating and Well-being for the Complementary Client – Level 3
Awarding body:
    VTCT

Helping Skills – Level 2
Awarding body:
    NCFE

Introduction to Childcare – Level 1
Awarding body:
    EDEXCEL

Less Common Pathology for Complementary Therapies – Level 3
Awarding body:
    VTCT

Listening Support Skills – Level 2
Awarding body:
    CPCAB

Lower Leg and Foot, Forearm and Hand Massage for Complementary Therapies – Level 2
Awarding body:
    VTCT

Managing Conflict in the Workplace – Level 2
Awarding body:
    ABC

Manual Handling – Principles and Practice – Level 2
Awarding body:
   CIEH

Paediatric First Aid – Level 2
Awarding body:
   FAQ

Preventing and Managing Physical Assault at Work – Level 2
Awarding body:
   ABC

Prevention and Control of Infection – Level 2
Awarding body:
   NCFE

Principles of Risk Assessment – Level 2
Awarding body:
   CIEH

Promoting the Mental Health and Well-being of Older People – Level 2
Awarding body:
   City & Guilds

Promoting the Mental Health and Well-being of Older People (Introductory) – Level 3
Awarding body:
   City & Guilds

Recognising and Responding to Substance Misuse – Level 2
Awarding body:
   City & Guilds

Risk Assessment Principles and Practice – Level 3
Awarding body:
   CIEH

School Choice Advisers – Level 2
Awarding body:
   ABC

Supervising Health and Safety in the Workplace – Level 3
Awarding body:
   HABC

Supporting People with a Learning Disability (induction) – Level 2
Awarding body:
   City & Guilds
   NOCN

Supporting People with a Learning Disability (induction) – Level 3
Awarding body:
   City & Guilds
   NOCN

Tackling Substance Misuse – Level 3
Awarding body:
   NOCN

The Prevention and Control of Infection – Level 2
Awarding body:
   ASCENTIS
   City & Guilds
   EDI
   FAQ

Understanding HIV and AIDS – Level 2
Awarding body:
   City & Guilds

Understanding Substance Misuse – Level 2
Awarding body:
   CPCAB

Working with Substance Misuse – Level 3
Awarding body:
   City & Guilds

Working with Substance Misuse – Level 4
Awarding body:
   City & Guilds

Working with Vulnerable Young People – Level 3
Awarding body:
   ABC

Working with Vulnerable Young People – Level 4
Awarding body:
   ABC

**Workplace Hazard Awareness –
Entry Level**
Awarding body:
  BSC

BTEC Award

Dementia Care – Level 2
Awarding body:
  EDEXCEL

Foster Care – Level 2
Awarding body:
  EDEXCEL

Foster Care – Level 3
Awarding body:
  EDEXCEL

**Health and Safety in the Workplace –
Level 3**
Awarding body:
  EDEXCEL

**Induction to Supporting People who
have Learning Disabilities – Level 2**
Awarding body:
  EDEXCEL

**Integrated Practice within Childrens'
Services – Level 3**
Awarding body:
  EDEXCEL

**Introduction to Counselling Skills –
Level 2**
Awarding body:
  EDEXCEL

Nutrition Awareness – Level 2
Awarding body:
  EDEXCEL

Paediatric First Aid – Level 2
Awarding body:
  EDEXCEL

**Prevention and Control of Infection –
Level 2**
Awarding body:
  EDEXCEL

**Professional Development for Working
in Children's Services – Level 3**
Awarding body:
  EDEXCEL

**Professional Development for Working
in Childrens' Services – Level 2**
Awarding body:
  EDEXCEL

**Safe Learning in the Workplace –
Level 2**
Awarding body:
  EDEXCEL

**Signing with Babies and Young Children
– Level 2**
Awarding body:
  EDEXCEL

**Signing with Babies and Young Children
– Level 3**
Awarding body:
  EDEXCEL

**Society, Health and Development –
Level 2**
Awarding body:
  EDEXCEL

**Society, Health and Development
(General) – Level 3**
Awarding body:
  EDEXCEL

**Supervising the Health and Safety of
Learners in the Workplace – Level 3**
Awarding body:
  EDEXCEL

Support Work in Social Care – Level 2
Awarding body:
  EDEXCEL

Working with Medication – Level 3
Awarding body:
  EDEXCEL

**Working with Substance Misuse –
Level 3**
Awarding body:
  EDEXCEL

**Working with Substance Misuse –
Level 4**
Awarding body:
EDEXCEL

BTEC Certificate

Ambulance Care Assistance – Level 2
Awarding body:
EDEXCEL

Health and Social Care – Level 2
Awarding body:
EDEXCEL

Health and Social Care – Level 3
Awarding body:
EDEXCEL

**Society, Health and Development –
Level 2**
Awarding body:
EDEXCEL

Working in the Health Sector – Level 2
Awarding body:
EDEXCEL

Working in the Health Sector – Level 3
Awarding body:
EDEXCEL

**Working with Substance Misuse –
Level 3**
Awarding body:
EDEXCEL

**Working with Substance Misuse –
Level 4**
Awarding body:
EDEXCEL

BTEC Diploma

Developing Counselling Skills – Level 3
Awarding body:
EDEXCEL

**Society, Health and Development
(General) – Level 3**
Awarding body:
EDEXCEL

**Society, Health and Development
(Health) – Level 3**
Awarding body:
EDEXCEL

BTEC Extended Certificate

**Society, Health and Development –
Level 2**
Awarding body:
EDEXCEL

**Society, Health and Development
(General) – Level 3**
Awarding body:
EDEXCEL

BTEC First Certificate

Health and Social Care – Level 2
Awarding body:
EDEXCEL

BTEC First Diploma

Health and Social Care – Level 2
Awarding body:
EDEXCEL

BTEC Higher National Certificate

Health and Social Care – Level 5
Awarding body:
EDEXCEL

BTEC Higher National Diploma

Health and Social Care – Level 5
Awarding body:
EDEXCEL

BTEC National Award

Health and Social Care – Level 3
Awarding body:
EDEXCEL

BTEC National Certificate

Health and Social Care – Level 3
Awarding body:
EDEXCEL

BTEC National Diploma

Health and Social Care – Level 3
Awarding body:
EDEXCEL

Certificate

Administration of Medicines – Level 3
Awarding body:
ASCENTIS

Administration of Medicines in Care Settings – Level 2
Awarding body:
FAQ

An Introduction to the Hair and Beauty Sector – Level 1
Awarding body:
ITEC

Anatomy and Physiology for Complementary Therapies – Level 2
Awarding body:
City & Guilds
VTCT

Basic First Aid – Level 2
Awarding body:
FAQ

Cognitive Behavioural Therapeutic Skills and Theory – Level 5
Awarding body:
CPCAB

Community Development – Level 1
Awarding body:
NOCN

Community Development – Level 2
Awarding body:
NOCN

Community Development – Level 3
Awarding body:
NOCN

Community Mental Health Care (for people aged 18-65 years) – Level 3
Awarding body:
City & Guilds

Community Mental Health Work – Level 2
Awarding body:
City & Guilds

Construction Health and Safety – Level 3
Awarding body:
NEBOSH

Contact Lens Practice – Level 6
Awarding body:
ABDO

COSHH Risk Assessment – Level 2
Awarding body:
BSC

Counselling – Level 3
Awarding body:
AQA

Counselling Concepts – Level 2
Awarding body:
ABC

Counselling Skills – Level 2
Awarding body:
AQA
CPCAB

Counselling Skills – Level 3
Awarding body:
ABC

Counselling Studies – Level 3
Awarding body:
CPCAB

Dementia Awareness – Level 2
Awarding body:
NCFE

Dementia Care – Level 2
Awarding body:
EDI
FAQ

**Developing Environmental Awareness –
Level 2**
Awarding body:
　ASCENTIS

**Developing Information, Advice or
Guidance – Level 2**
Awarding body:
　NOCN

**Developing Personal Safety and Security
Skills – Level 2**
Awarding body:
　EDI

**Diabetic Retinopathy Screening
(Administration) – Level 3**
Awarding body:
　City & Guilds

**Diabetic Retinopathy Screening
(Grading) – Level 3**
Awarding body:
　City & Guilds

**Diabetic Retinopathy Screening
(Imaging) – Level 3**
Awarding body:
　City & Guilds

**Drug and Substance Awareness –
Level 1**
Awarding body:
　EDI

Drug Awareness – Level 1
Awarding body:
　CCEA
　NCFE

**Drug Awareness Studies and their
Applications – Level 2**
Awarding body:
　CCEA
　NCFE

DSE Risk Assessment – Level 2
Awarding body:
　BSC

**Faith Community Development –
Level 1**
Awarding body:
　NOCN

**Faith Community Development –
Level 2**
Awarding body:
　NOCN

Fire Risk Assessment – Level 2
Awarding body:
　BSC
　NCFE

**Fire Safety and Risk Management –
Level 3**
Awarding body:
　NEBOSH

First Aid for Sport – Level 2
Awarding body:
　ITC

**Head and Scalp Massage within
Complementary Therapies – Level 2**
Awarding body:
　City & Guilds

Health and Safety – Level 1
Awarding body:
　ASCENTIS

Health and Safety at Work – Level 1
Awarding body:
　BSC

**Health and Safety in the Workplace –
Level 2**
Awarding body:
　ABC
　ASCENTIS

Health and Social Care – Level 1
Awarding body:
　EDEXCEL

Health and Social Care – Level 2
Awarding body:
　City & Guilds
　EDI
　OCR

Health and Social Care – Level 3
Awarding body:
　City & Guilds
　EDI
　OCR

Health Trainers – Level 3
Awarding body:
City & Guilds

Housing – Level 4
Awarding body:
CIH

Housing (NVQ) – Level 3
Awarding body:
City & Guilds

Independent Advocacy – Level 3
Awarding body:
City & Guilds

Information, Advice or Guidance – Level 3
Awarding body:
NOCN

Introduction to Caring for Adults – Level 1
Awarding body:
EDI

Introduction to Counselling Concepts – Level 2
Awarding body:
AQA

Introduction to Counselling Skills – Level 2
Awarding body:
CPCAB

Introduction to Youth Work – Level 1
Awarding body:
ABC

Manual Handling Risk Assessment – Level 2
Awarding body:
BSC

Mental Health Awareness – Level 1
Awarding body:
NCFE

Mental Health Awareness – Level 2
Awarding body:
ASCENTIS

Mental Health Helpline Workers – Level 2
Awarding body:
City & Guilds

Moving and Handling – Level 2
Awarding body:
EDI

Non-Care Staff in the Care Environment – Level 2
Awarding body:
EDI

Non-Care Workers in Care Settings – Level 2
Awarding body:
NCFE

Nutrition and Health – Level 2
Awarding body:
NCFE

Occupational Health and Safety – Level 2
Awarding body:
NCFE

Occupational Health and Safety – Level 3
Awarding body:
NEBOSH

Occupational Safety and Health – Level 3
Awarding body:
BSC

Optical Practice Support – Level 2
Awarding body:
WCSM

Optical Practice Support – Level 3
Awarding body:
WCSM

Outdoor First Aid – Level 2
Awarding body:
ITC

Paediatric First Aid – Level 2
Awarding body:
FAQ

Palliative Care – Level 3
Awarding body:
    NCFE

Personal Safety Awareness – Level 1
Awarding body:
    EDI

**Preparing for Work in the Care Sector –
Entry Level**
Awarding body:
    City & Guilds

**Promoting the Mental Health and
Well-being of Older People – Level 3**
Awarding body:
    City & Guilds

Risk Assessment – Level 2
Awarding body:
    BSC

Safe Handling of Medicines – Level 2
Awarding body:
    NCFE

**Safer Moving and Handling (Including
People) – Level 2**
Awarding body:
    NCFE

Sports First Aid – Level 2
Awarding body:
    FAQ

Supervising Staff Safely – Level 2
Awarding body:
    BSC

**Supporting the Development Needs of
Vulnerable People – Level 2**
Awarding body:
    City & Guilds

Supporting Youth Work – Level 2
Awarding body:
    City & Guilds

Supporting Youth Work – Level 3
Awarding body:
    City & Guilds

**The Introduction to Healthy Eating –
Level 2**
Awarding body:
    City & Guilds

**The Managing and Safe Handling of
Medicines – Level 2**
Awarding body:
    EDI

Training for Youth Work – Level 3
Awarding body:
    NOCN

**Understanding Substance Misuse –
Level 3**
Awarding body:
    ASCENTIS

Working in the Health Sector – Level 2
Awarding body:
    City & Guilds
    EDI
    NCFE

Working in the Health Sector – Level 3
Awarding body:
    City & Guilds
    EDI
    NCFE

**Working with People who have Learning
Disabilities – Level 2**
Awarding body:
    City & Guilds

**Working with People who have Learning
Disabilities – Level 3**
Awarding body:
    City & Guilds

**Working with People with Mental
Health Issues – Level 2**
Awarding body:
    NCFE

**Working with Substance Misuse –
Level 3**
Awarding body:
    City & Guilds

**Working with Substance Misuse –
Level 4**
Awarding body:
    City & Guilds

**Working with Vulnerable Young People
– Level 3**
Awarding body:
    ABC

**Working with Vulnerable Young People
– Level 4**
Awarding body:
  ABC

Youth Work – Level 2
Awarding body:
  ABC
  City & Guilds

Youth Work – Level 3
Awarding body:
  City & Guilds
  NOCN

Diploma

**Additional Aromatherapy Techniques –
Level 3**
Awarding body:
  VTCT

**Additional Reflexology Techniques –
Level 3**
Awarding body:
  VTCT

**Advanced Contact Lens Practice –
Level 7**
Awarding body:
  ABDO

**Anatomy, Physiology and Pathology –
Level 3**
Awarding body:
  City & Guilds
  ITEC

**Anatomy, Physiology and Pathology for
Complementary Therapies – Level 3**
Awarding body:
  VTCT

Aromatherapy – Level 3
Awarding body:
  City & Guilds
  ITEC
  VTCT

Aromatherapy Techniques – Level 3
Awarding body:
  City & Guilds
  ITEC

Basic Aromatherapy – Level 2
Awarding body:
  VTCT

**Basic Aromatherapy Techniques –
Level 2**
Awarding body:
  City & Guilds

**Basic Massage for Complementary
Therapies – Level 2**
Awarding body:
  VTCT

Basic Massage Techniques – Level 2
Awarding body:
  City & Guilds

Basic Reflexology – Level 2
Awarding body:
  VTCT

Basic Reflexology Techniques – Level 2
Awarding body:
  City & Guilds

Body Massage – Level 3
Awarding body:
  City & Guilds
  VTCT

**Body Massage for Complementary
Therapies – Level 3**
Awarding body:
  VTCT

Body Massage Techniques – Level 3
Awarding body:
  City & Guilds

Cervical Cytology – Level 3
Awarding body:
  City & Guilds

Complementary Therapies – Level 2
Awarding body:
  CIBTAC
  City & Guilds
  ITEC
  VTCT

Complementary Therapies – Level 3
Awarding body:
CIBTAC
City & Guilds
ITEC
VTCT

Complementary Therapies Techniques – Level 3
Awarding body:
City & Guilds

Complementary Therapy Techniques – Level 3
Awarding body:
ITEC

Counselling – Level 3
Awarding body:
AQA

Counselling Practice – Level 5
Awarding body:
AQA

Diabetic Retinopathy Screening – Level 3
Awarding body:
City & Guilds

Health and Social Care – Level 1
Awarding body:
EDEXCEL

Health, Safety, Security and Employment Standards – Level 3
Awarding body:
VTCT

Holistic Massage – Level 3
Awarding body:
ITEC

Holistic Therapies – Level 3
Awarding body:
VTCT

Housing – Level 4
Awarding body:
CIH

Housing (NVQ) – Level 3
Awarding body:
City & Guilds

Independent Mental Capacity Advocacy – Deprivation of Liberty Safeguards – Level 3
Awarding body:
City & Guilds

Infant and Child Massage – Level 3
Awarding body:
ITEC

Lymphatic Drainage Massage – Level 3
Awarding body:
ITEC

Massage – Level 3
Awarding body:
ITEC

Massage Techniques – Level 3
Awarding body:
ITEC

Non-Medical Nutritional Advice – Level 3
Awarding body:
VTCT

Occupational Health and Safety – Level 6
Awarding body:
NEBOSH

Occupational Safety and Health – Level 6
Awarding body:
BSC

On Site Massage – Level 3
Awarding body:
ITEC

Ophthalmic Dispensing – Level 6
Awarding body:
ABDO

Psychotherapeutic Counselling – Level 5
Awarding body:
CPCAB

Reflexology – Level 3
Awarding body:
ABC
City & Guilds
ITEC
VTCT

Reflexology Techniques – Level 3
Awarding body:
   City & Guilds
   ITEC

Remedial Massage – Level 3
Awarding body:
   VTCT

Thai Massage – Level 3
Awarding body:
   ITEC

The Assessment and Management of Low Vision – Level 6
Awarding body:
   ABDO

The Geometric Optics of Ophthalmic Lens – Level 7
Awarding body:
   ABDO

The Theory and Practice of Counselling – Level 4
Awarding body:
   ABC

Therapeutic Counselling – Level 4
Awarding body:
   CPCAB

Therapeutic Counselling Supervision – Level 6
Awarding body:
   CPCAB

Understanding the Healthcare Environment for Providers of Complementary Therapies – Level 3
Awarding body:
   VTCT

Workplace Massage – Level 3
Awarding body:
   VTCT

Youth Work – Level 3
Awarding body:
   ABC

Foundation Diploma

Society, Health and Development – Level 1
Awarding body:
   AQA
   City & Guilds
   EDEXCEL
   EDI
   OCR

Higher Diploma

Society, Health and Development – Level 2
Awarding body:
   AQA
   City & Guilds
   EDEXCEL
   EDI
   OCR

Higher Professional Diploma

Counselling – Level 4
Awarding body:
   City & Guilds

Health and Well-being – Level 4
Awarding body:
   City & Guilds

Learning Disability Services – Level 4
Awarding body:
   City & Guilds

Introductory Certificate

Health and Social Care – Level 1
Awarding body:
   EDEXCEL

Introductory Diploma

Health and Social Care – Level 1
Awarding body:
   EDEXCEL

IVQ Diploma

Health Care – Level 2
Awarding body:
   City & Guilds

IVQ Specialist Diploma

Health Care – Level 2
Awarding body:
   City & Guilds

National Award

Health and Social Care – Level 1
Awarding body:
   OCR

Health and Social Care – Level 2
Awarding body:
   OCR

National Certificate

Health and Social Care – Level 1
Awarding body:
   OCR

Health and Social Care – Level 2
Awarding body:
   OCR

Health, Social Care and Early Years – Level 3
Awarding body:
   OCR

National Diploma

Health, Social Care and Early Years – Level 3
Awarding body:
   OCR

National Extended Diploma

Health, Social Care and Early Years – Level 3
Awarding body:
   OCR

National First Award

Health and Social Care – Level 1
Awarding body:
   OCR

National Vocational Qualification

Advice and Guidance – Level 3
Awarding body:
   City & Guilds
   EDEXCEL
   EDI
   NCFE
   OCR
   OU
   SQA

Advice and Guidance – Level 4
Awarding body:
   City & Guilds
   EDEXCEL
   EDI
   NCFE
   OCR
   OU

Advice and Guidance Support – Level 2
Awarding body:
   City & Guilds
   EDEXCEL
   EDI
   NCFE
   OCR
   OU
   SQA

Commissioning, Procurement and Contracting for Social Care – Level 3
Awarding body:
   OU

Commissioning, Procurement and Contracting for Social Care – Level 4
Awarding body:
   OU

Commissioning, Procurement and Contracting for Social Care – Level 5
Awarding body:
   OU

Community Development Work – Level 2
Awarding body:
City & Guilds

Community Development Work – Level 3
Awarding body:
City & Guilds

Community Development Work – Level 4
Awarding body:
City & Guilds

Health – Level 2
Awarding body:
City & Guilds
EDEXCEL

Health – Level 3
Awarding body:
City & Guilds
EDEXCEL

Health and Safety Regulation – Level 5
Awarding body:
City & Guilds
OCR

Health and Social Care – Level 2
Awarding body:
CACHE
City & Guilds
EDEXCEL
EDI
NCFE
OCR
OU

Health and Social Care – Level 3
Awarding body:
CACHE
City & Guilds
EDEXCEL
EDI
NCFE
OCR
OU

Health and Social Care – Level 4
Awarding body:
City & Guilds
EDEXCEL
EDI
NCFE
OCR
OU

Health and Social Care (Adults) – Level 3
Awarding body:
CACHE

Housing – Level 2
Awarding body:
City & Guilds

Housing – Level 3
Awarding body:
City & Guilds

Housing – Level 4
Awarding body:
City & Guilds

Leadership and Management for Care Services – Level 4
Awarding body:
City & Guilds
CMI
EDEXCEL
EDI
OCR
OU

Learning, Development and Support Services for Children, Young People and Those who Care for Them – Level 3
Awarding body:
EDEXCEL
OCR

Learning, Development and Support Services for Children, Young People and Those who Care for Them – Level 4
Awarding body:
EDEXCEL
OCR

Management of Health and Safety – Level 5
Awarding body:
City & Guilds
OCR

Occupational Health and Safety – Level 3
Awarding body:
City & Guilds
EAL
NCFE
OCR

Occupational Health and Safety Practice – Level 4
Awarding body:
City & Guilds
NCFE
OCR

Support Services in Health Care – Level 2
Awarding body:
City & Guilds
EDEXCEL
EDI

Youth Work – Level 2
Awarding body:
ABC
City & Guilds

Youth Work – Level 3
Awarding body:
ABC
City & Guilds

Principal Learning

Society, Health & Development – Level 1
Awarding body:
AQA
City & Guilds

Society, Health & Development – Level 2
Awarding body:
AQA
City & Guilds

Society, Health & Development – Level 3
Awarding body:
AQA
City & Guilds

Society, Health and Development – Level 1
Awarding body:
EDEXCEL
EDI
OCR

Society, Health and Development – Level 2
Awarding body:
EDEXCEL
EDI
OCR

Society, Health and Development – Level 3
Awarding body:
EDEXCEL
EDI
OCR

Professional Diploma

Therapeutic Counselling – Level 5
Awarding body:
EDEXCEL

Progression Award

Health and Safety in the Workplace – Level 2
Awarding body:
City & Guilds

Progression Diploma

Society, Health and Development – Level 3
Awarding body:
AQA
City & Guilds
EDEXCEL
EDI
OCR

Medicine and Dentistry

Award

Dental Nursing – Level 3
Awarding body:
City & Guilds

BTEC National Award

Dental Technology – Level 3
Awarding body:
EDEXCEL

BTEC National Diploma

Dental Technology – Level 3
Awarding body:
EDEXCEL

Nursing and Subjects and Vocations Allied to Medicine

BTEC National Certificate

Pharmacy Services – Level 3
Awarding body:
EDEXCEL

Certificate

Pharmacy Services – Level 3
Awarding body:
City & Guilds

Supporting Users of Assistive Technology – Level 2
Awarding body:
City & Guilds

Diploma

Anatomy and Physiology – Level 3
Awarding body:
VTCT

National Vocational Qualification

Dental Nursing – Level 3
Awarding body:
City & Guilds

Pharmacy Services – Level 2
Awarding body:
City & Guilds
EDEXCEL

Pharmacy Services – Level 3
Awarding body:
City & Guilds
EDEXCEL

Public Services

Advanced Certificate

Public Relations – Level 5
Awarding body:
City & Guilds

Advanced Diploma

Public Services – Level 3
Awarding body:
AQA
City & Guilds
EDEXCEL
OCR

Award

Cash and Valuables in Transit – Level 2
Awarding body:
NOCN

CCTV Operations (Public Space Surveillance) – Level 2
Awarding body:
NOCN

Civil Enforcement Officers (Parking) – Level 2
Awarding body:
City & Guilds

Community Action in Housing – Level 2
Awarding body:
CIH

Door Supervision – Level 2
Awarding body:
NOCN

Door Supervision (Northern Ireland) – Level 2
Awarding body:
NOCN

Governance for Housing – Level 4
Awarding body:
CIH

Housing – Level 3
Awarding body:
CIH

Management of Built Assets – Level 2
Awarding body:
CIH

Management of Built Assets – Level 3
Awarding body:
CIH

Principles and Application of Coaching Skills – Level 3
Awarding body:
NOCN

Professional Investigators – Level 3
Awarding body:
EDI

Public Services – Entry Level
Awarding body:
EDEXCEL

Public Services – Level 1
Awarding body:
EDEXCEL

Security Guarding – Level 2
Awarding body:
NOCN

BTEC Award

CCTV Operations (Public Space Surveillance) – Level 2
Awarding body:
EDEXCEL

Community Safety for Accredited Persons – Level 2
Awarding body:
EDEXCEL

Compartment Fire Behaviour Training – Level 3
Awarding body:
EDEXCEL

Disengagement and Non-Restrictive Physical Intervention Skills – Level 2
Awarding body:
EDEXCEL

Disengagement and Physical Intervention Skills – Level 2
Awarding body:
EDEXCEL

Door Supervision – Level 2
Awarding body:
EDEXCEL

Fire and Rescue Services in the Community – Level 2
Awarding body:
EDEXCEL

Security Operations – Level 2
Awarding body:
EDEXCEL

The Delivery of Conflict Management Training – Level 3
Awarding body:
EDEXCEL

BTEC Certificate

Compartment Fire Behaviour Training – Level 3
Awarding body:
EDEXCEL

Emergency Fire Services Operations in the Community – Level 3
Awarding body:
EDEXCEL

Fire and Rescue Services in the Community – Level 2
Awarding body:
EDEXCEL

BTEC Diploma

Fire and Rescue Services in the Community – Level 2
Awarding body:
EDEXCEL

BTEC First Certificate

Public Services – Level 2
Awarding body:
EDEXCEL

BTEC First Diploma

Public Services – Level 2
Awarding body:
EDEXCEL

BTEC Higher National Certificate

Public Services – Level 5
Awarding body:
EDEXCEL

BTEC Higher National Diploma

Public Services – Level 5
Awarding body:
EDEXCEL

BTEC National Award

Central and Local Government – Level 3
Awarding body:
EDEXCEL

Uniformed Public Services – Level 3
Awarding body:
EDEXCEL

BTEC National Certificate

Uniformed Public Services – Level 3
Awarding body:
EDEXCEL

BTEC National Diploma

Uniformed Public Services – Level 3
Awarding body:
EDEXCEL

Certificate

Access to Housing – Level 4
Awarding body:
CIH

CCTV Operatives (Public Space Surveillance) – Level 2
Awarding body:
EDI

CCTV Operators (Public Space Surveillance) – Level 2
Awarding body:
City & Guilds

Close Protection – Level 3
Awarding body:
City & Guilds

Community Justice – Level 3
Awarding body:
City & Guilds

Community Safety for Accredited Persons – Level 2
Awarding body:
City & Guilds
EDI

Conflict Management – Level 2
Awarding body:
City & Guilds
NCFE

Conflict Management – Level 3
Awarding body:
City & Guilds

Deliverers of Conflict Management Training – Level 3
Awarding body:
City & Guilds

Door Supervisors – Level 2
Awarding body:
EDI

Entry to the Uniformed Services – Level 1
Awarding body:
NCFE

Entry to the Uniformed Services – Level 2
Awarding body:
NCFE

Entry to the Uniformed Services – Level 3
Awarding body:
NCFE

Fire Risk Assessment – Level 3
Awarding body:
ABBE

Fire Science and Fire Safety – Level 4
Awarding body:
IFE

Fire Science, Operations and Safety – Level 2
Awarding body:
IFE

Fire Science, Operations, Safety and Management – Level 3
Awarding body:
IFE

Housing – Level 2
Awarding body:
CIH

Housing – Level 3
Awarding body:
CIH

Housing Maintenance – Level 2
Awarding body:
CIOB
CIH

Housing Maintenance – Level 3
Awarding body:
CIOB
CIH

Housing Maintenance Management – Level 4
Awarding body:
CIOB
CIH

Knowledge of Electronic Security and Emergency Systems – Level 2
Awarding body:
City & Guilds

Knowledge of Security and Emergency Alarm Systems – Level 3
Awarding body:
City & Guilds

Licensing Practitioners (Principles of Licensing) – Level 2
Awarding body:
BIIAB

Public Services – Level 1
Awarding body:
EDEXCEL

Security Guards – Level 2
Awarding body:
BIIAB
City & Guilds
EDI

Security Practitioners – Level 2
Awarding body:
City & Guilds
NOCN

Tenant Participation and Neighbourhood Renewal – Level 3
Awarding body:
CIH

Working in the Community – Level 2
Awarding body:
CCEA

Development Award

Work with Offending Behaviour – Level 3
Awarding body:
City & Guilds

Diploma

Fire Science and Fire Safety – Level 3
Awarding body:
IFE

Fire Science and Fire Service Operations. – Level 3
Awarding body:
IFE

Fire Science, Operations and Safety. – Level 3
Awarding body:
IFE

Health Emergency Planning – Level 4
Awarding body:
RSPH

Housing Development – Level 4
Awarding body:
CIOB
CIH

Housing Maintenance and Asset Management – Level 4
Awarding body:
CIOB
CIH

Public Services – Level 1
Awarding body:
EDEXCEL

Foundation Diploma

Public Services – Level 1
Awarding body:
AQA
City & Guilds
EDEXCEL
OCR

Higher Diploma

Public Services – Level 2
Awarding body:
AQA
City & Guilds
EDEXCEL
OCR

Introductory Certificate

Neighbourhood Management – Level 3
Awarding body:
CMI

National Award

Public Services – Level 2
Awarding body:
OCR

National Certificate

CCTV Operators (Public Space Surveillance) – Level 2
Awarding body:
BIIAB

Door Supervisors – Level 2
Awarding body:
BIIAB
City & Guilds

Door Supervisors (Northern Ireland) – Level 2
Awarding body:
BIIAB

Licensing Practitioners (Gambling) – Level 2
Awarding body:
BIIAB

Public Services – Level 2
Awarding body:
OCR

Public Services – Level 3
Awarding body:
OCR

National Diploma

Public Services – Level 3
Awarding body:
OCR

National Extended Diploma

Public Services – Level 3
Awarding body:
OCR

National Vocational Qualification

Community Justice: Community Safety and Crime Reduction – Level 3
Awarding body:
City & Guilds

Community Justice: Community Safety and Crime Reduction – Level 4
Awarding body:
City & Guilds

Community Justice: Work with Offending Behaviour – Level 3
Awarding body:
City & Guilds

Community Justice: Work with Offending Behaviour – Level 4
Awarding body:
City & Guilds

Community Justice: Work with Victims, Survivors and Witnesses – Level 3
Awarding body:
City & Guilds

Community Justice: Work with Victims, Survivors and Witnesses – Level 4
Awarding body:
City & Guilds

Community Wardens – Level 2
Awarding body:
City & Guilds

Controlling Parking Areas – Level 2
Awarding body:
City & Guilds
EDEXCEL

Court Administration – Level 2
Awarding body:
SQA

Custodial Care – Level 2
Awarding body:
City & Guilds
EDEXCEL

Custodial Care – Level 3
Awarding body:
City & Guilds
EDEXCEL

Democratic Services – Level 3
Awarding body:
OU

Democratic Services – Level 4
Awarding body:
OU

Emergency Fire Services – Operations in the Community – Level 3
Awarding body:
EDEXCEL

Emergency Fire Services – Watch Management – Level 3
Awarding body:
EDEXCEL

Fire and Rescue Sector Control Operations – Level 3
Awarding body:
EDEXCEL

Fire Safety – Level 2
Awarding body:
EDEXCEL

Fire Safety – Level 3
Awarding body:
EDEXCEL

Fire Safety – Level 4
Awarding body:
EDEXCEL

Intelligence Analysis – Level 3
Awarding body:
City & Guilds
OCR
OU

Legal Advice – Level 3
Awarding body:
OU

Legal Advice – Level 4
Awarding body:
OU

Local Land Charges and Property Information – Level 3
Awarding body:
City & Guilds

Local Land Charges and Property Information – Level 4
Awarding body:
City & Guilds

Police Operational Management – Level 4
Awarding body:
City & Guilds
CMI
EDEXCEL
OCR

Police Operational Management – Level 5
Awarding body:
CMI
EDEXCEL

Police Organisational Management – Level 4
Awarding body:
City & Guilds
CMI
EDEXCEL

Police Strategic Management – Level 5
Awarding body:
CMI
EDEXCEL

Police Supervisory Management – Level 3
Awarding body:
City & Guilds
CMI
EDEXCEL
OCR

Policing – Level 3
Awarding body:
City & Guilds
EDEXCEL
OCR

Policing – Level 4
Awarding body:
City & Guilds
EDEXCEL
OCR

Providing Security Services – Level 2
Awarding body:
City & Guilds
EDEXCEL
EDI
NCFE

Public Services – Level 2
Awarding body:
City & Guilds
EDEXCEL
SQA

Supporting Legal Advice Provision – Level 2
Awarding body:
OU

Witness Care – Level 3
Awarding body:
NCFE
OU

Youth Justice Services – Level 3
Awarding body:
City & Guilds

Youth Justice Services – Level 4
Awarding body:
City & Guilds

Principal Learning

Public Services – Level 1
Awarding body:
AQA
City & Guilds
EDEXCEL
OCR

Public Services – Level 2
Awarding body:
AQA
City & Guilds
EDEXCEL
OCR

Public Services – Level 3
Awarding body:
AQA
City & Guilds
EDEXCEL
OCR

Progression Diploma

Public Services – Level 3
Awarding body:
AQA
City & Guilds
EDEXCEL
OCR

History, Philosophy and Theology

Archaeology and Archaeological Sciences

National Vocational Qualification

Archaeological Practice – Level 3
Awarding body:
  EDI

Archaeological Practice – Level 4
Awarding body:
  EDI

History

Certificate

History – Entry Level
Awarding body:
  AQA
  CCEA
  EDEXCEL
  OCR
  WJEC

History – Level 1,2
Awarding body:
  Cambridge International

Pre-U Certificate

Classical Heritage (Principal) – Level 3
Awarding body:
  Cambridge International

History (Principal) – Level 3
Awarding body:
  Cambridge International

Philosophy

Award

Thinking and Reasoning Skills (Pilot) – Level 2
Awarding body:
  OCR

Theology and Religious Studies

Award

**General Religious Education –
Entry Level**
Awarding body:
NOCN

General Religious Education – Level 1
Awarding body:
NOCN

General Religious Education – Level 2
Awarding body:
NOCN

General Religious Education – Level 3
Awarding body:
NOCN

Certificate

Applied Christian Studies – Level 3
Awarding body:
ABC

Religious Education – Entry Level
Awarding body:
WJEC

Religious Studies – Entry Level
Awarding body:
AQA
CCEA
EDEXCEL
WJEC

**Religious Studies (Philosophy and Ethics)
– Entry Level**
Awarding body:
OCR

**Religious Studies (World Religions) –
Entry Level**
Awarding body:
OCR

The Way of Faith (Horizons) – Level 3
Awarding body:
EDI

Information and Communication Technology

ICT for Users

Advanced Diploma

Computer Studies – Level 5
Awarding body:
NCC

IT Users (e-Quals) – Enhanced – Level 3
Awarding body:
City & Guilds

IT Users (e-Quals) – Standard – Level 3
Awarding body:
City & Guilds

Award

Creative Digital Media (Digital Cre8or Full Award) – Level 2
Awarding body:
BCS

Creative Digital Media (Digital Cre8or) – Level 2
Awarding body:
BCS

Digital Applications for IT Users – Level 1
Awarding body:
EDEXCEL

Digital Applications for IT Users – Level 2
Awarding body:
EDEXCEL

Digital Literacy – Entry Level
Awarding body:
OCR

Information and Communication Technology – Level 2
Awarding body:
IAM

Introduction to Contact Centres – Level 1
Awarding body:
EDEXCEL

IT User Skills – Level 1
Awarding body:
ASCENTIS

IT User Skills – Level 2
Awarding body:
ASCENTIS

IT User Skills – Level 3
Awarding body:
OCR

IT User Skills (ECDL Essentials) (ITQ) – Level 1
Awarding body:
BCS

IT User Skills (ITQ) – Level 1
Awarding body:
BCS

IT User Skills (ITQ) – Level 2
Awarding body:
BCS

IT User Skills (ITQ) – Level 3
Awarding body:
BCS

IT Users (ITQ) – Entry Level
Awarding body:
EDEXCEL

IT Users (ITQ) – Level 1
Awarding body:
EDEXCEL

IT Users (Start IT – iTQ) – Entry Level
Awarding body:
City & Guilds

IT Users – ITQ – Level 1
Awarding body:
City & Guilds

IT Users – ITQ – Level 2
Awarding body:
City & Guilds

IT Users – ITQ – Level 3
Awarding body:
City & Guilds

Using ICT – Entry Level
Awarding body:
OCR

BTEC Award

Contact Centre Skills – Level 2
Awarding body:
EDEXCEL

Certificate

Communication and Presentation – Level 1
Awarding body:
ICAAE

Communication and Presentation – Level 2
Awarding body:
ICAAE

Communication Technology – Level 2
Awarding body:
ICAAE

Contact Centre Skills – Level 2
Awarding body:
City & Guilds

Contact Centre Skills – Level 3
Awarding body:
City & Guilds

Digital Applications for IT Users – Level 1
Awarding body:
EDEXCEL

Digital Applications for IT Users – Level 2
Awarding body:
EDEXCEL

Essential Skills – Information and Communication Technology – Level 1
Awarding body:
City & Guilds

Essential Skills – Information and Communication Technology – Level 2
Awarding body:
City & Guilds

Essential Skills ICT – Level 1
Awarding body:
CCEA

Essential Skills ICT – Level 2
Awarding body:
CCEA

Handling Data and Information – Level 1
Awarding body:
ICAAE

Handling Data and Information – Level 2
Awarding body:
ICAAE

ICT Applications – Level 1
Awarding body:
EDI

ICT Applications – Level 2
Awarding body:
EDI

ICT Applications – Level 3
Awarding body:
EDI

ICT Open Systems and Office Applications – Entry Level
Awarding body:
TLM

ICT Open Systems and Office Applications – Level 1
Awarding body:
TLM

ICT Open Systems and Office Applications – Level 2
Awarding body:
TLM

ICT Open Systems, Enterprise and Business Growth – Level 1
Awarding body:
TLM

ICT Open Systems, Enterprise and Business Growth – Level 2
Awarding body:
TLM

ICT Skills for Life – Entry Level
Awarding body:
ASCENTIS
City & Guilds
OCR

Information and Communication Technology – Entry Level
Awarding body:
AQA

Information and Communication Technology – Level 3
Awarding body:
IAM

IT User Skills – Level 1
Awarding body:
ASCENTIS

IT User Skills – Level 2
Awarding body:
ASCENTIS

IT User Skills – Level 3
Awarding body:
OCR

IT User Skills (Digital Creator) (ITQ) – Level 1
Awarding body:
BCS

IT User Skills (Digital Creator) (ITQ) – Level 2
Awarding body:
BCS

IT User Skills (ECDL Advanced) (ITQ) – Level 3
Awarding body:
BCS

IT User Skills (ECDL Extra) (ITQ) – Level 2
Awarding body:
BCS

IT User Skills (ITQ) – Level 1
Awarding body:
BCS

IT User Skills (ITQ) – Level 2
Awarding body:
BCS

IT User Skills (ITQ) – Level 3
Awarding body:
BCS

IT Users (CLAiT Advanced) – Level 3
Awarding body:
OCR

IT Users (CLAiT Plus) – Level 2
Awarding body:
OCR

IT Users (ECDL Part 1) – Level 1
Awarding body:
BCS

IT Users (ECDL Part 2) – Level 2
Awarding body:
BCS

IT Users (ITQ) – Entry Level
Awarding body:
EDEXCEL

IT Users (ITQ) – Level 1
Awarding body:
City & Guilds
EDEXCEL

IT Users (ITQ) – Level 2
Awarding body:
City & Guilds

IT Users (New CLAiT) – Level 1
Awarding body:
OCR

IT Users (Start IT – iTQ) – Entry Level
Awarding body:
City & Guilds

IT Users – (e-Quals) – Enhanced – Level 1
Awarding body:
City & Guilds

IT Users – (e-Quals) – Standard – Level 1
Awarding body:
City & Guilds

IT Users – ITQ – Level 1
Awarding body:
City & Guilds

IT Users – ITQ – Level 2
Awarding body:
City & Guilds

IT Users – ITQ – Level 3
Awarding body:
City & Guilds

IT Users – ITQ for Life – Level 1
Awarding body:
City & Guilds

IT Users Apprentices – ITQ – Level 2
Awarding body:
City & Guilds

Systems and Control – Level 2
Awarding body:
ICAAE

Using ICT – Entry Level
Awarding body:
City & Guilds

Diploma

Computer Studies – Level 4
Awarding body:
NCC

Digital Applications for IT Users – Level 1
Awarding body:
EDEXCEL

Digital Applications for IT Users – Level 2
Awarding body:
EDEXCEL

ICT Applications – Level 1
Awarding body:
EDI

ICT Applications – Level 2
Awarding body:
EDI

ICT Applications – Level 3
Awarding body:
EDI

IT User Skills – Level 1
Awarding body:
ASCENTIS

IT User Skills – Level 2
Awarding body:
ASCENTIS

IT User Skills – Level 3
Awarding body:
OCR

IT User Skills (ITQ) – Level 1
Awarding body:
BCS

IT User Skills (ITQ) – Level 2
Awarding body:
BCS

IT User Skills (ITQ) – Level 3
Awarding body:
BCS

IT Users (CLAiT Advanced) – Level 3
Awarding body:
OCR

IT Users (CLAiT Plus) – Level 2
Awarding body:
OCR

IT Users (e-Quals) – Enhanced – Level 2
Awarding body:
City & Guilds

IT Users (e-Quals) – Standard – Level 2
Awarding body:
City & Guilds

IT Users (ITQ) – Level 1
Awarding body:
EDEXCEL

IT Users (ITQ) – Level 3
Awarding body:
City & Guilds

IT Users (New CLAiT) – Level 1
Awarding body:
OCR

IT Users – ITQ – Level 1
Awarding body:
City & Guilds

IT Users – ITQ – Level 2
Awarding body:
City & Guilds

IT Users – ITQ – Level 3
Awarding body:
City & Guilds

Extended Certificate

Digital Applications for IT Users – Level 1
Awarding body:
EDEXCEL

Digital Applications for IT Users – Level 2
Awarding body:
EDEXCEL

Foundation Award

Information and Communication Technology – Level 1
Awarding body:
IAM

Higher Professional Diploma

Information Management Using ICT – Level 4
Awarding body:
City & Guilds

Introductory Certificate

IT @ Work – Level 1
Awarding body:
EDEXCEL

Introductory Diploma

IT @ Work – Level 1
Awarding body:
EDEXCEL

ITQ Award

IT User Skills – Level 1
Awarding body:
OCR

IT User Skills – Level 2
Awarding body:
OCR

ITQ Certificate

IT User Skills – Level 1
Awarding body:
OCR

IT User Skills – Level 2
Awarding body:
OCR

ITQ Diploma

IT User Skills – Level 1
Awarding body:
OCR

IT User Skills – Level 2
Awarding body:
OCR

National Award

ICT – Level 1
Awarding body:
  OCR

ICT – Level 2
Awarding body:
  OCR

National Certificate

ICT – Level 1
Awarding body:
  OCR

ICT – Level 2
Awarding body:
  OCR

ICT – Level 3
Awarding body:
  OCR

National Diploma

ICT – Level 3
Awarding body:
  OCR

National Extended Diploma

ICT – Level 3
Awarding body:
  OCR

National First Award

ICT – Level 1
Awarding body:
  OCR

ICT – Level 2
Awarding body:
  OCR

National First Certificate

ICT – Level 2
Awarding body:
  OCR

National Vocational Qualification

Contact Centre Operations – Level 1
Awarding body:
  EDI

Contact Centre Operations – Level 2
Awarding body:
  EDI

Contact Centre Professionals – Level 3
Awarding body:
  EDI

IT Users – Level 1
Awarding body:
  BCS
  EDEXCEL
  EDI
  SQA

IT Users – Level 2
Awarding body:
  BCS
  EDEXCEL
  EDI
  SQA

IT Users – Level 3
Awarding body:
  BCS
  EDEXCEL
  EDI
  SQA

IT Users (ITQ) – Level 1
Awarding body:
  City & Guilds
  OCR

IT Users (ITQ) – Level 2
Awarding body:
  City & Guilds
  OCR

IT Users (ITQ) – Level 3
Awarding body:
City & Guilds
OCR

Principal Learning

**Information Technology (Wales) –
Level 1**
Awarding body:
WJEC-EDEXCEL

**Information Technology (Wales) –
Level 2**
Awarding body:
WJEC-EDEXCEL

**Information Technology (Wales) –
Level 3**
Awarding body:
WJEC-EDEXCEL

ICT Practitioners

Advanced Diploma

Business Information Systems – Level 6
Awarding body:
ABE

ICT Software Developer – Level 3
Awarding body:
City & Guilds

ICT Systems Support – Level 3
Awarding body:
City & Guilds

Information Technology – Level 3
Awarding body:
AQA
City & Guilds
EDEXCEL
OCR

IT Professionals – Level 3
Awarding body:
City & Guilds

Award

Apprentice IT Practitioners – Level 2
Awarding body:
OCR

**Digital Home Technology Integrators –
Level 2**
Awarding body:
City & Guilds

**ICT Systems and Principles for
Apprentices – Level 2**
Awarding body:
City & Guilds

IT Service Management (ISEB) – Level 3
Awarding body:
BCS

BTEC Award

**Contact Centre Supervisory Skills –
Level 3**
Awarding body:
EDEXCEL

**Information Technology (Specialist) –
Level 2**
Awarding body:
EDEXCEL

**Information Technology (Specialist) –
Level 3**
Awarding body:
EDEXCEL

BTEC Certificate

Customer Contact – Level 2
Awarding body:
  EDEXCEL

ICT Systems and Principles for Apprentices – Level 2
Awarding body:
  EDEXCEL

ICT Systems and Principles for Apprentices – Level 3
Awarding body:
  EDEXCEL

Information Technology (Specialist) – Level 2
Awarding body:
  EDEXCEL

BTEC Diploma

ICT Professional Competence – Level 2
Awarding body:
  EDEXCEL

ICT Professional Competence – Level 3
Awarding body:
  EDEXCEL

ICT Systems and Principles for Apprentices – Level 3
Awarding body:
  EDEXCEL

Information Technology (Specialist) – Level 3
Awarding body:
  EDEXCEL

Professional Software Development – Level 5
Awarding body:
  EDEXCEL

BTEC Extended Certificate

Information Technology (Specialist) – Level 2
Awarding body:
  EDEXCEL

Information Technology (Specialist) – Level 3
Awarding body:
  EDEXCEL

BTEC First Certificate

ICT Practitioners – Level 2
Awarding body:
  EDEXCEL

BTEC First Diploma

ICT Practitioners – Level 2
Awarding body:
  EDEXCEL

BTEC Higher National Certificate

Computing (General) – Level 5
Awarding body:
  EDEXCEL

Computing (ICT Systems Support) – Level 5
Awarding body:
  EDEXCEL

Computing (Software Development) – Level 5
Awarding body:
  EDEXCEL

BTEC Higher National Diploma

Computing (General) – Level 5
Awarding body:
  EDEXCEL

Computing (ICT Systems Support) – Level 5
Awarding body:
  EDEXCEL

Computing (Software Development) – Level 5
Awarding body:
  EDEXCEL

BTEC National Award

Communications Technology – Level 3
Awarding body:
EDEXCEL

IT Practitioners – Level 3
Awarding body:
EDEXCEL

BTEC National Certificate

Communications Technology – Level 3
Awarding body:
EDEXCEL

IT Practitioners – Level 3
Awarding body:
EDEXCEL

BTEC National Diploma

Communications Technology – Level 3
Awarding body:
EDEXCEL

IT Practitioners – Level 3
Awarding body:
EDEXCEL

Certificate

Apprentice IT Professionals – Level 3
Awarding body:
OCR

Communications Cabling – Level 2
Awarding body:
City & Guilds

Contact Centre Skills – Level 1
Awarding body:
City & Guilds

Home Technology Integrators – Level 2
Awarding body:
City & Guilds

ICT Systems and Principles for Advanced Apprentices – Level 3
Awarding body:
City & Guilds

Information and Communication Technology – Entry Level
Awarding body:
CCEA
EDEXCEL
OCR

Information and Communication Technology – Level 1,2
Awarding body:
Cambridge International

Information Technology – Entry Level
Awarding body:
WJEC

IT – Level 4
Awarding body:
BCS

IT Practitioners – Level 1
Awarding body:
OCR

IT Practitioners – Level 2
Awarding body:
OCR

IT Professionals – Level 3
Awarding body:
OCR

IT Systems Support – PC Maintenance – Level 1
Awarding body:
City & Guilds

Diploma

Apprentice IT Practitioners – Level 2
Awarding body:
OCR

Apprentice IT Practitioners (Skills) – Level 2
Awarding body:
OCR

Apprentice IT Professionals – Level 3
Awarding body:
OCR

Apprentice IT Professionals (Skills) – Level 3
Awarding body:
OCR

Business Information Systems – Level 5
Awarding body:
ABE

Designing and Planning Communications Networks – Level 3
Awarding body:
City & Guilds

Digital Home Technology Integrators – Level 2
Awarding body:
City & Guilds

ICT Communications Systems – Level 3
Awarding body:
City & Guilds

ICT Professional Competence – Level 2
Awarding body:
City & Guilds

ICT Professional Competence – Level 3
Awarding body:
City & Guilds

ICT Systems Support – Level 2
Awarding body:
City & Guilds

IT – Level 5
Awarding body:
BCS

IT Practitioners – Level 1
Awarding body:
OCR

IT Practitioners – Level 2
Awarding body:
City & Guilds
OCR

IT Professionals – Level 3
Awarding body:
OCR

Software Developers – Level 2
Awarding body:
City & Guilds

Foundation Diploma

Information Technology – Level 1
Awarding body:
AQA
City & Guilds
EDEXCEL
OCR

Higher Diploma

Information Technology – Level 2
Awarding body:
AQA
City & Guilds
EDEXCEL
OCR

Higher Professional Diploma

IT Practitioners – Level 4
Awarding body:
City & Guilds

National Vocational Qualification

Communication Technologies Practitioners – Level 2
Awarding body:
City & Guilds

Communication Technologies Professionals – Level 3
Awarding body:
City & Guilds

Communication Technologies Professionals – Level 4
Awarding body:
City & Guilds

Communication Technology Practitioners – Level 2
Awarding body:
EDEXCEL

Communication Technology Professionals – Level 3
Awarding body:
EDEXCEL

Communication Technology Professionals – Level 4
Awarding body:
  EDEXCEL

Contact Centre Operations – Level 1
Awarding body:
  City & Guilds
  EDEXCEL
  OCR

Contact Centre Operations – Level 2
Awarding body:
  City & Guilds
  EDEXCEL
  OCR

Contact Centre Professionals – Level 3
Awarding body:
  City & Guilds
  EDEXCEL
  OCR

Contact Centre Professionals – Level 4
Awarding body:
  City & Guilds
  EDEXCEL
  OCR

Contact Centre Professionals – Level 5
Awarding body:
  OCR

IT Practitioners – Level 1
Awarding body:
  City & Guilds
  EDEXCEL
  OCR
  SQA

IT Practitioners – Level 2
Awarding body:
  City & Guilds
  EDEXCEL
  OCR
  SQA

IT Professionals – Level 3
Awarding body:
  City & Guilds
  EDEXCEL
  OCR
  SQA

IT Professionals – Level 4
Awarding body:
  City & Guilds
  OCR

Postgraduate Diploma

Strategic Business Information Technology – Level 7
Awarding body:
  NCC

Principal Learning

IT – Level 1
Awarding body:
  AQA
  City & Guilds
  EDEXCEL
  OCR

IT – Level 2
Awarding body:
  AQA
  City & Guilds
  EDEXCEL
  OCR

IT – Level 3
Awarding body:
  AQA
  City & Guilds
  EDEXCEL
  OCR

IT (Wales) – Level 1
Awarding body:
  OCR

IT (Wales) – Level 2
Awarding body:
  OCR

IT (Wales) – Level 3
Awarding body:
  OCR

Professional Graduate Diploma

IT – Level 6
Awarding body:
  BCS

Progression Diploma

Information Technology – Level 3
Awarding body:
  AQA
  City & Guilds
  EDEXCEL
  OCR

Languages, Literature and Culture

Languages, Literature and Culture of the British Isles

Award

Defnyddio'r Gymraeg gyda Phlant Bach (Gweithle) – Level 1
Awarding body:
  NOCN

Defnyddio'r Gymraeg gyda Phlant Bach (i'r teulu) – Level 1
Awarding body:
  NOCN

Yr Iaith ar Waith – Entry Level
Awarding body:
  WJEC

Yr Iaith ar Waith – Level 1
Awarding body:
  WJEC

Yr Iaith ar Waith – Level 2
Awarding body:
  WJEC

Yr Iaith ar Waith – Level 3
Awarding body:
  WJEC

Certificate

Cornish Listening (Breakthrough) (Asset Languages) – Entry Level
Awarding body:
  OCR

Cornish Listening (Preliminary) (Asset Languages) – Level 1
Awarding body:
  OCR

Cornish Reading (Breakthrough) (Asset Languages) – Entry Level
Awarding body:
  OCR

Cornish Reading (Preliminary) (Asset Languages) – Level 1
Awarding body:
  OCR

Cornish Speaking (Breakthrough) (Asset Languages) – Entry Level
Awarding body:
  OCR

Cornish Speaking (Preliminary) (Asset Languages) – Level 1
Awarding body:
  OCR

Cornish Writing (Breakthrough) (Asset Languages) – Entry Level
Awarding body:
  OCR

Cornish Writing (Preliminary) (Asset Languages) – Level 1
Awarding body:
  OCR

Cymraeg Ail Iaith (Mynediad 3) (Peilot Llwybrau Credyd) (Pilot) – Entry Level
Awarding body:
  WJEC

Cymraeg yn Ail Iaith (Llwybr Credydau) (Pilot) – Level 1
Awarding body:
  WJEC

Cymraeg yn Ail Iaith (Llwybr Credydau) (Pilot) – Level 2
Awarding body:
WJEC

English – Entry Level
Awarding body:
AQA
CCEA
EDEXCEL
OCR
WJEC

English (IELTS 4/4.5) – Entry Level
Awarding body:
Cambridge ESOL

English (IELTS 5/5.5) – Level 1
Awarding body:
Cambridge ESOL

English (IELTS 6/6.5) – Level 2
Awarding body:
Cambridge ESOL

English (IELTS 7/7.5) – Level 3
Awarding body:
Cambridge ESOL

English as a Second Language – Level 1,2
Awarding body:
Cambridge International

English Language and Literature – Level 3
Awarding body:
ASCENTIS

ESOL International – Entry Level
Awarding body:
Cambridge ESOL

ESOL International – Level 1
Awarding body:
Cambridge ESOL

ESOL International – Level 2
Awarding body:
Cambridge ESOL

ESOL International – Level 3
Awarding body:
Cambridge ESOL

ESOL International (Spoken) – Level 1
Awarding body:
City & Guilds

ESOL International (BULATS) – Level 1
Awarding body:
Cambridge ESOL

ESOL International (BULATS) – Level 2
Awarding body:
Cambridge ESOL

ESOL International (BULATS) – Level 3
Awarding body:
Cambridge ESOL

ESOL International (Business English) – Entry Level
Awarding body:
Cambridge ESOL

ESOL International (Business English) – Level 1
Awarding body:
Cambridge ESOL

ESOL International (Business English) – Level 2
Awarding body:
Cambridge ESOL

ESOL International (Financial English) – Level 1
Awarding body:
Cambridge ESOL

ESOL International (Financial English) – Level 2
Awarding body:
Cambridge ESOL

ESOL International (LCCI EfB) – Entry Level
Awarding body:
EDI

ESOL International (LCCI EfB) – Level 1
Awarding body:
EDI

ESOL International (LCCI EfB) – Level 2
Awarding body:
EDI

**ESOL International (Legal English) –
Level 1**
Awarding body:
Cambridge ESOL

**ESOL International (Legal English) –
Level 2**
Awarding body:
Cambridge ESOL

**ESOL International (reading, writing and
listening) – Entry Level**
Awarding body:
City & Guilds

**ESOL International (reading, writing and
listening) – Level 1**
Awarding body:
City & Guilds

**ESOL International (reading, writing and
listening) – Level 2**
Awarding body:
City & Guilds

**ESOL International (reading, writing and
listening) – Level 3**
Awarding body:
City & Guilds

**ESOL International (Spoken) –
Entry Level**
Awarding body:
City & Guilds

ESOL International (Spoken) – Level 2
Awarding body:
City & Guilds

ESOL International (Spoken) – Level 3
Awarding body:
City & Guilds

**ESOL International All Modes –
Entry Level**
Awarding body:
ESB

ESOL International All Modes – Level 1
Awarding body:
ESB

ESOL International All Modes – Level 2
Awarding body:
ESB

ESOL International All Modes – Level 3
Awarding body:
ESB

First Language English – Level 1,2
Awarding body:
Cambridge International

Irish – Entry Level
Awarding body:
CCEA

**Irish Listening (Breakthrough) (Asset
Languages) – Entry Level**
Awarding body:
OCR

**Irish Listening (Intermediate) (Asset
Languages) – Level 2**
Awarding body:
OCR

**Irish Reading (Breakthrough) (Asset
Languages) – Entry Level**
Awarding body:
OCR

**Irish Reading (Intermediate) (Asset
Languages) – Level 2**
Awarding body:
OCR

**Irish Speaking (Breakthrough) (Asset
Languages) – Entry Level**
Awarding body:
OCR

**Irish Speaking (Intermediate) (Asset
Languages) – Level 2**
Awarding body:
OCR

**Irish Writing (Breakthrough) (Asset
Languages) – Entry Level**
Awarding body:
OCR

**Irish Writing (Intermediate) (Asset
Languages) – Level 2**
Awarding body:
OCR

**Language Proficiency (Using Welsh) –
Level 4**
Awarding body:
WJEC

Literature (English) – Level 1,2
Awarding body:
Cambridge International

Teaching English as a Foreign Language – Level 4
Awarding body:
EDI

Welsh – Entry Level
Awarding body:
WJEC

Welsh as a Second Language – Entry Level
Awarding body:
WJEC

Welsh Listening (Breakthrough) (Asset Languages) – Entry Level
Awarding body:
OCR

Welsh Listening (Intermediate) (Asset Languages) – Level 2
Awarding body:
OCR

Welsh Listening (Preliminary) (Asset Languages) – Level 1
Awarding body:
OCR

Welsh Reading (Breakthrough) (Asset Languages) – Entry Level
Awarding body:
OCR

Welsh Reading (Intermediate) (Asset Languages) – Level 2
Awarding body:
OCR

Welsh Reading (Preliminary) (Asset Languages) – Level 1
Awarding body:
OCR

Welsh Second Language (Using Welsh) – Entry Level
Awarding body:
WJEC

Welsh Second Language (Using Welsh) – Level 1
Awarding body:
WJEC

Welsh Second Language: The Use of Welsh – Level 2
Awarding body:
WJEC

Welsh Second Language: The Use of Welsh – Level 3
Awarding body:
WJEC

Welsh Speaking (Breakthrough) (Asset Languages) – Entry Level
Awarding body:
OCR

Welsh Speaking (Intermediate) (Asset Languages) – Level 2
Awarding body:
OCR

Welsh Speaking (Preliminary) (Asset Languages) – Level 1
Awarding body:
OCR

Welsh Writing (Breakthrough) (Asset Languages) – Entry Level
Awarding body:
OCR

Welsh Writing (Intermediate) (Asset Languages) – Level 2
Awarding body:
OCR

Welsh Writing (Preliminary) (Asset Languages) – Level 1
Awarding body:
OCR

National Vocational Qualification

English Language Units – Level 1
Awarding body:
OCR

English Language Units – Level 2
Awarding body:
  OCR

English Language Units – Level 3
Awarding body:
  OCR

English Language Units – Level 4
Awarding body:
  OCR

Irish Language Units – Level 1
Awarding body:
  OCR

Irish Language Units – Level 2
Awarding body:
  OCR

Irish Language Units – Level 3
Awarding body:
  OCR

Irish Language Units – Level 4
Awarding body:
  OCR

Irish Sign Language – Level 4
Awarding body:
  Signature

Welsh – Level 1
Awarding body:
  EDEXCEL

Welsh – Level 2
Awarding body:
  EDEXCEL

Welsh – Level 3
Awarding body:
  EDEXCEL

Welsh Language Units – Level 1
Awarding body:
  EDEXCEL
  OCR

Welsh Language Units – Level 2
Awarding body:
  EDEXCEL
  OCR

Welsh Language Units – Level 3
Awarding body:
  EDEXCEL
  OCR

Welsh Language Units – Level 4
Awarding body:
  OCR

Pre-U Certificate

Literature in English (Principal) – Level 3
Awarding body:
  Cambridge International

Other Languages, Literature and Culture

Award

British Sign Language – Level 1
Awarding body:
  Signature

Introduction to Community Interpreting Skills – Level 3
Awarding body:
  ASCENTIS

Irish Sign Language – Level 1
Awarding body:
  Signature

Language Skills – Entry Level
Awarding body:
  NOCN

Language Skills – Level 1
Awarding body:
  NOCN

Language Skills – Level 2
Awarding body:
    NOCN

Language Skills – Level 3
Awarding body:
    NOCN

**Languages for Travel and Leisure
(Reading and Writing) – Entry Level**
Awarding body:
    ASCENTIS

**Languages for Travel and Leisure
(Reading and Writing) – Level 1**
Awarding body:
    ASCENTIS

**Languages for Travel and Leisure
(Reading and Writing) – Level 2**
Awarding body:
    ASCENTIS

**Languages for Travel and Leisure
(Speaking and Listening) – Entry Level**
Awarding body:
    ASCENTIS

**Languages for Travel and Leisure
(Speaking and Listening) – Level 1**
Awarding body:
    ASCENTIS

**Languages for Travel and Leisure
(Speaking and Listening) – Level 2**
Awarding body:
    ASCENTIS

Modern Language – Entry Level
Awarding body:
    CCEA

Modern Languages – Entry Level
Awarding body:
    CCEA

Modern Languages – Level 1
Awarding body:
    CCEA

Modern Languages – Level 2
Awarding body:
    CCEA

**Reading and Writing in Arabic –
Entry Level**
Awarding body:
    ABC

Reading and Writing in Arabic – Level 1
Awarding body:
    ABC

Reading and Writing in Arabic – Level 2
Awarding body:
    ABC

**Reading and Writing in Bengali –
Entry Level**
Awarding body:
    ABC

**Reading and Writing in French –
Entry Level**
Awarding body:
    ABC

Reading and Writing in French – Level 1
Awarding body:
    ABC

Reading and Writing in French – Level 2
Awarding body:
    ABC

Reading and Writing in French – Level 3
Awarding body:
    ABC

**Reading and Writing in German –
Entry Level**
Awarding body:
    ABC

**Reading and Writing in German –
Level 1**
Awarding body:
    ABC

**Reading and Writing in German –
Level 2**
Awarding body:
    ABC

**Reading and Writing in German –
Level 3**
Awarding body:
    ABC

**Reading and Writing in Greek –
Entry Level**
Awarding body:
 ABC

Reading and Writing in Greek – Level 1
Awarding body:
 ABC

Reading and Writing in Greek – Level 2
Awarding body:
 ABC

**Reading and Writing in Italian –
Entry Level**
Awarding body:
 ABC

Reading and Writing in Italian – Level 1
Awarding body:
 ABC

Reading and Writing in Italian – Level 2
Awarding body:
 ABC

Reading and Writing in Italian – Level 3
Awarding body:
 ABC

**Reading and Writing in Japanese –
Entry Level**
Awarding body:
 ABC

**Reading and Writing in Japanese –
Level 1**
Awarding body:
 ABC

**Reading and Writing in Japanese –
Level 2**
Awarding body:
 ABC

**Reading and Writing in Mandarin
Chinese – Entry Level**
Awarding body:
 ABC

**Reading and Writing in Mandarin
Chinese – Level 1**
Awarding body:
 ABC

**Reading and Writing in Mandarin
Chinese – Level 2**
Awarding body:
 ABC

**Reading and Writing in Polish –
Entry Level**
Awarding body:
 ABC

Reading and Writing in Polish – Level 1
Awarding body:
 ABC

Reading and Writing in Polish – Level 2
Awarding body:
 ABC

**Reading and Writing in Portuguese –
Entry Level**
Awarding body:
 ABC

**Reading and Writing in Portuguese –
Level 1**
Awarding body:
 ABC

**Reading and Writing in Portuguese –
Level 2**
Awarding body:
 ABC

**Reading and Writing in Portuguese –
Level 3**
Awarding body:
 ABC

**Reading and Writing in Punjabi –
Entry Level**
Awarding body:
 ABC

**Reading and Writing in Russian –
Entry Level**
Awarding body:
 ABC

**Reading and Writing in Russian –
Level 1**
Awarding body:
 ABC

Reading and Writing in Russian – Level 2
Awarding body:
ABC

Reading and Writing in Spanish – Entry Level
Awarding body:
ABC

Reading and Writing in Spanish – Level 1
Awarding body:
ABC

Reading and Writing in Spanish – Level 2
Awarding body:
ABC

Reading and Writing in Spanish – Level 3
Awarding body:
ABC

Reading and Writing in Tajweed – Entry Level
Awarding body:
ABC

Reading and Writing in Turkish – Entry Level
Awarding body:
ABC

Reading and Writing in Urdu – Entry Level
Awarding body:
ABC

Reading and Writing in Urdu – Level 1
Awarding body:
ABC

Signing and Receiving Skills in British Sign Language – Entry Level
Awarding body:
ABC

Signing and Receiving Skills in British Sign Language – Level 1
Awarding body:
ABC

Signing and Receiving Skills in British Sign Language – Level 2
Awarding body:
ABC

Signing and Receiving Skills in British Sign Language – Level 3
Awarding body:
ABC

Speaking and Listening in Arabic – Entry Level
Awarding body:
ABC

Speaking and Listening in Arabic – Level 1
Awarding body:
ABC

Speaking and Listening in Arabic – Level 2
Awarding body:
ABC

Speaking and Listening in Bengali – Entry Level
Awarding body:
ABC

Speaking and Listening in Dutch – Entry Level
Awarding body:
ABC

Speaking and Listening in French – Entry Level
Awarding body:
ABC

Speaking and Listening in French – Level 1
Awarding body:
ABC

Speaking and Listening in French – Level 2
Awarding body:
ABC

Speaking and Listening in French – Level 3
Awarding body:
ABC

Speaking and Listening in German – Entry Level
Awarding body:
ABC

Speaking and Listening in German – Level 1
Awarding body:
ABC

Speaking and Listening in German – Level 2
Awarding body:
ABC

Speaking and Listening in German – Level 3
Awarding body:
ABC

Speaking and Listening in Greek – Entry Level
Awarding body:
ABC

Speaking and Listening in Greek – Level 1
Awarding body:
ABC

Speaking and Listening in Greek – Level 2
Awarding body:
ABC

Speaking and Listening in Greek – Level 3
Awarding body:
ABC

Speaking and Listening in Italian – Entry Level
Awarding body:
ABC

Speaking and Listening in Italian – Level 1
Awarding body:
ABC

Speaking and Listening in Italian – Level 2
Awarding body:
ABC

Speaking and Listening in Italian – Level 3
Awarding body:
ABC

Speaking and Listening in Japanese – Entry Level
Awarding body:
ABC

Speaking and Listening in Japanese – Level 1
Awarding body:
ABC

Speaking and Listening in Japanese – Level 2
Awarding body:
ABC

Speaking and Listening in Japanese – Level 3
Awarding body:
ABC

Speaking and Listening in Mandarin Chinese – Entry Level
Awarding body:
ABC

Speaking and Listening in Mandarin Chinese – Level 1
Awarding body:
ABC

Speaking and Listening in Mandarin Chinese – Level 2
Awarding body:
ABC

Speaking and Listening in Polish – Entry Level
Awarding body:
ABC

Speaking and Listening in Polish – Level 1
Awarding body:
ABC

Speaking and Listening in Polish – Level 2
Awarding body:
ABC

**Speaking and Listening in Portuguese –
Entry Level**
Awarding body:
ABC

**Speaking and Listening in Portuguese –
Level 1**
Awarding body:
ABC

**Speaking and Listening in Portuguese –
Level 2**
Awarding body:
ABC

**Speaking and Listening in Portuguese –
Level 3**
Awarding body:
ABC

**Speaking and Listening in Punjabi –
Entry Level**
Awarding body:
ABC

**Speaking and Listening in Russian –
Entry Level**
Awarding body:
ABC

**Speaking and Listening in Russian –
Level 1**
Awarding body:
ABC

**Speaking and Listening in Russian –
Level 2**
Awarding body:
ABC

**Speaking and Listening in Spanish –
Entry Level**
Awarding body:
ABC

**Speaking and Listening in Spanish –
Level 1**
Awarding body:
ABC

**Speaking and Listening in Spanish –
Level 2**
Awarding body:
ABC

**Speaking and Listening in Spanish –
Level 3**
Awarding body:
ABC

**Speaking and Listening in Turkish –
Entry Level**
Awarding body:
ABC

**Speaking and Listening in Urdu –
Entry Level**
Awarding body:
ABC

Speaking and Listening in Urdu – Level 1
Awarding body:
ABC

Certificate

**Arabic Listening (Advanced) (Asset
Languages) – Level 3**
Awarding body:
OCR

**Arabic Listening (Breakthrough) (Asset
Languages) – Entry Level**
Awarding body:
OCR

**Arabic Listening (Intermediate) (Asset
Languages) – Level 2**
Awarding body:
OCR

**Arabic Listening (Preliminary) (Asset
Languages) – Level 1**
Awarding body:
OCR

**Arabic Reading (Advanced) (Asset
Languages) – Level 3**
Awarding body:
OCR

**Arabic Reading (Breakthrough) (Asset
Languages) – Entry Level**
Awarding body:
OCR

Arabic Reading (Intermediate) (Asset Languages) – Level 2
Awarding body:
OCR

Arabic Reading (Preliminary) (Asset Languages) – Level 1
Awarding body:
OCR

Arabic Speaking (Advanced) (Asset Languages) – Level 3
Awarding body:
OCR

Arabic Speaking (Breakthrough) (Asset Languages) – Entry Level
Awarding body:
OCR

Arabic Speaking (Intermediate) (Asset Languages) – Level 2
Awarding body:
OCR

Arabic Speaking (Preliminary) (Asset Languages) – Level 1
Awarding body:
OCR

Arabic Writing (Advanced) (Asset Languages) – Level 3
Awarding body:
OCR

Arabic Writing (Breakthrough) (Asset Languages) – Entry Level
Awarding body:
OCR

Arabic Writing (Intermediate) (Asset Languages) – Level 2
Awarding body:
OCR

Arabic Writing (Preliminary) (Asset Languages) – Level 1
Awarding body:
OCR

Bengali Listening (Breakthrough) (Asset Languages) – Entry Level
Awarding body:
OCR

Bengali Listening (Intermediate) (Asset Languages) – Level 2
Awarding body:
OCR

Bengali Listening (Preliminary) (Asset Languages) – Level 1
Awarding body:
OCR

Bengali Reading (Breakthrough) (Asset Languages) – Entry Level
Awarding body:
OCR

Bengali Reading (Intermediate) (Asset Languages) – Level 2
Awarding body:
OCR

Bengali Reading (Preliminary) (Asset Languages) – Level 1
Awarding body:
OCR

Bengali Speaking (Preliminary) (Asset Languages) – Level 1
Awarding body:
OCR

Bengali Speaking (Breakthrough) (Asset Languages) – Entry Level
Awarding body:
OCR

Bengali Speaking (Intermediate) (Asset Languages) – Level 2
Awarding body:
OCR

Bengali Writing (Breakthrough) (Asset Languages) – Entry Level
Awarding body:
OCR

Bengali Writing (Intermediate) (Asset Languages) – Level 2
Awarding body:
OCR

Bengali Writing (Preliminary) (Asset Languages) – Level 1
Awarding body:
OCR

Bilingual Skills – Level 3
Awarding body:
   IoLET

British Sign Language – Level 2
Awarding body:
   Signature

British Sign Language – Level 3
Awarding body:
   Signature

Business Chinese (Speaking, Listening and Culture) – Entry Level
Awarding body:
   ICAAE

Business Chinese (Speaking, Listening and Culture) – Level 1
Awarding body:
   ICAAE

Business Language Competence – Entry Level
Awarding body:
   OCR

Business Language Competence – Level 1
Awarding body:
   OCR

Business Language Competence – Level 2
Awarding body:
   OCR

Business Language Competence – Level 3
Awarding body:
   OCR

Chinese (Cantonese) Listening (Advanced) (Asset Languages) – Level 3
Awarding body:
   OCR

Chinese (Cantonese) Listening (Breakthrough) (Asset Languages) – Entry Level
Awarding body:
   OCR

Chinese (Cantonese) Listening (Intermediate) (Asset Languages) – Level 2
Awarding body:
   OCR

Chinese (Cantonese) Listening (Preliminary) (Asset Languages) – Level 1
Awarding body:
   OCR

Chinese (Cantonese) Speaking (Advanced) (Asset Languages) – Level 3
Awarding body:
   OCR

Chinese (Cantonese) Speaking (Breakthrough) (Asset Languages) – Entry Level
Awarding body:
   OCR

Chinese (Cantonese) Speaking (Intermediate) (Asset Languages) – Level 2
Awarding body:
   OCR

Chinese (Cantonese) Speaking (Preliminary) (Asset Languages) – Level 1
Awarding body:
   OCR

Chinese (Mandarin) – Entry Level
Awarding body:
   AQA

Chinese (Mandarin) – Level 1
Awarding body:
   AQA

Chinese (Mandarin) Listening (Advanced) (Asset Languages) – Level 3
Awarding body:
   OCR

Chinese (Mandarin) Listening (Breakthrough) (Asset Languages) – Entry Level
Awarding body:
   OCR

Chinese (Mandarin) Listening (Intermediate) (Asset Languages) – Level 2
Awarding body:
OCR

Chinese (Mandarin) Listening (Preliminary) (Asset Languages) – Level 1
Awarding body:
OCR

Chinese (Mandarin) Speaking (Breakthrough) (Asset Languages) – Entry Level
Awarding body:
OCR

Chinese (Mandarin) Speaking (Preliminary) (Asset Languages) – Level 1
Awarding body:
OCR

Chinese (Mandarin) Speaking (Advanced) (Asset Languages) – Level 3
Awarding body:
OCR

Chinese (Mandarin) Speaking (Intermediate) (Asset Languages) – Level 2
Awarding body:
OCR

Chinese (Simplified) Reading (Advanced) (Asset Languages) – Level 3
Awarding body:
OCR

Chinese (Simplified) Reading (Breakthrough) (Asset Languages) – Entry Level
Awarding body:
OCR

Chinese (Simplified) Reading (Intermediate) (Asset Languages) – Level 2
Awarding body:
OCR

Chinese (Simplified) Reading (Preliminary) (Asset Languages) – Level 1
Awarding body:
OCR

Chinese (Simplified) Writing (Advanced) (Asset Languages) – Level 3
Awarding body:
OCR

Chinese (Simplified) Writing (Breakthrough) (Asset Languages) – Entry Level
Awarding body:
OCR

Chinese (Simplified) Writing (Intermediate) (Asset Languages) – Level 2
Awarding body:
OCR

Chinese (Simplified) Writing (Preliminary) (Asset Languages) – Level 1
Awarding body:
OCR

Chinese (Traditional) Reading (Advanced) (Asset Languages) – Level 3
Awarding body:
OCR

Chinese (Traditional) Reading (Breakthrough) (Asset Languages) – Entry Level
Awarding body:
OCR

Chinese (Traditional) Reading (Intermediate) (Asset Languages) – Level 2
Awarding body:
OCR

Chinese (Traditional) Reading (Preliminary) (Asset Languages) – Level 1
Awarding body:
OCR

Chinese (Traditional) Writing (Advanced) (Asset Languages) – Level 3
Awarding body:
OCR

Chinese (Traditional) Writing (Breakthrough) (Asset Languages) – Entry Level
Awarding body:
OCR

Chinese (Traditional) Writing (Intermediate) (Asset Languages) – Level 2
Awarding body:
OCR

Chinese (Traditional) Writing (Preliminary) (Asset Languages) – Level 1
Awarding body:
OCR

Communication with Deaf People – Level 2
Awarding body:
Signature

Communication with Deafblind People – Level 2
Awarding body:
Signature

Communication with Deafblind People (Manual) – Level 2
Awarding body:
Signature

Facilitating Communication with Deaf People – Level 3
Awarding body:
Signature

Facilitating Communication with Deafblind People (Manual) – Level 3
Awarding body:
Signature

French – Entry Level
Awarding body:
AQA
CCEA
OCR
WJEC

French – Level 1
Awarding body:
AQA

French – Level 1,2
Awarding body:
Cambridge International

French Listening (Advanced) (Asset Languages) – Level 3
Awarding body:
OCR

French Listening (Breakthrough) (Asset Languages) – Entry Level
Awarding body:
OCR

French Listening (Intermediate) (Asset Languages) – Level 2
Awarding body:
OCR

French Listening (Mastery) (Asset Languages) – Level 6
Awarding body:
OCR

French Listening (Preliminary) (Asset Languages) – Level 1
Awarding body:
OCR

French Listening (Proficiency) (Asset Languages) – Level 4
Awarding body:
OCR

French Reading (Advanced) (Asset Languages) – Level 3
Awarding body:
OCR

French Reading (Breakthrough) (Asset Languages) – Entry Level
Awarding body:
OCR

French Reading (Intermediate) (Asset Languages) – Level 2
Awarding body:
OCR

French Reading (Mastery) (Asset Languages) – Level 6
Awarding body:
OCR

French Reading (Preliminary) (Asset Languages) – Level 1
Awarding body:
OCR

French Reading (Proficiency) (Asset Languages) – Level 4
Awarding body:
OCR

French Speaking (Advanced) (Asset Languages) – Level 3
Awarding body:
OCR

French Speaking (Breakthrough) (Asset Languages) – Entry Level
Awarding body:
OCR

French Speaking (Intermediate) (Asset Languages) – Level 2
Awarding body:
OCR

French Speaking (Mastery) (Asset Languages) – Level 6
Awarding body:
OCR

French Speaking (Preliminary) (Asset Languages) – Level 1
Awarding body:
OCR

French Speaking (Proficiency) (Asset Languages) – Level 4
Awarding body:
OCR

French Writing (Advanced) (Asset Languages) – Level 3
Awarding body:
OCR

French Writing (Breakthrough) (Asset Languages) – Entry Level
Awarding body:
OCR

French Writing (Intermediate) (Asset Languages) – Level 2
Awarding body:
OCR

French Writing (Mastery) (Asset Languages) – Level 6
Awarding body:
OCR

French Writing (Preliminary) (Asset Languages) – Level 1
Awarding body:
OCR

French Writing (Proficiency) (Asset Languages) – Level 4
Awarding body:
OCR

German – Entry Level
Awarding body:
AQA
CCEA
OCR
WJEC

German – Level 1
Awarding body:
AQA

German Listening (Advanced) (Asset Languages) – Level 3
Awarding body:
OCR

German Listening (Breakthrough) (Asset Languages) – Entry Level
Awarding body:
OCR

German Listening (Intermediate) (Asset Languages) – Level 2
Awarding body:
OCR

German Listening (Preliminary) (Asset Languages) – Level 1
Awarding body:
OCR

German Listening (Proficiency) (Asset Languages) – Level 4
Awarding body:
OCR

German Reading (Advanced) (Asset Languages) – Level 3
Awarding body:
OCR

German Reading (Breakthrough) (Asset Languages) – Entry Level
Awarding body:
OCR

German Reading (Intermediate) (Asset Languages) – Level 2
Awarding body:
OCR

German Reading (Preliminary) (Asset Languages) – Level 1
Awarding body:
OCR

German Reading (Proficiency) (Asset Languages) – Level 4
Awarding body:
OCR

German Speaking (Advanced) (Asset Languages) – Level 3
Awarding body:
OCR

German Speaking (Breakthrough) (Asset Languages) – Entry Level
Awarding body:
OCR

German Speaking (Intermediate) (Asset Languages) – Level 2
Awarding body:
OCR

German Speaking (Preliminary) (Asset Languages) – Level 1
Awarding body:
OCR

German Speaking (Proficiency) (Asset Languages) – Level 4
Awarding body:
OCR

German Writing (Advanced) (Asset Languages) – Level 3
Awarding body:
OCR

German Writing (Breakthrough) (Asset Languages) – Entry Level
Awarding body:
OCR

German Writing (Intermediate) (Asset Languages) – Level 2
Awarding body:
OCR

German Writing (Preliminary) (Asset Languages) – Level 1
Awarding body:
OCR

German Writing (Proficiency) (Asset Languages) – Level 4
Awarding body:
OCR

Greek – Level 1,2
Awarding body:
Cambridge International

Gujarati Listening (Breakthrough) (Asset Languages) – Entry Level
Awarding body:
OCR

Gujarati Listening (Intermediate) (Asset Languages) – Level 2
Awarding body:
OCR

Gujarati Listening (Preliminary) (Asset Languages) – Level 1
Awarding body:
OCR

Gujarati Reading (Breakthrough) (Asset Languages) – Entry Level
Awarding body:
OCR

Gujarati Reading (Intermediate) (Asset Languages) – Level 2
Awarding body:
OCR

Gujarati Reading (Preliminary) (Asset Languages) – Level 1
Awarding body:
OCR

Gujarati Speaking (Breakthrough) (Asset Languages) – Entry Level
Awarding body:
OCR

Gujarati Speaking (Intermediate) (Asset Languages) – Level 2
Awarding body:
OCR

Gujarati Speaking (Preliminary) (Asset Languages) – Level 1
Awarding body:
OCR

Gujarati Writing (Breakthrough) (Asset Languages) – Entry Level
Awarding body:
OCR

Gujarati Writing (Intermediate) (Asset Languages) – Level 2
Awarding body:
OCR

Gujarati Writing (Preliminary) (Asset Languages) – Level 1
Awarding body:
OCR

Hindi as a Second Language – Level 1,2
Awarding body:
Cambridge International

Hindi Listening (Breakthrough) (Asset Languages) – Entry Level
Awarding body:
OCR

Hindi Listening (Intermediate) (Asset Languages) – Level 2
Awarding body:
OCR

Hindi Listening (Preliminary) (Asset Languages) – Level 1
Awarding body:
OCR

Hindi Reading (Breakthrough) (Asset Languages) – Entry Level
Awarding body:
OCR

Hindi Reading (Intermediate) (Asset Languages) – Level 2
Awarding body:
OCR

Hindi Reading (Preliminary) (Asset Languages) – Level 1
Awarding body:
OCR

Hindi Speaking (Breakthrough) (Asset Languages) – Entry Level
Awarding body:
OCR

Hindi Speaking (Intermediate) (Asset Languages) – Level 2
Awarding body:
OCR

Hindi Speaking (Preliminary) (Asset Languages) – Level 1
Awarding body:
OCR

Hindi Writing (Breakthrough) (Asset Languages) – Entry Level
Awarding body:
OCR

Hindi Writing (Intermediate) (Asset Languages) – Level 2
Awarding body:
OCR

Hindi Writing (Preliminary) (Asset Languages) – Level 1
Awarding body:
OCR

Insights into Communication with Congenitally Deafblind People – Level 3
Awarding body:
Signature

Irish Listening (Preliminary) (Asset Languages) – Level 1
Awarding body:
OCR

Irish Reading (Preliminary) (Asset Languages) – Level 1
Awarding body:
OCR

Irish Sign Language – Level 2
Awarding body:
Signature

Irish Sign Language – Level 3
Awarding body:
Signature

Irish Speaking (Preliminary) (Asset Languages) – Level 1
Awarding body:
OCR

Irish Writing (Preliminary) (Asset Languages) – Level 1
Awarding body:
OCR

Italian – Entry Level
Awarding body:
AQA

Italian – Level 1
Awarding body:
AQA

Italian Listening (Advanced) (Asset Languages) – Level 3
Awarding body:
OCR

Italian Listening (Breakthrough) (Asset Languages) – Entry Level
Awarding body:
OCR

Italian Listening (Intermediate) (Asset Languages) – Level 2
Awarding body:
OCR

Italian Listening (Preliminary) (Asset Languages) – Level 1
Awarding body:
OCR

Italian Reading (Advanced) (Asset Languages) – Level 3
Awarding body:
OCR

Italian Reading (Breakthrough) (Asset Languages) – Entry Level
Awarding body:
OCR

Italian Reading (Intermediate) (Asset Languages) – Level 2
Awarding body:
OCR

Italian Reading (Preliminary) (Asset Languages) – Level 1
Awarding body:
OCR

Italian Speaking (Advanced) (Asset Languages) – Level 3
Awarding body:
OCR

Italian Speaking (Breakthrough) (Asset Languages) – Entry Level
Awarding body:
OCR

Italian Speaking (Intermediate) (Asset Languages) – Level 2
Awarding body:
OCR

Italian Speaking (Preliminary) (Asset Languages) – Level 1
Awarding body:
OCR

Italian Writing (Advanced) (Asset Languages) – Level 3
Awarding body:
OCR

Italian Writing (Breakthrough) (Asset Languages) – Entry Level
Awarding body:
OCR

Italian Writing (Intermediate) (Asset Languages) – Level 2
Awarding body:
OCR

Italian Writing (Preliminary) (Asset Languages) – Level 1
Awarding body:
OCR

Japanese Listening (Advanced) (Asset Languages) – Level 3
Awarding body:
OCR

Japanese Listening (Breakthrough) (Asset Languages) – Entry Level
Awarding body:
    OCR

Japanese Listening (Intermediate) (Asset Languages) – Level 2
Awarding body:
    OCR

Japanese Listening (Preliminary) (Asset Languages) – Level 1
Awarding body:
    OCR

Japanese Reading (Advanced) (Asset Languages) – Level 3
Awarding body:
    OCR

Japanese Reading (Breakthrough) (Asset Languages) – Entry Level
Awarding body:
    OCR

Japanese Reading (Intermediate) (Asset Languages) – Level 2
Awarding body:
    OCR

Japanese Reading (Preliminary) (Asset Languages) – Level 1
Awarding body:
    OCR

Japanese Speaking (Advanced) (Asset Languages) – Level 3
Awarding body:
    OCR

Japanese Speaking (Breakthrough) (Asset Languages) – Entry Level
Awarding body:
    OCR

Japanese Speaking (Intermediate) (Asset Languages) – Level 2
Awarding body:
    OCR

Japanese Speaking (Preliminary) (Asset Languages) – Level 1
Awarding body:
    OCR

Japanese Writing (Advanced) (Asset Languages) – Level 3
Awarding body:
    OCR

Japanese Writing (Breakthrough) (Asset Languages) – Entry Level
Awarding body:
    OCR

Japanese Writing (Intermediate) (Asset Languages) – Level 2
Awarding body:
    OCR

Japanese Writing (Preliminary) (Asset Languages) – Level 1
Awarding body:
    OCR

Language Service Professionals Working with Deaf and Deafblind People – Level 3
Awarding body:
    Signature

Language Skills – Level 1
Awarding body:
    NOCN

Language Skills – Level 2
Awarding body:
    NOCN

Language Skills – Level 3
Awarding body:
    NOCN

Languages for Travel and Leisure (Speaking and Listening, Reading and Writing) – Entry Level
Awarding body:
    ASCENTIS

Languages for Travel and Leisure (Speaking and Listening, Reading and Writing) – Level 1
Awarding body:
    ASCENTIS

Languages for Travel and Leisure (Speaking and Listening, Reading and Writing) – Level 2
Awarding body:
    ASCENTIS

Latin Language – Level 1
Awarding body:
  WJEC

Latin Language – Level 2
Awarding body:
  WJEC

Latin Language and Roman Civilisation – Level 1
Awarding body:
  WJEC

Latin Language and Roman Civilisation – Level 2
Awarding body:
  WJEC

Latin Literature – Level 1
Awarding body:
  WJEC

Latin Literature – Level 2
Awarding body:
  WJEC

Modern Foreign Languages – Entry Level
Awarding body:
  EDEXCEL

Modern Greek Listening (Advanced) (Asset Languages) – Level 3
Awarding body:
  OCR

Modern Greek Listening (Breakthrough) (Asset Languages) – Entry Level
Awarding body:
  OCR

Modern Greek Listening (Intermediate) (Asset Languages) – Level 2
Awarding body:
  OCR

Modern Greek Listening (Preliminary) (Asset Languages) – Level 1
Awarding body:
  OCR

Modern Greek Reading (Advanced) (Asset Languages) – Level 3
Awarding body:
  OCR

Modern Greek Reading (Breakthrough) (Asset Languages) – Entry Level
Awarding body:
  OCR

Modern Greek Reading (Intermediate) (Asset Languages) – Level 2
Awarding body:
  OCR

Modern Greek Reading (Preliminary) (Asset Languages) – Level 1
Awarding body:
  OCR

Modern Greek Speaking (Advanced) (Asset Languages) – Level 3
Awarding body:
  OCR

Modern Greek Speaking (Breakthrough) (Asset Languages) – Entry Level
Awarding body:
  OCR

Modern Greek Speaking (Intermediate) (Asset Languages) – Level 2
Awarding body:
  OCR

Modern Greek Speaking (Preliminary) (Asset Languages) – Level 1
Awarding body:
  OCR

Modern Greek Writing (Advanced) (Asset Languages) – Level 3
Awarding body:
  OCR

Modern Greek Writing (Breakthrough) (Asset Languages) – Entry Level
Awarding body:
  OCR

Modern Greek Writing (Intermediate) (Asset Languages) – Level 2
Awarding body:
  OCR

Modern Greek Writing (Preliminary) (Asset Languages) – Level 1
Awarding body:
  OCR

Modifying Written English Texts for Deaf People – Level 3
Awarding body:
Signature

Panjabi Listening (Breakthrough) (Asset Languages) – Entry Level
Awarding body:
OCR

Panjabi Listening (Intermediate) (Asset Languages) – Level 2
Awarding body:
OCR

Panjabi Listening (Preliminary) (Asset Languages) – Level 1
Awarding body:
OCR

Panjabi Reading (Breakthrough) (Asset Languages) – Entry Level
Awarding body:
OCR

Panjabi Reading (Intermediate) (Asset Languages) – Level 2
Awarding body:
OCR

Panjabi Reading (Preliminary) (Asset Languages) – Level 1
Awarding body:
OCR

Panjabi Speaking (Breakthrough) (Asset Languages) – Entry Level
Awarding body:
OCR

Panjabi Speaking (Intermediate) (Asset Languages) – Level 2
Awarding body:
OCR

Panjabi Speaking (Preliminary) (Asset Languages) – Level 1
Awarding body:
OCR

Panjabi Writing (Breakthrough) (Asset Languages) – Entry Level
Awarding body:
OCR

Panjabi Writing (Intermediate) (Asset Languages) – Level 2
Awarding body:
OCR

Panjabi Writing (Preliminary) (Asset Languages) – Level 1
Awarding body:
OCR

Polish Listening (Advanced) (Asset Languages) – Level 3
Awarding body:
OCR

Polish Listening (Breakthrough) (Asset Languages) – Entry Level
Awarding body:
OCR

Polish Listening (Intermediate) (Asset Languages) – Level 2
Awarding body:
OCR

Polish Listening (Preliminary) (Asset Languages) – Level 1
Awarding body:
OCR

Polish Reading (Advanced) (Asset Languages) – Level 3
Awarding body:
OCR

Polish Reading (Breakthrough) (Asset Languages) – Entry Level
Awarding body:
OCR

Polish Reading (Intermediate) (Asset Languages) – Level 2
Awarding body:
OCR

Polish Reading (Preliminary) (Asset Languages) – Level 1
Awarding body:
OCR

Polish Speaking (Advanced) (Asset Languages) – Level 3
Awarding body:
OCR

Polish Speaking (Breakthrough) (Asset Languages) – Entry Level
Awarding body:
OCR

Polish Speaking (Intermediate) (Asset Languages) – Level 2
Awarding body:
OCR

Polish Speaking (Preliminary) (Asset Languages) – Level 1
Awarding body:
OCR

Polish Writing (Advanced) (Asset Languages) – Level 3
Awarding body:
OCR

Polish Writing (Breakthrough) (Asset Languages) – Entry Level
Awarding body:
OCR

Polish Writing (Intermediate) (Asset Languages) – Level 2
Awarding body:
OCR

Polish Writing (Preliminary) (Asset Languages) – Level 1
Awarding body:
OCR

Portuguese Listening (Advanced) (Asset Languages) – Level 3
Awarding body:
OCR

Portuguese Listening (Breakthrough) (Asset Languages) – Entry Level
Awarding body:
OCR

Portuguese Listening (Intermediate) (Asset Languages) – Level 2
Awarding body:
OCR

Portuguese Listening (Preliminary) (Asset Languages) – Level 1
Awarding body:
OCR

Portuguese Reading (Advanced) (Asset Languages) – Level 3
Awarding body:
OCR

Portuguese Reading (Breakthrough) (Asset Languages) – Entry Level
Awarding body:
OCR

Portuguese Reading (Intermediate) (Asset Languages) – Level 2
Awarding body:
OCR

Portuguese Reading (Preliminary) (Asset Languages) – Level 1
Awarding body:
OCR

Portuguese Speaking (Advanced) (Asset Languages) – Level 3
Awarding body:
OCR

Portuguese Speaking (Breakthrough) (Asset Languages) – Entry Level
Awarding body:
OCR

Portuguese Speaking (Intermediate) (Asset Languages) – Level 2
Awarding body:
OCR

Portuguese Speaking (Preliminary) (Asset Languages) – Level 1
Awarding body:
OCR

Portuguese Writing (Advanced) (Asset Languages) – Level 3
Awarding body:
OCR

Portuguese Writing (Breakthrough) (Asset Languages) – Entry Level
Awarding body:
OCR

Portuguese Writing (Intermediate) (Asset Languages) – Level 2
Awarding body:
OCR

Portuguese Writing (Preliminary) (Asset Languages) – Level 1
Awarding body:
OCR

Practical Arabic – Entry Level
Awarding body:
ABC

Practical Arabic – Level 1
Awarding body:
ABC

Practical Arabic – Level 2
Awarding body:
ABC

Practical Bengali – Entry Level
Awarding body:
ABC

Practical French – Entry Level
Awarding body:
ABC

Practical French – Level 1
Awarding body:
ABC

Practical French – Level 2
Awarding body:
ABC

Practical French – Level 3
Awarding body:
ABC

Practical German – Entry Level
Awarding body:
ABC

Practical German – Level 1
Awarding body:
ABC

Practical German – Level 2
Awarding body:
ABC

Practical German – Level 3
Awarding body:
ABC

Practical Greek – Entry Level
Awarding body:
ABC

Practical Greek – Level 1
Awarding body:
ABC

Practical Greek – Level 2
Awarding body:
ABC

Practical Greek – Level 3
Awarding body:
ABC

Practical Italian – Entry Level
Awarding body:
ABC

Practical Italian – Level 1
Awarding body:
ABC

Practical Italian – Level 2
Awarding body:
ABC

Practical Italian – Level 3
Awarding body:
ABC

Practical Japanese – Entry Level
Awarding body:
ABC

Practical Japanese – Level 1
Awarding body:
ABC

Practical Japanese – Level 2
Awarding body:
ABC

Practical Japanese – Level 3
Awarding body:
ABC

Practical Mandarin Chinese – Entry Level
Awarding body:
ABC

Practical Mandarin Chinese – Level 1
Awarding body:
ABC

Practical Mandarin Chinese – Level 2
Awarding body:
ABC

Practical Polish – Entry Level
Awarding body:
 ABC

Practical Polish – Level 1
Awarding body:
 ABC

Practical Polish – Level 2
Awarding body:
 ABC

Practical Portuguese – Entry Level
Awarding body:
 ABC

Practical Portuguese – Level 1
Awarding body:
 ABC

Practical Portuguese – Level 2
Awarding body:
 ABC

Practical Portuguese – Level 3
Awarding body:
 ABC

Practical Punjabi – Entry Level
Awarding body:
 ABC

Practical Russian – Entry Level
Awarding body:
 ABC

Practical Russian – Level 1
Awarding body:
 ABC

Practical Russian – Level 2
Awarding body:
 ABC

Practical Spanish – Entry Level
Awarding body:
 ABC

Practical Spanish – Level 1
Awarding body:
 ABC

Practical Spanish – Level 2
Awarding body:
 ABC

Practical Spanish – Level 3
Awarding body:
 ABC

Practical Turkish – Entry Level
Awarding body:
 ABC

Practical Urdu – Entry Level
Awarding body:
 ABC

Practical Urdu – Level 1
Awarding body:
 ABC

Reading and Writing in Greek – Level 3
Awarding body:
 ABC

Reading and Writing in Japanese – Level 3
Awarding body:
 ABC

Russian Listening (Advanced) (Asset Languages) – Level 3
Awarding body:
 OCR

Russian Listening (Breakthrough) (Asset Languages) – Entry Level
Awarding body:
 OCR

Russian Listening (Intermediate) (Asset Languages) – Level 2
Awarding body:
 OCR

Russian Listening (Preliminary) (Asset Languages) – Level 1
Awarding body:
 OCR

Russian Reading (Advanced) (Asset Languages) – Level 3
Awarding body:
 OCR

Russian Reading (Breakthrough) (Asset Languages) – Entry Level
Awarding body:
 OCR

Russian Reading (Intermediate) (Asset Languages) – Level 2
Awarding body:
OCR

Russian Reading (Preliminary) (Asset Languages) – Level 1
Awarding body:
OCR

Russian Speaking (Advanced) (Asset Languages) – Level 3
Awarding body:
OCR

Russian Speaking (Breakthrough) (Asset Languages) – Entry Level
Awarding body:
OCR

Russian Speaking (Intermediate) (Asset Languages) – Level 2
Awarding body:
OCR

Russian Speaking (Preliminary) (Asset Languages) – Level 1
Awarding body:
OCR

Russian Writing (Advanced) (Asset Languages) – Level 3
Awarding body:
OCR

Russian Writing (Breakthrough) (Asset Languages) – Entry Level
Awarding body:
OCR

Russian Writing (Intermediate) (Asset Languages) – Level 2
Awarding body:
OCR

Russian Writing (Preliminary) (Asset Languages) – Level 1
Awarding body:
OCR

Somali Listening (Breakthrough) (Asset Languages) – Entry Level
Awarding body:
OCR

Somali Listening (Intermediate) (Asset Languages) – Level 2
Awarding body:
OCR

Somali Listening (Preliminary) (Asset Languages) – Level 1
Awarding body:
OCR

Somali Reading (Breakthrough) (Asset Languages) – Entry Level
Awarding body:
OCR

Somali Reading (Intermediate) (Asset Languages) – Level 2
Awarding body:
OCR

Somali Reading (Preliminary) (Asset Languages) – Level 1
Awarding body:
OCR

Somali Speaking (Breakthrough) (Asset Languages) – Entry Level
Awarding body:
OCR

Somali Speaking (Intermediate) (Asset Languages) – Level 2
Awarding body:
OCR

Somali Speaking (Preliminary) (Asset Languages) – Level 1
Awarding body:
OCR

Somali Writing (Breakthrough) (Asset Languages) – Entry Level
Awarding body:
OCR

Somali Writing (Intermediate) (Asset Languages) – Level 2
Awarding body:
OCR

Somali Writing (Preliminary) (Asset Languages) – Level 1
Awarding body:
OCR

Spanish – Entry Level
Awarding body:
AQA
CCEA
OCR
WJEC

Spanish – Level 1
Awarding body:
AQA

Spanish Listening (Intermediate) (Asset Languages) – Level 2
Awarding body:
OCR

Spanish Listening (Advanced) (Asset Languages) – Level 3
Awarding body:
OCR

Spanish Listening (Breakthrough) (Asset Languages) – Entry Level
Awarding body:
OCR

Spanish Listening (Preliminary) (Asset Languages) – Level 1
Awarding body:
OCR

Spanish Listening (Proficiency) (Asset Languages) – Level 4
Awarding body:
OCR

Spanish Reading (Advanced) (Asset Languages) – Level 3
Awarding body:
OCR

Spanish Reading (Breakthrough) (Asset Languages) – Entry Level
Awarding body:
OCR

Spanish Reading (Intermediate) (Asset Languages) – Level 2
Awarding body:
OCR

Spanish Reading (Preliminary) (Asset Languages) – Level 1
Awarding body:
OCR

Spanish Reading (Proficiency) (Asset Languages) – Level 4
Awarding body:
OCR

Spanish Speaking (Advanced) (Asset Languages) – Level 3
Awarding body:
OCR

Spanish Speaking (Breakthrough) (Asset Languages) – Entry Level
Awarding body:
OCR

Spanish Speaking (Intermediate) (Asset Languages) – Level 2
Awarding body:
OCR

Spanish Speaking (Preliminary) (Asset Languages) – Level 1
Awarding body:
OCR

Spanish Speaking (Proficiency) (Asset Languages) – Level 4
Awarding body:
OCR

Spanish Writing (Advanced) (Asset Languages) – Level 3
Awarding body:
OCR

Spanish Writing (Breakthrough) (Asset Languages) – Entry Level
Awarding body:
OCR

Spanish Writing (Intermediate) (Asset Languages) – Level 2
Awarding body:
OCR

Spanish Writing (Preliminary) (Asset Languages) – Level 1
Awarding body:
OCR

Spanish Writing (Proficiency) (Asset Languages) – Level 4
Awarding body:
OCR

Swedish Listening (Breakthrough) (Asset Languages) – Entry Level
Awarding body:
   OCR

Swedish Listening (Intermediate) (Asset Languages) – Level 2
Awarding body:
   OCR

Swedish Listening (Preliminary) (Asset Languages) – Level 1
Awarding body:
   OCR

Swedish Reading (Breakthrough) (Asset Languages) – Entry Level
Awarding body:
   OCR

Swedish Reading (Intermediate) (Asset Languages) – Level 2
Awarding body:
   OCR

Swedish Reading (Preliminary) (Asset Languages) – Level 1
Awarding body:
   OCR

Swedish Speaking (Breakthrough) (Asset Languages) – Entry Level
Awarding body:
   OCR

Swedish Speaking (Intermediate) (Asset Languages) – Level 2
Awarding body:
   OCR

Swedish Speaking (Preliminary) (Asset Languages) – Level 1
Awarding body:
   OCR

Swedish Writing (Breakthrough) (Asset Languages) – Entry Level
Awarding body:
   OCR

Swedish Writing (Intermediate) (Asset Languages) – Level 2
Awarding body:
   OCR

Swedish Writing (Preliminary) (Asset Languages) – Level 1
Awarding body:
   OCR

Tamil Listening (Intermediate) (Asset Languages) – Level 2
Awarding body:
   OCR

Tamil Listening (Preliminary) (Asset Languages) – Level 1
Awarding body:
   OCR

Tamil Reading (Breakthrough) (Asset Languages) – Entry Level
Awarding body:
   OCR

Tamil Reading (Intermediate) (Asset Languages) – Level 2
Awarding body:
   OCR

Tamil Reading (Preliminary) (Asset Languages) – Level 1
Awarding body:
   OCR

Tamil Speaking (Breakthrough) (Asset Languages) – Entry Level
Awarding body:
   OCR

Tamil Speaking (Intermediate) (Asset Languages) – Level 2
Awarding body:
   OCR

Tamil Speaking (Preliminary) (Asset Languages) – Level 1
Awarding body:
   OCR

Tamil Writing (Breakthrough) (Asset Languages) – Entry Level
Awarding body:
   OCR

Tamil Writing (Intermediate) (Asset Languages) – Level 2
Awarding body:
   OCR

Tamil Writing (Preliminary) (Asset Languages) – Level 1
Awarding body:
  OCR

Turkish Listening (Advanced) (Asset Languages) – Level 3
Awarding body:
  OCR

Turkish Listening (Breakthrough) (Asset Languages) – Entry Level
Awarding body:
  OCR

Turkish Listening (Intermediate) (Asset Languages) – Level 2
Awarding body:
  OCR

Turkish Listening (Preliminary) (Asset Languages) – Level 1
Awarding body:
  OCR

Turkish Reading (Advanced) (Asset Languages) – Level 3
Awarding body:
  OCR

Turkish Reading (Breakthrough) (Asset Languages) – Entry Level
Awarding body:
  OCR

Turkish Reading (Intermediate) (Asset Languages) – Level 2
Awarding body:
  OCR

Turkish Reading (Preliminary) (Asset Languages) – Level 1
Awarding body:
  OCR

Turkish Speaking (Advanced) (Asset Languages) – Level 3
Awarding body:
  OCR

Turkish Speaking (Breakthrough) (Asset Languages) – Entry Level
Awarding body:
  OCR

Turkish Speaking (Intermediate) (Asset Languages) – Level 2
Awarding body:
  OCR

Turkish Speaking (Preliminary) (Asset Languages) – Level 1
Awarding body:
  OCR

Turkish Writing (Advanced) (Asset Languages) – Level 3
Awarding body:
  OCR

Turkish Writing (Breakthrough) (Asset Languages) – Entry Level
Awarding body:
  OCR

Turkish Writing (Intermediate) (Asset Languages) – Level 2
Awarding body:
  OCR

Turkish Writing (Preliminary) (Asset Languages) – Level 1
Awarding body:
  OCR

Urdu Listening (Advanced) (Asset Languages) – Level 3
Awarding body:
  OCR

Urdu Listening (Breakthrough) (Asset Languages) – Entry Level
Awarding body:
  OCR

Urdu Listening (Intermediate) (Asset Languages) – Level 2
Awarding body:
  OCR

Urdu Listening (Preliminary) (Asset Languages) – Level 1
Awarding body:
  OCR

Urdu Reading (Advanced) (Asset Languages) – Level 3
Awarding body:
  OCR

Urdu Reading (Breakthrough) (Asset Languages) – Entry Level
Awarding body:
  OCR

Urdu Reading (Intermediate) (Asset Languages) – Level 2
Awarding body:
  OCR

Urdu Reading (Preliminary) (Asset Languages) – Level 1
Awarding body:
  OCR

Urdu Speaking (Advanced) (Asset Languages) – Level 3
Awarding body:
  OCR

Urdu Speaking (Breakthrough) (Asset Languages) – Entry Level
Awarding body:
  OCR

Urdu Speaking (Intermediate) (Asset Languages) – Level 2
Awarding body:
  OCR

Urdu Speaking (Preliminary) (Asset Languages) – Level 1
Awarding body:
  OCR

Urdu Writing (Advanced) (Asset Languages) – Level 3
Awarding body:
  OCR

Urdu Writing (Breakthrough) (Asset Languages) – Entry Level
Awarding body:
  OCR

Urdu Writing (Intermediate) (Asset Languages) – Level 2
Awarding body:
  OCR

Urdu Writing (Preliminary) (Asset Languages) – Level 1
Awarding body:
  OCR

Working in French – Level 1
Awarding body:
  DefAB

Working in French – Level 2
Awarding body:
  DefAB

Working in French (Relaying information) – Level 2
Awarding body:
  DefAB

Working in French (Writing and Relaying information) – Level 2
Awarding body:
  DefAB

Working in French (Writing) – Level 2
Awarding body:
  DefAB

Yoruba Listening (Breakthrough) (Asset Languages) – Entry Level
Awarding body:
  OCR

Yoruba Listening (Intermediate) (Asset Languages) – Level 2
Awarding body:
  OCR

Yoruba Listening (Preliminary) (Asset Languages) – Level 1
Awarding body:
  OCR

Yoruba Reading (Breakthrough) (Asset Languages) – Entry Level
Awarding body:
  OCR

Yoruba Reading (Intermediate) (Asset Languages) – Level 2
Awarding body:
  OCR

Yoruba Reading (Preliminary) (Asset Languages) – Level 1
Awarding body:
  OCR

Yoruba Speaking (Breakthrough) (Asset Languages) – Entry Level
Awarding body:
  OCR

Yoruba Speaking (Intermediate) (Asset Languages) – Level 2
Awarding body:
OCR

Yoruba Speaking (Preliminary) (Asset Languages) – Level 1
Awarding body:
OCR

Yoruba Writing (Breakthrough) (Asset Languages) – Entry Level
Awarding body:
OCR

Yoruba Writing (Intermediate) (Asset Languages) – Level 2
Awarding body:
OCR

Yoruba Writing (Preliminary) (Asset Languages) – Level 1
Awarding body:
OCR

Diploma

Public Service Interpreting – Level 6
Awarding body:
IoLET

Translation – Level 7
Awarding body:
IoLET

National Vocational Qualification

Arabic – Level 1
Awarding body:
EDEXCEL

Arabic – Level 2
Awarding body:
EDEXCEL

Arabic – Level 3
Awarding body:
EDEXCEL

Arabic Language Units – Level 1
Awarding body:
EDEXCEL

Arabic Language Units – Level 2
Awarding body:
EDEXCEL

Arabic Language Units – Level 3
Awarding body:
EDEXCEL

British Sign Language – Level 3
Awarding body:
Signature

British Sign Language – Level 4
Awarding body:
Signature

Chinese – Level 1
Awarding body:
EDEXCEL

Chinese – Level 2
Awarding body:
EDEXCEL

Chinese – Level 3
Awarding body:
EDEXCEL

Chinese Language Units – Level 1
Awarding body:
EDEXCEL

Chinese Language Units – Level 2
Awarding body:
EDEXCEL

Chinese Language Units – Level 3
Awarding body:
EDEXCEL

French – Level 1
Awarding body:
EDEXCEL

French – Level 2
Awarding body:
EDEXCEL

French – Level 3
Awarding body:
EDEXCEL

French Language Units – Level 1
Awarding body:
EDEXCEL
OCR

French Language Units – Level 2
Awarding body:
  EDEXCEL

French Language Units – Level 3
Awarding body:
  EDEXCEL
  OCR

French Language Units – Level 4
Awarding body:
  OCR

German – Level 1
Awarding body:
  EDEXCEL

German – Level 2
Awarding body:
  EDEXCEL

German – Level 3
Awarding body:
  EDEXCEL

German Language Units – Level 1
Awarding body:
  EDEXCEL
  OCR

German Language Units – Level 2
Awarding body:
  EDEXCEL
  OCR

German Language Units – Level 3
Awarding body:
  EDEXCEL
  OCR

German Language Units – Level 4
Awarding body:
  OCR

Interpreting (BSL/English) – Level 4
Awarding body:
  Signature

Irish Sign Language – Level 3
Awarding body:
  Signature

Italian – Level 1
Awarding body:
  EDEXCEL

Italian – Level 2
Awarding body:
  EDEXCEL

Italian – Level 3
Awarding body:
  EDEXCEL

Italian Language Units – Level 1
Awarding body:
  EDEXCEL
  OCR

Italian Language Units – Level 2
Awarding body:
  EDEXCEL
  OCR

Italian Language Units – Level 3
Awarding body:
  EDEXCEL
  OCR

Italian Language Units – Level 4
Awarding body:
  OCR

Spanish – Level 1
Awarding body:
  EDEXCEL

Spanish – Level 2
Awarding body:
  EDEXCEL

Spanish – Level 3
Awarding body:
  EDEXCEL

Spanish Language Units – Level 1
Awarding body:
  EDEXCEL
  OCR

Spanish Language Units – Level 2
Awarding body:
  EDEXCEL
  OCR

Spanish Language Units – Level 3
Awarding body:
  EDEXCEL
  OCR

Spanish Language Units – Level 4
Awarding body:
  OCR

Pre-U Certificate

Classical Greek (Principal) – Level 3
Awarding body:
  Cambridge International

French (Principal) – Level 3
Awarding body:
  Cambridge International

French (Short Course) – Level 3
Awarding body:
  Cambridge International

German (Principal) – Level 3
Awarding body:
  Cambridge International

German (Short Course) – Level 3
Awarding body:
  Cambridge International

Italian – Level 3
Awarding body:
  Cambridge International

Italian (Short Course) – Level 3
Awarding body:
  Cambridge International

Latin (Principal) – Level 3
Awarding body:
  Cambridge International

Mandarin Chinese (Principal) – Level 3
Awarding body:
  Cambridge International

Mandarin Chinese (Short Course) – Level 3
Awarding body:
  Cambridge International

Russian (Principal) – Level 3
Awarding body:
  Cambridge International

Russian (Short Course) – Level 3
Awarding body:
  Cambridge International

Spanish (Principal) – Level 3
Awarding body:
  Cambridge International

Spanish (Short Course) – Level 3
Awarding body:
  Cambridge International

Leisure, Travel and Tourism

Sport, Leisure and Recreation

Advanced Diploma

Sport and Active Leisure – Level 3
Awarding body:
 AQA
 City & Guilds
 EDEXCEL
 OCR

Award

Active, Healthy Living – Level 1
Awarding body:
 Active IQ

Activity Leadership – Level 2
Awarding body:
 EDI

Adapting Fitness Instruction for Adolescents – Level 2
Awarding body:
 Active IQ

Adapting Gym Instruction for Adolescents – Level 2
Awarding body:
 Active IQ

Adapting Physical Activity for Antenatal and Postnatal Clients – Level 3
Awarding body:
 VTCT

Assisting Health Related Activity Sessions – Level 1
Awarding body:
 Active IQ

Basic Expedition Leadership – Level 2
Awarding body:
 Sports Leaders UK

Basic Health and Fitness – Entry Level
Awarding body:
 Active IQ

Basic Pool Plant Operations – Level 2
Awarding body:
 Active IQ

Chair Based Exercise for the Frailer Older Person – Level 2
Awarding body:
 CYQ

Circuit Training – Level 2
Awarding body:
 CYQ

Coaching Studies – Level 2
Awarding body:
 1st4sport

Community Sports Leadership – Level 2
Awarding body:
 Sports Leaders UK

Customer Care for the Active Leisure Sector – Level 2
Awarding body:
 Active IQ

Dance Leadership – Level 1
Awarding body:
 Sports Leaders UK

Designing Pre and Post Natal Exercise Programmes – Level 3
Awarding body:
 Active IQ

Employment Awareness in Active Leisure and Learning – Level 2
Awarding body:
1st4sport
Active IQ
City & Guilds
CYQ
LTAO
VTCT

Employment Awareness in Active Leisure and Learning – Level 3
Awarding body:
1st4sport
Active IQ
City & Guilds
CYQ
LTAO
VTCT

Functional Training for the Independent Older Adult – Level 3
Awarding body:
CYQ

Group Indoor Cycling – Level 2
Awarding body:
CYQ

Healthy Living – Level 1
Awarding body:
EDI

Higher Sports Leadership – Level 3
Awarding body:
Sports Leaders UK

Instructing Circuit Sessions – Level 2
Awarding body:
Active IQ

Instructing Circuit Training Sessions – Level 2
Awarding body:
VTCT

Instructing Physical Activity for Ante/Post Natal Exercise – Level 3
Awarding body:
CYQ

Instructing Sports Specific Conditioning – Level 3
Awarding body:
VTCT

Leading Health Related Activity Sessions – Level 2
Awarding body:
Active IQ

Lifestyle Management – Level 1
Awarding body:
CYQ

Mountain Leadership – Level 3
Awarding body:
MLTE

Preparation for Event Volunteering – Entry Level
Awarding body:
1st4sport
Active IQ
NOCN
VTCT

Preparation for Event Volunteering (Personal Best) – Level 1
Awarding body:
1st4sport
Active IQ
City & Guilds
EDI
NOCN
VTCT

Single Pitch Rock Climbing Supervision – Level 3
Awarding body:
MLTE

Sport and Active Leisure – Entry Level
Awarding body:
EDEXCEL

Sport and Active Leisure – Level 1
Awarding body:
EDEXCEL

Sport and Leisure Industry Awareness – Level 1
Awarding body:
1st4sport

Sports Leadership – Level 1
Awarding body:
Sports Leaders UK

Step Exercise to Music – Level 2
Awarding body:
CYQ

Studio Resistance Training – Level 2
Awarding body:
CYQ

Swimming Pool Operations – Level 2
Awarding body:
Active IQ

Swimming Pool Operations – Level 3
Awarding body:
Active IQ

**The Principles and Practice of
Swimming Pool Water Testing – Level 2**
Awarding body:
Active IQ

**The Principles of Health and Fitness –
Entry Level**
Awarding body:
Active IQ

**Understanding Stewarding at Spectator
Events – Level 2**
Awarding body:
1st4sport
City & Guilds
EDI
NCFE

Walk Leading – Level 2
Awarding body:
CYQ

Walking Group Leadership – Level 3
Awarding body:
MLTE

**Working with Participants with
Disabilities in Sport and Active Leisure –
Level 2**
Awarding body:
City & Guilds

BTEC Award

**Understanding Stewarding at Spectator
Events – Level 2**
Awarding body:
EDEXCEL

**Understanding the Laws of Sport –
Level 2**
Awarding body:
EDEXCEL

BTEC Certificate

Sailing and Watersports – Level 2
Awarding body:
EDEXCEL

Sailing and Watersports – Level 3
Awarding body:
EDEXCEL

Sport – Level 2
Awarding body:
EDEXCEL

Sport – Level 3
Awarding body:
EDEXCEL

Sport and Exercise Sciences – Level 3
Awarding body:
EDEXCEL

BTEC Diploma

Sailing and Watersports – Level 3
Awarding body:
EDEXCEL

Sport – Level 3
Awarding body:
EDEXCEL

Sport and Exercise Sciences – Level 3
Awarding body:
EDEXCEL

BTEC Extended Diploma

Sport – Level 3
Awarding body:
EDEXCEL

Sport and Exercise Sciences – Level 3
Awarding body:
EDEXCEL

BTEC First Certificate

Sport – Level 2
Awarding body:
  EDEXCEL

BTEC First Diploma

Sport – Level 2
Awarding body:
  EDEXCEL

BTEC Higher National Certificate

Sport and Exercise Sciences – Level 5
Awarding body:
  EDEXCEL

Sport and Leisure Management – Level 5
Awarding body:
  EDEXCEL

BTEC Higher National Diploma

Sport and Exercise Sciences – Level 5
Awarding body:
  EDEXCEL

Sport and Leisure Management – Level 5
Awarding body:
  EDEXCEL

BTEC National Award

Sport – Level 3
Awarding body:
  EDEXCEL

Sport and Exercise Sciences – Level 3
Awarding body:
  EDEXCEL

BTEC National Certificate

Sport – Level 3
Awarding body:
  EDEXCEL

Sport and Exercise Sciences – Level 3
Awarding body:
  EDEXCEL

BTEC National Diploma

Sport – Level 3
Awarding body:
  EDEXCEL

Sport and Exercise Sciences – Level 3
Awarding body:
  EDEXCEL

BTEC Subsidiary Certificate

Sailing and Watersports – Level 2
Awarding body:
  EDEXCEL

BTEC Subsidiary Diploma

Sport – Level 3
Awarding body:
  EDEXCEL

Sport and Exercise Sciences – Level 3
Awarding body:
  EDEXCEL

Certificate

Active Leisure Industry and Organisational Awareness – Level 2
Awarding body:
  VTCT

Active Leisure Industry and Organisational Awareness – Level 3
Awarding body:
  VTCT

Advanced Fitness Instructing – Level 3
Awarding body:
  Active IQ
  CYQ
  NCFE

Advanced Fitness Instructing (Gym) – Level 3
Awarding body:
  Active IQ
  City & Guilds
  CYQ
  OCR
  VTCT

Assessing in the Active Leisure Sector – Level 3
Awarding body:
  CYQ

Coaching – Level 1
Awarding body:
  1st4sport
  ASA

Coaching – Level 2
Awarding body:
  1st4sport
  ASA
  EQL

Coaching – Level 3
Awarding body:
  1st4sport
  ASA
  EQL

Coaching (Assistant) – Level 1
Awarding body:
  EQL

Coaching Athletics – Level 2
Awarding body:
  ASQ

Coaching Athletics – Level 3
Awarding body:
  ASQ

Coaching Athletics (Assistant Coach) – Level 1
Awarding body:
  ASQ

Coaching Golf – Level 1
Awarding body:
  ASQ

Coaching Golf – Level 2
Awarding body:
  ASQ

Coaching Golf – Level 3
Awarding body:
  ASQ

Coaching Gymnastics – Level 1
Awarding body:
  BG

Coaching Gymnastics – Level 2
Awarding body:
  BG

Coaching Gymnastics – Level 3
Awarding body:
  BG

Coaching Paddlesport – Level 1
Awarding body:
  BCU

Coaching Paddlesport – Level 2
Awarding body:
  BCU

Coaching Paddlesport – Level 3
Awarding body:
  BCU

Community Sports Work – Level 3
Awarding body:
  Sports Leaders UK

Developing Personal Health and Fitness – Level 1
Awarding body:
  ABC

Developing Personal Health and Fitness – Level 2
Awarding body:
  ABC

Event and Match Day Stewarding – Level 2
Awarding body:
  1st4sport

Event Management – Level 3
Awarding body:
  NCFE

Event Planning – Level 2
Awarding body:
  NCFE

Exercise for the Management of Low Back Pain – Level 4
Awarding body:
　Active IQ

Exercise Referral – Level 3
Awarding body:
　Active IQ

Exercise Referral for Clients with Specific Controlled Conditions – Level 3
Awarding body:
　CYQ

Exercise Studies – Level 1
Awarding body:
　NCFE

First Aid for Sport – Level 2
Awarding body:
　1st4sport

Fitness Industry Studies – Level 2
Awarding body:
　NCFE

Fitness Instructing – Level 2
Awarding body:
　Active IQ
　City & Guilds
　CYQ
　NCFE
　OCR
　VTCT

Fitness Management – Level 3
Awarding body:
　Active IQ

Health & Fitness – Level 1
Awarding body:
　VTCT

Improving Personal Exercise and Nutrition – Level 2
Awarding body:
　NCFE

Improving the Customer Experience in the Active Leisure Sector (Fitness Instructing Context) – Level 2
Awarding body:
　CYQ

Industry and Organisational Awareness for the Active Leisure and Learning Industry – Level 2
Awarding body:
　1st4sport
　Active IQ

Industry and Organisational Awareness for the Active Leisure and Learning Industry – Level 3
Awarding body:
　1st4sport
　Active IQ

Instructing Circuit Sessions – Level 2
Awarding body:
　Active IQ

Instructing Health Related Exercise for Children – Level 2
Awarding body:
　CYQ

Instructing Mat-based Pilates – Level 3
Awarding body:
　OCR

Internal Verifying in the Active Leisure Sector – Level 3
Awarding body:
　CYQ

Leading Health Related Activity Sessions – Level 2
Awarding body:
　Active IQ

Managing Community Sport – Level 3
Awarding body:
　Sports Leaders UK

Managing Sports Volunteers – Level 3
Awarding body:
　1st4sport

Motorsports Incident Marshalling – Level 2
Awarding body:
　ASCENTIS

National Rescue Standard – Level 2
Awarding body:
　STA

National Rescue Standard – Poolside Helper – Level 2
Awarding body:
  STA

Nutrition for a Healthy Lifestyle – Level 2
Awarding body:
  CYQ

Outdoor Activity Leadership – Level 2
Awarding body:
  NCFE

Outdoor Industry – Level 3
Awarding body:
  NCFE

Personal Development for the Outdoor Industry – Level 1
Awarding body:
  NCFE

Personal Training – Level 3
Awarding body:
  Active IQ
  CYQ

Physical Education – Entry Level
Awarding body:
  AQA
  CCEA
  EDEXCEL
  OCR
  WJEC

Pool Plant Operations – Level 3
Awarding body:
  Active IQ

Scuba Instruction – Level 3
Awarding body:
  PADI

Sport and Active Leisure – Level 1
Awarding body:
  EDEXCEL

Sport and Leisure – Level 1
Awarding body:
  City & Guilds

Sport and Leisure Studies – Level 1
Awarding body:
  NCFE

Sport and Recreation Operations – Level 2
Awarding body:
  Active IQ

Sport, Recreation and Allied Occupation Industry and Organisational Awareness – Level 3
Awarding body:
  City & Guilds

Sport, Recreation and Allied Occupations Industry and Organisational Awareness – Level 2
Awarding body:
  City & Guilds

Sports and Fitness Therapies – Level 2
Awarding body:
  VTCT

Sports Coaching – Level 2
Awarding body:
  NCFE

Sports Massage – Level 3
Awarding body:
  CYQ

Sports Massage Therapy – Level 3
Awarding body:
  Active IQ

Sports Officials – Level 2
Awarding body:
  1st4sport

Supervisory Management in Sport and Recreation – Level 3
Awarding body:
  Active IQ

Swimming Pool and Spa Water Treatment – Level 2
Awarding body:
  STA

Swimming Pool Supervision and Rescue (National Pool Lifeguard Qualification – NPLQ) – Level 2
Awarding body:
  IQL

**Talented Athlete Lifestyle Support –
Level 3**
Awarding body:
　1st4sport

Teaching (Aquatics) – Level 1
Awarding body:
　ASA

Teaching Aquatics – Level 2
Awarding body:
　ASA

Teaching Mat Pilates – Level 3
Awarding body:
　CYQ

**Teaching Physical Activity to Children –
Level 2**
Awarding body:
　Active IQ

Teaching Swimming – Level 2
Awarding body:
　STA

Teaching Yoga – Level 3
Awarding body:
　CYQ

**The Treatment and Management of
Injury in Football – Level 3**
Awarding body:
　1st4sport

**Training and Development in the Active
Leisure Sector – Level 3**
Awarding body:
　CYQ

**Treatment and Management of Injury in
Sport – Level 2**
Awarding body:
　1st4sport

**Understanding the Fitness, Leisure and
Recreation Industry – Level 2**
Awarding body:
　CYQ

**Understanding the Fitness, Leisure and
Recreation Industry – Level 3**
Awarding body:
　CYQ

Working in the Outdoors – Level 2
Awarding body:
　1st4sport

Working in the Outdoors – Level 3
Awarding body:
　1st4sport

Diploma

**Exercise and Fitness Instructing –
Level 2**
Awarding body:
　CYQ

Pilates Teaching – Level 3
Awarding body:
　ITEC

Sport and Active Leisure – Level 1
Awarding body:
　EDEXCEL

Sport and Leisure – Level 2
Awarding body:
　City & Guilds

Sport and Recreation – Level 2
Awarding body:
　Active IQ

**Sports and Fitness Therapy Techniques –
Level 3**
Awarding body:
　VTCT

Sports Massage – Level 3
Awarding body:
　ITEC

Sports Massage Therapy – Level 3
Awarding body:
　VTCT

Yoga Teaching – Level 3
Awarding body:
　ITEC

Foundation Certificate

**Swimming Pool and Spa Water
Treatment – Level 1**
Awarding body:
　STA

Foundation Diploma

Sport and Active Leisure – Level 1
Awarding body:
AQA
City & Guilds
EDEXCEL
EDI
OCR

Higher Diploma

Sport and Active Leisure – Level 2
Awarding body:
AQA
City & Guilds
EDEXCEL
EDI
OCR

Higher Professional Diploma

Sport and Recreation Management – Level 4
Awarding body:
City & Guilds

Introductory Certificate

Exercise and Fitness Instructing – Level 1
Awarding body:
CYQ

Sport and Leisure – Level 1
Awarding body:
EDEXCEL

Introductory Diploma

Sport and Leisure – Level 1
Awarding body:
EDEXCEL

National Award

Sport – Level 2
Awarding body:
OCR

National Certificate

Sport – Level 2
Awarding body:
OCR

Sport – Level 3
Awarding body:
OCR

National Diploma

Sport – Level 3
Awarding body:
OCR

National Extended Diploma

Sport – Level 3
Awarding body:
OCR

National Vocational Qualification

Achieving Excellence in Sports Performance – Level 3
Awarding body:
1st4sport
City & Guilds
EDEXCEL

Coaching – Level 3
Awarding body:
City & Guilds

Cultural Heritage – Level 4
Awarding body:
EDI

Cultural Heritage Management – Level 5
Awarding body:
EDI

Cultural Heritage Operations – Level 3
Awarding body:
EDI

Instructing Exercise and Fitness – Level 2
Awarding body:
  Active IQ
  City & Guilds
  CYQ
  EDEXCEL
  NCFE
  OCR
  VTCT

Instructing Physical Activity and Exercise – Level 3
Awarding body:
  Active IQ
  City & Guilds
  CYQ
  NCFE
  OCR
  VTCT

Leisure Management – Level 3
Awarding body:
  Active IQ
  City & Guilds
  CYQ
  EDEXCEL
  OCR
  VTCT

Managing Sport and Active Leisure – Level 4
Awarding body:
  City & Guilds

Mechanical Ride Operations (Leisure Parks, Piers and Attractions) – Level 2
Awarding body:
  City & Guilds

Museums, Galleries and Heritage (Heritage Care and Visitor Services) – Level 2
Awarding body:
  EDI

Outdoor Programmes – Level 3
Awarding body:
  City & Guilds

Spectator Safety – Level 2
Awarding body:
  1st4sport
  City & Guilds
  EDEXCEL
  EDI
  NCFE

Spectator Safety – Level 3
Awarding body:
  1st4sport
  City & Guilds
  EDEXCEL
  EDI
  NCFE

Spectator Safety Management – Level 4
Awarding body:
  City & Guilds
  EDEXCEL
  EDI
  NCFE

Sport and Play Surfaces – Level 2
Awarding body:
  EDEXCEL

Sport, Recreation and Allied Occupations – Level 1
Awarding body:
  City & Guilds
  EDEXCEL
  OCR

Sport, Recreation and Allied Occupations: Activity Leadership – Level 2
Awarding body:
  Active IQ
  City & Guilds
  CYQ
  EDEXCEL
  NCFE
  OCR
  VTCT

Sport, Recreation and Allied Occupations: Coaching, Teaching and Instructing – Level 2
Awarding body:
  1st4sport
  EDEXCEL

Sport, Recreation and Allied Occupations: Coaching, Teaching and Instructing – Level 3
Awarding body:
City & Guilds

Sport, Recreation and Allied Occupations: Coaching, Teaching, Instructing – Level 2
Awarding body:
City & Guilds
OCR

Sport, Recreation and Allied Occupations: Operational Services – Level 2
Awarding body:
Active IQ
City & Guilds
CYQ
EDEXCEL
NCFE
OCR
VTCT

Sports Development – Level 3
Awarding body:
City & Guilds
EDEXCEL
OCR

Pre-U Certificate

Sports Science (Principal) – Level 3
Awarding body:
Cambridge International

Principal Learning

Sport and Active Leisure – Level 1
Awarding body:
EDEXCEL
EDI
OCR

Sport and Active Leisure – Level 2
Awarding body:
EDEXCEL
EDI
OCR

Sport and Active Leisure – Level 3
Awarding body:
EDEXCEL
EDI

Sports and Active Leisure – Level 1
Awarding body:
AQA
City & Guilds

Sports and Active Leisure – Level 2
Awarding body:
AQA
City & Guilds

Sports and Active Leisure – Level 3
Awarding body:
AQA
City & Guilds

Progression Award

Sport and Recreation – Level 3
Awarding body:
City & Guilds

Progression Diploma

Sport and Active Leisure – Level 3
Awarding body:
AQA
City & Guilds
EDEXCEL
EDI
OCR

Teaching and Lecturing

Certificate

Mentoring in Sport – Level 3
Awarding body:
   1st4sport

Travel and Tourism

Advanced Diploma

Tourism Management – Level 5
Awarding body:
   CTH

Travel and Tourism – Level 3
Awarding body:
   AQA
   City & Guilds
   EDEXCEL
   OCR

Advanced National Diploma

Travel and Tourism – Level 3
Awarding body:
   City & Guilds

BTEC Certificate

Preparation for Air Cabin Crew Service – Level 2
Awarding body:
   EDEXCEL

Preparation for Tourist Guiding – Level 2
Awarding body:
   EDEXCEL

Transporting Passengers by Bus and Coach – Level 2
Awarding body:
   EDEXCEL

Travel and Tourism Services – Level 2
Awarding body:
   EDEXCEL

Travel and Tourism Services – Level 3
Awarding body:
   EDEXCEL

BTEC Diploma

Travel Operations – Level 2
Awarding body:
   EDEXCEL

Travel Operations – Level 3
Awarding body:
   EDEXCEL

BTEC First Certificate

Travel and Tourism – Level 2
Awarding body:
   EDEXCEL

BTEC First Diploma

Travel and Tourism – Level 2
Awarding body:
  EDEXCEL

BTEC Higher National Certificate

Travel and Tourism Management – Level 5
Awarding body:
  EDEXCEL

BTEC Higher National Diploma

Travel and Tourism Management – Level 5
Awarding body:
  EDEXCEL

BTEC Intermediate Diploma

Overseas Resort Operations – Level 2
Awarding body:
  EDEXCEL

BTEC National Award

Aviation Operations – Level 3
Awarding body:
  EDEXCEL

Travel and Tourism – Level 3
Awarding body:
  EDEXCEL

BTEC National Certificate

Aviation Operations – Level 3
Awarding body:
  EDEXCEL

Travel and Tourism – Level 3
Awarding body:
  EDEXCEL

BTEC National Diploma

Aviation Operations – Level 3
Awarding body:
  EDEXCEL

Travel and Tourism – Level 3
Awarding body:
  EDEXCEL

Certificate

Air Cabin Crew Skills – Level 2
Awarding body:
  ASCENTIS

Airline Cabin Crew – Level 2
Awarding body:
  NCFE

Airport Customer Service Agent Skills – Level 2
Awarding body:
  ASCENTIS

Airport Operations – Level 2
Awarding body:
  NCFE

Airport Passenger Services Agents – Level 2
Awarding body:
  NCFE

Customer Service for Hospitality, Leisure, Travel and Tourism – Level 2
Awarding body:
  NCFE

Event Planning – Level 2
Awarding body:
  EDI

Organising Conferences, Leisure or Hospitality Events – Level 3
Awarding body:
  EDI

Principles of Aviation First Aid – Level 2
Awarding body:
  ASCENTIS

Resort Representatives – Level 2
Awarding body:
  NCFE

Sustainable Tourism – Level 2
Awarding body:
  NCFE

Sustainable Tourism – Level 3
Awarding body:
  NCFE

Tour Management – Level 3
Awarding body:
  NCFE

Travel – Level 1
Awarding body:
  NCFE

Travel and Tourism – Level 1
Awarding body:
  City & Guilds

Travel and Tourism – Level 2
Awarding body:
  City & Guilds
  NCFE

Travel and Tourism – Level 3
Awarding body:
  City & Guilds

Travel and Tourism (Additional Services) – Level 2
Awarding body:
  City & Guilds

Travel and Tourism (Air Fares and Ticketing) – Level 1
Awarding body:
  City & Guilds

Travel and Tourism (Air Fares and Ticketing) – Level 2
Awarding body:
  City & Guilds

Travel and Tourism (Children's Resort Representatives) – Level 2
Awarding body:
  City & Guilds

Travel and Tourism (Introduction to Business Travel Practices) – Level 2
Awarding body:
  City & Guilds

Travel and Tourism (Introduction to Responsible Tourism) – Level 2
Awarding body:
  City & Guilds

Travel and Tourism (Meet and Greet) – Level 2
Awarding body:
  City & Guilds

Travel and Tourism (Resort Representatives) – Level 2
Awarding body:
  City & Guilds

Travel and Tourism (UK Destinations) – Level 1
Awarding body:
  City & Guilds

Travel and Tourism (UK Destinations) – Level 2
Awarding body:
  City & Guilds

Travel and Tourism Communication Skills – Overseas Resort Representative Pathway – Level 3
Awarding body:
  ESB

Travel and Tourism Communication Skills – Overseas Resort Reps Pathway – Level 2
Awarding body:
  ESB

Travel and Tourism for all – Level 1
Awarding body:
  City & Guilds

Diploma

Tourism Management – Level 4
Awarding body:
  CTH

Travel Agency Management – Level 4
Awarding body:
  CTH

First Award

Travel and Tourism – Level 2
Awarding body:
City & Guilds

First Diploma

Travel and Tourism – Level 2
Awarding body:
City & Guilds

Foundation Diploma

Travel and Tourism – Level 1
Awarding body:
AQA
City & Guilds
EDEXCEL
OCR

Higher Diploma

Travel and Tourism – Level 2
Awarding body:
AQA
City & Guilds
EDEXCEL
OCR

Intermediate Certificate

Air Cabin Crewing – Level 2
Awarding body:
EAL

Introductory Award

Travel and Tourism – Level 1
Awarding body:
City & Guilds

Introductory Certificate

Hospitality, Travel and Tourism – Level 1
Awarding body:
EDEXCEL

Introductory Diploma

Hospitality, Travel and Tourism – Level 1
Awarding body:
EDEXCEL

Travel and Tourism – Level 1
Awarding body:
City & Guilds

IVQ Advanced Diploma

International Tourism – Level 3
Awarding body:
City & Guilds

IVQ Certificate

International Tourism – Level 1
Awarding body:
City & Guilds

IVQ Diploma

International Tourism – Level 2
Awarding body:
City & Guilds

National Award

Leisure and Tourism – Level 1
Awarding body:
OCR

Travel and Tourism – Level 2
Awarding body:
OCR

Travel and Tourism – Level 3
Awarding body:
City & Guilds

National Certificate

Leisure and Tourism – Level 1
Awarding body:
OCR

Travel and Tourism – Level 2
Awarding body:
  OCR

Travel and Tourism – Level 3
Awarding body:
  OCR

National Diploma

Travel and Tourism – Level 3
Awarding body:
  City & Guilds
  OCR

National Extended Diploma

Travel and Tourism – Level 3
Awarding body:
  OCR

National First Award

Leisure and Tourism – Level 1
Awarding body:
  OCR

National Vocational Qualification

Travel and Tourism – Level 2
Awarding body:
  City & Guilds

Travel and Tourism – Level 3
Awarding body:
  City & Guilds

Travel and Tourism Services – Level 2
Awarding body:
  EDEXCEL

Travel and Tourism Services – Level 3
Awarding body:
  EDEXCEL

Principal Learning

Travel and Tourism – Level 1
Awarding body:
  AQA
  City & Guilds
  EDEXCEL
  OCR

Travel and Tourism – Level 2
Awarding body:
  AQA
  City & Guilds
  EDEXCEL
  OCR

Travel and Tourism – Level 3
Awarding body:
  AQA
  City & Guilds
  EDEXCEL
  OCR

Progression Diploma

Travel and Tourism – Level 3
Awarding body:
  AQA
  City & Guilds
  EDEXCEL
  OCR

Preparation for Life and Work

Foundations for Learning and Life

Award

Communication Skills – Entry Level
Awarding body:
EDEXCEL

Community Volunteering – Level 1
Awarding body:
ASDAN

Community Volunteering – Level 2
Awarding body:
ASDAN

Community Volunteering – Level 3
Awarding body:
ASDAN

Employability – Entry Level
Awarding body:
ASDAN

Employability – Level 1
Awarding body:
ASDAN

Employability – Level 2
Awarding body:
ASDAN

Employability – Level 3
Awarding body:
ASDAN

English – Level 2
Awarding body:
WJEC

Financial Literacy – Entry Level
Awarding body:
NOCN

Financial Literacy – Level 1
Awarding body:
NOCN

Functional Skills English – Entry Level
Awarding body:
ASCENTIS
ASDAN
City & Guilds
EDEXCEL
EDI
NCFE
NOCN
OCR
VTCT
WJEC

Functional Skills English – Level 1
Awarding body:
AQA
ASCENTIS
ASDAN
City & Guilds
EDEXCEL
EDI
NCFE
OCR
VTCT
WJEC

Functional Skills English – Level 2
Awarding body:
AQA
ASCENTIS
ASDAN
City & Guilds
EDEXCEL
EDI
NCFE
OCR
VTCT

Functional Skills ICT – Entry Level
Awarding body:
EDEXCEL

Functional Skills Information and Communication Technology – Entry Level
Awarding body:
ASCENTIS
ASDAN
City & Guilds
EDI
NCFE
OCR
VTCT
WJEC

Functional Skills Information and Communication Technology – Level 1
Awarding body:
AQA
ASCENTIS
ASDAN
City & Guilds
EDEXCEL
EDI
NCFE
OCR
VTCT
WJEC

Functional Skills Information and Communication Technology – Level 2
Awarding body:
AQA
ASCENTIS
ASDAN
City & Guilds
EDEXCEL
EDI
NCFE
OCR
VTCT

Functional Skills Information and Communication Technology (ICT) – Entry Level
Awarding body:
NOCN

Functional Skills Mathematics – Entry Level
Awarding body:
ASCENTIS
ASDAN
City & Guilds
EDEXCEL
EDI
NCFE
NOCN
OCR
VTCT
WJEC

Functional Skills Mathematics – Level 1
Awarding body:
AQA
ASCENTIS
ASDAN
City & Guilds
EDEXCEL
EDI
NCFE
OCR
VTCT
WJEC

Functional Skills Mathematics – Level 2
Awarding body:
AQA
ASCENTIS
ASDAN
City & Guilds
EDEXCEL
EDI
NCFE
OCR
VTCT
WJEC

ICT Skills – Entry Level
Awarding body:
EDEXCEL

Information and Communication Technology – Level 2
Awarding body:
WJEC

Information, Advice or Guidance (Introduction) – Level 1
Awarding body:
NOCN

**Introduction to Hair and Beauty –
Entry Level**
Awarding body:
  EDEXCEL

**Introduction to Hair and Beauty –
Level 1**
Awarding body:
  EDEXCEL

Land-based Studies – Entry Level
Awarding body:
  EDEXCEL

Land-based Studies – Level 1
Awarding body:
  EDEXCEL

Managing Personal Finance – Level 1
Awarding body:
  ASCENTIS

Mathematical Skills – Entry Level
Awarding body:
  EDEXCEL

Media Literacy – Entry Level
Awarding body:
  NOCN

Parenting – Level 1
Awarding body:
  EDEXCEL

Parents to Be – Entry Level
Awarding body:
  EDEXCEL

Parents to Be – Level 1
Awarding body:
  EDEXCEL

**Personal and Social Development –
Entry Level**
Awarding body:
  ASDAN
  City & Guilds
  EDI

**Personal and Social Development –
Level 1**
Awarding body:
  ASDAN
  City & Guilds
  EDI

**Personal and Social Development –
Level 2**
Awarding body:
  ASDAN

Personal Development – Entry Level
Awarding body:
  ASCENTIS

Personal Development – Level 1
Awarding body:
  ASCENTIS

Personal Effectiveness – Level 1
Awarding body:
  ASDAN

**Personal Employability, Achievement
and Reflection for Learning (Pilot) –
Entry Level**
Awarding body:
  GQAL

**Personal Employability, Achievement
and Reflection for Learning (Pilot) –
Level 1**
Awarding body:
  GQAL

**Personal Employability, Achievement
and Reflection for Learning (Pilot) –
Level 2**
Awarding body:
  GQAL

**Personal Employability, Achievement
and Reflection for Learning (Pilot) –
Level 3**
Awarding body:
  GQAL

Personal Finance – Level 1
Awarding body:
  BCS

Personal Finance – Level 2
Awarding body:
  BCS

Personal Financial Planning – Level 2
Awarding body:
  IFS

Personal Money Management – Level 1
Awarding body:
  CCEA

Personal Progress – Entry Level
Awarding body:
ASCENTIS
ASDAN
City & Guilds
EDEXCEL
NOCN

Personal, Social and Health Education – Level 1
Awarding body:
AQA

Progression – Entry Level
Awarding body:
NOCN

Progression – Level 1
Awarding body:
NOCN

Progression – Level 2
Awarding body:
NOCN

Progression – Level 3
Awarding body:
NOCN

Safe Road User Award – Level 1
Awarding body:
SQA

Skills for Independent Living – Entry Level
Awarding body:
EDEXCEL

Skills for Supported Employment – Entry Level
Awarding body:
EDEXCEL

Skills Towards Enabling Progression (Step-UP) – Entry Level
Awarding body:
NOCN

Skills Towards Enabling Progression (Step-UP) – Level 1
Awarding body:
NOCN

Supporting a Child's Learning and Development – Entry Level
Awarding body:
ASCENTIS

Supporting a Child's Learning and Development – Level 1
Awarding body:
ASCENTIS

Volunteering at an Event – Level 1
Awarding body:
ASDAN

Volunteering at an Event – Level 2
Awarding body:
ASDAN

Certificate

Adult Literacy – Entry Level
Awarding body:
ABC
AQA
ASCENTIS
EDEXCEL
EDI
NCFE
NOCN
OCR
VTCT
WAMITAB

Adult Literacy – Level 1
Awarding body:
AQA
ASCENTIS
ASDAN
CACHE
EAL
EDEXCEL
EDI
IMIAL
NCFE
NOCN
OCR
VTCT
WAMITAB

Adult Literacy – Level 2
Awarding body:
AQA
ASCENTIS
ASDAN
CACHE
City & Guilds
EAL
EDEXCEL
EDI
IMIAL
NCFE
NOCN
OCR
VTCT
WAMITAB

Adult Numeracy – Entry Level
Awarding body:
ABC
AQA
ASCENTIS
City & Guilds
EDEXCEL
EDI
NCFE
NOCN
OCR
VTCT
WAMITAB

Adult Numeracy – Level 1
Awarding body:
AQA
ASCENTIS
ASDAN
CACHE
City & Guilds
EAL
EDEXCEL
EDI
IMIAL
NCFE
NOCN
OCR
VTCT
WAMITAB

Adult Numeracy – Level 2
Awarding body:
AQA
ASCENTIS
ASDAN
CACHE
City & Guilds
EAL
EDEXCEL
EDI
IMIAL
NCFE
NOCN
OCR
VTCT
WAMITAB

Citizenship Studies – Entry Level
Awarding body:
OCR

City & Guilds Entry Level Certificate in Adult Literacy – Entry Level
Awarding body:
City & Guilds

City & Guilds Level 1 Certificate in Adult Literacy – Level 1
Awarding body:
City & Guilds

Communication Skills – Entry Level
Awarding body:
EDEXCEL

Community Volunteering – Level 1
Awarding body:
ASDAN

Community Volunteering – Level 2
Awarding body:
ASDAN

Community Volunteering – Level 3
Awarding body:
ASDAN

Employability – Entry Level
Awarding body:
ASDAN

Employability – Level 1
Awarding body:
ASDAN

Employability – Level 2
Awarding body:
ASDAN

Employability – Level 3
Awarding body:
ASDAN

Equality and Diversity – Level 2
Awarding body:
NCFE

ESOL for Work – Entry Level
Awarding body:
ASCENTIS
Cambridge ESOL
City & Guilds
EDEXCEL
ESB
NOCN
SQA
TCL

ESOL for Work – Level 1
Awarding body:
ASCENTIS
Cambridge ESOL
City & Guilds
EDEXCEL
ESB
NOCN
SQA
TCL

ESOL International – Entry Level
Awarding body:
Cambridge ESOL
EDEXCEL
TCL

ESOL International – Level 1
Awarding body:
EDEXCEL
EDI
TCL

ESOL International – Level 2
Awarding body:
EDEXCEL
EDI
TCL

ESOL International – Level 3
Awarding body:
EDEXCEL
TCL

ESOL International (Anglia) – Entry Level
Awarding body:
ASCENTIS

ESOL International (Anglia) – Level 1
Awarding body:
ASCENTIS

ESOL International (Anglia) – Level 2
Awarding body:
ASCENTIS

ESOL International (Anglia) – Level 3
Awarding body:
ASCENTIS

ESOL International (BULATS) – Entry Level
Awarding body:
Cambridge ESOL

ESOL International (Business English) – Entry Level
Awarding body:
Cambridge ESOL

ESOL International (CEF A1) – Entry Level
Awarding body:
EDI

ESOL International (CEF A2) – Entry Level
Awarding body:
EDI

ESOL International (CEF B1) – Entry Level
Awarding body:
EDI

ESOL International (SEW 1) – Entry Level
Awarding body:
TCL

ESOL International (SEW 2) (SEW 3) – Level 1
Awarding body:
TCL

ESOL International (SEW 4) – Level 2
Awarding body:
 TCL

ESOL International – Speaking and Listening – Entry Level
Awarding body:
 TCL

ESOL International – Speaking and Listening – Level 1
Awarding body:
 TCL

ESOL International – Speaking and Listening – Level 2
Awarding body:
 TCL

ESOL International – Speaking and Listening – Level 3
Awarding body:
 TCL

ESOL Skills for Life – Entry Level
Awarding body:
 ASCENTIS
 Cambridge ESOL
 City & Guilds
 EDEXCEL
 EDI
 NOCN
 TCL

ESOL Skills for Life – Level 1
Awarding body:
 ASCENTIS
 Cambridge ESOL
 City & Guilds
 EDEXCEL
 EDI
 TCL

ESOL Skills for Life – Level 2
Awarding body:
 ASCENTIS
 Cambridge ESOL
 City & Guilds
 EDEXCEL
 EDI
 TCL

ESOL Skills for Life (Speaking and Listening) – Entry Level
Awarding body:
 ASCENTIS
 Cambridge ESOL
 City & Guilds
 EDEXCEL
 ESB
 TCL

ESOL Skills for Life (Speaking and Listening) – Level 1
Awarding body:
 ASCENTIS
 Cambridge ESOL
 City & Guilds
 EDEXCEL
 ESB
 TCL

ESOL Skills for Life (Speaking and Listening) – Level 2
Awarding body:
 ASCENTIS
 Cambridge ESOL
 City & Guilds
 EDEXCEL
 ESB
 TCL

Essential Skills – Adult Literacy – Entry Level
Awarding body:
 CCEA
 City & Guilds
 NOCN

Essential Skills – Adult Numeracy – Entry Level
Awarding body:
 CCEA
 City & Guilds
 NOCN

Essential Skills – Application of Number – Level 1
Awarding body:
 CCEA
 City & Guilds

Essential Skills – Application of Number – Level 2
Awarding body:
   CCEA
   City & Guilds

Essential Skills – Communication – Level 1
Awarding body:
   CCEA
   City & Guilds

Essential Skills – Communication – Level 2
Awarding body:
   CCEA
   City & Guilds

Financial Literacy – Entry Level
Awarding body:
   NOCN

Financial Literacy – Level 1
Awarding body:
   NOCN

Healthy Living (Eating and Exercise) – Level 1
Awarding body:
   ASCENTIS

Healthy Living (Eating and Exercise) – Level 2
Awarding body:
   ASCENTIS

HL Biology – Level 3
Awarding body:
   IBO

HL Business and Management – Level 3
Awarding body:
   IBO

HL Chemistry – Level 3
Awarding body:
   IBO

HL Classical Languages – Level 3
Awarding body:
   IBO

HL Computer Science – Level 3
Awarding body:
   IBO

HL Design Technology – Level 3
Awarding body:
   IBO

HL Economics – Level 3
Awarding body:
   IBO

HL Geography – Level 3
Awarding body:
   IBO

HL History – Level 3
Awarding body:
   IBO

HL Information Technology in a Global Society – Level 3
Awarding body:
   IBO

HL Language A1 – Level 3
Awarding body:
   IBO

HL Language B – Level 3
Awarding body:
   IBO

HL Mathematics – Level 3
Awarding body:
   IBO

HL Music – Level 3
Awarding body:
   IBO

HL Philosophy – Level 3
Awarding body:
   IBO

HL Physics – Level 3
Awarding body:
   IBO

HL Psychology – Level 3
Awarding body:
   IBO

HL Social and Cultural Anthropology – Level 3
Awarding body:
   IBO

HL Theatre – Level 3
Awarding body:
   IBO

HL Visual Arts – Level 3
Awarding body:
  IBO

ICT – Entry Level
Awarding body:
  NCFE

ICT Skills for Life – Entry Level
Awarding body:
  ABC
  VTCT

**Introduction to Hair and Beauty –
Entry Level**
Awarding body:
  EDEXCEL

**Introduction to Hair and Beauty –
Level 1**
Awarding body:
  EDEXCEL

Land-based Studies – Level 1
Awarding body:
  EDEXCEL

Learning Skills – Entry Level
Awarding body:
  OCR

Life Skills – Entry Level
Awarding body:
  ABC
  EDEXCEL
  NPTC
  WJEC

Life Skills (Entry 1 and 2) – Entry Level
Awarding body:
  ASCENTIS

Making Progress – Entry Level
Awarding body:
  NCFE

Managing Diversity – Level 3
Awarding body:
  NCFE

Media Literacy – Entry Level
Awarding body:
  NOCN

**Occupational Studies (Double Award) –
Level 1**
Awarding body:
  CCEA

**Occupational Studies (Double Award) –
Level 2**
Awarding body:
  CCEA

**Occupational Studies (Single Award) –
Level 1**
Awarding body:
  CCEA

**Occupational Studies (Single Award) –
Level 2**
Awarding body:
  CCEA

Oral Skills for Interviews – Level 1
Awarding body:
  ESB

Oral Skills for Interviews – Level 2
Awarding body:
  ESB

Oral Skills for Interviews – Level 3
Awarding body:
  ESB

Parents to Be and in Parenting – Level 1
Awarding body:
  EDEXCEL

**Personal and Social Development –
Entry Level**
Awarding body:
  ASDAN
  City & Guilds
  EDI

**Personal and Social Development –
Level 1**
Awarding body:
  ASDAN
  City & Guilds
  EDI

**Personal and Social Development –
Level 2**
Awarding body:
  ASDAN

Personal and Social Skills – Entry Level
Awarding body:
WJEC

Personal Development and Learning for Unpaid Carers – Level 2
Awarding body:
City & Guilds

Personal Development for Progression – Level 3
Awarding body:
ASCENTIS

Personal Effectiveness – Level 1
Awarding body:
ASDAN

Personal Effectiveness – Level 2
Awarding body:
ASDAN

Personal Effectiveness – Level 3
Awarding body:
ASDAN
CCEA

Personal Effectiveness (Seven Habits) – Level 2
Awarding body:
QNUK

Personal Effectiveness at Work – Level 3
Awarding body:
NCFE

Personal Finance – Level 2
Awarding body:
BCS

Personal Financial Planning – Level 2
Awarding body:
IFS

Personal Money Management – Level 1
Awarding body:
NCFE

Personal Progress – Entry Level
Awarding body:
ASCENTIS
ASDAN
City & Guilds
EDEXCEL
NOCN

Personal, Social and Health Education – Entry Level
Awarding body:
AQA

Progression – Entry Level
Awarding body:
NOCN

Progression – Level 1
Awarding body:
NOCN

Progression – Level 2
Awarding body:
NOCN

Progression – Level 3
Awarding body:
NOCN

Self Development through Learning – Entry Level
Awarding body:
City & Guilds

Self Development through Learning – Level 1
Awarding body:
City & Guilds

Skills for Independent Living – Entry Level
Awarding body:
EDEXCEL

Skills Towards Enabling Progression (Step-UP) – Entry Level
Awarding body:
NOCN

Skills Towards Enabling Progression (Step-UP) – Level 1
Awarding body:
NOCN

SL Biology – Level 3
Awarding body:
IBO

SL Business and Management – Level 3
Awarding body:
IBO

SL Chemistry – Level 3
Awarding body:
  IBO

SL Classical Languages – Level 3
Awarding body:
  IBO

SL Computer Science – Level 3
Awarding body:
  IBO

SL Design Technology – Level 3
Awarding body:
  IBO

SL Economics – Level 3
Awarding body:
  IBO

SL Further Mathematics – Level 3
Awarding body:
  IBO

SL Geography – Level 3
Awarding body:
  IBO

SL History – Level 3
Awarding body:
  IBO

SL Information Technology in a Global Society – Level 3
Awarding body:
  IBO

SL Language A1 – Level 3
Awarding body:
  IBO

SL Language Ab Initio – Level 2
Awarding body:
  IBO

SL Language B – Level 3
Awarding body:
  IBO

SL Mathematical Studies – Level 3
Awarding body:
  IBO

SL Mathematics – Level 3
Awarding body:
  IBO

SL Music – Level 3
Awarding body:
  IBO

SL Philosophy – Level 3
Awarding body:
  IBO

SL Physics – Level 3
Awarding body:
  IBO

SL Psychology – Level 3
Awarding body:
  IBO

SL Social and Cultural Anthropology – Level 3
Awarding body:
  IBO

SL Theatre – Level 3
Awarding body:
  IBO

SL Visual Arts – Level 3
Awarding body:
  IBO

Solving Problems – Entry Level
Awarding body:
  NCFE

Speaking and Listening Skills for Adult Learners – Level 1
Awarding body:
  ESB

Speaking and Listening Skills for Adult Learners – Level 2
Awarding body:
  ESB

Speaking and Listening Skills for Adult Learners – Level 3
Awarding body:
  ESB

Sustainable Development – Level 1
Awarding body:
  NCFE

Sustainable Development – Level 2
Awarding body:
  NCFE

Travel and Tourism Communication Skills – Level 1
Awarding body:
ESB

Volunteering – Level 2
Awarding body:
NCFE

Working Together – Entry Level
Awarding body:
NCFE

Diploma

Land-based Studies – Level 1
Awarding body:
EDEXCEL

Personal Finance – Level 2
Awarding body:
BCS

Personal Progress – Entry Level
Awarding body:
ASCENTIS
ASDAN
City & Guilds
EDEXCEL
NOCN

Progression – Level 1
Awarding body:
NOCN

Progression – Level 2
Awarding body:
NOCN

Skills Towards Enabling Progression (Step-UP) – Entry Level
Awarding body:
NOCN

Skills Towards Enabling Progression (Step-UP) – Level 1
Awarding body:
NOCN

Essential Skills (Wales)

Application of Number – Level 1
Awarding body:
City & Guilds
EAL
EDI
IMIAL
VTCT
WJEC

Application of Number – Level 2
Awarding body:
City & Guilds
EAL
EDI
IMIAL
VTCT
WJEC

Application of Number – Level 3
Awarding body:
EAL
EDI
VTCT
WJEC

Application of Number – Level 4
Awarding body:
WJEC

Communication – Level 1
Awarding body:
City & Guilds
EAL
EDI
IMIAL
VTCT
WJEC

Communication – Level 2
Awarding body:
City & Guilds
EAL
EDI
IMIAL
VTCT
WJEC

Communication – Level 3
Awarding body:
  City & Guilds
  EAL
  EDI
  VTCT
  WJEC

Communication – Level 4
Awarding body:
  WJEC

Information and Communication Technology – Level 1
Awarding body:
  City & Guilds
  EAL
  EDI
  IMIAL
  VTCT
  WJEC

Information and Communication Technology – Level 2
Awarding body:
  City & Guilds
  EAL
  EDI
  IMIAL
  VTCT
  WJEC

Information and Communication Technology – Level 3
Awarding body:
  City & Guilds
  EAL
  EDI
  VTCT
  WJEC

Information and Communication Technology – Level 4
Awarding body:
  WJEC

Introductory Certificate

Vocational Studies – Level 1
Awarding body:
  EDEXCEL

Introductory Diploma

Vocational Studies – Level 1
Awarding body:
  EDEXCEL

Key Skills

Application of Number – Level 1
Awarding body:
  AQA
  ASDAN
  BHEST
  CACHE
  CCEA
  City & Guilds
  EAL
  EDEXCEL
  EDI
  ETCAL
  HAB
  IMIAL
  NCFE
  OCR
  VTCT
  WJEC

Application of Number – Level 2
Awarding body:
  AQA
  ASDAN
  BHEST
  CACHE
  CCEA
  City & Guilds
  EAL
  EDEXCEL
  EDI
  ETCAL
  HAB
  IMIAL
  NCFE
  OCR
  VTCT
  WJEC

Application of Number – Level 3

Awarding body:
AQA
ASDAN
CACHE
CCEA
City & Guilds
EAL
EDEXCEL
EDI
HAB
IMIAL
NCFE
OCR
VTCT
WJEC

Application of Number – Level 4

Awarding body:
AQA
ASDAN
CACHE
CCEA
City & Guilds
EDEXCEL
EDI
HAB
NCFE
OCR
VTCT
WJEC

Communication – Level 1

Awarding body:
AQA
ASDAN
BHEST
CACHE
CCEA
City & Guilds
EAL
EDEXCEL
EDI
ETCAL
HAB
IMIAL
NCFE
OCR
VTCT
WJEC

Communication – Level 2

Awarding body:
AQA
ASDAN
BHEST
CACHE
CCEA
City & Guilds
EAL
EDEXCEL
EDI
ETCAL
HAB
IMIAL
NCFE
OCR
VTCT
WJEC

Communication – Level 3

Awarding body:
AQA
ASDAN
CACHE
CCEA
City & Guilds
EAL
EDEXCEL
EDI
HAB
IMIAL
NCFE
OCR
VTCT
WJEC

Communication – Level 4

Awarding body:
AQA
ASDAN
CACHE
CCEA
City & Guilds
EDEXCEL
EDI
HAB
NCFE
OCR
VTCT
WJEC

Improving Own Learning and Performance – Level 1
Awarding body:
AQA
ASDAN
BHEST
CACHE
CCEA
City & Guilds
EAL
EDEXCEL
EDI
ETCAL
HAB
IMIAL
NCFE
OCR
VTCT
WJEC

Improving Own Learning and Performance – Level 2
Awarding body:
AQA
ASDAN
BHEST
CACHE
CCEA
City & Guilds
EAL
EDEXCEL
EDI
ETCAL
HAB
IMIAL
NCFE
OCR
VTCT
WJEC

Improving Own Learning and Performance – Level 3
Awarding body:
AQA
ASDAN
CACHE
CCEA
City & Guilds
EAL
EDEXCEL
EDI
HAB
IMIAL
NCFE
OCR
VTCT
WJEC

Improving Own Learning and Performance – Level 4
Awarding body:
AQA
ASDAN
CACHE
CCEA
City & Guilds
EDEXCEL
EDI
HAB
NCFE
OCR
VTCT
WJEC

Information and Communication Technology – Level 1
Awarding body:
AQA
ASDAN
BHEST
CACHE
CCEA
City & Guilds
EAL
EDEXCEL
EDI
ETCAL
HAB
IMIAL
NCFE
OCR
VTCT
WJEC

Information and Communication Technology – Level 2
Awarding body:
AQA
ASDAN
BHEST
CACHE
CCEA
City & Guilds
EAL
EDEXCEL
EDI
ETCAL
HAB
IMIAL
NCFE
OCR
VTCT
WJEC

Information and Communication Technology – Level 3
Awarding body:
AQA
ASDAN
CACHE
CCEA
City & Guilds
EAL
EDEXCEL
EDI
HAB
IMIAL
NCFE
OCR
VTCT
WJEC

Information and Communication Technology – Level 4
Awarding body:
AQA
ASDAN
CACHE
CCEA
City & Guilds
EDEXCEL
EDI
HAB
NCFE
OCR
VTCT
WJEC

Problem Solving – Level 1
Awarding body:
  AQA
  ASDAN
  BHEST
  CACHE
  CCEA
  City & Guilds
  EAL
  EDEXCEL
  EDI
  ETCAL
  HAB
  IMIAL
  NCFE
  OCR
  VTCT
  WJEC

Problem Solving – Level 2
Awarding body:
  AQA
  ASDAN
  BHEST
  CACHE
  CCEA
  City & Guilds
  EAL
  EDEXCEL
  EDI
  ETCAL
  HAB
  IMIAL
  NCFE
  OCR
  VTCT
  WJEC

Problem Solving – Level 3
Awarding body:
  AQA
  ASDAN
  CACHE
  CCEA
  City & Guilds
  EAL
  EDEXCEL
  EDI
  HAB
  IMIAL
  NCFE
  OCR
  VTCT
  WJEC

Problem Solving – Level 4
Awarding body:
  AQA
  ASDAN
  CACHE
  CCEA
  City & Guilds
  EDEXCEL
  EDI
  HAB
  NCFE
  OCR
  VTCT
  WJEC

Working with Others – Level 1
Awarding body:
  AQA
  ASDAN
  BHEST
  CACHE
  CCEA
  City & Guilds
  EAL
  EDEXCEL
  EDI
  ETCAL
  HAB
  IMIAL
  NCFE
  OCR
  WJEC

Working with Others – Level 2
Awarding body:
AQA
ASDAN
BHEST
CACHE
CCEA
City & Guilds
EAL
EDEXCEL
EDI
ETCAL
HAB
IMIAL
NCFE
OCR
WJEC

Working with Others – Level 3
Awarding body:
AQA
ASDAN
CACHE
CCEA
City & Guilds
EAL
EDEXCEL
EDI
HAB
NCFE
OCR
WJEC

Working with Others – Level 4
Awarding body:
AQA
ASDAN
CACHE
CCEA
City & Guilds
EDEXCEL
EDI
HAB
NCFE
OCR
WJEC

Pre-U Certificate

Global Perspectives and Independent Research – Level 3
Awarding body:
Cambridge International

Philosophy and Theology (Principal) – Level 3
Awarding body:
Cambridge International

Preparation for Work

Award

An Introduction to the Hair and Beauty Sector – Entry Level
Awarding body:
ASCENTIS

An Introduction to the Hair and Beauty Sector – Level 1
Awarding body:
ASCENTIS

Business Administration – Level 1
Awarding body:
ASCENTIS

Developing Enterprise Capabilities – Level 2
Awarding body:
NCFE

Employability – Level 2
Awarding body:
NOCN

Employability and Personal Development – Entry Level
Awarding body:
City & Guilds

Employability and Personal Development – Level 1
Awarding body:
City & Guilds

Employability and Work Skills – Entry Level
Awarding body:
ASCENTIS

Employability and Work Skills – Level 1
Awarding body:
ASCENTIS

Employability Skills – Level 1
Awarding body:
NCFE

Employability Skills – Level 2
Awarding body:
NCFE

Employability Skills – Level 3
Awarding body:
NCFE

Exploring Employability Skills – Entry Level
Awarding body:
NCFE

Exploring Enterprise Capabilities – Level 1
Awarding body:
NCFE

Introduction to the Hospitality Industry – Entry Level
Awarding body:
ASCENTIS

Introduction to the Hospitality Industry – Level 1
Awarding body:
ASCENTIS

Personal Advancement – Level 1
Awarding body:
ASCENTIS

Personal Advancement – Level 2
Awarding body:
ASCENTIS

Personal Advancement – Level 3
Awarding body:
ASCENTIS

Personal and Social Development – Entry Level
Awarding body:
EDEXCEL

Personal and Social Development – Level 1
Awarding body:
EDEXCEL

Personal and Social Development – Level 2
Awarding body:
EDEXCEL

Personal Development and Contributing to the Community – Entry Level
Awarding body:
City & Guilds

Personal Development and Contributing to the Community – Level 1
Awarding body:
City & Guilds

Skills for Working Life – Entry Level
Awarding body:
NPTC

Travel and Tourism – Entry Level
Awarding body:
EDEXCEL

Travel and Tourism – Level 1
Awarding body:
EDEXCEL

WorkSkills – Entry Level
Awarding body:
EDEXCEL

WorkSkills – Level 1
Awarding body:
EDEXCEL

BTEC Award

WorkSkills – Level 2
Awarding body:
 EDEXCEL

WorkSkills – Level 3
Awarding body:
 EDEXCEL

BTEC Certificate

Employability Skills – Level 2
Awarding body:
 EDEXCEL

WorkSkills – Level 2
Awarding body:
 EDEXCEL

WorkSkills – Level 3
Awarding body:
 EDEXCEL

BTEC Diploma

WorkSkills – Level 2
Awarding body:
 EDEXCEL

BTEC Extended Certificate

WorkSkills – Level 2
Awarding body:
 EDEXCEL

Certificate

An Introduction to the Hair and Beauty Sector – Entry Level
Awarding body:
 ASCENTIS

An Introduction to the Hair and Beauty Sector – Level 1
Awarding body:
 ASCENTIS

Career Planning – Level 1
Awarding body:
 ASDAN

Career Planning – Level 2
Awarding body:
 ASDAN

Career Planning – Level 3
Awarding body:
 ASDAN

Developing Enterprise Capabilities – Level 2
Awarding body:
 NCFE

Employability – Level 2
Awarding body:
 NOCN

Employability and Personal Development – Entry Level
Awarding body:
 City & Guilds

Employability and Personal Development – Level 1
Awarding body:
 City & Guilds

Employability Skills – Entry Level
Awarding body:
 OCR

Employability Skills – Level 1
Awarding body:
 NCFE
 OCR

Employability Skills – Level 2
Awarding body:
 NCFE
 OCR

Employability Skills – Level 3
Awarding body:
 NCFE

Employment Skills – Level 1
Awarding body:
 CCEA
 NCFE

Employment Skills – Level 2
Awarding body:
 CCEA
 NCFE

Engineering – Entry Level
Awarding body:
    ASCENTIS

Enterprise and Employability – Level 1
Awarding body:
    AQA

Enterprise and Employability – Level 2
Awarding body:
    AQA

**Exploring Employability Skills –
Entry Level**
Awarding body:
    NCFE

**Exploring Enterprise Capabilities –
Level 1**
Awarding body:
    NCFE

ICT Skills for Life – Entry Level
Awarding body:
    EDEXCEL

**Introduction to Employment in the
Construction Industries – Entry Level**
Awarding body:
    ASCENTIS

**Introduction to Motor Vehicle
Maintenance and Repair – Entry Level**
Awarding body:
    ASCENTIS

**Introduction to Motor Vehicle
Maintenance and Repair – Level 1**
Awarding body:
    ASCENTIS

**Introduction to the Hospitality Industry
– Entry Level**
Awarding body:
    ASCENTIS

**Introduction to the Hospitality Industry
– Level 1**
Awarding body:
    ASCENTIS

Peer Support and Mentoring – Level 1
Awarding body:
    NCFE

**Personal and Professional Development
– Entry Level**
Awarding body:
    ASCENTIS

**Personal and Professional Development
– Level 1**
Awarding body:
    ASCENTIS

**Personal and Social Development –
Entry Level**
Awarding body:
    EDEXCEL

**Personal and Social Development –
Level 1**
Awarding body:
    EDEXCEL

**Personal and Social Development –
Level 2**
Awarding body:
    EDEXCEL

**Personal Development and Contributing
to the Community – Entry Level**
Awarding body:
    City & Guilds

**Personal Development and Contributing
to the Community – Level 1**
Awarding body:
    City & Guilds

**Personal Progression through
Employment – Entry Level**
Awarding body:
    City & Guilds

Preparation for Childcare – Entry Level
Awarding body:
    ASCENTIS

**Preparation for Employment –
Entry Level**
Awarding body:
    City & Guilds

Preparation for Employment – Level 1
Awarding body:
    City & Guilds

**Preparation for Employment in
Construction Industries – Entry Level**
Awarding body:
    ASCENTIS

**Preparation for Employment in
Plastering – Entry Level**
Awarding body:
    ABC

**Preparation for Employment in the
Construction Industries – Level 1**
Awarding body:
    ASCENTIS

Preparation for Work – Level 1
Awarding body:
    EDI

**Preparation for Working Life –
Entry Level**
Awarding body:
    AQA

Preparation for Working Life – Level 1
Awarding body:
    AQA

Preparation for Working Life – Level 2
Awarding body:
    AQA

Salon Work – Entry Level
Awarding body:
    ASCENTIS

**Science, Technology, Engineering and
Maths Leadership Skills – Level 1**
Awarding body:
    EDEXCEL

**Science, Technology, Engineering and
Maths Leadership Skills – Level 2**
Awarding body:
    EDEXCEL

Skills for Working Life – Entry Level
Awarding body:
    ABC
    EDEXCEL
    EDI
    NPTC
    VTCT

**Skills for Working Life (Hair & Beauty) –
Entry Level**
Awarding body:
    VTCT

**Skills for Working Life (Health &
Fitness) – Entry Level**
Awarding body:
    VTCT

**Skills for Working Life – Craft, Design
and Technology – Entry Level**
Awarding body:
    NPTC

**Skills for Working Life – Hospitality,
Catering and Retail – Entry Level**
Awarding body:
    NPTC

**Skills for Working Life – Land-based
(Animals) – Entry Level**
Awarding body:
    NPTC

**Skills for Working Life – Land-Based
(land and plants) – Entry Level**
Awarding body:
    NPTC

**Teamwork and Personal Skills for Cadets
– Level 1**
Awarding body:
    EDEXCEL

Travel and Tourism – Level 1
Awarding body:
    EDEXCEL

**Work Based Support and Mentoring –
Level 2**
Awarding body:
    NCFE

Work Skills – Entry Level
Awarding body:
    WJEC

WorkSkills – Entry Level
Awarding body:
    EDEXCEL

WorkSkills – Level 1
Awarding body:
    EDEXCEL

Diploma

Skills for Working Life – Entry Level
Awarding body:
  NPTC

Skills for Working Life – Craft, Design and Technology – Entry Level
Awarding body:
  NPTC

Skills for Working Life – Land-based (Animals) – Entry Level
Awarding body:
  NPTC

Skills for Working Life – Land-Based (land and plants) – Entry Level
Awarding body:
  NPTC

Travel and Tourism – Level 1
Awarding body:
  EDEXCEL

WorkSkills – Level 1
Awarding body:
  EDEXCEL

Foundation Award

Careers Education and Preparation for Working Life – Level 1
Awarding body:
  NOCN

Intermediate Award

Careers Education and Preparation for Working Life – Level 2
Awarding body:
  NOCN

Key Skills

Working with Others – Level 1
Awarding body:
  VTCT

Working with Others – Level 2
Awarding body:
  VTCT

Working with Others – Level 3
Awarding body:
  IMIAL
  VTCT

Working With Others – Level 4
Awarding body:
  VTCT

Retail and Commercial Enterprise

Hospitality and Catering

Advanced Certificate

Licensed Hospitality – Level 3
Awarding body:
    BIIAB

Wines and Spirits – Level 3
Awarding body:
    WSET

Advanced Diploma

Hospitality – Level 3
Awarding body:
    AQA
    City & Guilds
    EDEXCEL
    OCR

Hotel Management – Level 5
Awarding body:
    CTH

Award

Alcohol Awareness – Level 1
Awarding body:
    BIIAB

Assessment of Licensed Premises (Social Responsibility) – Level 2
Awarding body:
    BIIAB

Barista Skills – Level 2
Awarding body:
    City & Guilds

Cooking Theory and Practice – Level 2
Awarding body:
    BIIAB

Designated Premises Supervisors – Level 2
Awarding body:
    BIIAB

Domestic Food Hygiene – Level 1
Awarding body:
    City & Guilds

Drugs Awareness for the Licensed Retail Sector – Level 2
Awarding body:
    EDI

Essentials of Catering – Level 1
Awarding body:
    BIIAB

Exploring the Hospitality Industry – Entry Level
Awarding body:
    EDEXCEL

Exploring the Hospitality Industry – Level 1
Awarding body:
    EDEXCEL

Food Safety for Catering – Level 2
Awarding body:
    City & Guilds

Food Safety in Catering – Level 2
Awarding body:
    CIEH
    City & Guilds
    EDI
    HABC
    RSPH

General Front Office Operations – Level 1
Awarding body:
    City & Guilds

**General Housekeeping Operations –
Level 1**
Awarding body:
City & Guilds

**Healthier Food and Special Diets –
Level 2**
Awarding body:
CIEH
City & Guilds
RSPH

**Healthier Foods and Special Diets –
Level 2**
Awarding body:
EDI

**Hospitality and Catering Principles
(Food and Drink Service) – Level 2**
Awarding body:
City & Guilds
EDI

**Hospitality and Catering Principles
(Front Office) – Level 2**
Awarding body:
City & Guilds
EDI

**Hospitality and Catering Principles
(Housekeeping) – Level 2**
Awarding body:
City & Guilds
EDI

**Hospitality and Catering Principles
(Multi-Skilled) – Level 2**
Awarding body:
City & Guilds
EDI

**Hospitality Supervision and Leadership
Principles – Level 3**
Awarding body:
City & Guilds
EDI

**Introduction to Front Office Operations
in Hospitality – Level 1**
Awarding body:
EDEXCEL

**Introduction to Housekeeping
Operations in Hospitality – Level 1**
Awarding body:
EDEXCEL

**Introduction to the Hospitality Industry
– Entry Level**
Awarding body:
City & Guilds

**Introduction to the Hospitality Industry
– Level 1**
Awarding body:
City & Guilds

**Managing Food Safety in Catering –
Level 4**
Awarding body:
CIEH
HABC
RSPH

Music Promoters – Level 2
Awarding body:
BIIAB

**Nutrition for Healthier Food and Special
Diets – Level 3**
Awarding body:
RSPH

Personal Licence Holders – Level 2
Awarding body:
BIIAB
HABC

**Practical Food Safety in Catering –
Level 2**
Awarding body:
ASCENTIS
EDI

**Practical Food Safety Supervision for
Catering – Level 3**
Awarding body:
EDI

**Practical Supervision of Food Safety in
Catering – Level 3**
Awarding body:
ASCENTIS

Principles of Customer Service in Hospitality, Leisure, Travel and Tourism – Level 2
Awarding body:
City & Guilds

Principles of Customer Service in the Hospitality, Leisure, Travel and Tourism Industry – Level 2
Awarding body:
EDI

Principles of Practical Food Safety for Catering – Level 2
Awarding body:
NCFE

Principles of Practical Food Safety Supervision for Catering – Level 3
Awarding body:
NCFE

Principles of Supervising Customer Service Performance in Hospitality, Leisure, Travel and Tourism – Level 3
Awarding body:
City & Guilds

Principles of Supervising Customer Service Performance in the Hospitality, Leisure, Travel and Tourism Industry – Level 3
Awarding body:
EDI

Professional Bartending (Cocktails) – Level 2
Awarding body:
City & Guilds

Providing a Healthier School Meals Service – Level 1
Awarding body:
EDI

Responsible Alcohol Retailing – Level 1
Awarding body:
BIIAB

Supervising Food Safety for Catering – Level 3
Awarding body:
City & Guilds

Supervising Food Safety in Catering – Level 3
Awarding body:
CIEH
City & Guilds
HABC
RSPH

Wines and Spirits – Level 2
Awarding body:
WSET

BTEC Award

Hospitality and Catering Principles (Food and Drink Service) – Level 2
Awarding body:
EDEXCEL

Hospitality and Catering Principles (Front Office) – Level 2
Awarding body:
EDEXCEL

Hospitality and Catering Principles (Housekeeping) – Level 2
Awarding body:
EDEXCEL

Hospitality and Catering Principles (Multi-Skilled) – Level 2
Awarding body:
EDEXCEL

Hospitality Supervision and Leadership – Level 3
Awarding body:
EDEXCEL

Principles of Customer Service in Hospitality, Leisure, Travel and Tourism – Level 2
Awarding body:
EDEXCEL

Principles of Supervising Customer Service Performance in Hospitality, Leisure, Travel and Tourism – Level 3
Awarding body:
EDEXCEL

BTEC Certificate

Food and Beverage Service – Level 3
Awarding body:
    EDEXCEL

Front Office Operations – Level 3
Awarding body:
    EDEXCEL

Hospitality and Catering Principles (Food Processing and Cooking) – Level 2
Awarding body:
    EDEXCEL

Hospitality and Catering Principles (Professional Cookery) – Level 2
Awarding body:
    EDEXCEL

Hospitality and Catering Principles (Professional Cookery) – Level 3
Awarding body:
    EDEXCEL

Hospitality Customer Relations – Level 3
Awarding body:
    EDEXCEL

Hospitality Small Business Operations – Level 3
Awarding body:
    EDEXCEL

International Cuisine – Level 3
Awarding body:
    EDEXCEL

BTEC Diploma

International Cuisine – Level 3
Awarding body:
    EDEXCEL

BTEC First Certificate

Hospitality – Level 2
Awarding body:
    EDEXCEL

BTEC First Diploma

Hospitality – Level 2
Awarding body:
    EDEXCEL

BTEC Higher National Certificate

Hospitality Management – Level 5
Awarding body:
    EDEXCEL

BTEC Higher National Diploma

Hospitality Management – Level 5
Awarding body:
    EDEXCEL

BTEC National Award

Hospitality – Level 3
Awarding body:
    EDEXCEL

BTEC National Certificate

Hospitality – Level 3
Awarding body:
    EDEXCEL

BTEC National Diploma

Hospitality – Level 3
Awarding body:
    EDEXCEL

Certificate

Alcohol Awareness – Level 1
Awarding body:
    BIIAB

Exploring the Hospitality Industry – Entry Level
Awarding body:
    EDEXCEL

**Exploring the Hospitality Industry –
Level 1**
Awarding body:
   EDEXCEL

Food Studies – Entry Level
Awarding body:
   WJEC

**Food Studies (Entry 1 and 2) –
Entry Level**
Awarding body:
   City & Guilds

General Cookery – Level 1
Awarding body:
   City & Guilds
   EDI

**General Food and Beverage Service –
Level 1**
Awarding body:
   City & Guilds
   EDI

Home Economics – Entry Level
Awarding body:
   CCEA

Hospitality and Catering – Entry Level
Awarding body:
   City & Guilds

**Hospitality and Catering Principles
(Food Processing and Cooking) – Level 2**
Awarding body:
   City & Guilds
   EDI

**Hospitality and Catering Principles
(Professional Cookery) – Level 2**
Awarding body:
   City & Guilds
   EDI

**Hospitality and Catering Principles
(Professional Cookery) – Level 3**
Awarding body:
   City & Guilds
   EDI

Hospitality and Catering Skills – Level 1
Awarding body:
   ABC

**Hospitality and Tourism Management –
Level 7**
Awarding body:
   CTH

**Hospitality, Leisure and Tourism –
Level 2**
Awarding body:
   Institute of Hospitality

**Introduction to Cookery in Hospitality –
Level 1**
Awarding body:
   EDEXCEL

**Introduction to Food and Beverage
Service in Hospitality – Level 1**
Awarding body:
   EDEXCEL

**Introduction to the Hospitality Industry
– Entry Level**
Awarding body:
   City & Guilds

**Introduction to the Hospitality Industry
– Level 1**
Awarding body:
   City & Guilds
   EDEXCEL

**Investigating the Hospitality Industry –
Level 1**
Awarding body:
   City & Guilds

**Management for Hospitality, Leisure
and Tourism – Level 3**
Awarding body:
   Institute of Hospitality

Pastry Chefs and Patissiers – Level 2
Awarding body:
   ABC

**Professional Food and Beverage Service
– Level 1**
Awarding body:
   City & Guilds

Diploma

Advanced Professional Cookery – Level 3
Awarding body:
City & Guilds

Butlers – Level 2
Awarding body:
City & Guilds

Butlers – Level 3
Awarding body:
City & Guilds

Designated Premises Supervisors – Level 3
Awarding body:
EDI

Hospitality Supervision and Leadership (NVQ) – Level 3
Awarding body:
City & Guilds

Hospitality Supervision and Leadership Skills (NVQ) – Level 3
Awarding body:
EDEXCEL
EDI

Hotel and Casino Management – Level 4
Awarding body:
CTH

Hotel Management – Level 4
Awarding body:
CTH

Introduction to Professional Cookery – Level 1
Awarding body:
City & Guilds
EDI

Licensed Hospitality – Level 3
Awarding body:
BIIAB

Management for Hospitality, Leisure and Tourism – Level 4
Awarding body:
Institute of Hospitality

Pastry Chefs and Patissiers – Level 3
Awarding body:
ABC

Professional Cookery – Level 2
Awarding body:
City & Guilds
EDI

Professional Food and Beverage Service – Level 2
Awarding body:
City & Guilds

Shift Management (McDonald's) – Level 3
Awarding body:
McDonald's

Foundation Certificate

Wines – Level 1
Awarding body:
WSET

Foundation Diploma

Hospitality – Level 1
Awarding body:
AQA
City & Guilds
EDEXCEL
EDI
OCR

Higher Diploma

Hospitality – Level 2
Awarding body:
AQA
City & Guilds
EDEXCEL
EDI
OCR

IVQ Advanced Diploma

Accommodation Operations and Services – Level 3
Awarding body:
City & Guilds

Culinary Arts – Level 3
Awarding body:
City & Guilds

Food and Beverage Service – Level 3
Awarding body:
City & Guilds

Reception Operations and Services – Level 3
Awarding body:
City & Guilds

IVQ Certificate

Accommodation Operations and Services – Level 1
Awarding body:
City & Guilds

Food and Beverage Service – Level 1
Awarding body:
City & Guilds

Food Preparation and Cooking – Level 1
Awarding body:
City & Guilds

Reception Operations and Services – Level 1
Awarding body:
City & Guilds

IVQ Diploma

Accommodation Operations and Services – Level 2
Awarding body:
City & Guilds

Food and Beverage Service – Level 2
Awarding body:
City & Guilds

Food Preparation and Cooking (Culinary Arts) – Level 2
Awarding body:
City & Guilds

Patisserie – Level 2
Awarding body:
City & Guilds

Reception Operations and Services – Level 2
Awarding body:
City & Guilds

National Certificate

Cellar Service, Installation and Maintenance – Level 2
Awarding body:
BIIAB

Designated Premises Supervisors – Level 2
Awarding body:
BIIAB

Licensed Retailing – Level 2
Awarding body:
BIIAB

Licensees (Drugs Awareness) – Level 2
Awarding body:
BIIAB

Licensing Practitioners – Level 2
Awarding body:
BIIAB

Personal Licence Holders – Level 2
Awarding body:
BIIAB
GQAL
NCFE

National Vocational Qualification

Drinks Dispense Systems – Level 3
Awarding body:
City & Guilds

Food and Drink Service – Level 2
Awarding body:
    City & Guilds
    EDEXCEL
    EDI

Food Processing and Cooking – Level 2
Awarding body:
    City & Guilds
    EDEXCEL
    EDI

Front Office – Level 2
Awarding body:
    City & Guilds
    EDEXCEL
    EDI

Gambling Operations – Level 2
Awarding body:
    City & Guilds

Gambling Operations – Level 3
Awarding body:
    City & Guilds

Hospitality – Level 1
Awarding body:
    City & Guilds
    EDEXCEL
    EDI

Housekeeping – Level 2
Awarding body:
    City & Guilds
    EDEXCEL
    EDI

Multi-Skilled Hospitality Services – Level 2
Awarding body:
    City & Guilds
    EDEXCEL
    EDI

Professional Cookery – Level 2
Awarding body:
    City & Guilds
    EDEXCEL
    EDI

Professional Cookery – Level 3
Awarding body:
    City & Guilds
    EDEXCEL
    EDI

Postgraduate Diploma

Hospitality and Tourism Management – Level 7
Awarding body:
    CTH

Principal Learning

Hospitality – Level 1
Awarding body:
    AQA
    City & Guilds
    EDEXCEL
    EDI
    OCR

Hospitality – Level 2
Awarding body:
    AQA
    City & Guilds
    EDEXCEL
    EDI
    OCR

Hospitality – Level 3
Awarding body:
    AQA
    City & Guilds
    EDEXCEL
    EDI
    OCR

Professional Certificate

Spirits – Level 2
Awarding body:
    WSET

Progression Diploma

Hospitality – Level 3
Awarding body:
   AQA
   City & Guilds
   EDEXCEL
   EDI
   OCR

Retailing and Wholesaling

Advanced Diploma

Retail Business – Level 3
Awarding body:
   AQA
   City & Guilds
   EDEXCEL
   OCR

Award

Food Safety for Retail – Level 2
Awarding body:
   CIEH
   HABC
   RSPH

Food Safety Supervision for Retail – Level 3
Awarding body:
   CIEH
   HABC
   RSPH

Home Improvement Knowledge – Level 2
Awarding body:
   City & Guilds

Home Improvement Knowledge (Building) – Level 2
Awarding body:
   City & Guilds

Home Improvement Knowledge (Gardening) – Level 2
Awarding body:
   City & Guilds

Home Improvement Knowledge (Room Solutions) – Level 2
Awarding body:
   City & Guilds

Introduction to Retail Skills – Entry Level
Awarding body:
   City & Guilds

Legislation for the Retail Environment – Level 2
Awarding body:
   City & Guilds

Marketing in the Retail Environment – Level 2
Awarding body:
   City & Guilds

Monitor Retail Operations – Level 2
Awarding body:
   City & Guilds

Product Range Planning in the Retail Environment – Level 2
Awarding body:
   City & Guilds

Retail Knowledge – Level 1
Awarding body:
ABC
EDEXCEL
EDI

Retail Knowledge – Level 2
Awarding body:
ABC
City & Guilds
OCR
VTCT

Retail Knowledge – Level 3
Awarding body:
ABC
City & Guilds
EDI
OCR

Retail Skills – Level 1
Awarding body:
ABC
City & Guilds
EDI
OCR

Retail Skills – Level 2
Awarding body:
ABC
City & Guilds
EDEXCEL
EDI
OCR

Security in a Retail Environment – Level 2
Awarding body:
City & Guilds

Serving Customers in the Retail Environment – Level 2
Awarding body:
City & Guilds

Underage Sales Prevention – Level 2
Awarding body:
EDI

Visual Merchandising – Level 2
Awarding body:
City & Guilds

BTEC Award

Retail Knowledge – Level 2
Awarding body:
EDEXCEL

Retail Knowledge – Level 3
Awarding body:
EDEXCEL

BTEC Certificate

Retail Beauty Consultancy – Level 2
Awarding body:
EDEXCEL

Retail Knowledge – Level 2
Awarding body:
EDEXCEL

Retail Knowledge – Level 3
Awarding body:
EDEXCEL

Retailing – Level 2
Awarding body:
EDEXCEL

Retailing – Level 3
Awarding body:
EDEXCEL

BTEC Diploma

Retail Beauty Consultancy – Level 2
Awarding body:
EDEXCEL

Retail Knowledge – Level 2
Awarding body:
EDEXCEL

Retail Knowledge – Level 3
Awarding body:
EDEXCEL

BTEC First Certificate

Retail – Level 2
Awarding body:
EDEXCEL

BTEC First Diploma

Retail – Level 2
Awarding body:
EDEXCEL

Certificate

Introduction to Retailing – Level 1
Awarding body:
EDI

Retail (Management) – Level 3
Awarding body:
ABC
City & Guilds
EDEXCEL
EDI
OCR

Retail (Sales Professional) – Level 3
Awarding body:
ABC
City & Guilds
EDEXCEL
EDI

Retail (Visual Merchandising) – Level 3
Awarding body:
ABC
City & Guilds
EDEXCEL
EDI
OCR

Retail Knowledge – Level 1
Awarding body:
ABC
EDEXCEL
EDI
VTCT

Retail Knowledge – Level 2
Awarding body:
ABC
City & Guilds
EDI
OCR
VTCT

Retail Knowledge – Level 3
Awarding body:
ABC
City & Guilds
EDI
OCR

Retail Knowledge (Construction and Electrical Merchanting – Building) – Level 2
Awarding body:
City & Guilds

Retail Principles – Level 2
Awarding body:
City & Guilds

Retail Skills – Level 1
Awarding body:
ABC
City & Guilds
EDI
OCR

Retail Skills – Level 2
Awarding body:
ABC
City & Guilds
EDEXCEL
EDI
OCR

Retail Skills (Sales Professional) – Level 3
Awarding body:
OCR

Visual Merchandising for Retail – Level 3
Awarding body:
ABC

Diploma

Buying and Merchandising for Fashion Retail – Level 4
Awarding body:
ABC

Fashion Retail – Level 2
Awarding body:
ABC

Fashion Retail – Level 3
Awarding body:
ABC

Retail (Management) – Level 3
Awarding body:
ABC
City & Guilds
EDEXCEL
EDI
OCR

Retail (Sales Professional) – Level 3
Awarding body:
ABC
City & Guilds
EDEXCEL
EDI
OCR

Retail (Visual Merchandising) – Level 3
Awarding body:
ABC
City & Guilds
EDEXCEL
EDI
OCR

Retail Knowledge (Garden Retail) – Level 3
Awarding body:
Lantra Awards

Retail Skills – Level 1
Awarding body:
ABC
City & Guilds
EDI
OCR

Retail Skills – Level 2
Awarding body:
ABC
City & Guilds
EDEXCEL
EDI
OCR

Visual Merchandising for Retail – Level 4
Awarding body:
ABC

Foundation Diploma

Retail Business – Level 1
Awarding body:
AQA
City & Guilds
EDEXCEL
EDI
OCR

Higher Diploma

Retail Business – Level 2
Awarding body:
AQA
City & Guilds
EDEXCEL
EDI
OCR

National Award

Retail – Level 3
Awarding body:
EDEXCEL

National Certificate

Personal Licence Holders – Level 2
Awarding body:
EDI

National Vocational Qualification

Optical Retailing – Level 2
Awarding body:
City & Guilds
EDEXCEL
SQA

Optical Retailing – Level 3
Awarding body:
City & Guilds

Principal Learning

Retail Business – Level 1
Awarding body:
  AQA
  City & Guilds
  EDEXCEL
  EDI
  OCR

Retail Business – Level 2
Awarding body:
  AQA
  City & Guilds
  EDEXCEL
  EDI
  OCR

Retail Business – Level 3
Awarding body:
  AQA
  City & Guilds
  EDEXCEL
  EDI
  OCR

Progression Diploma

Retail Business – Level 3
Awarding body:
  AQA
  City & Guilds
  EDEXCEL
  EDI
  OCR

Service Enterprises

Advanced Diploma

Beauty Therapy – Level 3
Awarding body:
  VTCT

Hair and Beauty Studies – Level 3
Awarding body:
  AQA
  City & Guilds
  EDEXCEL
  OCR
  VTCT

Hair and Beauty Therapy Studies – Level 3
Awarding body:
  ITEC

Award

Chattels Auctioneering – Level 3
Awarding body:
  NFOPP

Cleaning in Food Premises – Level 2
Awarding body:
  CIEH

Cleaning Principles (Confined Spaces) – Level 2
Awarding body:
  City & Guilds

Cleaning Principles (Deep Cleaning of Internal Equipment Surfaces and Areas) – Level 2
Awarding body:
  City & Guilds

Cleaning Principles (External Surfaces and Areas) – Level 2
Awarding body:
  City & Guilds

Cleaning Principles (Food Areas) – Level 2
Awarding body:
  City & Guilds

Cleaning Principles (Glazed Surfaces and Facades) – Level 2
Awarding body:
 City & Guilds

Cleaning Principles (High Risk Areas; Controlled Environments) – Level 2
Awarding body:
 City & Guilds

Cleaning Principles (Interiors and Washrooms) – Level 2
Awarding body:
 City & Guilds

Cleaning Principles (Maintenance and Minor Repairs of Property) – Level 2
Awarding body:
 City & Guilds

Cleaning Principles (Manual Street Cleaning) – Level 2
Awarding body:
 City & Guilds

Cleaning Principles (Mechanical Street Cleaning) – Level 2
Awarding body:
 City & Guilds

Cleaning Principles (Passenger Transport Interiors) – Level 2
Awarding body:
 City & Guilds

Cleaning Principles (Periodic Cleaning of Hard and Semi-hard Floors) – Level 2
Awarding body:
 City & Guilds

Cleaning Principles (Periodic Cleaning of Soft Floors and Furnishings) – Level 2
Awarding body:
 City & Guilds

Cleaning Principles (Specialist Electronic Equipment) – Level 2
Awarding body:
 City & Guilds

Cleaning Principles (Water-Fed Pole Systems) – Level 2
Awarding body:
 City & Guilds

Cleaning Principles (Working Safely at Heights) – Level 2
Awarding body:
 City & Guilds

Colouring and Styling Men's Hair – Level 1
Awarding body:
 City & Guilds

Colouring and Styling Women's Hair – Level 1
Awarding body:
 City & Guilds

Commercial Property Agency – Level 3
Awarding body:
 NFOPP

Contact Dermatitis Prevention – Level 2
Awarding body:
 City & Guilds

Creative Hair Styling – Level 3
Awarding body:
 ABC

Hair Styling – Level 1
Awarding body:
 City & Guilds

Historical Hair Styling Techniques – Level 3
Awarding body:
 ABC

Introduction to the Hair and Beauty Sector – Entry Level
Awarding body:
 City & Guilds
 VTCT

Introduction to the Hair and Beauty Sector – Level 1
Awarding body:
 City & Guilds
 VTCT

Make-up and Face Painting – Level 1
Awarding body:
 City & Guilds

Nail Art and Face Painting – Level 1
Awarding body:
 City & Guilds

Nail Art and Make-Up – Level 1
Awarding body:
   City & Guilds

Real Property Auctioneering – Level 3
Awarding body:
   NFOPP

Residential Letting and Property Management – Level 3
Awarding body:
   NFOPP

Residential Letting and Property Management Northern Ireland – Level 3
Awarding body:
   NFOPP

Retail Knowledge – Level 1
Awarding body:
   VTCT

Sale of Residential Property – Level 3
Awarding body:
   NFOPP

Styling, Plaiting and Twisting Hair – Level 1
Awarding body:
   City & Guilds

BTEC Certificate

Close Protection Operations – Level 3
Awarding body:
   EDEXCEL

Hairdressing – Level 2
Awarding body:
   EDEXCEL

BTEC Higher National Certificate

Beauty Therapy Sciences – Level 5
Awarding body:
   EDEXCEL

BTEC Higher National Diploma

Beauty Therapy Sciences – Level 5
Awarding body:
   EDEXCEL

BTEC National Award

Beauty Therapy Sciences – Level 3
Awarding body:
   EDEXCEL

Hairdressing – Level 3
Awarding body:
   EDEXCEL

BTEC National Certificate

Hairdressing – Level 3
Awarding body:
   EDEXCEL

BTEC National Diploma

Beauty Therapy Sciences – Level 3
Awarding body:
   EDEXCEL

Certificate

African-Caribbean Hairdressing – Level 2
Awarding body:
   VTCT

Anatomy, Physiology, Complementary Medicine and Massage – Level 3
Awarding body:
   City & Guilds

Aromatherapy Massage Using Pre-blended Oils – Level 3
Awarding body:
   City & Guilds

Artificial Nail Structures – Level 3
Awarding body:
   City & Guilds

Barbering – Level 2
Awarding body:
  VTCT

Beauty Salon Reception – Level 2
Awarding body:
  City & Guilds

Body Art – Level 2
Awarding body:
  City & Guilds

Body Massage – Level 3
Awarding body:
  City & Guilds

Cleaning Principles – Level 2
Awarding body:
  City & Guilds
  EDI

Cleaning Science – Level 2
Awarding body:
  City & Guilds

Colouring and Dressing Hair – Level 2
Awarding body:
  City & Guilds

Colouring Hair – Level 3
Awarding body:
  City & Guilds

Complementary Medicine and Principles of Massage – Level 3
Awarding body:
  City & Guilds

Cosmetic Make-Up – Level 2
Awarding body:
  VTCT

Creative Hair Design and Make-Up – Level 3
Awarding body:
  City & Guilds

Cutting African Caribbean Women's Hair – Level 3
Awarding body:
  City & Guilds

Cutting Beards and Moustaches – Level 3
Awarding body:
  City & Guilds

Cutting Men's Hair – Level 3
Awarding body:
  City & Guilds

Dressing Hair – Level 2
Awarding body:
  City & Guilds

Ear Piercing – Level 2
Awarding body:
  VTCT

Electrical Epilation Treatments – Level 3
Awarding body:
  City & Guilds

Eyelash and Eyebrow Treatments – Level 2
Awarding body:
  City & Guilds

Face and Body Painting – Level 2
Awarding body:
  VTCT

Face and Skin Conditioning using Electrotherapy – Level 3
Awarding body:
  City & Guilds

Facial Care and Scalp Massage for Men – Level 2
Awarding body:
  City & Guilds

Facial Treatments – Level 2
Awarding body:
  City & Guilds

Fashion and Photographic Make-Up – Level 2
Awarding body:
  VTCT

Hair & Beauty Salon Services – Level 1
Awarding body:
  ITEC

Hairdressing – Level 1
Awarding body:
  EDEXCEL

Hairdressing – Level 2
Awarding body:
  VTCT

Hairdressing African Type Hair – Level 1
Awarding body:
 VTCT

Hairdressing and Barbering – Level 1
Awarding body:
 VTCT

Hairdressing Salon Reception – Level 2
Awarding body:
 City & Guilds

Indian Head Massage – Level 3
Awarding body:
 City & Guilds

Introduction to the Hair and Beauty Sector – Entry Level
Awarding body:
 City & Guilds
 VTCT

Introduction to the Hair and Beauty Sector – Level 1
Awarding body:
 City & Guilds
 VTCT

Introduction to Therapies – Level 1
Awarding body:
 VTCT

Making a Hair Addition and Styling – Level 3
Awarding body:
 City & Guilds

Manicure – Level 2
Awarding body:
 City & Guilds

Massage, Anatomy and Physiology – Level 3
Awarding body:
 City & Guilds

Mendhi and Henna Skin Decoration – Level 2
Awarding body:
 VTCT

Nail Art – Level 2
Awarding body:
 City & Guilds
 VTCT

Nail Design and Make-Up – Level 3
Awarding body:
 City & Guilds

Nail Technologies – Level 2
Awarding body:
 City & Guilds

Nail Technology – Level 2
Awarding body:
 VTCT

Nail Treatments – Level 2
Awarding body:
 VTCT

Pedicure – Level 2
Awarding body:
 City & Guilds

Perm and Neutralise African Caribbean Women's Hair – Level 3
Awarding body:
 City & Guilds

Perming Hair – Level 3
Awarding body:
 City & Guilds

Pest Control – Level 2
Awarding body:
 RSPH

Pest Control – Level 3
Awarding body:
 RSPH

Photographic Make-Up – Level 2
Awarding body:
 City & Guilds

Photographic Make-Up and Body Art Design – Level 2
Awarding body:
 City & Guilds

Photographic Make-Up and Dressing Hair – Level 2
Awarding body:
 City & Guilds

Principles of Cleaning – Level 2
Awarding body:
 FDQ

Providing Face Massage – Level 3
Awarding body:
  City & Guilds

Providing Professional Shaving Services – Level 3
Awarding body:
  City & Guilds

Relax African Caribbean Women's Hair – Level 3
Awarding body:
  City & Guilds

Salon Services – Level 1
Awarding body:
  City & Guilds

Self Tanning – Level 3
Awarding body:
  City & Guilds

Service Sector Receptionists – Level 2
Awarding body:
  VTCT

Skin Care and Make-up Treatments – Level 2
Awarding body:
  City & Guilds

Style and Finish African Caribbean Women's Hair – Level 3
Awarding body:
  City & Guilds

Styling Women's Hair – Level 3
Awarding body:
  City & Guilds

Swedish Massage – Level 3
Awarding body:
  VTCT

Threading Depilation – Level 2
Awarding body:
  VTCT

UV Tanning – Level 3
Awarding body:
  City & Guilds

Wax Depilation – Level 2
Awarding body:
  VTCT

Waxing Techniques – Level 2
Awarding body:
  City & Guilds

Women's Hair Cutting – Level 3
Awarding body:
  City & Guilds

Working in the Beauty Industry – Level 2
Awarding body:
  City & Guilds

Working in the Nail Industry – Level 2
Awarding body:
  City & Guilds

Working in the Professional Beauty Industry – Level 3
Awarding body:
  City & Guilds

Working in the Professional Hairdressing Industry – Level 3
Awarding body:
  City & Guilds

Diploma

Advanced Beauty Therapy – Level 3
Awarding body:
  City & Guilds

Advanced Creative Hair and Beauty Studies – Level 3
Awarding body:
  City & Guilds

Advanced Hairdressing – Level 3
Awarding body:
  City & Guilds

African Caribbean Women's Hairdressing – Level 2
Awarding body:
  City & Guilds

African Caribbean Women's Hairdressing – Level 3
Awarding body:
  City & Guilds

African Caribbean Women's Hairdressing Services – Level 2
Awarding body:
   City & Guilds

Barbering – Level 2
Awarding body:
   VTCT

Barbering – Level 3
Awarding body:
   VTCT

Barbering African Type Hair – Level 2
Awarding body:
   VTCT

Barbering African Type Hair – Level 3
Awarding body:
   VTCT

Barbering Services – Level 2
Awarding body:
   City & Guilds

Beauty Consultancy – Level 2
Awarding body:
   City & Guilds

Beauty Consultancy Services – Level 2
Awarding body:
   City & Guilds

Beauty Specialist Techniques – Level 2
Awarding body:
   VTCT

Beauty Specialists – Level 2
Awarding body:
   ITEC

Beauty Therapy – Level 2
Awarding body:
   CIBTAC
   City & Guilds

Beauty Therapy – Level 3
Awarding body:
   City & Guilds
   ITEC

Beauty Therapy Services – Level 2
Awarding body:
   City & Guilds

Body Treatments – Level 3
Awarding body:
   City & Guilds
   ITEC

Chemically Treated African Type Hair – Level 2
Awarding body:
   VTCT

Chemically Treated African Type Hair – Level 3
Awarding body:
   VTCT

Cleaning Principles – Level 2
Awarding body:
   City & Guilds

Cleaning Services Supervision – Level 3
Awarding body:
   City & Guilds

Ear Piercing – Level 2
Awarding body:
   ITEC

Epilation – Level 3
Awarding body:
   ITEC
   VTCT

Facial Electrical Treatments – Level 3
Awarding body:
   ITEC

Fashion, Theatre and Media Make-Up – Level 3
Awarding body:
   ITEC

Hair and Make-up Styling – Level 3
Awarding body:
   ABC

Hairdressing – Level 2
Awarding body:
   City & Guilds
   VTCT

Hairdressing – Level 3
Awarding body:
   City & Guilds
   VTCT

Hairdressing (Combined Hair Types) – Level 2
Awarding body:
ITEC
VTCT

Hairdressing (Combined Hair Types) – Level 3
Awarding body:
VTCT

Indian Head Massage – Level 3
Awarding body:
ITEC
VTCT

Introduction to the Hair and Beauty Sector – Level 1
Awarding body:
City & Guilds

Laser and Intense Pulsed Light Treatments – Level 4
Awarding body:
ITEC

Microdermabrasion Treatments – Level 3
Awarding body:
ITEC

Nail Art – Level 2
Awarding body:
ITEC

Nail Art – Level 3
Awarding body:
ITEC

Nail Technology – Level 2
Awarding body:
City & Guilds

Nail Technology – Level 3
Awarding body:
ITEC

Nail Technology Services – Level 2
Awarding body:
City & Guilds

Red Vein Treatment – Level 3
Awarding body:
ITEC

Salon Services (Beauty) – Level 1
Awarding body:
City & Guilds

Salon Services (Hair and Beauty) – Level 1
Awarding body:
City & Guilds

Salon Services (Hairdressing) – Level 1
Awarding body:
City & Guilds

Spa Treatments – Level 3
Awarding body:
ITEC

Stone Therapy – Level 3
Awarding body:
VTCT

Stone Therapy Massage – Level 3
Awarding body:
ITEC

Tanning Treatments – Level 3
Awarding body:
ITEC

Theatrical and Media Make-Up – Level 3
Awarding body:
VTCT

Treating Natural African Type Hair – Level 2
Awarding body:
VTCT

Treating Natural African Type Hair – Level 3
Awarding body:
VTCT

Using Therapy Techniques as an Aid to Stress Management – Level 3
Awarding body:
VTCT

Women's Hairdressing Services – Level 2
Awarding body:
City & Guilds

Foundation Diploma

Creative Hair and Beauty Studies – Level 1
Awarding body:
City & Guilds

Hair and Beauty Studies – Level 1
Awarding body:
AQA
City & Guilds
EDEXCEL
OCR
VTCT

Hair and Beauty Therapy Studies – Level 1
Awarding body:
ITEC

Higher Diploma

Creative Hair and Beauty Studies – Level 2
Awarding body:
City & Guilds

Hair and Beauty Studies – Level 2
Awarding body:
AQA
City & Guilds
EDEXCEL
OCR
VTCT

Hair and Beauty Therapy Studies – Level 2
Awarding body:
ITEC

Higher Professional Certificate

Technical Salon Management – Level 4
Awarding body:
City & Guilds

Higher Professional Diploma

Technical Salon Management – Level 4
Awarding body:
City & Guilds

IVQ Advanced Diploma

African Caribbean Women's Hairdressing – Level 3
Awarding body:
City & Guilds

Beauty Therapy – Level 3
Awarding body:
City & Guilds

Body Treatments – Level 3
Awarding body:
City & Guilds

Hairdressing – Level 3
Awarding body:
City & Guilds

IVQ Certificate

Beauty Therapy – Level 1
Awarding body:
City & Guilds

Hairdressing – Level 1
Awarding body:
City & Guilds

IVQ Diploma

African Caribbean Women's Hairdressing – Level 2
Awarding body:
City & Guilds

Beauty Consultancy – Level 2
Awarding body:
City & Guilds

Beauty Therapy – Level 2
Awarding body:
City & Guilds

Hairdressing – Level 2
Awarding body:
City & Guilds

Nail Technology – Level 2
Awarding body:
City & Guilds

National Certificate

Beauty Therapy Sciences – Level 3
Awarding body:
    EDEXCEL

National Vocational Qualification

Barbering – Level 2
Awarding body:
    City & Guilds
    EDEXCEL
    VTCT

Barbering – Level 3
Awarding body:
    City & Guilds
    EDEXCEL
    VTCT

Beauty Therapy – Level 1
Awarding body:
    City & Guilds
    EDEXCEL
    VTCT

Beauty Therapy – Level 2
Awarding body:
    City & Guilds
    EDEXCEL
    VTCT

Beauty Therapy – Level 3
Awarding body:
    City & Guilds
    EDEXCEL
    VTCT

Cleaning and Support Services – Level 1
Awarding body:
    City & Guilds
    EDI
    HAB
    NCFE

Cleaning and Support Services – Level 2
Awarding body:
    City & Guilds
    EDI
    FDQ
    NCFE

Facilities Management – Level 3
Awarding body:
    FDQ

Forecourt Operations – Level 2
Awarding body:
    City & Guilds

Hairdressing – Level 1
Awarding body:
    City & Guilds
    EDEXCEL
    VTCT

Hairdressing – Level 2
Awarding body:
    City & Guilds
    EDEXCEL
    ITEC
    VTCT

Hairdressing – Level 3
Awarding body:
    City & Guilds
    EDEXCEL
    VTCT

Hairdressing (Combined Hair Types) – Level 2
Awarding body:
    City & Guilds

Hairdressing and Barbering – Level 1
Awarding body:
    City & Guilds

Local Environmental Services – Level 2
Awarding body:
    City & Guilds
    FDQ
    NCFE

Nail Services – Level 2
Awarding body:
    City & Guilds
    EDEXCEL
    VTCT

Nail Services – Level 3
Awarding body:
    City & Guilds
    EDEXCEL
    VTCT

Sale of Residential Property – Level 2
Awarding body:
  ABBE
  EDEXCEL

Sale of Residential Property – Level 3
Awarding body:
  ABBE
  EDEXCEL

Spa Therapy – Level 3
Awarding body:
  City & Guilds
  EDEXCEL
  VTCT

Principal Learning

Hair and Beauty Studies – Level 1
Awarding body:
  AQA
  City & Guilds
  VTCT

Hair and Beauty Studies – Level 2
Awarding body:
  AQA
  City & Guilds
  VTCT

Hair and Beauty Studies – Level 3
Awarding body:
  AQA
  City & Guilds
  VTCT

Progression Diploma

Hair and Beauty Studies – Level 3
Awarding body:
  AQA
  City & Guilds
  EDEXCEL
  OCR
  VTCT

Warehousing and Distribution

Advanced Diploma

Logistics and Transport – Level 6
Awarding body:
  CILT(UK)

Award

The Safe Loading and Securing of Steel Products for Road Transportation – Level 2
Awarding body:
  EDI

BTEC Award

Carry and Deliver Goods – Level 2
Awarding body:
  EDEXCEL

Certificate

Logistics and Transport – Level 3
Awarding body:
  CILT(UK)

Warehousing and Storage Principles – Level 2
Awarding body:
  City & Guilds
  EDI

Diploma

Bulk Liquid Operations – Level 2
Awarding body:
  PAA\VQSET

Introductory Certificate

Logistics and Transport – Level 2
Awarding body:
   CILT(UK)

National Vocational Qualification

Bulk Liquid Warehousing – Level 2
Awarding body:
   City & Guilds
   PAA\VQSET

Carry and Deliver Goods – Level 2
Awarding body:
   City & Guilds
   EDEXCEL
   EDI
   OCR
   SQA

Driving Goods Vehicles – Level 2
Awarding body:
   City & Guilds
   EDEXCEL
   EDI
   OCR
   PAA\VQSET
   SQA

Driving Goods Vehicles – Level 3
Awarding body:
   City & Guilds
   EDEXCEL
   EDI
   OCR
   PAA\VQSET
   SQA

Integrated Logistics Support Management – Level 4
Awarding body:
   EAL

Logistics Operations Management – Level 3
Awarding body:
   City & Guilds
   EAL
   EDEXCEL
   EDI
   OCR
   PAA\VQSET
   SQA

Mail Services – Level 2
Awarding body:
   City & Guilds

Traffic Office – Level 2
Awarding body:
   City & Guilds

Traffic Office – Level 3
Awarding body:
   City & Guilds

Transportation – Level 3
Awarding body:
   OU

Transportation – Level 4
Awarding body:
   OU

Transportation – Level 5
Awarding body:
   OU

Warehousing and Storage – Level 1
Awarding body:
   City & Guilds
   EAL
   EDEXCEL
   EDI
   OCR
   PAA\VQSET
   SQA

Warehousing and Storage – Level 2
Awarding body:
    City & Guilds
    EAL
    EDEXCEL
    EDI
    NCFE
    OCR
    PAA\VQSET
    SQA

Professional Diploma

Logistics and Transport – Level 5
Awarding body:
    CILT(UK)

Science and Mathematics

Mathematics and Statistics

Advanced Extension Award

Mathematics – Level 3
Awarding body:
EDEXCEL

Advanced Free-Standing Mathematics Qualification

Data Analysis (Pilot) – Level 3
Awarding body:
AQA

Dynamics (Pilot) – Level 3
Awarding body:
AQA

Mathematical Principles for Personal Finance (Pilot) – Level 3
Awarding body:
AQA

Modelling with calculus – Level 3
Awarding body:
AQA

Using and Applying Decision Mathematics – Level 3
Awarding body:
AQA

Using and applying statistics – Level 3
Awarding body:
AQA

Working with algebraic and graphical techniques – Level 3
Awarding body:
AQA

Award

Mathematical Applications (Pilot) – Level 1
Awarding body:
EDEXCEL

Mathematics in Engineering – Level 3
Awarding body:
EDEXCEL

BTEC Award

Mathematical Applications (Pilot) – Level 2
Awarding body:
EDEXCEL

Certificate

Mathematical techniques and applications for engineers – Level 3
Awarding body:
OCR

Mathematics – Entry Level
Awarding body:
AQA
EDEXCEL
WJEC

Mathematics – Level 1,2
Awarding body:
Cambridge International

Mathematics A – Entry Level
Awarding body:
OCR

Mathematics B – Entry Level
Awarding body:
OCR

Mathematics for Engineering – Level 3
Awarding body:
OCR

Mathematics for Life – Entry Level
Awarding body:
CCEA

Foundation Level Free-Standing Mathematics Qualification

Making sense of data – Level 1
Awarding body:
AQA

Managing money – Level 1
Awarding body:
AQA

Money Management (Pilot) – Level 1
Awarding body:
AQA

Using Data (Pilot) – Level 1
Awarding body:
AQA

Using Spatial Techniques (Pilot) – Level 1
Awarding body:
AQA

Working in 2 and 3 Dimensions – Level 1
Awarding body:
AQA

Free-Standing Mathematics Qualification

Calculus (Pilot) – Level 3
Awarding body:
AQA

Decision Mathematics (Pilot) – Level 3
Awarding body:
AQA

Dynamics (Pilot) – Level 3
Awarding body:
AQA

Hypothesis Testing (Pilot) – Level 3
Awarding body:
AQA

Mathematical Principles for Personal Finance (Pilot) – Level 3
Awarding body:
AQA

Intermediate Level Free-Standing Mathematics Qualification

Algebra and Graphs (Pilot) – Level 2
Awarding body:
AQA

Calculating finances – Level 2
Awarding body:
AQA

Data Handling (Pilot) – Level 2
Awarding body:
AQA

Financial Calculations (Pilot) – Level 2
Awarding body:
AQA Foundation Level
Free-Standing Mathematics
Qualification:

Foundations of Advanced Mathematics – Level 2
Awarding body:
OCR

Handling and interpreting data – Level 2
Awarding body:
AQA

Shape and Space (Pilot) – Level 2
Awarding body:
AQA

Using algebra, functions and graphs – Level 2
Awarding body:
AQA

Pre-U Certificate

Further Mathematics (Principal) – Level 3
Awarding body:
Cambridge International

Mathematics (Principal) – Level 3
Awarding body:
Cambridge International

Science

Award

Chemical and Pharmaceutical Based Process Support (Sample and Test Materials) – Level 2
Awarding body:
PAA\VQSET

Nuclear Industry Awareness – Level 2
Awarding body:
PAA\VQSET

Polymer and Composites Based Process Support (Complex Sampling Operations) – Level 3
Awarding body:
PAA\VQSET

Polymer and Composites Based Process Support (Testing Operations) – Level 2
Awarding body:
PAA\VQSET

BTEC Certificate

Applied Science – Level 2
Awarding body:
EDEXCEL

Applied Science – Level 3
Awarding body:
EDEXCEL

BTEC Diploma

Applied Science – Level 2
Awarding body:
EDEXCEL

Applied Science – Level 3
Awarding body:
EDEXCEL

BTEC Extended Certificate

Applied Science – Level 2
Awarding body:
EDEXCEL

BTEC Extended Diploma

Applied Science – Level 3
Awarding body:
EDEXCEL

BTEC First Certificate

Applied Science – Level 2
Awarding body:
EDEXCEL

BTEC First Diploma

Applied Science – Level 2
Awarding body:
EDEXCEL

BTEC Higher National Certificate

Applied Biology – Level 5
Awarding body:
EDEXCEL

Applied Chemistry – Level 5
Awarding body:
EDEXCEL

BTEC Higher National Diploma

Applied Biology – Level 5
Awarding body:
EDEXCEL

Applied Chemistry – Level 5
Awarding body:
EDEXCEL

Nautical Science – Level 5
Awarding body:
EDEXCEL

BTEC National Award

Applied Science – Level 3
Awarding body:
EDEXCEL

BTEC National Certificate

Applied Science – Level 3
Awarding body:
EDEXCEL

BTEC National Diploma

Applied Science – Level 3
Awarding body:
EDEXCEL

BTEC Subsidiary Diploma

Applied Science – Level 3
Awarding body:
EDEXCEL

Certificate

Biology – Level 1,2
Awarding body:
Cambridge International

Biology – Level 3
Awarding body:
ASCENTIS

Chemistry – Level 1,2
Awarding body:
Cambridge International

Gemmology – Level 3
Awarding body:
Gem-A

Human Physiology – Level 2
Awarding body:
ASCENTIS

Laboratory Technical Skills – Level 1
Awarding body:
PAA\VQSET

Laboratory Technical Skills – Level 2
Awarding body:
PAA\VQSET

Laboratory Technical Skills – Level 3
Awarding body:
PAA\VQSET

Physics – Level 1,2
Awarding body:
Cambridge International

Psychological Perspectives – Level 3
Awarding body:
ASCENTIS

Psychology – Level 2
Awarding body:
ASCENTIS

Science – Entry Level
Awarding body:
AQA
EDEXCEL
OCR

Science (Double Award) – Entry Level
Awarding body:
WJEC

Science (Single Award) – Entry Level
Awarding body:
CCEA
WJEC

Diploma

Gem Diamond – Level 4
Awarding body:
   Gem-A

Gemmology – Level 5
Awarding body:
   Gem-A

Introductory Certificate

Applied Science – Level 1
Awarding body:
   EDEXCEL

Introductory Diploma

Applied Science – Level 1
Awarding body:
   EDEXCEL

National Award

Science – Level 2
Awarding body:
   OCR

National Certificate

Science – Level 2
Awarding body:
   OCR

National Vocational Qualification

Analytical Chemistry – Level 5
Awarding body:
   PAA\VQSET

Clinical Laboratory Support – Level 2
Awarding body:
   City & Guilds
   EDEXCEL

Weather Forecasting – Level 4
Awarding body:
   PAA\VQSET

Weather Observing – Level 3
Awarding body:
   PAA\VQSET

Pre-U Certificate

Biology (Principal) – Level 3
Awarding body:
   Cambridge International

Chemistry (Principal) – Level 3
Awarding body:
   Cambridge International

Physics (Principal) – Level 3
Awarding body:
   Cambridge International

Psychology (Principal) – Level 3
Awarding body:
   Cambridge International

Social Sciences

Economics

Certificate

Business Studies – Level 1,2
Awarding body:
   Cambridge International

Pre-U Certificate

Economics (Principal) – Level 3
Awarding body:
   Cambridge International

Geography

Certificate

Geographical Information Systems – Level 3
Awarding body:
   EDI

Geography – Entry Level
Awarding body:
   AQA
   CCEA
   EDEXCEL

Geography – Level 1,2
Awarding body:
   Cambridge International

Geography (A) – Entry Level
Awarding body:
   WJEC

Geography A – Entry Level
Awarding body:
   OCR

Geography C – Entry Level
Awarding body:
   OCR

Diploma

Aeronautical Cartography – Level 4
Awarding body:
   DefAB

Pre-U Certificate

Geography (Principal) – Level 3
Awarding body:
   Cambridge International

Politics

Pre-U Certificate

**Comparative Government and Politics
(Principal) – Level 3**
Awarding body:
    Cambridge International

Sociology and Social Policy

Award

**Deaf Awareness and Communication –
Level 1**
Awarding body:
    Signature

Certificate

Humanities – Entry Level
Awarding body:
    WJEC

**Introduction to Principles of
Criminology – Level 2**
Awarding body:
    ASCENTIS

Sociology – Level 2
Awarding body:
    ASCENTIS

Part 3

Sources of Information

Introduction

The acronyms listed at the beginning of this section are mainly quoted in those entries to be found in Part Two – The Directory of Vocational Qualifications – and the full addresses of most of these bodies will be found in the list that follows, together with other relevant useful addresses.

Acronyms

14–19	14–19 year olds
AAT	Association of Accounting Technicians
ABBE	Awarding Body for the Built Environment
ABC	Awarding Body Consortium
ABDO	Association of British Dispensing Opticians
ABE	Association of Building Engineers
ABLS	Association of British Language Schools
ABRSM	Associated Board of the Royal Schools of Music
ACCA	Association of Chartered Certified Accountants
ACE	Adult and Community Learning
ACRIB	Air Conditioning and Refrigeration Industry Board
AEB	Associates Examining Board
AMSPAR	Association of Medical Secretaries, Practice Managers, Administrators and Receptionists
APL	Accreditation of Prior Learning
AP(E)L	Accreditation of Prior Experiential Learning
APCL	Accreditation of Prior Certificated Learning
AQA	Assessment and Qualifications Alliance
ASA	Amateur Swimming Association
ASDAN	Award Scheme Development and Accreditation Network
ASQ	Association of Sports Qualifications
BA	Bachelor of Arts
BA (Hons)	Bachelor of Arts (Honours)
BAAL	British Association for Applied Linguistics
BAC	British Accreditation Council for Independent Further and Higher Education
BAGMA	British Agricultural and Garden Machinery Association
BBO	British Ballet Organisation
BC	British Council
BCF	British Coatings Federation
BCS	British Computer Society
BCU	British Canoe Union
BDS	British Driving Society
BECTA	British Educational Communications and Technology Agency
BG	British Gymnastics
BHEST	British Horseracing Education and Standards Trust
BHS	British Horse Society
BII	British Institute of Innkeeping
BIS	Department for Business, Innovation and Skills
BSc	Bachelor of Science
BSc (Hons)	Bachelor of Science (Honours)
BSC	British Safety Council
BSGA	British Sign and Graphics Association
BST	British Sports Trust

BTDA	British Theatre Dance Association
BVC	Bar Vocational Course
C&G	City and Guilds
CACDP	The Council for the Advancement of Communication between Deaf and Hearing People
CACHE	Council for Awards in Children's Care and Education
CALL	Computer Assisted Language Learning
CAMBRIDGE ESOL	University of Cambridge ESOL Examinations
CAP	Common Application Process
CCEA	Council for Curriculum, Examinations and Assessment
CCN	City College Norwich
CfBT	Centre for British Teachers
CIAT	Chartered Institute of Architectural Technologists
CIBTAC	Confederation of International Beauty Therapy and Cosmetology
CIEH	Chartered Institute of Environmental Health
CIH	Chartered Institute of Housing
CII	Chartered Insurance Institute
CILT	Chartered Institute of Logistics and Transport (UK)
CIM	Chartered Institute of Marketing
CIOB	Chartered Institute of Building
CIoBS	Chartered Institute of Bankers In Scotland
CIPD	Chartered Institute of Personnel and Development
CIPR	Chartered Institute of Public Relations
CIPS	Chartered Institute of Purchasing and Supply
CITB	Construction Skills
CMI	Chartered Management Institute
COTAC	Conference on Training in Architectural Conservation
CPCAB	Counselling and Psychotherapy Central Awarding Body
CYQ	Central YMCA Qualifications
DCSF	Department for Children, Schools and Families
DIVQ	Distilling Industry Vocational Qualifications Group
EAL	EMTA Awards Ltd
ECITB	Engineering Construction Industry Training Board
EDI	Education Development International Plc
EMP	Engineering Management Partnership
ESB	English Speaking Board (International) Ltd
ESTTL	Engineering Services Training Trust Ltd
ETCAL	Engineering Training Council Awards Ltd
FAQ	First Aid Qualifications
FD	Foundation Degree
FDQ	Food and Drink Qualifications
FE	Further Education
GCSE	General Certificate of Secondary Education
GEM-A	Gemmological Association of Great Britain

GERI	Gender, Race, Equality and Inclusion
GNVQ	General National Vocational Qualification
GQA	Glass Qualifications Authority
GQAL	Graded Qualifications Alliance
GSMD	Guildhall School of Music and Drama Examination Service
HAB	Hospitality Awarding Body
HE	Higher Education
HLSPP	Higher Level Skills Pathfinder Project
HNC	Higher National Certificate
HND	Higher National Diploma
IAB	International Association of Book-Keepers
IAG	Information, Advice and Guidance
IAM	Institute of Advanced Motorists
IBO	International Baccalaureate Organisation
ICAA	International Curriculum and Assessment Agency
ICE	Institution of Civil Engineers
ICG	Institute of Career Guidance
ICM	Institute of Credit Management
ICT	Information, Communication and Technology
ICoW	Institute of Clerks of Works of Great Britain Incorporated
IDTA	International Dance Teachers Association
IFE	Institution of Fire Engineers
IFS	Institute of Financial Services
IH	Institute of Hospitality
ILEX	Institute of Legal Executives
ILM	Institute of Leadership and Management
IMI	Institute of the Motor Industry
IOCM	Institute of Commercial Management
IoL	Chartered Institute of Linguists
IOLET	Institute of Linguists Educational Trust
IOM	Institute of Operations Management
IQL	Institute of Qualified Lifeguards
IRRV	Institute of Revenues, Rating and Valuation
ISMM	Institute of Sales and Marketing Management
ISTD	Imperial Society of Teachers of Dancing
ITEC	International Therapy Examination Council
LA	Lantra
LAMDA	London Academy of Music and Dramatic Art
LANTRA	The Sector Skills Council for the Environmental and Land-based Sector
LCCI	London Chamber of Commerce and Industry Examinations Board
LLN	Lifelong Learning Network
MIAP	Managing Information Across Partners
MLTE	Mountain Leader Training England
MOD	Ministry of Defence
MPQC	Mineral Products Qualification Council

| MRS | Market Research Society |
| MSc | Master of Science |

NAEA	National Association of Estate Agents
NEA	National Energy Action
NEBDN	National Examining Board for Dental Nurses
NEBOSH	National Examination Board in Occupational Safety and Health
NEET	Not in Employment, Education or Training
NFOPP	National Federation of Property Professionals
NIACE	National Institute of Adult Continuing Education
NGO	Non-governmental Organisation
NOCN	National Open College Network
NPTC	National Proficiency Tests Council
NQF	National Qualifications Framework
NVQ	National Vocational Qualification

OCR	Oxford, Cambridge and Royal School of Arts Examinations
ODL	Open and Distance Learning
OL	Open Learning
OLASS	Offender Learning and Skills Service
OPITO	Offshore Petroleum Industry Training Organisation
OU	Open University

PAA/VQSET	Process Awards Authority/Vocational Qualifications in Science, Engineering and Technology
PADI	Professional Association of Dive Instructors
PhP	Doctor of Philosophy
PIABC	Packaging Industry Awarding Body Company
PMI	The Pensions Management Institute
PREMIER TI	Premier Training International

QCA	Qualification and Curriculum Authority
QCDA	Qualifications and Curriculum Development Agency
QCF	Qualifications and Credit Framework
QNUK	Qualifications Network UK
QTS	Qualified Teacher Status

RAD	Royal Academy of Dance
RCVS	The Royal College of Veterinary Surgeons
RHS	Royal Horticultural Society
RIPH	Royal Institute of Public Health
RSL	Rock School Ltd
RSPH	Royal Society for the Promotion of Health

SAMB	Scottish Association of Master Bakers
SBATC	Scottish Building Apprenticeship and Training Council
SCITT	School Centred Initial Teacher Training
SfL	Skills for Logistics
SII	Securities & Investment Institute
SfS	Skills for Security

SJIB	Scottish Joint Industry Board for the Electrical Contracting Industry
SNIJIBPI	Scottish and Northern Ireland Joint Industry Board for the Plumbing Industry
SNVQ	Scottish National Vocational Qualification
SPEF	Scottish Print Employers Federation
SQA	Scottish Qualifications Authority
SSCS	Sector Skills Council
STA	Swimming Teachers Association
TCL	Trinity College London
TLM	The Learning Machine
TTF	Timber Trade Federation
TVU	Thames Valley University
UAL	University of the Arts London
UKCES	UK Commission for Employment and Skills
UKRLP	UK Register of Learning Providers
UKSIP	UK Society of Investment Professionals
VSO	Voluntary Service Overseas
VT	Vocational Training
VTCT	Vocational Training Charitable Trust
WAMITAB	Waste Management Industry Training and Advisory Board
WBL	Work-based Learning
WCF	Worshipful Company of Farriers
WCSM	Worshipful Company of Spectacle Makers
WJEC	Welsh Joint Education Committee
WSET	Wine & Spirit Education Trust

Awarding Bodies and Sources of Further Information

1st4Sport Qualifications
Coachwise Ltd
Chelsea Close
Off Amberley Road
Armley
Leeds LS12 4HP
Tel: 0113 290 7610
Fax: 0113 231 9606
enquiries@1st4sportqualifications.com
www.1st4sportqualifications.com

ABDO College Distance Learning Institute
Godmersham Park
Godmersham
Canterbury
Kent CT4 7DT
Tel: 01227 733910
Fax: 01227 733900
general@abdo.org.uk
www.abdo.org.uk

Active IQ
Suite 3, Unit 4
Cromwell Business Centre
New Road
St Ives
Cambridgeshire
PE27 5BG
Tel: 01480 467950
Fax: 01480 467997
info@activeiq.co.uk

AFAQ-ETA
185 Park Street
Bankside
London SE1 9DY
Tel: 020 7922 1630
Fax: 020 7922 1627
www.eta.org.uk

Air Conditioning and Refrigeration Industry Board
Kelvin House
76 Mill Lane
Carshalton
Surrey SM5 2JR
Tel: 020 8254 7842
Fax: 020 8773 0165
www.acrib.org.uk

Amateur Swimming Association
Harold Fern House, Derby Square
Loughborough
Leicestershire LE11 5AL
Tel: 01509 618 700
Fax: 01509 618 701
customerservices@swimming.org
www.britishswimming.org

ASET
124 Micklegate
York YO1 6XJ
Tel: 0845 45 89 500
Fax: 01904 677042
customer.services@aset.ac.uk
www.aset.ac.uk

Assessment and Qualifications Alliance
Stag Hill House
Guildford
Surrey GU2 7XJ
Tel: 01483 506506
Fax: 01483 300152
mailbox@aqa.org.uk
www.aqa.org.uk

Associated Board of the Royal Schools of Music
24 Portland Place
London W1B 1LU
Tel: 020 7636 5400
Fax: 020 7637 0234
www.abrsm.org

Association of Accounting Technicians
140 Aldersgate Street
London
EC1A 4HY
Tel: 0845 863 0800 or 020 7397 3000
www.aat.org.uk

Association of Building Engineers
Lutyens House
Billing Brook Road
Weston Favell
Northampton
Northamptonshire
NN3 8NW
Tel: 0845 126 1058
Fax: 01604 784220
building.engineers@abe.org.uk

Association of Chartered Certified Accountants
29 Lincolns Inn Fields
London
United Kingdom
WC2A 3EE
Tel: 020 7059 5000
info@accaglobal.com
www.accaglobal.com

Association of Medical Secretaries, Practice Managers, Administrators and Receptionists
Tavistock House North
Tavistock Square
London WC1H 9LN
Tel: 020 7387 6005
Fax: 020 7388 2648
info@amspar.co.uk
www.amspar.co.uk

Association of Sports Qualifications
Ping House
The Belfry
Sutton Coldfield
West Midlands
United Kingdom
B76 9PW
info@asq.org.uk

Awarding Body Consortium
Duxbury Park
Duxbury Hall Road
Chorley
Lancashire PR7 4AT
Tel: 01257 241428
Fax: 01257 260357
enquiries_chorley@abcawards.co.uk
www.abcawards.co.uk

Award Scheme Development and Accreditation Network (ASDAN)
Wainbrook House
Hudds Vale Road
St George
Bristol BS5 7HY
Tel: 0117 9411126
Fax: 0117 9351112
info@asdan.co.uk
www.asdan.co.uk

British Agricultural and Garden Machinery Association (BAGMA)
Entrance B, Level 1
Salamander Quay West
Park Lane
Harefield UB9 6NZ
Tel: 0870 205 2834
Fax: 0870 205 2835
info@bagma.com
www.bagma.com

British Ballet Organisation (BBO)
Woolborough House
39 Lonsdale Road
Barnes
London SW13 9JP
Tel: 020 8748 1241
Fax: 020 8748 1301
info@bbo.org.uk
www.bbo.org.uk

British Canoe Union
18 Market Place
Bingham
Nottinghamshire
United Kingdom
NG13 8AP
Tel: 0845 370 9503
bcuawarding@bcu.co.uk
www.bcu.org.uk

British Coatings Federation Ltd
James House
Bridge Street
Leatherhead
Surrey KT22 7EP
Tel: 01372 360660
Fax: 01372 376069
enquiry@bcf.co.uk
www.coatings.org.uk

British Computer Society
First Floor, Block D
North Star House
North Star Avenue
Swindon
Wiltshire SN2 1FA
Tel: 01793 417417
Fax: 01793 417444
www.bcs.org.uk

British Driving Society
83 New Road
Helmingham
Stowmarket
Suffolk
United Kingdom
IP14 6EA
email@britishdrivingsociety.co.uk
www.britishdrivingsociety.co.uk

British Gymnastics
Ford Hall
Lilleshall National Sports Centre
Newport
Shropshire TF10 9NB
Tel: 0845 1297129
Fax: 0845 1249089
information@british-gymnastics.org
www.british-gymnastics.org

British Horse Society
Stoneleigh Deer Park
Kenilworth
Warwickshire CV8 2XZ
Tel: 0844 848 1666
Fax: 01926 707800
enquiry@bhs.org.uk
www.bhs.org.uk

British Horseracing Education and Standards Trust
Suite 16, Unit 8, Kings Court
Willie Snaith Road
Newmarket
Suffolk CB8 7SG
Tel: 01638 565130
Fax: 01638 660932
www.bhtb.co.uk

British Institute of Cleaning Science
9 Premier Court
Boarden Close
Moulton Park
Northampton NN3 6LF
Tel: 01604 678710
www.bics.org.uk

British Institute of Innkeeping Awarding Body
Wessex House
80 Park Street
Camberley
Surrey GU15 3PT
Tel: 01276 684449
Fax: 01276 23045
reception@bii.org
www.bii.org

British Safety Council
70 Chancellors Road
London W6 9RS
Tel: 020 8741 1231
Fax: 020 8741 4555
mail@britsafe.org
www.britishsafetycouncil.co.uk

British Sign and Graphics Association
5 Orton Enterprise Centre
Bakewell Road, Orton Southgate
Peterborough PE2 6XU
Tel: 01733 230033
info@bsga.co.uk
www.bsga.co.uk

British Theatre Dance Association
The International Arts Centre
Garden Street
Leicester LE1 3UA
Tel: 0845 166 2179
Fax: 0116 251 4781
info@btda.org.uk
www.btda.org.uk

CABWI Awarding Body
1 Queen Anne's Gate
London SW1H 9BT
Tel: 020 7957 4523
Fax: 020 7957 4641
enquiries@cabwi.co.uk
www.cabwi.co.uk

Cambridge, University of, ESOL Examinations
1 Hills Road
Cambridge CB1 2EU
Tel: 01223 553355
Fax: 01223 460278
esolhelpdesk@ucles.org.uk
www.cambridgeesol.org

Central YMCA Qualifications (CYQ)
112 Great Russell Street
London WC1B 3NQ
Tel: 020 7343 1800
Fax: 020 7436 2687
info@cyq.org.uk
www.cyq.org.uk

The CFA Society of the UK
4th Floor
90 Basinghall Street
London EC2V 5AY
Tel: 020 7796 3000
Fax: 020 7796 3333
info@cfauk.org
www.cfauk.org

Chartered Institute of Architectural Technologists
397 City Road
London EC1V 1NH
Tel: 020 7278 2206
Fax: 020 7837 3194
info@ciat.org.uk
www.ciat.org.uk

Chartered Institute of Bankers In Scotland
Drumsheugh House
38b Drumsheugh Gardens
Edinburgh EH3 7SW
Tel: 0131 473 7777
Fax: 0131 473 7788
info@ciobs.org.uk
www.ciobs.org.uk

Chartered Institute of Building
Englemere
Kings Ride
Ascot
Berks SL5 7TB
Tel: 01344 630700
Fax: 01344 630777
reception@ciob.org.uk
www.ciob.org.uk

Chartered Institute of Environmental Health
Chadwick Court
15 Hatfields
London SE1 8DJ
Tel: 020 7928 6006
Fax: 020 7827 5862
www.cieh.org

Chartered Institute of Housing
Octavia House
Westwood Way
Coventry CV4 8JP
Tel: 024 7685 1700
Fax: 024 7669 5110
customer.services@cih.org
www.cih.org

Chartered Institute of Logistics and Transport (UK)
Logistics and Transport Centre
Earlstrees Court
Earlstrees Road
Corby, Northants
NN17 4AX
Tel: 01536 740100
Fax: 01536 740101
enquiry@ciltuk.org.uk
www.ciltuk.org.uk

Chartered Institute of Marketing
Moor Hall
Cookham
Maidenhead
Berks SL6 9QH
Tel: 01628 427500
Fax: 01628 472499
membershipinfo@cim.co.uk
www.cim.co.uk

Chartered Institute of Personnel and Development (CIPD)
151 The Broadway
London SW19 1JQ
Tel: 020 8612 6200
Fax: 020 8612 6201
www.cipd.co.uk

Chartered Institute of Public Relations
CIPR PR Centre
32 St James's Square
London SW1Y 4JR
Tel: 020 7766 3333
Fax: 020 7766 3334
info@cipr.co.uk
www.cipr.co.uk

Chartered Institute of Purchasing and Supply
Easton House
Church Street
Easton on the Hill
Stamford
Lincolnshire PE9 3NZ
Tel: 01780 756777
Fax: 01780 751610
info@cips.org
www.cips.org

Chartered Insurance Institute
42–48 High Road
South Woodford
London E18 2JP
Tel: 020 8989 8464
Fax: 020 8530 3052
customer.serv@cii.co.uk
www.cii.co.uk

Chartered Management Institute
3rd Floor
2 Savoy Court
Strand
London WC2R 0EZ
Tel: 020 7497 0580
Fax: 020 7497 0463
enquiries@managers.org.uk
www.managers.org.uk

CILT (UK)
Earlstrees Court
Earlstrees Road
Corby
Northants NN17 4AX
Tel: 01536 740105
Fax: 01536 740101

CITB-ConstructionSkills
Bircham Newton
Kings Lynn
Norfolk PE31 6RH
Tel: 01485 577577
call.centre@skills.org
www.citb.co.uk

City and Guilds
1 Giltspur Street
London EC1A 9DD
Tel: 020 7294 2800
Fax: 020 7294 2400
www.cityandguilds.com

City College Norwich
Ipswich Road
Norwich
United Kingdom
NR2 2LJ
Tel: 01603 773311
info@ccn.ac.uk
www.ccn.ac.uk

Confederation of International Beauty Therapy & Cosmetology
Meteor Court
Barnett Way
Gloucester
GL4 3GG
Tel: 01452 623114
Fax   01452 611724
ameena@cibtac.com
www.cibtac.com

Conference on Training in Architectural Conservation
The Building Crafts College
Kennard Road
Stratford
London E15 1AH
Tel: 020 8522 1705
Fax: 020 8522 1309
cotac@thebcc.co.uk
www.cotac.org.uk

The Council for the Advancement of Communication between Deaf and Hearing People
Mersey House
Mandale Business Park
Belmont
Durham DH1 1TH
Tel: 0191 383 1155
Fax: 0191 383 7914
durham@cacdp.org.uk
www.cacdp.org.uk

Council for Awards in Children's Care and Education
Beaufort House
Grosvenor Road
St Albans
Herts AL1 3AW
Tel: 0845 347 2123
Fax: 01727 818618
info@cache.org.uk
www.cache.org.uk

Council for the Curriculum, Examinations and Assessment
29 Clarendon Road
Clarendon Dock
Belfast BT1 3BG
Tel: 028 9026 1200
Fax: 028 9026 1234
info@ccea.org.uk
www.ccea.org.uk

Counselling and Psychotherapy Central Awarding Body (CPCAB)

PO Box 1768
Glastonbury
Somerset BA6 8YP
Tel: 01458 850350
Fax: 01458 852055
admin@cpcab.co.uk
www.cpcab.co.uk

Distilling Industry Vocational Qualifications Group

20 Atholl Crescent
Edinburgh EH3 8HF
Tel: 0131 222 9200
Fax: 0131 222 9237
info@swa.org.uk
www.scotch-whisky.org.uk

Edexcel

One90 High Holborn
London WC1V 7BH
Tel: 0870 240 9800
Fax: 020 7190 5706
www.edexcel.org.uk

EDI Plc

International House
Siskin Parkway East
Middlemarch Business Park
Coventry CV3 4PE
Tel: 08707 202909
Fax: 024 7651 6505
enquiries@ediplc.com
www.ediplc.com

EMP Awarding Body Limited

Knowledge Centre
Wyboston Lane
Great North Road
Wyboston
Bedfordshire
MK44 3BY
Tel: 01480 479267
Fax: 01480 213854
info@empawards.com
www.empawards.com

EMTA Awards Ltd

SEMTA House
14 Upton Road
Watford
Hertfordshire WD18 0JT
Tel: 01923 652 400
Fax: 01923 652 401
customercare@eal.org.uk
www.eal.org.uk

Engineering Construction Industry Training Board

Blue Court
Church Lane
Kings Langley
Hertfordshire WD4 8JP
Tel: 01923 260000
Fax: 01923 270969
ecitb@ecitb.org.uk
www.ecitb.org.uk

Engineering Management Partnership

School of Management
University of Bath
Bath BA2 7AY
Tel: 01225 384245
Fax: 01225 386473
emp@management.bath.ac.uk
www.emp.ac.uk

Engineering Training Council Awards Ltd

Interpoint
20–24 York Street
Belfast BT15 1AQ
Tel: 028 9032 9878
Fax: 028 9031 0301
www.etcni.org.uk

English Speaking Board (International) Ltd

26a Princes Street
Southport PR8 1EQ
Tel: 01704 501730
Fax: 01704 539637
admin@esbuk.org
www.esbuk.org

First Aid Qualifications

EMP House
Telford Way
Coalville
Leicestershire
LE67 3HB
Tel: 0845 029 1905
Fax: 0845 029 1906
info@firstaidqualifications.com
www.firstaidqualifications.com

Food and Drink Qualifications
PO Box 141
Winterhill House
Snowdon Drive
Milton Keynes MK6 1YY
Tel: 01908 231 062
Fax: 01908 231 063
info@fdq.org.uk
www.fdq.org.uk

Gemmological Association of Great Britain
27 Greville Street
London EC1N 8TN
Tel: 020 7404 3334
Fax: 020 7404 8843
information@gem-a.info
www.gem-a.info

Glass Qualifications Authority Ltd
Provincial House
Solly Street
Sheffield S1 4BA
Tel: 0114 272 0033
Fax: 0114 272 0060
info@gqualifications.com
www.glassqualificationsauthority.com

Graded Qualifications Alliance
Garden Street
Leicester
United Kingdom
LE1 3UA
Tel: 0116 262 4122
info@btda.org.uk
www.btda.org.uk

Guildhall School of Music and Drama Examination Service
Silk Street
Barbican
London EC2Y 8DT
Tel: 020 7628 2571
Fax: 020 7256 9438
registry@gsmd.ac.uk
www.gsmd.ac.uk

Hospitality Awarding Body (HAB)
c/o City and Guilds
1 Giltspur Street
London EC1A 9DD
Tel: 0870 060 2556
Fax: 0870 060 2555
info@hab.org.uk
www.hab.org.uk

Imperial Society of Teachers of Dancing
22/26 Paul Street
London EC2A 4QE
Tel: 020 7377 1577
www.istd.org

Institute of Advanced Motorists
IAM House
510 Chiswick High Road
London
W4 5RG
Tel: 020 8996 9600
Fax: 020 8996 9601
www.iam.org.uk

Institute of Career Guidance
Third Floor, Copthall House
1 New Road
Stourbridge
West Midlands DY8 1PH
Tel: 01384 376464
www.icg-uk.org

Institute of Clerks of Works of Great Britain Incorporated
Equinox
28 Commerce Road
Lynch Wood
Peterborough PE2 6LR
Tel: 01733 405160
Fax: 01733 405161
info@icwgb.co.uk
www.icwgb.org

Institute of Commercial Management
The Fusee
20a Bargates
Christchurch
Dorset
United Kingdom
BH23 1QL
Tel: 01202 490 555
Fax   01202 490 666
info@icm.ac.uk
www.icm.ac.uk

Institute of Credit Management
The Water Mill
Station Road
South Luffenham
Oakham
Leicestershire LE15 8NB
Tel: 01780 722900
Fax: 01780 721333
info@icm.org.uk
www.icm.org.uk

Institute of Financial Services (IFS)
4–9 Burgate Lane
Canterbury
Kent CT1 2XJ
Tel: 01227 818609
Fax: 01227 784331
customerservices@ifslearning.com
www.ifslearning.com

Institution of Fire Engineers
London Road
Moreton-in-Marsh
United Kingdom
GL56 0RH
Tel: 01608 812 580
Fax: 01608 812 581
info@ife.org.uk
www.ife.org.uk

Institute of Hospitality
Trinity Court
34 West Street
Sutton
Surrey SM1 1SH
Tel: 020 8661 4900
Fax: 020 8661 4901
commdept@instituteofhospitality.org
www.instituteofhospitality.org

Institute of Leadership and Management
Stowe House
Netherstowe
Lichfield
Staffordshire WS13 6TJ
Tel: 01543 266 867
Fax: 01543 266 811
customer@i-l-m.com
www.i-l-m.com

Institute of Legal Executives
Kempston Manor
Kempston
Bedfordshire MK42 7AB
Tel: 01234 841000
Fax: 01234 840373
info@ilex.org.uk
www.ilex.org.uk

Institute of Linguists Educational Trust
Chartered Institute of Linguists
Saxon House
48 Southwark Street
London SE1 1UN
Tel: 020 7940 3100
Fax: 020 7940 3101
info@iol.org.uk
www.iol.org.uk

Institute of the Motor Industry
Fanshaws
Brickendon
Hertford SG13 8PQ
Tel: 01992 511 521
Fax: 01992 511 548
imi@motor.org.uk
www.motor.org.uk

Institute of Revenues, Rating and Valuation
41 Doughty Street
London WC1N 2LF
Tel: 020 7831 3505
www.irrv.org.uk

Institute of Sales and Marketing Management
Harrier Court
Lower Woodside
Bedfordshire LU1 4DQ
Tel: 01582 840001
Fax: 01582 849142
www.ismm.co.uk

Institution of Civil Engineers
One Great George Street
Westminster
London SW1P 3AA
Tel: 020 7222 7722
communications@ice.org.uk
www.ice.org.uk

International Association of Book-Keepers
Burford House
44 London Road
Sevenoaks
Kent TN13 1AS
Tel: 01732 458080
Fax: 01732 455848
mail@iab.org.uk
www.iab.org.uk

International Curriculum and Assessment Agency Ltd
The ICAA Education Centre
Bighton, Alresford
Hants SO24 9RE
Tel: 01962 735801
Fax: 01962 735597
info@icaa.com
www.icaag.com

International Dance Teachers Association

International House
76 Bennett Road
Brighton
East Sussex BN2 5JL
Tel: 01273 685652
Fax: 01273 674388
www.idta.co.uk

International Therapy Examination Council (ITEC)

2nd Floor, Chiswick Gate
598–608 Chiswick High Road
London W4 5RT
Tel: 020 8994 4141
Fax: 020 8994 7880
info@itecworld.co.uk
www.itecworld.co.uk

Lantra

Lantra House
Stoneleigh Park, Nr Coventry
Warwickshire CV8 2LG
Tel: 0845 707 8067
connect@lantra.co.uk
www.lantra.co.uk

Lifesavers The Royal Life Saving Society UK

River House
High Street
Broom, Alcester
Warwickshire B50 4HN
Tel: 01789 773994
Fax: 01789 773995
lifesavers@rlss.org.uk
www.lifesavers.org.uk

London Academy of Music and Dramatic Art (LAMDA)

155 Talgarth Road
London W14 9DA
Tel: 020 8834 0500
Fax: 020 8834 0501
enquiries@lamda.org.uk
www.lamda.org.uk

Market Research Society

15 Northburgh Street
London EC1V 0JR
Tel: 020 7490 4911
Fax: 020 7490 0608
info@mrs.org.uk
www.mrs.org.uk

Mineral Products Qualification Council

Knowledge Centre
Wyboston Lakes
Great North Road
Wyboston
Bedfordshire
United Kingdom
MK44 3BY

Ministry of Defence

Whitehall
London SW1A 2HB
Tel: 0870 607 4455
www.mod.uk

Mountain Leader Training England

Capel Curig
Betws-y-Coed
Gwynedd
United Kingdom
LL24 0ET
Tel: 01690 720 314
Fax: 01690 720248
info@mlte.org
www.mlte.org

National Association of Estate Agents

Arbon House
6 Tournament Court
Edgehill Drive
Warwick
CV34 6LG
Tel: 01926 496800
Fax: 01926 417788
info@naea.co.uk
www.naea.co.uk

National Energy Action

St Andrew's House
90–92 Pilgrim Street
Newcastle upon Tyne NE1 6SG
Tel: 0191 261 5677
Fax: 0191 261 6496
info@nea.org.uk
www.nea.org.uk

National Examination Board in Occupational Safety and Health

Dominus Way
Meridian Business Park
Leicester LE19 1QW
Tel: 0116 263 4700
Fax: 0116 282 4000
info@nebosh.org.uk
www.nebosh.org.uk

National Examining Board for Dental Nurses
110 London Street
Fleetwood
Lancashire FY7 6EU
Tel: 01253 778417
Fax: 01253 777268
info@nebdn.org

National Federation of Property Professionals
6 Tournament Court
Edgehill Drive
Warwick
United Kingdom
CV32 6LG
quals@nfopp.co.uk
www.nfopp.co.uk

National Open College Network
The Quadrant
Parkway Business Park
99 Parkway Avenue
Sheffield S9 4WG
Tel: 0114 227 0500
Fax: 0114 227 0501
nocn@nocn.org.uk
www.nocn.org.uk

National Proficiency Tests Council
Stoneleigh Park
Stoneleigh
Warwickshire CV8 2LG
Tel: 024 7685 7300
Fax: 024 7669 6128
information@nptc.org.uk
www.nptc.org.uk

NCFE
Citygate
St James' Boulevard
Newcastle upon Tyne NE1 4JE
Tel: 0191 239 8000
Fax: 0191 239 8001
info@ncfe.org.uk
www.ncfe.org.uk

The Oil and Gas Academy
First Floor, Block 2
The Altec Centre
Minto Drive
Altens
Aberdeen AB12 3LW

Open College of the North West
West Lodge
Quernmore Road
Lancaster LA1 3JT
Tel: 01524 845046
Fax: 01524 388467
accreditation@ocnw.com
www.ocnw.com

Open University
PO Box 197
Milton Keynes MK7 6AA
Tel: 0845 300 6090
www.open.ac.uk

Oxford, Cambridge and Royal School of Arts Examinations (OCR)
(Vocational qualifications)
Progress House
Westwood Way
Coventry CV4 8JQ
Tel: 02476 851509
Fax: 02476 421944
vocationalqualifications@ocr.org.uk
(Head Office)
1 Hills Road
Cambridge CB1 2EU
Tel: 01223 553 998
Fax: 01223 552 627
general.qualifications@ocr.org.uk
www.ocr.org.uk

Packaging Industry Awarding Body Company
Springfield House
Springfield Business Park
Grantham
Lincolnshire NG31 7BG
Tel: 01476 514595
Fax: 01476 514591
info@piabc.org.uk
www.piabc.org.uk

The Pensions Management Institute
PMI House
4/10 Artillery Lane
London E1 7LS
Tel: 020 7247 1452
Fax: 020 7375 0603
enquiries@pensions-pmi.org.uk
www.pensions-pmi.org.uk

Premier Training International
Premier House
Willowside Park
Canal Road
Trowbridge
Wiltshire BA14 8RH
Tel: 0845 909090
www.premierglobal.co.uk

Process Awards Authority/Vocational Qualifications in Science, Engineering and Technology
Brooke House
24 Dam Street
Lichfield
Staffordshire WS13 6AA
Tel: 01543 254223
Fax: 01543 257848
info@paa-uk.org
www.paa-uk.org

Professional Association of Dive Instructors (PADI) International Ltd
Unit 7, St Philips Central
Albert Road
St Philips
Bristol BS2 0PD
Tel: 0117 300 7234
Fax: 0117 971 0400
general@padi.co.uk
www.padi.co.uk

Qualifications Network
Colwell Lodge
110 Lewes Road
Haywards Heath
West Sussex
United Kingdom
RH17 7TB
Tel: 0845 121 8328
Fax: 0845 121 8327
info@qualificationsnetwork.co.uk
www.qualificationsnetwork.co.uk

Rock School Ltd
Evergreen House
2–4 King Street
Twickenham
Middlesex TW1 3RZ
Tel: 0845 460 4747
Fax: 0845 460 1960
info@rockschool.co.uk
www.rockschool.co.uk

Royal Academy of Dance
36 Battersea Square
London SW11 3RA
Tel: 020 7326 8000
Fax: 020 7924 3129
info@rad.org.uk
www.rad.org.uk

The Royal College of Veterinary Surgeons
Belgravia House
62–64 Horseferry Road
London SW1P 2AF
Tel: 020 7222 2001
Fax: 020 7222 2004
admin@rcvs.org.uk
www.rcvs.org.uk

Royal Horticultural Society
80 Vincent Square
London SW1P 2PE
Tel: 0845 260 5000
info@rhs.org.uk
www.rhs.org.uk

Royal Institute of Public Health
28 Portland Place
London W1B 1DE
Tel: 020 7580 2731
Fax: 020 7580 6157
examinations@riph.org.uk
www.riph.org.uk

Royal Society for the Promotion of Health
38A St George's Drive
London SW1V 4BH
Tel: 020 7630 0121
Fax: 020 7976 6847
rsph@rsph.org
www.rsph.org

Scottish Association of Master Bakers
Atholl House
4 Torphichen Street
Edinburgh EH3 8JQ
Tel: 0131 229 1401
Fax: 0131 229 8239
master.bakers@samb.co.uk
www.samb.co.uk

Scottish Building Apprenticeship and Training Council
Carron Grange
Carrongrange Avenue
Stenhousemuir FK5 3BQ
Tel: 01324 555550
Fax: 01324 555551
info@scottish-building.co.uk
www.sbatc.co.uk

Scottish Joint Industry Board of the Electrical Contracting Industry
The Walled Garden
Bush Estate
Midlothian EH26 0SB
Tel: 0131 445 9216
grading@sjib.org.uk
www.sjib.org.uk

Scottish and Northern Ireland Joint Industry Board for the Plumbing Industry
2 Walker Street
Edinburgh EH3 7LB
Tel: 0131 225 2255
info@snipef.org
www.snipef.org

Scottish Print Employers Federation
48 Palmerston Place
Edinburgh EH12 5DE
Tel: 0131 220 4353
Fax: 0131 220 4344
info@spef.org.uk
www.spef.org.uk

Scottish Qualifications Authority
The Optima Building
58 Robertson Street
Glasgow G2 8DQ
Tel: 0845 279 1000
Fax: 0845 213 5000
customer@sqa.org.uk
www.sqa.org.uk

Securities & Investment Institute
8 Eastcheap
London EC3M 1AF
Tel: 020 7645 0600
Fax: 020 7645 0601
clientservices@sii.org.uk
www.sii.org.uk

Single Subject Qualifications
1 Giltspur Street
London EC1A 9DD
Tel: 020 7294 2800
Fax: 020 7294 2400
www.cityandguilds.com

Skillset
Focus Point
21 Caledonian Road
London N1 9GB
Tel: 020 7713 9800
www.skillset.org

Skills for Logistics
12 Warren Yard
Warren Farm Office Village
Stratford Road
Milton Keynes MK12 5NW
Tel: 01908 313360
Fax: 01908 313006
info@skillsforlogistics.org
www.skillsforlogistics.org

Skills for Security
Security House
Barbourne Road
Worcester WR1 1RS
Tel: 08450 750111
Fax: 01905 724949
info@skillsforsecurity.org.uk
www.skillsforsecurity.org.uk

Sports Leaders UK
23–25 Linford Forum
Rockingham Drive
Linford Wood
Milton Keynes MK14 6LY
Tel: 01908 689180
Fax: 01908 393744
info@sportsleaders.org
www.sportsleaders.org

SummitSkills
Vega House
Opal Drive
Fox Milne
Milton Keynes MK15 0DF
Tel: 01908 303960
enquiries@summitskills.org.uk
www.summitskills.org.uk

Swimming Teachers Association
Anchor House
Birch Street
Walsall
West Midlands WS2 8HZ
Tel: 01922 645097
Fax: 01922 720628
sta@sta.co.uk
www.sta.co.uk

Thames Valley University
St Mary's Road
Ealing
London W5 5RF
Tel: 020 8579 5000
Fax: 020 8566 1353
www.tvu.ac.uk

The Learning Machine
36 Ashby Road
Tamworth
Staffordshire
United Kingdom
B79 8AQ
www.theINGOTs.org

Timber Trade Federation
The Building Centre
26 Store Street
London WC1E 7BT
Tel: 020 3205 0067
ttf@ttf.co.uk
www.ttf.co.uk

Trinity College London
89 Albert Embankment
London SE1 7TP
Tel: 020 7820 6100
Fax: 020 7820 6161
info@trinitycollege.co.uk
www.trinitycollege.co.uk

Vocational Training Charitable Trust
3rd Floor, Eastleigh House
Upper Market Street
Eastleigh
Hampshire SO50 9FD
Tel: 023 8068 4500
Fax: 023 8065 1493
customerservice@vtct.org.uk
www.vtct.org.uk

Waste Management Industry Training and Advisory Board
Peterbridge House
3 The Lakes
Northampton NN4 7HE
Tel: 01604 231950
Fax: 01604 232457
info.admin@wamitab.org.uk.
www.wamitab.org.uk

Welsh Joint Education Committee
245 Western Avenue
Cardiff CF5 2YX
Tel: 029 2026 5000
info@wjec.co.uk
www.wjec.co.uk

Wine & Spirit Education Trust
International Wine & Spirit Centre
39–45 Bermondsey Street
London SE1 3XF
Tel: 020 7089 3800
Fax: 020 7089 3845
wset@wset.co.uk
www.wset.co.uk

Worshipful Company of Farriers
19 Queen Street
Chipperfield
Kings Langley
Herts WD4 9BT
Tel: 01923 260747
Fax: 01923 261677
theclerk@wcf.org.uk
www.wcf.org.uk

Worshipful Company of Spectacle Makers
Apothecaries' Hall
Black Friars Lane
London EC4V 6EL
Tel: 020 7236 2932
Fax: 020 7329 3249
www.spectaclemakers.com

Part 4

Directory of Colleges Offering Vocational Qualifications

Introduction

Within the last decade the provision of vocational qualifications has been radically restructured. Qualifications are now offered in further education colleges, higher education institutions (see *British Qualifications* also published by Kogan Page), in the workplace and delivered by distance learning to students in their homes. To list the complete range of course providers within this book would not be possible. However, the addresses of active Further Education colleges have been included as a starting point for readers to identify providers of vocational qualifications. Awarding bodies may also provide details of the full range of different study opportunities (see Part Three for full contact details of Awarding Bodies).

Avon

Bristol Old Vic Theatre School
2 Downside Road
Clifton
Bristol
Avon BS8 2XF
Tel: 0117 9733535
Fax: 0117 9739371
enquiries@oldvic.ac.uk
www.oldvic.ac.uk

City of Bristol College
Marksbury Road
Bristol
Avon BS3 5JL
Tel: 0117 3125000
Fax: 0117 3125051
enquiries@cityofbristol.ac.uk
www.cityofbristol.ac.uk

Filton College
Filton Avenue
Filton
Bristol
Avon BS34 7AT
Tel: 0117 9312121
Fax: 0117 9312233
info@filton.ac.uk
www.filton.ac.uk

Bedfordshire

Barnfield College
New Bedford Road
Luton
Bedfordshire LU2 7BF
Tel: 01582 569600
enquiries@barnfield.ac.uk
www.barnfield.ac.uk

Bedford College
Cauldwell Street
Bedford
Bedfordshire MK42 9AH
Tel: 0800 074 0234
Fax: 01234 342674
info@bedford.ac.uk
www.bedford.ac.uk

Dunstable College
Kingsway
Dunstable
Bedfordshire LU5 4HG
Tel: 01582 477776
Fax: 01582 478801
enquiries@dunstable.ac.uk
www.dunstable.ac.uk

Belfast

Belfast Metropolitan College
Montgomery Road
Belfast BT6 9JD
Tel: 028 9026 5265
central-admissions@ belfastinstitute.ac.uk
www.belfastmet.ac.uk

Berkshire

Berkshire College of Agriculture
Hall Place
Burchetts Green
Maidenhead
Berkshire SL6 6QR
Tel: 01628 824444
Fax: 01628 824695
enquiries@bca.ac.uk
www.bca.ac.uk

Bracknell and Wokingham College
Church Road
Bracknell
Berkshire RG12 1DJ
Tel: 0845 330 3343
study@bracknell.ac.uk
www.bracknell.ac.uk

East Berkshire College
Langley Campus
Station Road
Langley
Berkshire SL3 8BY
Tel: 0845 373 2500
info@eastberks.ac.uk
www.eastberks.ac.uk

Newbury College
Monks Lane
Newbury
Berkshire RG14 7TD
Tel: 01635 845000
Fax: 01635 845312
info@newbury-college.ac.uk
www.newbury-college.ac.uk

Thames Valley University
St Mary's Road
Ealing
London W5 5RF
Tel: 020 8579 5000
Fax: 020 8566 1353
www.tvu.ac.uk

Buckinghamshire

Amersham and Wycombe College
Stanley Hill
Amersham
Buckinghamshire HP7 9HN
Tel: 0800 614 016
Fax: 01494 585566
www.amersham.ac.uk

Aylesbury College
Oxford Road
Aylesbury
Buckinghamshire HP21 8PD
Tel: 01296 588588
Fax: 01296 588589
customerservices@aylesbury.ac.uk
www.aylesbury.ac.uk

Buckingham Chilterns University College
Queen Alexandra Road
High Wycombe
Buckinghamshire HP11 2JZ
Tel: 0800 0565 660
Fax: 01494 524392
advice@bcuc.ac.uk
www.bcuc.ac.uk

Milton Keynes College
Woughton Campus West
Leadenhall
Milton Keynes
Buckinghamshire MK6 5LP
Tel: 01908 684444
Fax: 01908 684399
info@mkcollege.ac.uk
www.mkcollege.ac.uk

Cambridgeshire

Cambridge Regional College
Kings Hedges Road
Cambridge
Cambridgeshire CB4 2QT
Tel: 01223 532240
enquiry@camre.ac.uk
www.camre.ac.uk

Huntingdonshire Regional College
California Road
Huntingdon
Cambridgeshire PE29 1BL
Tel: 01480 379100
Fax: 01480 379127
college@huntingdon.ac.uk
www.huntingdon.ac.uk

Isle College
Ramnoth Road
Wisbech
Cambridgeshire PE13 2JE
Tel: 01945 582561
Fax: 01945 582706
courses@isle.ac.uk
www.isle.ac.uk

Peterborough Regional College
Park Crescent
Peterborough
Cambridgeshire PE1 4DZ
Tel: 0845 872 8722
Fax: 01733 767986
info@peterborough.ac.uk
www.peterborough.ac.uk

Cheshire

Cheadle & Marple Sixth Form College
Cheadle Campus
Cheadle Road
Cheadle Hulme
Cheshire SK8 5HA
Tel: 0161 486 4600
Fax: 0161 482 8129
info@camsfc.ac.uk
www.camsfc.ac.uk

Cheadle & Marple Sixth Form College
Marple Campus
Hibbert Lane
Marple
Stockport
Cheshire SK6 7PA
Tel: 0161 484 6600
Fax: 0161 484 6602
www.camsfc.ac.uk

Riverside College Halton
Kingsway
Widnes
Cheshire WA8 7QQ
Tel: 0151 257 2800
www.haltoncollege.ac.uk

Macclesfield College
Park Lane
Macclesfield
Cheshire SK11 8LF
Tel: 01625 410000
Fax: 01625 410001
info@macclesfield.ac.uk
www.macclesfield.ac.uk

Mid-Cheshire College
Hartford Campus
Chester Road
Northwich
Cheshire CW8 1LJ
Tel: 01606 74444
info@midchesh.ac.uk
www.midchesh.ac.uk

North Area College
Buckingham Road
Heaton Moor
Stockport
Cheshire SK4 4RA
Tel: 0161 442 7494
Fax: 0161 442 2166
www.nacstock.ac.uk

Priestley College
Loushers Lane
Warrington
Cheshire WA4 6RD
Tel: 01925 633591
Fax: 01925 413887
enquiries@priestley.ac.uk
www.priestleycollege.ac.uk

Reaseheath College
Nantwich
Cheshire CW5 6DF
Tel: 01270 625131
Fax: 01270 625665
enquiries@reaseheath.ac.uk
www.reaseheath.ac.uk

Sir John Deane's College
Monarch Drive
Northwich
Cheshire CW9 8AF
Tel: 01606 46011
Fax: 01606 353939
www.sjd.ac.uk

South Cheshire College
Dane Bank Avenue
Crewe
Cheshire CW2 8AB
Tel: 01270 654654
Fax: 01270 651515
info@s-cheshire.ac.uk
www.s-cheshire.ac.uk

South Trafford College
Manchester Rd
West Timperley
Altrincham
Cheshire WA14 5PQ
Tel: 0161 952 4600
Fax: 0161 952 4672
enquiries@stcoll.ac.uk
www.stcoll.ac.uk

Warrington Collegiate
Winwick Road Campus
Winwick Road
Warrington
WA2 8QA
Tel: 01925 494494
Fax: 01925 418328
learner.services@warrington.ac.uk
www.warrington.ac.uk

West Cheshire College
Handbridge Centre
Eaton Road
Handbridge
Chester CH4 7ER
Tel: 01244 670600
Fax: 01244 670676
info@west-cheshire.ac.uk
www.west-cheshire.ac.uk

Cleveland

Hartlepool College of Further Education
Stockton Street
Hartlepool
Cleveland TS24 7NT
Tel: 01429 295000
Fax: 01429 292999
enquiries@hartlepoolfe.ac.uk
www.hartlepoolfe.ac.uk

Prior Pursglove College
Church Walk
Guisborough
Cleveland TS14 6BU
Tel: 01287 280800
Fax: 01287 280280
www.pursglove.ac.uk

Redcar and Cleveland College
Corporation Road
Redcar
Cleveland TS10 1EZ
Tel: 01642 473132
Fax: 01642 490856
webenquiry@cleveland.ac.uk
www.cleveland.ac.uk

Stockton Riverside College
Harvard Avenue
Stockton-on-Tees
Cleveland TS17 6FB
Tel: 01642 865400
Fax: 01642 865470
www.stockton.ac.uk

Cornwall

Cornwall College Camborne
Trevenson Road
Pool
Redruth
Cornwall TR15 3RD
Tel: 01209 616161
Fax: 01209 611612
enquiries@cornwall.ac.uk
www.camborne.ac.uk

Cornwall College, St Austell
Tregonnisey Road
St Austell
Cornwall PL25 4DJ
Tel: 01726 226626
Fax: 01726 226627
info@st-austell.ac.uk
www.st-austell.ac.uk

Duchy College
Rosewarne Campus
Camborne
Cornwall TR14 OAB
Tel: 01209 722100
Fax: 01209 722159
rosewarne.enquiries@duchy.ac.uk
www.cornwall.ac.uk/duchy

Duchy College
Stoke Campus
Stoke Climsland
Callington
Cornwall PL17 8PB
Tel: 01579 372233
Fax: 01579 372200
stoke.enquiries@duchy.ac.uk
www.cornwall.ac.uk/duchy

Falmouth Marine School
Killigrew Street
Falmouth
Cornwall TR11 3QS
Tel: 01326 310310
Fax: 01326 310300
falenquiries@cornwall.ac.uk
www.falmouthmarineschool.ac.uk

Penwith College
St Clare Street
Penzance
Cornwall TR18 2SA
Tel: 01736 335000
Fax: 01736 335100
enquire@penwith.ac.uk
www.itsgot2bpenwith.ac.uk

Truro College
College Road
Truro
Cornwall TR1 3XX
Tel: 01872 267000
enquiry@trurocollege.ac.uk
www.trurocollege.ac.uk

Cumbria

Carlisle College
Victoria Place
Carlisle
Cumbria CA1 1HS
Tel: 01228 822703
Fax: 01228 822710
info@carlisle.ac.uk
www.carlisle.ac.uk

Furness College
Channelside
Barrow-in-Furness
Cumbria LA14 2PJ
Tel: 01229 825017
Fax: 01229 870964
info@furness.ac.uk
www.furness.ac.uk

Kendal College
Milnthorpe Road
Kendal
Cumbria LA9 5AY
Tel: 01539 814700
Fax: 01539 814701
enquiries@kendal.ac.uk
www.kendal.ac.uk

Lakes College West Cumbria
Hallwood Road
Lillyhall Business Park
Workington
Cumbria CA14 4JN
Tel: 01946 839300
Fax: 01946 839302
info@lcwc.ac.uk
www.westcumbcoll.ac.uk

Derbyshire

Chesterfield College
Infirmary Road
Chesterfield
Derbyshire S41 7NG
Tel: 01246 500500
advice@chesterfield.ac.uk
www.chesterfield.ac.uk

Derby College
Morley Ilkeston
Derbyshire DE7 6DN
Tel: 01332 520200
Fax: 01332 510548
enquiries@derby-college.ac.uk
www.derby-college.ac.uk

South East Derbyshire College
Field Road
Ilkeston
Derbyshire DE7 5RS
Tel: 0115 849 2000
Fax: 0115 849 2121
admissions@sedc.ac.uk
www.sedc.ac.uk

Devon

Bicton College
East Budleigh
Budleigh Salterton
Devon EX9 7BY
Tel: 01395 562400
Fax: 01395 567502
enquiries@bicton.ac.uk
www.bicton.ac.uk

East Devon College
Bolham Road
Tiverton
Devon EX16 6SH
Tel: 01884 235200
Fax: 01884 235262
enquiries@admin.eastdevon.ac.uk
www.edc.ac.uk

Exeter College
Victoria House
33–36 Queen Street
Exeter
Devon EX4 3SR
Tel: 01392 205223
Fax: 01392 205225
info@exe-coll.ac.uk
www.exe-coll.ac.uk

North Devon College
Old Sticklepath Hill
Barnstaple
Devon EX31 2BQ
Tel: 01271 345291
Fax: 01271 338121
postbox@ndevon.ac.uk
www.ndevon.ac.uk

Plymouth College of Art and Design
Tavistock Place
Plymouth
Devon PL4 8AT
Tel: 01752 203434
Fax: 01752 203444
enquiries@pcad.ac.uk
www.pcad.ac.uk

City College Plymouth
Kings Road Centre
Devonport
Plymouth
PL1 5QG
Tel: 01752 305300
Fax: 01752 305343
reception@cityplym.ac.uk
www.cityplym.ac.uk

South Devon College
Vantage Point
Long Road
Paignton
TQ4 7EJ
Tel: 01803 540540
enquiries@southdevon.ac.uk
www.southdevon.ac.uk

Dorset

Bournemouth and Poole College
North Road
Poole
Dorset BH14 0LS
Tel: 01202 205205
enquiries@thecollege.co.uk
www.thecollege.co.uk

Kingston Maurward College
Dorchester
Dorset DT2 8PY
Tel: 01305 215000
Fax: 01305 215001
administration@kmc.ac.uk
www.kmc.ac.uk

Weymouth College
Cranford Avenue
Weymouth
Dorset DT4 7LQ
Tel: 01305 761100
Fax: 01305 208892
igs@weymouth.ac.uk
www.weymouth.ac.uk

Durham

Bishop Auckland College
Woodhouse Lane
Bishop Auckland
County Durham DL14 6JZ
Tel: 01388 443000
Fax: 01388 609294
enquiries@bacoll.ac.uk
www.bacoll.ac.uk

Darlington College
Central Park
Haughton Road
Darlington
DL1 1DR
Tel: 01325 503030
Fax: 01325 503000
enquire@darlington.ac.uk
www.darlington.ac.uk

Derwentside College
Consett Campus
Front Street
Consett
County Durham DH8 5EE
Tel: 01207 585900
Fax: 01207 585991
enquiries@derwentside.ac.uk
www.derwentside.ac.uk

East Durham and Houghall Community College
Burnhope Way Centre
Burnhope Way
Peterlee
County Durham SR8 1NU
Tel: 0191 518 2000
Fax: 0191 586 7125
enquiries@edhcc.ac.uk
www.edhcc.ac.uk

New College Durham
Framwellgate Moor Campus
Framwellgate Moor
Durham
DH1 5ES
Tel: 0191 375 4000
Fax: 0191 375 4222
help@newdur.ac.uk
www.newdur.ac.uk

East Sussex

Bexhill College
Penland Road
Bexhill-on-Sea
East Sussex TN40 2LG
Tel: 01424 214545
Fax: 01424 215050
enquiries@bexhillcollege.ac.uk
www.bexhillcollege.ac.uk

City College Brighton and Hove
Pelham Street
Brighton
East Sussex BN1 4FA
Tel: 01273 667788
info@ccb.ac.uk
www.ccb.ac.uk

Hastings College of Arts & Technology
Archery Road
St. Leonards on Sea
East Sussex TN38 0HX
Tel: 01424 442222
Fax: 01424 721763
studentadvisers@hastings.ac.uk
www.hastings.ac.uk

Plumpton College
Ditchling Road
Nr Lewes
East Sussex BN7 3AE
Tel: 01273 890454
Fax: 01273 890071
enquiries@plumpton.ac.uk
www.plumpton.ac.uk

Sussex Downs College
Cross Levels Way
Eastbourne
East Sussex BN21 2UF
Tel: 01323 637637
Fax: 01323 637472
info@sussexdowns.ac.uk
www.sussexdowns.ac.uk

Varndean College
Surrenden Road
Brighton
East Sussex BN1 6WQ
Tel: 01273 508011
Fax: 01273 542950
www.varndean.ac.uk

Essex

Barking College
Dagen
Dagenham Road
Romford
Essex RM7 0XU
Tel: 01708 770000
Fax: 01708 770007
admissions@barkingcollege.ac.uk
www.barkingcollege.ac.uk

Braintree College
1 Church Lane
Braintree
Essex CM7 5SN
Tel: 01376 321711
Fax: 01376 340799
enquiries@braintree.ac.uk
www.braintree.ac.uk

Chelmsford College
Princes Road Campus
Princes Road
Chelmsford
Essex CM2 9DE
Tel: 01245 265611
Fax: 01245 346615
www.chelmsford-college.ac.uk

Colchester Institute
Sheepen Road
Colchester
Essex CO3 3LL
Tel: 01206 518777
www.colchester.ac.uk

Epping Forest College
Borders Lane
Loughton
Essex IG10 3SA
Tel: 020 8508 8311
informationcentre@epping-forest.ac.uk
www.epping-forest.ac.uk

Harlow College
Velizy Avenue
Town Centre
Harlow
Essex CM20 3LH
Tel: 01279 868000
Fax: 01279 868260
full-time@harlow-college.ac.uk
www.harlow-college.ac.uk

Havering College

Ardleigh Green Campus
Ardleigh Green Road
Hornchurch
Essex RM11 2LL
Tel: 01708 455011
www.havering-college.ac.uk

Palmer's College

Chadwell Road
Grays
Essex RM17 5TD
Tel: 01375 370121
enquiries@palmers.ac.uk
www.palmers.ac.uk

Redbridge College

Little Heath
Barley Lane
Romford
Essex RM6 4XT
Tel: 020 8548 7400
Fax: 020 8599 8224
info@redbridge-college.ac.uk
www.redbridge-college.ac.uk

Seevic College

Runnymede Chase
Benfleet
Essex SS7 1TW
Tel: 01268 756 111
Fax: 01268 565 515
info@seevic-college.ac.uk
www.seevic-college.ac.uk

South East Essex College of Arts and Technology

Luker Road
Southend-on-Sea
Essex SS1 1ND
Tel: 01702 220400
Fax: 01702 432320
admissions@southend.ac.uk
www.southend.ac.uk

Thurrock and Basildon College

Nethermayne Campus
Nethermayne
Basildon
Essex SS16 5NN
Tel: 0845 6015746
Fax: 01375 373356
enquire@tab.ac.uk
www.tab.ac.uk

Writtle College

Chelmsford
Essex CM1 3RR
Tel: 01245 424200
Fax: 01245 420456
info@writtle.ac.uk
www.writtle.ac.uk

Gloucestershire

Cirencester College

Fosse Way Campus
Stroud Road
Cirencester
Gloucestershire GL7 1XA
Tel: 01285 640994
Fax: 01285 644171
student.services@cirencester.ac.uk
www.cirencester.ac.uk

Gloucestershire College of Arts and Technology

Gloucester Campus
Brunswick Road
Gloucester
Gloucestershire GL1 1HU
Tel: 01452 532000
Fax: 01452 563441
info@gloscat.ac.uk
www.gloscat.ac.uk

Hartpury College

Hartpury House
Gloucester
Gloucestershire GL19 3BE
Tel: 01452 702132
Fax: 01452 700629
enquire@hartpury.ac.uk
www.hartpury.ac.uk

Royal Forest of Dean College

Five Acres Campus
Berry Hill
Coleford
Gloucestershire GL16 7JT
Tel: 01594 883416
Fax: 01594 837497
enquiries@rfdc.ac.uk
www.rfdc.ac.uk

Stroud College in Gloucestershire
Stratford Road
Stroud
Gloucestershire GL5 4AH
Tel: 01453 763424
Fax: 01453 753543
enquire@stroudcol.ac.uk
www.stroud.ac.uk

Hampshire

Alton College
Old Odiham Road
Alton
Hampshire GU34 2LX
Tel: 01420 592200
Fax: 01420 592253
enquiries@altoncollege.ac.uk
www.altoncollege.ac.uk

Barton Peveril College
Chestnut Avenue
Eastleigh
Hampshire SO50 5ZA
Tel: 023 8061 7200
enquiries@barton.ac.uk
www.barton-peveril.ac.uk

Basingstoke College of Technology
Worting Road
Basingstoke
Hampshire RG21 8TN
Tel: 01256 354141
Fax: 01256 306444
information@bcot.ac.uk
www.bcot.ac.uk

Brockenhurst College
Lyndhurst Road
Brockenhurst
Hampshire SO42 7ZE
Tel: 01590 625555
enquiries@brock.ac.uk
www.brock.ac.uk

Cricklade College
Charlton Road
Andover
Hampshire SP10 1EJ
Tel: 01264 360000
Fax: 01264 360010
www.cricklade.ac.uk

Eastleigh College
Chestnut Avenue
Eastleigh
Hampshire SO50 5FS
Tel: 023 8091 1000
goplaces@eastleigh.ac.uk
www.eastleigh.ac.uk

Fareham College
Bishopsfield Road
Fareham
Hampshire PO14 1NH
Tel: 01329 815200
Fax: 01329 822483
info@fareham.ac.uk
www.fareham.ac.uk

Farnborough College of Technology
Boundary Road
Farnborough
Hampshire GU14 6SB
Tel: 01252 407040
info@farn-ct.ac.uk
www.farn-ct.ac.uk

Havant College
New Road
Havant
Hampshire PO9 1QL
Tel: 023 9248 3856
Fax: 023 9247 0621
enquiries@havant.ac.uk
www.havant.ac.uk

Highbury College
Dovercourt Road
Highbury
Portsmouth
Hampshire PO6 2SA
Tel: 023 9238 3131
Fax: 023 9232 5551
info@highbury.ac.uk
www.highbury.ac.uk

Itchen College
Middle Road
Bitterne
Southampton
Hampshire SO19 7TB
Tel: 023 8043 5636
Fax: 023 8042 1911
info@itchen.ac.uk
www.itchen.ac.uk

Peter Symonds College
Owens Road
Winchester
Hampshire SO22 6RX
Tel: 01962 857500
Fax: 01962 857501
www.psc.ac.uk

Portsmouth College
Tangier Road
Portsmouth
Hampshire PO3 6PZ
Tel: 023 9266 7521
Fax: 023 9234 4363
registry@portsmouth-college.ac.uk
www.portsmouth-college.ac.uk

Queen Mary's College
Cliddesden Road
Basingstoke
Hampshire RG21 3HF
Tel: 01256 417500
Fax: 01256 417501
info@qmc.ac.uk
www.qmc.ac.uk

South Downs College
College Road
Waterlooville
Hampshire PO7 8AA
Tel: 023 9279 7979
Fax: 023 9279 7940
college@southdowns.ac.uk
www.southdowns.ac.uk

Southampton City College
St Mary Street
Southampton
Hampshire SO14 1AR
Tel: 023 8048 4848
Fax: 023 8057 7473
www.southampton-city.ac.uk

Southampton Solent University
East Park Terrace
Southampton
Hampshire S014 OYN
Tel: 023 8031 9000
Fax: 023 8033 4161
postmaster@solent.ac.uk
www.solent.ac.uk

Sparsholt College
Westley Lane
Sparsholt
Winchester
SO21 2NF
Tel: 01962 776441
enquiries@sparsholt.ac.uk
www.sparsholt.ac.uk

St Vincent College
Mill Lane
Gosport
Hampshire PO12 4QA
Tel: 023 9258 8311
Fax: 023 9251 1186
info@stvincent.ac.uk
www.stvincent.ac.uk

Taunton's College
Hill Lane
Southampton
Hampshire SO15 5RL
Tel: 023 8051 1811
Fax: 023 8051 1991
admissions@tauntons.ac.uk
www.tauntons.ac.uk

Totton College
Calmore Road
Totton
Southampton
Hampshire SO40 3ZX
Tel: 023 8087 4874
Fax: 023 8087 4879
info@totton.ac.uk
www.totton.ac.uk

Herefordshire

Hereford College of Arts Folly Lane
Hereford
Herefordshire HR1 1LT
Tel: 01432 273359
Fax: 01432 341099
enquiries@hereford-art-col.ac.uk
www.hereford-art-col.ac.uk

Herefordshire College of Technology
Folly Lane
Hereford
Herefordshire HR1 1LS
Tel: 0800 032 1986
enquiries@hct.ac.uk
www.hct.ac.uk

Hertfordshire

Barnet College
Wood Street Centre
Wood Street
Barnet
Hertfordshire EN5 4AZ
Tel: 020 8266 4000
Fax: 020 8441 5236
www.barnet.ac.uk

Hertford Regional College
Broxbourne Centre
Turnford
Broxbourne
Hertfordshire EN10 6AE
Tel: 01992 411411
info@hertreg.ac.uk
www.hertreg.ac.uk

North Hertfordshire College
Stevenage Centre
Monkswood Way
Stevenage
Hertfordshire SG1 1LA
Tel: 01462 424239
enquiries@nhc.ac.uk
www.nhc.ac.uk

Oaklands College
St Albans Smallford Campus
Hatfield Road
St Albans
Hertfordshire AL4 0JA
Tel: 01727 737 080
advice.centre@oaklands.ac.uk
www.oaklands.ac.uk

West Herts College
Hempstead Road
Watford
Hertfordshire WD17 3EZ
Tel: 01923 812000
admissions@westherts.ac.uk
www.westherts.ac.uk

Isle of Wight

Isle of Wight College
Medina Way
Newport
Isle of Wight PO30 5TA
Tel: 01983 526631
Fax: 01983 521707
www.iwcollege.ac.uk

Kent

Bexley College
Tower Road
Belvedere
Kent DA17 6JA
Tel: 01322 422331
Fax: 01322 448403
enquiries@bexley.ac.uk
www.bexley.ac.uk

Bromley College
Rookery Lane Campus
Rookery Lane
Bromley
Kent BR2 8HE
Tel: 020 8295 7000
Fax: 020 8295 7099
info@bromley.ac.uk
www.bromley.ac.uk

Canterbury College
New Dover Road
Canterbury
Kent CT1 3AJ
Tel: 01227 811111
Fax: 01227 811101
courseenquiries@cant-col.ac.uk
www.cant-col.ac.uk

Dartford Technology College
Heath Lane
Dartford
Kent DA1 2LY
Tel: 01322 224309
Fax: 01322 222445
admin@dtc.kent.sch.uk
www.dtc.kent.sch.uk

Hadlow College
Hadlow
Tonbridge
Kent TN11 0AL
Tel: 01732 850551
enquiries@hadlow.ac.uk
www.hadlow.ac.uk

Hilderstone College
Broadstairs
Kent CT10 2JW
Tel: 01843 869171
Fax: 01843 603877
info@hilderstone.ac.uk
www.hilderstone.ac.uk

Mid-Kent College
Horsted Centre
Maidstone Road
Chatham
Kent ME5 9UQ
Tel:　01634 830633
Fax:　01634 830224
www.midkent.ac.uk

North West Kent College
Dartford Campus
Oakfield Lane
Dartford
Kent DA1 2JT
Tel:　0800 074 1447
Fax:　01322 629468
course.enquiries@nwkcollege.ac.uk
www.nwkcollege.ac.uk

Orpington College
The Walnuts
Orpington
Kent BR6 0TE
Tel:　01689 899700
Fax:　01689 877949
guidance@orpington.ac.uk
www.orpington.ac.uk

Ravensbourne College of Design and Communication
Walden Road
Chislehurst
Kent BR7 5SN
Tel:　020 8289 4900
Fax:　020 8325 8320
info@rave.ac.uk
www.rave.ac.uk

South Kent College
Folkestone Campus
Shorncliffe Road
Folkestone
Kent CT20 2NA
Tel:　01303 858200
www.southkent.ac.uk

Thanet College
Ramsgate Road
Broadstairs
Kent CT10 1PN
Tel:　01843 605040
student_admissions@thanet.ac.uk
www.thanet.ac.uk

West Kent College
Brook Street
Tonbridge
Kent TN9 2PW
Tel:　01732 358101
Fax:　01732 7714415
enquiries@wkc.ac.uk
www.wkc.ac.uk

Lancashire

Accrington and Rossendale College
Sandy Lane Campus
Sandy Lane
Accrington
Lancashire BB5 2AW
Tel:　01254 389933
Fax:　01254 354001
info@accross.ac.uk
www.accross.ac.uk

Adult College
White Cross Education Centre
Quarry Road
Lancaster
Lancashire LA1 3SE
Tel:　01524 60141
Fax:　01524 581137
adcollege.info@ed.lancscc.gov.uk
www.theadultcollege.org

Aquinas College
Nangreave Road
Stockport
Lancashire SK2 6TH
Tel:　0161 483 3237
Fax:　0161 487 4072
enquiries@aquinas.ac.uk
www.aquinas.ac.uk

Blackburn College
Feilden Street
Blackburn
Lancashire BB2 1LH
Tel:　01254 292929
studentservices@blackburn.ac.uk
www.blackburn.ac.uk

Blackpool and The Fylde College
Ashfield Road
Bispham
Blackpool
Lancashire FY2 0HB
Tel: 01253 352352
Fax: 01253 356127
visitors@blackpool.ac.uk
www.blackpool.ac.uk

Bolton Community College
Manchester Road Centre
Manchester Road
Bolton
Lancashire BL2 1ER
Tel: 01204 907000
Fax: 01204 907321
info@bolton-community-college.ac.uk
www.bolton-community-college.ac.uk

Burnley College
Shorey Bank
off Ormerod Road
Burnley
Lancashire BB11 2RX
Tel: 01282 711200
Fax: 01282 415063
student.services@burnley.ac.uk
www.burnley.ac.uk

Bury College
Woodbury Centre
Market Street
Bury
Manchester
Lancashire BL9 0BG
Tel: 0161 280 8280
information@burycollege.ac.uk
www.burycollege.ac.uk

Cardinal Newman College
Lark Hill
Preston
Lancashire PR1 4HD
Tel: 01772 460181
Fax: 01772 204671
admissions@cnc.hope.ac.uk
www.cardinalnewman.org.uk

City College Manchester
Abraham Moss Campus
Crescent Road
Crumpsall
Manchester
Lancashire M8 5UF
Tel: 0800 013 0123
www.manchester-city-coll.ac.uk

Cooperative College
Holyoake House
Hanover Street
Manchester
M60 0AS
Tel: 0161 246 2926
Fax: 0161 246 2946
enquiries@co-op.ac.uk
www.co-op.ac.uk

Eccles College
Chatsworth Road
Eccles
Salford
Lancashire M30 9FJ
Tel: 0161 789 5876
Fax: 0161 789 1123
admin@ecclescollege.ac.uk
www.ecclescollege.ac.uk

Hopwood Hall College
St Mary's Gate
Rochdale
Lancashire OL12 6RY
Tel: 01706 345346
Fax: 01706 641426
enquiries@hopwood.ac.uk
www.hopwood.ac.uk

Hugh Baird College
Balliol Road
Bootle
Liverpool
L20 7EW
Tel: 0151 353 4444
Fax: ˙ 0151 353 4469
info@hughbaird.ac.uk
www.hughbaird.ac.uk

Lancaster and Morecambe College
Morecambe Road
Lancaster
LA1 2TY
Tel: 01524 66215
Fax: 01524 843078
info@lmc.ac.uk
www.lmc.ac.uk

Liverpool Community College
Bankfield Road
Liverpool
L13 0BQ
Tel: 0151 252 3800
enquiry@liv-coll.ac.uk
www.liv-coll.ac.uk

Loreto College
Chichester Road
Manchester
M15 5PB
Tel: 0161 226 5156
Fax: 0161 227 9174
enquiries@loreto.ac.uk
www.loreto.ac.uk

Manchester College of Arts and Technology
Openshaw Campus
Ashton Old Road
Openshaw
Manchester
M11 2WH
Tel: 0161 953 5995
Fax: 0161 953 3909
enquiries@mancat.ac.uk
www.mancat.ac.uk

Myerscough College
Myerscough Hall
St Michael's Road
Bilsborrow
Preston
Lancashire PR3 0RY
Tel: 01995 642222
Fax: 01995 642333
enquiries@myerscough.ac.uk
www.myerscough.ac.uk

Nelson & Colne College
Scotland Road
Nelson
Lancashire BB9 7YT
Tel: 01282 440 200
Fax: 01282 440 274
info-officer@nelson.ac.uk
www.nelson.ac.uk

North Trafford College of Further Education
Talbot Road
Stretford
Manchester
M32 0XH
Tel: 0161 886 7000
Fax: 0161 872 7921
admissions@ntc.ac.uk
www.northtrafford.ac.uk

The Oldham College
Rochdale Road
Oldham
Lancashire OL9 6AA
Tel: 0161 624 5214
Fax: 0161 785 4234
info@oldham.ac.uk
www.oldham.ac.uk

Ormskirk College
Hants Lane
Ormskirk
Lancashire L39 1PX
Tel: 01695 577140
www.skelmersdale.ac.uk

Pendleton College
Pendleton Centre
Dronfield Road
Salford
Lancashire M6 7FR
Tel: 0161 736 5074
Fax: 0161 737 4103
www.pendcoll.ac.uk

Preston College
Fulwood Campus
St Vincents Road
Preston
Lancashire PR2 8UR
Tel: 01772 225000
Fax: 01772 225002
pc4u@preston.ac.uk
www.preston.ac.uk

Runshaw College
Langdale Road
Leyland
Lancashire PR25 3DQ
Tel: 01772 622677
Fax: 01772 642009
www.runshaw.ac.uk

Salford College
Worsley Campus
Walkden Road
Worsley
Lancashire M28 7QD
Tel: 0161 211 5001
Fax: 0161 211 5020
www.salford-col.ac.uk

Skelmersdale College
Westbank Campus
Yewdale
Skelmersdale
Lancashire WN8 6JA
Tel: 01695 728 744
www.skelmersdale.ac.uk

St Mary's College
Shear Brow
Blackburn
Lancashire BB1 8DX
Tel: 01254 580464
reception@stmarysblackburn.ac.uk
www.stmarysblackburn.ac.uk

Stockport College
Wellington Road South
Stockport
Lancashire SK1 3UQ
Tel: 0161 958 3100
Fax: 0161 480 6636
admissions@stockport.ac.uk
www.stockport.ac.uk

Tameside College
Beaufort Road
Ashton-under-Lyne
Greater Manchester
Lancashire OL6 6NX
Tel: 0161 908 6789
Fax: 0161 908 6612
www.tameside.ac.uk

Wigan and Leigh College
PO Box 53
Parsons Walk
Wigan
Lancashire WN1 1RS
Tel: 01942 761600
Fax: 01942 761603
www.wigan-leigh.ac.uk

Winstanley College
Billinge
Wigan
Lancashire WN5 7XF
Tel: 01695 633244
Fax: 01695 633409
www.winstanley.ac.uk

Xaverian College
Lower Park Road
Manchester
M14 5RB
Tel: 0161 224 1781
Fax: 0161 248 9039
college@xaverian.ac.uk
www.xaverian.ac.uk

Leicestershire

Brooksby Melton College
Brooksby
Melton Mowbray
Leicestershire LE14 2LJ
Tel: 01664 850850
Fax: 01664 855444
course.enquiries@brooksbymelton.ac.uk
www.brooksbymelton.ac.uk

Leicester Adult Education College
2 Wellington Street
Leicester
Leicestershire LE1 6HL
Tel: 0116 233 4343
Fax: 0116 233 4344
admin@laec.ac.uk
www.laec.ac.uk

Leicester College
Painter Street
Leicester
Leicestershire LE1 3WA
Tel: 0116 224 4100
Fax: 0116 253 6553
info@leicestercollege.ac.uk
www.leicestercollege.ac.uk

Loughborough College
Radmoor Road
Loughborough
Leicestershire LE11 3BT
Tel: 0845 166 2950
loucoll@loucoll.ac.uk
www.loucoll.ac.uk

North Warwickshire and Hinckley College
Hinckley College
London Road
Hinckley
Leicestershire LE10 1HQ
Tel: 024 7624 3000
the.college@nwhc.ac.uk
www.nwhc.ac.uk

Regent College
Regent Road
Leicester
Leicestershire LE1 7LW
Tel: 0116 255 4629
Fax: 0116 254 5680
support@regent-college.ac.uk
www.regent-college.ac.uk

South Leicestershire College
Station Road
Wigston
Leicestershire LE18 2DW
Tel: 0116 288 5051
Fax: 0116 288 0823
enquiries@slcollege.ac.uk
www.slcollege.ac.uk

Stephenson College
Thornborough Road
Coalville
Leicestershire LE67 3TN
Tel: 01530 836136
www.stephensoncoll.ac.uk

Lincolnshire

Bishop Grosseteste College
Newport
Lincoln
Lincolnshire LN1 3DY
Tel: 01522 527347
Fax: 01522 530243
info@bgc.ac.uk
www.bishopg.ac.uk

Boston College
Main Campus
Skirbeck Road
Boston
Lincolnshire PE21 6JF
Tel: 01205 365701
Fax: 01205 313252
info@boston.ac.uk
www.boston.ac.uk

Franklin College
Chelmsford Avenue
Grimsby
Lincolnshire DN34 5BY
Tel: 01472 875000
Fax: 01472 875019
college@franklin.ac.uk
www.franklin.ac.uk

Grantham College
Stonebridge Road
Grantham
Lincolnshire NG31 9AP
Tel: 01476 400200
Fax: 01476 400291
enquiry@grantham.ac.uk
www.grantham.ac.uk

Grimsby Institute of Further & Higher Education
Nuns Corner
Grimsby
North East Lincolnshire DN34 5BQ
Tel: 01472 311222
Fax: 01472 879924
infocent@grimsby.ac.uk
www.grimsby.ac.uk

Lincoln College
Monks Road
Lincoln
Lincolnshire LN2 5HQ
Tel: 01522 876000
Fax: 01522 876200
enquiries@lincolncollege.ac.uk
www.lincolncollege.ac.uk

North Lindsey College
Kingsway
Scunthorpe
North Lincolnshire DN17 1AJ
Tel: 01724 281111
Fax: 01724 294020
info@northlindsey.ac.uk
www.northlindsey.ac.uk

Stamford College
Drift Road
Stamford
Lincolnshire PE9 1XA
Tel: 01780 764141
Fax: 01780 763313
enquiries@stamford.ac.uk
www.stamford.ac.uk

London

Albany College
Main Campus
21–24 Queens Road
Hendon
London NW4 2TL
Tel: 020 8202 5965
Fax: 020 8202 8460
info@albany-college.co.uk
www.albany-college.co.uk

Ashbourne College
17 Old Court Place
Kensington
London W8 4PL
Tel: 020 7937 3858
Fax: 020 7937 2207
admin@ashbournecollege.co.uk
www.ashbournecollege.co.uk

Central School of Speech and Drama
Embassy Theatre
Eton Avenue
London NW3 3HY
Tel: 020 7722 8183
enquiries@cssd.ac.uk
www.cssd.ac.uk

City & Islington College
The Marlborough Building
383 Holloway Road
London N7 0RN
Tel: 020 7700 9333
www.candi.ac.uk

City of Westminster College
25 Paddington Green
London W2 1NB
Tel: 020 7723 8826
Fax: 020 7258 2700
www.cwc.ac.uk

College of Central London
73 Great Eastern Street
London EC2A 3HR
Tel: 020 7739 5555
www.central-college.co.uk

College of North East London
High Road
Tottenham
London N15 4RU
Tel: 020 8442 3055
admissions@staff.conel.ac.uk
www.conel.ac.uk

College of North West London
Willesden Centre
Dudden Hill Lane
London NW10 2XD
Tel: 020 8208 5050
courenq@cnwl.ac.uk
www.cnwl.ac.uk

Ealing, Hammersmith & West London College
Gliddon Road
Barons Court
London W14 9BL
Tel: 020 8741 1688
Fax: 020 8563 8247
cic@wlc.ac.uk
www.wlc.ac.uk

Greenwich Community College
95 Plumstead Road
London SE18 7DQ
Tel: 020 8488 4800
Fax: 020 8488 4899
info@gcc.ac.uk
www.gcc.ac.uk

Hackney, The Community College
Shoreditch Campus
Falkirk Street
London N1 6HQ
Tel: 020 7613 9123
enquiries@tcch.ac.uk
www.tcch.ac.uk

Kensington and Chelsea College
Hortensia Road
London SW10 0QS
Tel: 020 7573 3600
Fax: 020 7351 0956
enquiries@kcc.ac.uk
www.kcc.ac.uk

Lambeth College
45 Clapham Common South Side
London SW4 9BL
Tel: 020 7501 5010
courses@lambethcollege.ac.uk
www.lambethcollege.ac.uk

Lewisham College
Lewisham Way
London SE4 1UT
Tel: 0800 834 545
info@lewisham.ac.uk
www.lewisham.ac.uk

Morley College
61 Westminister Bridge Road
London SE1 7HT
Tel: 020 7928 8501
Fax: 020 7928 4074
enquiries@morleycollege.ac.uk
www.morleycollege.ac.uk

Newham College of Further Education
East Ham Campus
High Street South
London E6 6ER
Tel: 020 8257 4000
on-line.enquiries@newham.ac.uk
www.newham.ac.uk

Sir George Monoux College
Chingford Road
Walthamstow
London E17 5AA
Tel: 020 8523 3544
Fax: 020 8498 2443
info@george-monoux.ac.uk
www.george-monoux.ac.uk

South Thames College
Wandsworth High Street
London SW18 2PP
Tel: 020 8918 7777
studentservices@south-thames.ac.uk
www.south-thames.ac.uk

Southgate College
High Street
Southgate
London N14 6BS
Tel: 020 8982 5050
Fax: 020 8982 5051
admiss@southgate.ac.uk
www.southgate.ac.uk

Southwark College
Camberwell Centre
Southampton Way
London SE5 7EW
Tel: 020 7815 1677
Fax: 020 7261 1301
www.southwark.ac.uk

Tower Hamlets College
Poplar Centre
Poplar High Street
London E14 0AF
Tel: 020 7510 7777
Fax: 020 7538 9153
www.tower.ac.uk

University of the Arts, London
65 Davies Street
London W1K 5DA
Tel: 020 7514 8073
www.arts.ac.uk

Waltham Forest College
Forest Building
Forest Road
Walthamstow
London E17 4JB
Tel: 020 8501 8000
Fax: 020 8501 8001
info@waltham.ac.uk
www.waltham.ac.uk

Westminster Kingsway College
Vincent Square
London SW1P 2PD
Tel: 020 7556 8001
courseinfo@westking.ac.uk
www.westking.ac.uk

Merseyside

Carmel College
Prescot Road
St Helens
Merseyside WA10 3AG
Tel: 01744 452200
Fax: 01744 452222
info@carmel.ac.uk
www.carmel.ac.uk

King George V College
Scarisbrick New Road
Southport
Merseyside PR8 6LR
Tel: 01704 530601
Fax: 01704 548656
enquiries@kgv.ac.uk
www.kgv.ac.uk

Knowsley Community College
Kirkby Campus
Cherryfield Drive
Kirkby
Merseyside L32 8SF
Tel: 0845 155 1055
Fax: 0151 477 5703
info@knowsleycollege.ac.uk
www.knowsleycollege.ac.uk

Southport College
Mornington Road
Southport
Merseyside PR9 0TT
Tel: 01704 500606
Fax: 01704 392794
www.southport-college.ac.uk

St Helens College
Water Street/Town Centre Campus
Water Street
St Helens
Merseyside WA10 1PP
Tel: 01744 733766
Fax: 01744 623400
www.sthelens.ac.uk

Wirral Metropolitan College
Conway Park Campus
Europa Boulevard
Conway Park
Birkenhead
Merseyside CH41 4NT
Tel: 0151 551 7777
Fax: 0151 551 7701
enquiries@wmc.ac.uk
www.wmc.ac.uk

Middlesex

Brooklands College
Church Road
Ashford
Middlesex TW15 2XD
Tel: 01784 248666
Fax: 01784 254132
info@brooklands.ac.uk
www.brooklands.ac.uk

Capel Manor College
Bullsmoor Lane
Enfield
Middlesex EN1 4RQ
Tel: 020 8366 4442
Fax: 01992 717544
enquiries@capel.ac.uk
www.capel.ac.uk

Enfield College
73 Hertford Road
Enfield
Middlesex EN3 5HA
Tel: 020 8443 3434
Fax: 020 8804 7028
courseinformation@enfield.ac.uk
www.enfield.ac.uk

Harrow College
Harrow Weald Campus
Brookshill
Harrow Weald
Middlesex HA3 6RR
Tel: 020 8909 6000
Fax: 020 8909 6050
enquiries@harrow.ac.uk
www.harrow.ac.uk

Richmond upon Thames College
Egerton Road
Twickenham
Middlesex TW2 7SJ
Tel: 020 8607 8000
Fax: 020 8744 9738
courses@rutc.ac.uk
www.rutc.ac.uk

Stanmore College
Elm Park
Stanmore
Middlesex HA7 4BQ
Tel: 020 8420 7700
Fax: 020 8420 6502
enquiry@stanmore.ac.uk
www.stanmore.ac.uk

Uxbridge College
Uxbridge Campus
Park Road
Uxbridge
Middlesex UB8 1NQ
Tel: 01895 853333
Fax: 01895 853377
enquiries@uxbridgecollege.ac.uk
www.uxbridge.ac.uk

West Thames College
London Road
Isleworth
Middlesex TW7 4HS
Tel: 020 8326 2020
info@west-thames.ac.uk
www.west-thames.ac.uk

Norfolk

City College Norwich
Ipswich Road
Norwich
Norfolk NR2 2LJ
Tel: 01603 773311
www.ccn.ac.uk

College of West Anglia

Tennyson Avenue
King's Lynn
Norfolk PE30 2QW
Tel: 01553 761144
Fax: 01553 764902
www.col-westanglia.ac.uk

Easton College

Easton
Norwich
Norfolk NR9 5DX
Tel: 01603 731200
Fax: 01603 741438
info@easton-college.ac.uk
www.easton-college.ac.uk

Great Yarmouth College

Southtown
Great Yarmouth
Norfolk NR31 0ED
Tel: 01493 655261
Fax: 01493 653423
info@gyc.ac.uk
www.gyc.ac.uk

Northamptonshire

Moulton College

West Street
Moulton
Northampton
Northamptonshire NN3 7RR
Tel: 01604 491131
Fax: 01604 491127
enquiries@moulton.ac.uk
www.moulton.ac.uk

Northampton College

Booth Lane
Northampton
Northamptonshire NN3 3RF
Tel: 01604 734567
Fax: 01604 734207
enquiries@northamptoncollege.ac.uk
www.northamptoncollege.ac.uk

Tresham Institute

Windmill Avenue
Kettering
Northamptonshire NN15 6ER
Tel: 0845 658 89 90
Fax: 01536 522500
info@tresham.ac.uk
www.tresham.ac.uk

Northern Ireland

Belfast Metropolitan College

Brunswick Street
Belfast
Northern Ireland BT2 7GX
Tel: 028 9026 5000
Fax: 028 9026 5101
central_admissions@belfastmet.ac.uk
www.belfastmet.ac.uk

Ballymoney and Coleraine Northern Regional College

Union Street
Coleraine
Co Londonderry
Northern Ireland BT52 1QA
Tel: 028 7035 4717
Fax: 028 7035 6377
admissions@causeway.ac.uk
www.causeway.ac.uk

College of Agriculture Food and Rural Enterprise

Greenmount Campus
22 Greenmount Road
Antrim
Co. Antrim
Northern Ireland BT41 4PU
Tel: 028 9442 6601
Fax: 028 9442 6606
enquiries@dardni.gov.uk
www.greenmount.ac.uk

Northern Regional College

400 Shore Road
Newtownabbey
County Antrim
Northern Ireland BT37 9RS
Tel: 028 9085 5000
Fax: 028 9086 2076
info@eaifhe.ac.uk
www.eaifhe.ac.uk

South Eastern Regional College

Market Street
Downpatrick
County Down
Northern Ireland BT30 6ND
Tel: 028 4461 5815
Fax: 028 4461 5817
info@serc.ac.uk
www.serc.ac.uk

East Tyrone College of Further & Higher Education
Circular Road
Dungannon
County Tyrone
Northern Ireland BT71 6BQ
Tel: 028 8772 2323
Fax: 028 8775 2018
info@etcfhe.ac.uk
www.etcfhe.ac.uk

Limavady College of Further & Higher Education
Main Street
Limavady
County Londonderry
Northern Ireland BT49 OEX
Tel: 028 777 62334
Fax: 028 777 61018
www.limavady.ac.uk

Lisburn Institute
39 Castle Street
Lisburn
County Antrim
Northern Ireland BT27 4SU
Tel: 028 9267 7225
Fax: 028 9267 7291
admissions@liscol.ac.uk
www.liscol.ac.uk

Northern Regional College
Trostan Avenue
Ballymena
County Antrim
Northern Ireland BT43 7BN
Tel: 028 2565 2871
Fax: 028 2565 9245
www.nrc.ac.uk

North West Institute of Further & Higher Education
Strand Rd
Derry
County Londonderry
Northern Ireland BT48 7BY
Tel: 028 7127 6000
Fax: 028 7126 0520
www.nwifhe.ac.uk

Southern Regional College
Lonsdale Street
Armagh
County Armagh
BT61 7HN
Tel: 028 3752 2205
www.src.ac.uk

South West College Omagh Campus
2 Mountjoy Road
Omagh
County Tyrone
Northern Ireland BT79 7AH
Tel: 028 8224 5433
Fax: 028 8224 1440
www.omagh.ac.uk

St Mary's College Belfast
191 Falls Road
Belfast
Northern Ireland BT12 6FE
Tel: 028 9032 7678
Fax: 028 9033 3719
www.stmarys-belfast.ac.uk

Stranmillis College
Stranmillis Road
Belfast
Northern Ireland BT9 5DY
Tel: 028 9038 1271
Fax: 028 9066 4423
www.stran.ac.uk

Northumberland

Northumberland College
College Road
Ashington
Northumberland NE63 9RG
Tel: 01670 841200
Fax: 01670 841201
advice.centre@northland.ac.uk
www.northland.ac.uk

Nottinghamshire

Bilborough College
Bilborough Road
Bilborough
Nottingham
Nottinghamshire NG8 4DQ
Tel: 0115 929 9436
Fax: 0115 942 5561
www.bilborough.ac.uk

Broxtowe College
High Road
Chilwell
Nottingham
Nottinghamshire NG9 4AH
Tel: 0115 917 5252
Fax: 0115 917 5200
learn@broxtowe.ac.uk
www.broxtowe.ac.uk

Castle College Nottingham
Maid Marian Way
Nottingham NG1 6AB
Tel: 0845 895 0500
www.castlecollege.ac.uk

New College Nottingham
The Adams Building
Stoney Street
Nottingham
Nottinghamshire NG1 1NG
Tel: 0115 9100 100
enquiries@ncn.ac.uk
www.ncn.ac.uk

Newark College
Friary Road
Newark-On-Trent
Nottinghamshire NG24 1PB
Tel: 01636 680680
Fax: 01636 680681
enquiries@newark.ac.uk
www.newark.ac.uk

North Nottinghamshire College
Carlton Road
Worksop
Nottinghamshire S81 7HP
Tel: 01909 504504
Fax: 01909 504505
contact@nnc.ac.uk
www.nnotts-col.ac.uk

South Nottingham College
Greythorn Drive
West Bridgford
Nottingham
Nottinghamshire NG2 7GA
Tel: 0115 914 6400
Fax: 0115 914 6444
enquiry@snc.ac.uk
www.snc.ac.uk

West Nottinghamshire College
Derby Road
Mansfield
Nottinghamshire NG18 5BH
Tel: 01623 627191
Fax: 01623 623063
www.wnc.ac.uk

Oxfordshire

Abingdon and Witney College
Wootton Road
Abingdon
Oxfordshire OX14 1GG
Tel: 01235 555585
Fax: 01235 553168
enquiry@abingdon-witney.ac.uk
www.abingdon-witney.ac.uk

Henley College
Deanfield Avenue
Henley-on-Thames
Oxfordshire RG9 1UH
Tel: 01491 579988
Fax: 01491 410099
info@henleycol.ac.uk
www.henleycol.ac.uk

Oxford & Cherwell Valley College
Oxpens Road
Oxford
Oxfordshire OX1 1SA
Tel: 01865 550550
Fax: 01865 551386
enquiries@ovc.ac.uk
www.ocvc.ac.uk

Ruskin College
Walton Street
Oxford
Oxfordshire OX1 2HE
Tel: 01865 554331
Fax: 01865 554372
enquiries@ruskin.ac.uk
www.ruskin.ac.uk

Scotland

Aberdeen College
Gallowgate Centre
Gallowgate
Aberdeen
Aberdeenshire
Scotland AB25 1BN
Tel: 01224 612000
Fax: 01224 612001
enquiry@abcol.ac.uk
www.abcol.ac.uk

Adam Smith College, Fife
Glenrothes Campus
Stenton Road
Glenrothes
Fife
Scotland KY6 2RA
Tel: 01592 772233
Fax: 01592 568182
enquiries@adamsmith.ac.uk
www.adamsmithcollege.ac.uk

Adam Smith College, Fife
Kirkcaldy Campus
St Brycedale Avenue
Kirkcaldy
Fife
Scotland KY1 1EX
Tel: 01592 268591
Fax: 01592 640225
enquiries@adamsmith.ac.uk
www.adamsmithcollege.ac.uk

Angus College
Keptie Road
Arbroath
Angus
Scotland DD11 3EA
Tel: 01241 432600
Fax: 01241 876169
marketing@angus.ac.uk
www.angus.ac.uk

Anniesland College
19 Hatfield Drive
Glasgow
Lanarkshire
Scotland G12 OYE
Tel: 0141 357 3969
Fax: 0141 357 6557
reception@anniesland.ac.uk
www.anniesland.ac.uk

Ayr College
Dam Park
Ayr
Ayrshire
Scotland KA8 0EU
Tel: 01292 265184
Fax: 01292 263889
information@ayrcoll.ac.uk
www.ayrcoll.ac.uk

Banff & Buchan College
Henderson Road
Fraserburgh
Aberdeenshire
Scotland AB43 9GA
Tel: 01346 586100
Fax: 01346 515370
info@banff-buchan.ac.uk
www.banff-buchan.ac.uk

Barony College
Parkgate
Dumfries
Dumfriesshire
Scotland DG1 3NE
Tel: 01387 860251
Fax: 01387 860395
admin@barony.ac.uk
www.barony.ac.uk

Borders College
Melrose Road
Galashiels
Scotland TD1 2AF
Tel: 08700 505152
Fax: 01896 758179
enquiries@borderscollege.ac.uk
www.borderscollege.ac.uk

Cardonald College
690 Mosspark Drive
Glasgow
Lanarkshire
Scotland G52 3AY
Tel: 0141 272 3333
Fax: 0141 272 3444
enquiries@cardonald.ac.uk
www.cardonald.ac.uk

Central College of Commerce

300 Cathedral Street
Glasgow
Lanarkshire
Scotland G1 2TA
Tel: 0141 552 3941
Fax: 0141 553 2368
information@central-glasgow.ac.uk
www.centralcollege.ac.uk

Clydebank College

College Square
2 Aurora Avenue
Clydebank
Scotland G81 1NX
Tel: 0141 951 7400
Fax: 0141 951 7401
www.clydebank.ac.uk

Coatbridge College

Kildonan Street
Coatbridge
North Lanarkshire
Scotland ML5 3LS
Tel: 01236 422316
Fax: 01236 440266
admissions@coatbridge.ac.uk
www.coatbridge.ac.uk

Cumbernauld College

Tryst Road
Cumbernauld
Lanarkshire
Scotland G67 1HU
Tel: 01236 731811
Fax: 01236 723416
cumbernauld_college@cumbernauld.ac.uk
www.cumbernauld.ac.uk

Dumfries and Galloway College

Herries Avenue
Heathhall
Dumfries
Scotland DG1 3QZ
Tel: 01387 261261
Fax: 01387 250006
info@dumgal.ac.uk
www.dumgal.ac.uk

Dundee College

Kingsway Campus
Old Glamis Road
Dundee
Scotland DD3 8LE
Tel: 01382 834834
Fax: 01382 858117
enquiry@dundeecoll.ac.uk
www.dundeecoll.ac.uk

Elmwood College

Carslogie Road
Cupar
Fife
Scotland KY15 4JB
Tel: 01334 658800
Fax: 01334 6558888
www.elmwood.ac.uk

Forth Valley College

Clackmannan Campus
Branshill Road
Alloa
Clackmannanshire
Scotland FK10 3BT
Tel: 01259 215121
Fax: 01259 222789
info@forthvalley.ac.uk
www.forthvalley.ac.uk

Forth Valley College

Falkirk Campus
Grangemouth Road
Falkirk
Stirlingshire
Scotland FK2 9AD
Tel: 01324 403000
Fax: 01324 403222
info@forthvalley.ac.uk
www.forthvalley.ac.uk

Forth Valley College

Stirling Campus
Kerse Road
Stirling
Stirlingshire
Scotland FK7 7QA
Tel: 01786 406000
Fax: 01786 406070
info@forthvalley.ac.uk
www.forthvalley.ac.uk

Glasgow Metropolitan College
North Hanover Street Campus
60 North Hanover Street
Glasgow
Lanarkshire
Scotland G1 2BP
Tel: 0141 566 6222
Fax: 0141 566 6226
enquiries@glasgowmet.ac.uk
www.glasgowmet.ac.uk

Glasgow Metropolitan College
60 North Hanover Street
Glasgow
Scotland G1 2BP
Tel: 0141 566 6222
Fax: 0141 566 6226
enquiries@glasgowmet.ac.uk
www.glasgowmet.ac.uk

Glasgow College of Nautical Studies
21 Thistle Street
Glasgow
Lanarkshire
Scotland G5 9XB
Tel: 0141 565 2500
Fax: 0141 565 2599
enquiries@gcns.ac.uk
www.glasgow-nautical.ac.uk

Inverness College
Longman Campus
3 Longman Road
Longman South
Inverness
Scotland IV1 1SA
Tel: 01463 273000
Fax: 01463 711977
info@inverness.uhi.ac.uk
www.inverness.uhi.ac.uk

James Watt College of Further & Higher Enducation
Finnart Street
Greenock
Scotland PA16 8HF
Tel: 01475 724433
Fax: 01475 888079
enquiries@jameswatt.ac.uk
www.jameswatt.ac.uk

Jewel and Esk Valley College
24 Milton Road East
Edinburgh
Scotland EH15 2PP
Tel: 0131 660 1010
Fax: 0131 657 2276
info@jevc.ac.uk
www.jevc.ac.uk

John Wheatley College
2 Haghill Road
Glasgow
Scotland G31 3SR
Tel: 0141 588 1500
Fax: 0141 763 2384
advice@jwheatley.ac.uk
www.jwheatley.ac.uk

Kilmarnock College
Holehouse Road
Kilmarnock
Ayrshire
Scotland KA3 7AT
Tel: 01563 523501
Fax: 01563 538182
enquiries@kilmarnock.ac.uk
www.kilmarnock.ac.uk

Langside College
50 Prospecthill Road
Glasgow
Scotland G42 9LB
Tel: 0141 636 3600
Fax: 0141 632 5252
enquireuk@langside.ac.uk
www.langside.ac.uk

Lauder College
Halbeath
Dunfermline
Fife
Scotland KY11 8DY
Tel: 01383 845000
Fax: 01383 845001
customerservices@lauder.ac.uk
www.lauder.ac.uk

Lews Castle College
Stornoway
Isle of Lewis
Scotland HS2 0XR
Tel: 01851 770000
Fax: 01851 770001
aofficele@lews.uhi.ac.uk
www.lews.uhi.ac.uk

Moray College
Moray Street
Elgin
Morayshire
Scotland IV30 1JJ
Tel: 01343 576000
Fax: 01343 576001
www.moray.ac.uk

Motherwell College
Dalzell Drive
Motherwell
Scotland ML1 2DD
Tel: 01698 232425
Fax: 01698 232527
information@motherwell.co.uk
www.motherwell.ac.uk

Newbattle Abbey College
Newbattle Road
Newbattle
Dalkeith
Midlothian
Scotland EH22 3LL
Tel: 0131 663 1921
Fax: 0131 654 0598
office@newbattleabbeycollege.ac.uk
www.newbattleabbeycollege.co.uk

North Glasgow College
110 Flemington St
Glasgow
Scotland G21 4BX
Tel: 0141 558 9001
Tel: 0141 588 9905
www.northglasgowcollege.ac.uk

North Highland College
Ormlie Road
Thurso
Caithness
Scotland KW14 7EE
Tel: 01847 889000
Fax: 01847 889001
northhighlandcollege@thurso.uhi.ac.uk
www.nhcscotland.com

Oatridge Agricultural College
Ecclesmachen
Broxburn
West Lothian
Scotland EH52 6NH
Tel: 01506 864800
Fax: 01506 853373
info@oatridge.ac.uk
www.oatridge.ac.uk

Orkney College
East Road
Kirkwall
Orkney
Scotland KW15 1LX
Tel: 01856 569000
Fax: 01856 569001
orkney.college@orkney.uhi.ac.uk
www.orkney.uhi.ac.uk

Perth College
Crieff Road
Perth
Perthshire
Scotland PH1 2NX
Tel: 01738 877000
Fax: 01738 877001
pc.enquiries@perth.uhi.ac.uk
www.perth.ac.uk

Queen Margaret University College
Corstorphine Campus
Clerwood Terrace
Edinburgh
Scotland EH12 8TS
Tel: 0131 317 3247
Fax: 0131 317 3248
admissions@qmuc.ac.uk
www.qmced.ac.uk

Reid Kerr College
Renfrew Road
Paisley
Renfrewshire
Scotland PA3 4DR
Tel: 0800 052 7343
sservices@reidkerr.ac.uk
www.reidkerr.ac.uk

Sabhal Mòr Ostaig
Sleat
Isle of Skye
Scotland IV44 8RQ
Tel: 01471 888000
Fax: 01471 888001
sm.oifis@groupwise.uhi.ac.uk
www.smo.uhi.ac.uk/beurla

Scottish Agricultural College
King's Buildings
West Mains Road
Edinburgh
Scotland EH9 3JG
Tel: 0131 535 4000
information@sac.co.uk
www.sac.ac.uk

Shetland College of Further Education

Gremista
Lerwick
Shetland
Scotland ZE1 OPX
Tel: 01595 771000
Fax: 01595 771001
www.shetland.uhi.ac.uk

South Lanarkshire College

Hamilton Road
Cambuslang
Scotland G72 7NY
Tel: 0141 641 6600
Fax: 0141 641 4296
admissions@slc.ac.uk
www.south-lanarkshire-college.ac.uk

Stevenson College

Bankhead Avenue
Edinburgh
Scotland EH11 4DE
Tel: 0131 535 4700
Fax: 0131 535 4708
info@stevenson.ac.uk
www.stevenson.ac.uk

Stow College

43 Shamrock Street
Glasgow
Lanarkshire
Scotland G4 9LD
Tel: 0141 332 1786
enquiries@stow.ac.uk
www.stow.ac.uk

Telford College

Crewe Toll
Edinburgh
Scotland EH4 2NZ
Tel: 0131 332 2491
Fax: 0131 343 1218
mail@ed-coll.ac.uk
www.ed-coll.ac.uk

West Lothian College

Almondvale Crescent
Livingston
West Lothian
Scotland EH54 7EP
Tel: 01506 418181
Fax: 01506 409980
enquiries@west-lothian.ac.uk
www.west-lothian.ac.uk

Shropshire

Harper Adams University College

Newport
Shropshire TF10 8NB
Tel: 01952 820280
Fax: 01952 814783
www.harper-adams.ac.uk

Ludlow College

Castle Square
Ludlow
Shropshire SY8 1GD
Tel: 01584 872846
Fax: 01584 876012
info@ludlow-college.ac.uk
www.ludlow-college.ac.uk

New College Telford

King Street
Wellington
Telford
Shropshire TF1 1NY
Tel: 01952 641892
www.newcollegetelford.ac.uk

Shrewsbury College of Arts and Technology

London Road
Shrewsbury
Shropshire SY2 6PR
Tel: 01743 342342
Fax: 01743 342343
prospects@shrewsbury.ac.uk
www.shrewsbury.ac.uk

Telford College of Arts & Technology

Haybridge Road
Wellington
Telford
Shropshire TF1 2NP
Tel: 01952 642200
Fax: 01952 642263
studserv@tcat.ac.uk
www.tcat.ac.uk

Walford and North Shropshire College

Shrewsbury Road
Oswestry
Shropshire SY11 4QB
Tel: 01691 688000
Fax: 01691 688001
enquiries@wnsc.ac.uk
www.wnsc.ac.uk

Somerset

Bath Spa University
Newton Park Campus
Newton St Loe
Bath
Somerset BA2 9BN
Tel: 01225 875875
Fax: 01225 875444
enquiries@bathspa.ac.uk
www.bathspa.ac.uk

Bridgwater College
Bath Road
Bridgwater
Somerset TA6 4PZ
Tel: 01278 455464
Fax: 01278 444363
information@bridgwater.ac.uk
www.bridgwater.ac.uk

City of Bath College
Avon Street
Bath
Somerset BA1 1UP
Tel: 01225 312191
Fax: 01225 444213
enquiries@citybathcoll.ac.uk
www.citybathcoll.ac.uk

Norton Radstock College
South Hill Park
Radstock
Bath
Somerset BA3 3RW
Tel: 01761 433161
Fax: 01761 436173
courses@nortcoll.ac.uk
www.nortcoll.ac.uk

Richard Huish College
South Road
Taunton
Somerset TA1 3DZ
Tel: 01823 320800
Fax: 01823 320801
enquiries@richuish.ac.uk
www.richuish.ac.uk

Somerset College of Arts and Technology
Wellington Road
Taunton
Somerset TA1 5AX
Tel: 01823 366366
enquiries@somerset.ac.uk
www.somerset.ac.uk

Strode College
Church Road
Street
Somerset BA16 0AB
Tel: 01458 844400
Fax: 01458 844411
courseinfo@strode-college.ac.uk
www.strode-college.ac.uk

Weston College
Knightstone Road
Weston-super-Mare
North Somerset BS23 2AL
Tel: 01934 411 411
Fax: 01934 411 410
www.weston.ac.uk

Yeovil College
Mudford Road
Yeovil
Somerset BA21 4DR
Tel: 01935 423921
info@yeovil.ac.uk
www.yeovil-college.ac.uk

Staffordshire

Burton College
Lichfield Street
Burton on Trent
Staffordshire DE14 3RL
Tel: 01283 494400
Fax: 01283 494800
www.burton-college.ac.uk

Cannock Chase Technical College
The Green
Cannock
Staffordshire WS11 1UE
Tel: 01543 462200
Fax: 01543 574223
enquiries@cannock.ac.uk
www.cannock.ac.uk

Leek College
Stockwell St
Leek
Staffordshire ST13 6DP
Tel: 01538 398866
Fax: 01538 399506
admissions@leek.ac.uk
www.leek.ac.uk

Newcastle-under-Lyme College
Liverpool Road
Newcastle-under-Lyme
Staffordshire ST5 2DF
Tel: 01782 715111
Fax: 01782 717396
enquiries@nulc.ac.uk
www.nulc.ac.uk

Rodbaston College
Rodbaston
Penkridge
Staffordshire ST19 5PH
Tel: 01785 712209
Fax: 01785 715701
rodenquiries@rodbaston.ac.uk
www.rodbaston.ac.uk

Stafford College
Earl Street
Stafford
Staffordshire ST16 2QR
Tel: 01785 223 800
Fax: 01785 259 953
enquiries@staffordcoll.ac.uk
www.staffordcoll.ac.uk

Stoke on Trent College
Cauldron Campus
Stoke Road
Shelton
Stoke on Trent
Staffordshire ST4 2DG
Tel: 01782 208208
info@stokecoll.ac.uk
www.stokecoll.ac.uk

Tamworth and Lichfield Colleges
Croft Street
Upper Gungate
Tamworth
Staffordshire B79 8AE
Tel: 01827 310202
Fax: 01827 59437
enquiries@tamworth.ac.uk
www.tlc.ac.uk

Suffolk

Lowestoft College
St Peters Street
Lowestoft
Suffolk NR32 2NB
Tel: 01502 583521
Fax: 01502 500031
info@lowestoft.ac.uk
www.lowestoft.ac.uk

Otley College
Charity Lane
Otley
Ipswich
Suffolk IP6 9EY
Tel: 01473 785543
info@otleycollege.ac.uk
www.otleycollege.ac.uk

Suffolk College
Ipswich
Suffolk IP4 1HY
Tel: 01473 255885
Fax: 01473 230054
info@suffolk.ac.uk
www.suffolk.ac.uk

West Suffolk College
Out Risbygate
Bury St Edmunds
Suffolk IP33 3RL
Tel: 01284 701301
info@westsuffolk.ac.uk
www.westsuffolk.ac.uk

Surrey

Brooklands College
Heath Road
Weybridge
Surrey KT13 8TT
Tel: 01932 797700
Fax: 01932 797800
info@brooklands.ac.uk
www.brooklands.ac.uk

Carshalton College
Nightingale Road
Carshalton
Surrey SM5 2EJ
Tel: 020 8544 4444
Fax: 020 8544 4440
cs@carshalton.ac.uk
www.carshalton.ac.uk

Coulsdon College
Placehouse Lane
Old Coulsdon
Surrey CR5 1YA
Tel: 01737 551176
Fax: 01737 551282
info@coulsdon.ac.uk
www.coulsdon.ac.uk

Croydon College
College Road
Croydon
Surrey CR0 1DX
Tel: 020 8686 5700
info@croydon.ac.uk
www.croydon.ac.uk

East Surrey College
Gatton Point
Claremont Road
Redhill
Surrey RH1 2JX
Tel: 01737 772611
Fax: 01737 768641
studentservices@esc.ac.uk
www.esc.ac.uk

Esher College
Weston Green Road
Thames Ditton
Surrey KT7 0JB
Tel: 020 8398 0291
Fax: 020 8339 0207
eshercollege@esher.ac.uk
www.esher.ac.uk

Farnham College
Morley Road
Farnham
Surrey GU9 8LU
Tel: 01252 716988
Fax: 01252 723969
enquiries@farnham.ac.uk
www.farnham.ac.uk

Godalming College
Tuesley Lane
Godalming
Surrey GU7 1RS
Tel: 01483 423526
Fax: 01483 417079
college@godalming.ac.uk
www.godalming.ac.uk

Guildford College
Stoke Park Campus
Stoke Road
Guildford
Surrey GU1 1EZ
Tel: 01483 448585
Fax: 01483 448600
info@guildford.ac.uk
www.guildford.ac.uk

Hillcroft College
South Bank
Surbiton
Surrey KT6 6DF
Tel: 020 8399 2688
Fax: 020 8390 9171
enquiry@hillcroft.ac.uk
www.hillcroft.ac.uk

John Ruskin College
Selsdon Park Road
South Croydon
Surrey CR2 8JJ
Tel: 020 8651 1131
Fax: 020 8651 4011
info@johnruskin.ac.uk
www.johnruskin.ac.uk

Kingston College
Kingston Hall Road
Kingston upon Thames
Surrey KT1 2AQ
Tel: 020 8546 2151
info@kingston-college.ac.uk
www.kingston-college.ac.uk

Guildford College
Merrist Wood Campus
Worplesdon
Guildford
Surrey GU3 3PE
Tel: 01483 884000
info@guildford.ac.uk
www.merristwood.ac.uk

Merton College
Morden Park
London Road
Morden
Surrey SM4 5QX
Tel: 020 8408 6400
Fax: 020 8408 6666
info@merton.ac.uk
www.merton.ac.uk

North East Surrey College of Technology
Reigate Road
Ewell
Epsom
Surrey KT17 3DS
Tel: 020 8394 1731
info@nescot.ac.uk
www.nescot.ac.uk

Reigate College
Castlefield Road
Reigate
Surrey RH2 0SD
Tel: 01737 221118
Fax: 01737 222657
enquiries@reigate.ac.uk
www.reigate.ac.uk

Richmond Adult and Community College
Parkshot
Richmond
Surrey TW9 2RE
Tel: 020 8891 5907
Fax: 020 8332 6560
info@racc.ac.uk
www.racc.ac.uk

Strode's College
High Street
Egham
Surrey TW20 9DR
Tel: 01784 437506
Fax: 01784 471794
info@strodes.ac.uk
www.strodes.ac.uk

Woking College
Rydens Way
Woking
Surrey GU22 9DL
Tel: 01483 761036
Fax: 01483 728144
wokingcoll@woking.ac.uk
www.woking.ac.uk

Tyne and Wear

City of Sunderland College
Bede Centre
Durham Road
Sunderland
Tyne and Wear SR3 4AH
Tel: 0191 511 6060
Fax: 0191 511 6380
www.citysun.ac.uk

Newcastle College
Rye Hill Campus
Scotswood Road
Newcastle upon Tyne
Tyne and Wear NE4 5BR
Tel: 0191 200 4000
Fax: 0191 200 4517
enquiries@ncl-coll.ac.uk
www.ncl.coll.ac.uk

South Tyneside College
St. George's Avenue
South Shields
Tyne and Wear NE34 6ET
Tel: 0191 427 3500
Fax: 0191 427 3535
info@stc.ac.uk
www.stc.ac.uk

Tyne Metropolitan College
Embleton Avenue
Wallsend
Tyne and Wear NE28 9NJ
Tel: 0191 229 5000
Fax: 0191 229 5301
enquiries@tynemet.ac.uk
www.tynemet.ac.uk

Wales

Aberdare College
Cwmdare Road
Aberdare
Rhondda Cynon Taff
Wales CF44 8BR
Tel: 01685 887511
Fax: 01865 876635
www.aberdare.ac.uk

Barry College
Colcot Road
Barry
Wales CF62 8YJ
Tel: 01446 725000
Fax: 01446 732667
enquiries@barry.ac.uk
www.barry.ac.uk

Bridgend College
Cowbridge Road
Bridgend
Mid Glamorgan
Wales CF31 3DF
Tel: 01656 302302
Fax: 01656 663912
enquiries@bridgend.ac.uk
www.bridgend.ac.uk

Coleg Ceredigion
Park Place
Cardigan
Ceredigion
Wales SA43 1AB
Tel: 01239 612032
www.ceredigion.ac.uk

Coleg Glan Hafren
Trowbridge Road
Rumney
Cardiff
Wales CF3 1XZ
Tel: 0845 045 0845
Fax: 029 20 250339
enquiries@glan-hafren.ac.uk
www.glan-hafren.ac.uk

Coleg Gwent
The Rhadyr
Usk
Wales NP15 1XJ
Tel: 01495 333333
Fax: 01495 333526
info@coleggwent.ac.uk
www.coleggwent.ac.uk

Coleg Harlech
Harlech
Gwynedd
Wales LL46 2PU
Tel: 01766 781900
Fax: 01766 780169
info@harlech.ac.uk
www.harlech.ac.uk

Coleg Llandrillo
Llandudno Road
Rhos-on-Sea
Colwyn Bay
North Wales LL28 4HZ
Tel: 01492 546666
Fax: 01492 543052
www.llandrillo.ac.uk

Coleg Llysfasi
Pentrecelyn
Ruthin
Denbighshire
Clwyd
Wales LL15 2LB
Tel: 01978 790263
Fax: 01978 790468
admin@llysfasi.ac.uk
www.llysfasi.ac.uk

Coleg Meirion-Dwyfor
Ffordd Ty'n y Coed
Dolgellau
Gwynedd
Wales LL40 2SW
Tel: 01341 422827
Fax: 01341 422393
coleg@meiriondwyfor.ac.uk
www.meirion-dwyfor.ac.uk

Coleg Menai
Ffriddoedd Road
Bangor
Gwynedd
North Wales LL57 2TP
Tel: 01248 370125
Fax: 01248 370052
www.menai.ac.uk

Coleg Powys
Brecon Campus
Penlan
Brecon
Powys
Wales LD3 9SR
Tel: 0845 4086400
Fax: 01874 622165
www.coleg-powys.ac.uk

Coleg Powys
Llandrindod Campus
Spa Road
Llandrindod Wells
Powys
Wales LD1 5ES
Tel: 0845 4086300
Fax: 01597 825122
www.coleg-powys.ac.uk

Coleg Powys
Newtown Campus
Llanidloes Road
Newtown
Powys
Wales SY16 4HU
Tel: 0845 4086200
Fax: 01686 622246
www.coleg-powys.ac.uk

Deeside College
Kelsterton Road
Connah's Quay
Deeside
Flintshire
Wales CH5 4BR
Tel: 01244 831531
Fax: 01244 814305
www.deeside.ac.uk

Gorseinon College
Belgrave Road
Gorseinon
Swansea
Wales SA4 6RD
Tel: 01792 890700
Fax: 01792 898729
admin@gorseinon.ac.uk
www.gorseinon.ac.uk

Merthyr Tydfil College
Ynysfach
Merthyr Tydfil
Wales CF48 1AR
Tel: 01685 726000
college@merthyr.ac.uk
www.merthyr.ac.uk

Neath Port Talbot College
Dwr-y-Felin Road
Neath
West Glamorgan
Wales SA10 7RF
Tel: 01639 648000
Fax: 01639 648009
enquiries@nptc.ac.uk
www.nptc.ac.uk

Pembrokeshire College
Haverfordwest
Pembrokeshire
Wales SA61 1ZZ
Tel: 01437 753000
Fax: 01437 753001
admissions@pembrokeshire.ac.uk
www.pembrokeshire.ac.uk

Pontypridd College
Ynys Terrace
Rhydyfelin
Pontypridd
Rhondda Cynon Taff
Wales CF37 5RN
Tel: 01443 662800
Fax: 01443 663028
www.pontypridd.ac.uk

Swansea College
Tycoch Road
Tycoch
Swansea
West Glamorgan
Wales SA2 9EB
Tel: 01792 284000
Fax: 01792 284074
enquiries@swancoll.ac.uk
www.swancoll.ac.uk

Welsh College of Horticulture
Northop
Mold
Flintshire
Wales CH7 6AA
Tel: 01352 841000
Fax: 01352 841031
info@wcoh.ac.uk
www.wcoh.ac.uk

Ystrad Mynach College
Twyn Road
Ystrad Mynach
Hengoed
Wales CF82 7XR
Tel: 01443 816888
Fax: 01443 816973
enquiries@ystrad-mynach.ac.uk
www.ystrad-mynach.ac.uk

Warwickshire

North Warwickshire and Hinckley College
Main Site
Hinckley Road
Nuneaton
Warwickshire CV11 6BH
Tel: 024 7624 3000
the.college@nwhc.ac.uk
www.nwhc.ac.uk

Stratford-upon-Avon College
The Willows North
Alcester Road
Stratford-Upon-Avon
Warwickshire CV37 9QR
Tel: 01789 266 245
Fax: 01789 267 524
college@stratford.ac.uk
www.stratford.ac.uk

Warwickshire College
Leamington Centre
Warwick New Road
Leamington Spa
Warwickshire CV32 5JE
Tel: 01926 318000
Fax: 01926 318111
www.warkscol.ac.uk

Warwickshire College
Rugby Centre
Lower Hillmorton Road
Rugby
Warwickshire CV21 3QS
Tel: 01788 338800/0800 834 254
Fax: 01788 338575
www.warkscol.ac.uk

West Midlands

Birmingham College of Food, Tourism and Creative Studies
Summer Row
Birmingham
West Midlands B3 1JB
Tel: 0121 604 1000
Fax: 0121 608 7100
marketing@bcftcs.ac.uk
www.bcftcs.ac.uk

Birmingham Community College
8 Colmore Row
Birmingham
West Midlands B3 2QX
Tel: 0121 694 6461
Fax: 0121 694 6463
www.bcomcol.ac.uk

Birmingham Institute of Art and Design (BIAD)
Grosta Green
Corporation Street
Birmingham
West Midlands B4 7DX
Tel: 0121 331 5800/01
Fax: 0121 331 7814
enquiries@students.uce.ac.uk
www.biad.uce.ac.uk

Bournville College of Further Education

Bristol Road South
Northfield
Birmingham
West Midlands B31 2AJ
Tel: 0121 483 1000
Fax: 0121 411 2231
info@bournville.ac.uk
www.bournville.ac.uk

City College Birmingham
Garretts Green Lane
Garretts Green
Birmingham
West Midlands B33 0TS
Tel: 0121 743 4471
Fax: 0121 743 9050
enquiries@citycol.ac.uk
www.citycol.ac.uk

Coventry City College
Butts Centre
Butts
Coventry
West Midlands CV1 3GD
Tel: 024 7679 1000
Fax: 024 7679 1670
info@staff.covcollege.ac.uk
www.covcollege.ac.uk

Dudley College of Technology
The Broadway
Dudley
West Midlands DY1 4AS
Tel: 01384 363000
Fax: 01384 363311
studentservices@dudleycol.ac.uk
www.dudleycol.ac.uk

Fircroft College of Adult Education
1018 Bristol Road
Selly Oak
Birmingham
West Midlands B29 6LH
Tel: 0121 472 0116
Fax: 0121 471 1503
www.fircroft.ac.uk

Halesowen College
Whittingham Road
Halesowen
West Midlands B63 3NA
Tel: 0121 602 7777
Fax: 0121 585 0369
info@halesowen.ac.uk
www.halesowen.ac.uk

Henley College Coventry
Henley Road
Bell Green
Coventry
West Midlands CV2 1ED
Tel: 024 7662 6300
Fax: 024 7661 1837
www.henley-cov.ac.uk

Hereward College
Bramston Crescent
Tile Hill Lane
Coventry
West Midlands CV4 9SW
Tel: 024 7646 1231
enquiries@hereward.ac.uk
www.hereward.ac.uk

Matthew Boulton College of Further & Higher Education
Jennens Road
Birmingham
West Midlands B4 7PS
Tel: 0121 446 4545
Fax: 0121 503 8590
ask@mbc.ac.uk
www.matthew-boulton.ac.uk

Queen Alexandra College
Court Oak Road
Harborne
Birmingham
West Midlands B17 9TG
Tel: 0121 428 5050
Fax: 0121 428 5048
enquiries@qac.ac.uk
www.qac.ac.uk

Sandwell College
Oldbury Campus
Pound Road
Oldbury
West Midlands B68 8NA
Tel: 0121 556 6000
Fax: 0121 253 6836
enquiries@sandwell.ac.uk
www.sandwell.ac.uk

Solihull College
Blossomfield Campus
Blossomfield Road
Solihull
West Midlands B91 1SB
Tel: 0121 678 7001
Fax: 0121 678 7200
enquiries@solihull.ac.uk
www.solihull.ac.uk

South Birmingham College
Hall Green Centre
Cole Bank Road
Birmingham
West Midlands B28 8ES
Tel: 0121 694 5000
info@sbc.ac.uk
www.sbirmc.ac.uk

Stourbridge College
Hagley Road
Stourbridge
West Midlands DY8 1QU
Tel: 01384 344344
Fax: 01384 344345
info@stourbridge.ac.uk
www.stourbridge.ac.uk

Sutton Coldfield College
Sutton Campus
34 Lichfield Road
Sutton Coldfield
West Midlands B74 2NW
Tel: 0121 355 5671
Fax: 0121 362 1192
infoc@sutcol.ac.uk
www.sutcol.ac.uk

Walsall College of Arts & Technology
St Paul's Street Campus
Walsall
West Midlands WS1 1XN
Tel: 01922 657000
Fax: 01922 657083
info@walcat.ac.uk
www.walcat.ac.uk

City of Wolverhampton College
Paget Road
Wolverhampton
West Midlands WV6 ODU
Tel: 01902 836000
Fax: 01902 423070
mail@wolvcoll.ac.uk
www.wolverhamptoncollege.ac.uk

West Sussex

Central Sussex College
College Road
Crawley
West Sussex RH10 1NR
Tel: 0845 1550043
Fax: 01293 442399
www.centralsussex.ac.uk

Chichester College
Westgate Fields
Chichester
West Sussex PO19 1SB
Tel: 01243 786321
Fax: 01243 539481
info@chichester.ac.uk
www.chichester.ac.uk

Northbrook College, Sussex
West Durrington Campus
Littlehampton Road
Worthing
West Sussex BN12 6NU
Tel: 01903 606060
Fax: 01903 606073
www.northbrook.ac.uk

The College of Richard Collyer
Hurst Road
Horsham
West Sussex RH12 2EJ
Tel: 01403 210822
admin@collyers.ac.uk
www.collyers.ac.uk

West Dean College
West Dean
Chichester
West Sussex PO18 0QZ
Tel: 01243 811301
enquiries@westdean.org.uk
www.westdean.org.uk

Wiltshire

New College
New College Drive
Swindon
Wiltshire SN3 1AH
Tel: 01793 611470
Fax: 01793 436437
admissions@newcollege.ac.uk
www.newcollege.co.uk

Salisbury College
Southampton Road
Salisbury
Wiltshire SP1 2LW
Tel: 01722 344344
Fax: 01722 344345
enquiries@salisbury.ac.uk
www.salisbury.ac.uk

Swindon College
North Star Avenue
Swindon
Wiltshire SN2 1DY
Tel: 01793 491591
admissions@swindon-college.ac.uk
www.swindon-college.ac.uk

Wiltshire College
Cocklebury Road
Chippenham
Wiltshire SN15 3QD
Tel: 01249 464644
Fax: 01249 465326
info@iltscoll.ac.uk
www.wiltscoll.ac.uk

Worcestershire

Evesham College
Davies Road
Evesham
Worcestershire WR11 1LP
Tel: 01386 712600
Fax: 01386 712640
information@evesham.ac.uk
www.evesham.ac.uk

Kidderminster College
Market Street
Kidderminster
Worcestershire DY10 1LX
Tel: 01562 820811
Fax: 01562 512006
studentservices@kidderminster.ac.uk
www.kidderminster.ac.uk

New College
Bromsgrove Campus
Blackwood Road
Bromsgrove
Worcestershire B60 1PQ
Tel: 01527 570020
Fax: 01527 572900
www.ne-worcs.ac.uk

Pershore Group of Colleges
Avonbank
Pershore
Worcestershire WR10 3JP
Tel: 01386 552443
Fax: 01386 556528
pershore@pershore.ac.uk
www.pershore.ac.uk

Worcester College of Technology
Deansway
Worcester
Worcestershire WR1 2JF
Tel: 01905 725555
Fax: 01905 28906
college@wortech.ac.uk
www.wortech.ac.uk

Yorkshire

Askham Bryan College
Askham Bryan
York
Yorkshire YO23 3FR
Tel: 01904 772211
www.askham-bryan.ac.uk

Barnsley College
PO Box 266
Church Street
Barnsley
South Yorkshire S70 2YW
Tel: 01226 216216
Fax: 01226 216553
programme.enquiries@barnsley.ac.uk
www.barnsley.ac.uk

Bishop Burton College
York Road
Bishop Burton
Beverley
Yorkshire HU17 8QG
Tel: 01964 553000
Fax: 01964 553101
www.bishopburton.ac.uk

Bradford College
Great Horton Road
Bradford
West Yorkshire BD7 1AY
Tel: 01274 433004
Fax: 01274 741060
admissions@bilk.ac.uk
www.bradfordcollege.ac.uk

Calderdale College
Francis Street
Halifax
Yorkshire HX1 3UZ
Tel: 01422 357357
www.calderdale.ac.uk

Castle College
Granville Road
Sheffield
Yorkshire S2 2RL
Tel: 0114 260 2600
Fax: 0114 260 2101
http://my.sheffcol.ac.uk

Cleveland College of Art and Design
Green Lane
Linthorpe
Middlesbrough
Yorkshire TS5 7RJ
Tel: 01642 288000
Fax: 01642 288828
www.ccad.ac.uk

Craven College
High Street
Skipton
North Yorkshire BD23 1JY
Tel: 01756 791411
Fax: 01756 794872
enquiries@craven-college.ac.uk
www.craven-college.ac.uk

Dearne Valley College
Manvers Centre
Manvers Park
Wath-upon-Dearne
Rotherham
Yorkshire S63 7EW
Tel: 01709 513333
Fax: 01709 513110
learn@dearne-coll.ac.uk
www.dearne-coll.ac.uk

Dewsbury College
Halifax Road
Dewsbury
Yorkshire WF13 2AS
Tel: 01924 436221
Fax: 01924 457047
info@dewsbury.ac.uk
www.dewsbury.ac.uk

Doncaster College
Waterdale
Doncaster
Yorkshire DN1 3EX
Tel: 0800 358 7575
Fax: 01302 553559
infocentre@don.ac.uk
www.don.ac.uk

East Riding College
Longcroft Hall
Gallows Lane
Beverley
Yorkshire HU17 7DT
Tel: 0845 1200037
Fax: 01482 866784
info@eastridingcollege.ac.uk
www.eastridingcollege.ac.uk

Greenhead College
Greenhead Road
Huddersfield
West Yorkshire HD1 4ES
Tel: 01484 422032
Fax: 01484 518025
college@greenhead.ac.uk
www.greenhead.ac.uk

Huddersfield New College
New Hey Road
Huddersfield
Yorkshire HD3 4GL
Tel: 01484 652341
Fax: 01484 649923
info@huddnewcoll.ac.uk
www.huddnewcoll.ac.uk

Huddersfield Technical College
New North Road
Huddersfield
Yorkshire HD1 5NN
Tel: 01484 536521
Fax: 01484 511885
info@huddcoll.ac.uk
www.huddcoll.ac.uk

Hull College
Park Street Centre
Park Street
Hull
Yorkshire HU2 8RR
Tel: 01482 329988
Fax: 01482 589989
info@hull-college.ac.uk
www.hull-college.ac.uk

Joseph Priestley College
Peel Street
Morley
Leeds
Yorkshire LS27 8QE
Tel: 0113 307 6111
helpline@joseph-priestley.ac.uk
www.joseph-priestley.ac.uk

Keighley College
Cavendish Street
Keighley
North Yorkshire BD21 3DF
Tel: 01535 618600
Fax: 01535 618556
info@keighley.ac.uk
www.keighley.ac.uk

Leeds College of Art and Design
Blenheim Walk
Leeds
West Yorkshire LS2 9AQ
Tel: 0113 202 8000
Fax: 0113 202 8001
info@leeds-art.ac.uk
www.leeds-art.ac.uk

Leeds College of Building

North Street
Leeds
West Yorkshire LS2 7QT
Tel: 0113 222 6000
Fax: 0113 222 6001
info@lcb.ac.uk
www.lcb.ac.uk

Leeds Thomas Danby

Roundhay Road
Leeds
West Yorkshire LS7 3BG
Tel: 0113 249 4912
Fax: 0113 240 1967
info@thomasdanby.ac.uk
www.leedsthomasdanby.ac.uk

Middlesbrough College

Roman Road
Linthorpe
Middlesbrough
Yorkshire TS5 5JP
Tel: 01642 333333
courseinfo@mbro.ac.uk
www.mbro.ac.uk

New College Pontefract

Park Lane
Pontefract
Yorkshire WF8 4QR
Tel: 01977 702139
Fax: 01977 600708
reception@newcollpont.ac.uk
www.newcollpont.ac.uk

Norton College

Dyche Lane
Sheffield
Yorkshire S8 8BR
Tel: 0114 260 3603
Fax: 0114 260 3655
marketing@sheffcol.ac.uk
www.sheffcol.ac.uk

Park Lane College

Park Lane
Leeds
Yorkshire LS3 1AA
Tel: 0845 045 7275
Fax: 0113 216 2020
course.enquiry@parklanecoll.ac.uk
www.parklanecoll.ac.uk

Parson Cross College

Remington Road
Sheffield
Yorkshire S5 9PB
Tel: 0114 260 3603
Fax: 0114 260 3655
www.sheffcol.ac.uk

Peaks Centre

Waterthorpe Greenway
Sheffield
Yorkshire S20 8LY
Tel: 0114 260 3603
Fax: 0114 260 3655
www.sheffcol.ac.uk

Rotherham College of Arts and Technology

Rother Valley Campus
Doe Quarry Lane
Dinnington
Yorkshire S25 2NF
Tel: 08080 722777
www.rotherham.ac.uk

Rotherham College of Arts and Technology

Town Centre Campus
Eastwood Lane
Rotherham
Yorkshire S65 1EG
Tel: 08080 722777
www.rotherham.ac.uk

Selby College

Abbott's Road
Selby
North Yorkshire YO8 8AT
Tel: 01757 211000
Fax: 01757 213137
info@selby.ac.uk
www.selby.ac.uk

Sheffield College

PO Box 345
Sheffield
Yorkshire S2 2YY
Tel: 0114 260 3603
Fax: 0114 260 3655
www.sheffcol.ac.uk

Shipley College
Exhibition Road
Saltaire
West Yorkshire BD18 3JW
Tel: 01274 327222
Fax: 01274 327201
enquiries@shipley.ac.uk
www.shipley.ac.uk

Thomas Rotherham College
Moorgate Road
Rotherham
Yorkshire S60 2BE
Tel: 01709 300600
Fax: 01709 300601
enquiries@thomroth.ac.uk
www.thomroth.ac.uk

Trinity and All Saints College
Brownberrie Lane
Horsforth
Leeds
Yorkshire LS18 5HD
Tel: 0113 283 7100
Fax: 0113 283 7200
enquiries@leedstrinity.ac.uk
www.tasc.ac.uk

Wakefield College
Whitewood Campus
Four Lane Ends
Castleford
West Yorkshire WF10 5NF
Tel: 01924 789 789
Fax: 01924 789 340
info@wakcoll.ac.uk
www.wakcoll.ac.uk

Wilberforce College
Saltshouse Road
Hull
Yorkshire HU8 9HD
Tel: 01482 711688
enquiry@wilberforce.ac.uk
www.wilberforce.ac.uk
York College
Tadcaster Road
York
Yorkshire YO24 1UA
Tel: 01904 770400
Fax: 01904 770499
www.yorkcollege.ac.uk

York St John University
Lord Mayor's Walk
York
YO31 7EX
Tel: 01904 624624
Fax: 01904 612512
admissions@yorksj.ac.uk
www.yorksj.ac.uk

Yorkshire Coast College
Lady Edith's Drive Campus
Lady Edith's Drive
Scarborough
Yorkshire YO12 5RN
Tel: 0800 731 7410
enquiries@ycoastco.ac.uk
www.yorkshirecoastcollege.ac.uk